Three Postwar Eras in Comparison

Also by Carl Levy

GRAMSCI AND THE ANARCHISTS

ITALIAN REGIONALISM: History, Identity and Politics

REFUGEES, CITIZENSHIP AND SOCIAL POLICY IN EUROPE (*with Alice Bloch*)

SOCIALISM AND THE INTELLIGENTSIA, 1880–1914

THE FUTURE OF EUROPE: Problems and Issues for the Twenty–First Century (*with Valerie Symes and Jane Littlewood*)

Also by Mark Roseman

GENERATIONS IN CONFLICT: Youth Rebellion and Generation Formation in Modern Germany 1770–1968

NEITHER PUNITIVE NOR POWERLESS: Western Europe and the Division of Germany

RECASTING THE RUHR 1945–1958: Manpower, Economic Recovery and Labour Relations

THE PAST IN HIDING

Three Postwar Eras in Comparison

Western Europe 1918–1945–1989

Edited by

Carl Levy
Senior Lecturer in European Politics
Goldsmiths College
University of London

and

Mark Roseman
Professor of Modern History
University of Southampton

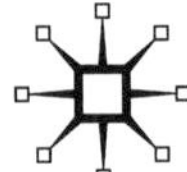

First published 2002 by
PALGRAVE
Houndmills, Basingstoke, Hampshire RG21 6XS and
175 Fifth Avenue, New York, N. Y. 10010
Companies and representatives throughout the world

PALGRAVE is the new global academic imprint of St. Martin's Press LLC Scholarly and Reference Division and Palgrave Publishers Ltd (formerly Macmillan Press Ltd).

ISBN 0–333–72103–9

This book is printed on paper suitable for recycling and made from fully managed and sustained forest sources.

A catalogue record for this book is available from the British Library.

Library of Congress Cataloging-in-Publication Data
Three post-war eras in comparison: western Europe, 1918—1945–
–1989/edited by Carl Levy and Mark Roseman
p. cm.
Rev. papers of a joint conference of the German History Society, the Association for the Study of Modern Italy, and the Association for the Study of Modern and Contemporary France, held 1995 at Keele University and co–hosted by the Goethe Institute Manchester; with several new papers added.
Includes bibliographical references and index.
ISBN 0–333–72103–9 (cloth)
1. Reconstruction (1914–1939)—Europe—Congresses. 2. Reconstruction (1939–1951)—Europe—Congresses. 3. Europe—Politics and government—20th century—Congresses. 4. Europe—Economic conditions—20th century—Congresses. I. Title: Western Europe, 1918—1945—1989. II. Title: Three postwar eras in comparison. III. Title: 3 post–war eras in comparison. IV. Levy, Carl, 1951– V. Roseman, Mark.

D653.T54 2001
940.5—dc21

2001036401

10 9 8 7 6 5 4 3 2 1
11 10 09 08 07 06 05 04 03 02

Printed and bound in Great Britain by
Antony Rowe Ltd, Chippenham, Wiltshire

Contents

List of Tables

List of Figures

Acknowledgements

This book has its origins in a joint conference of the German History Society, the Association for the Study of Modern Italy and the Association for the Study of Modern and Contemporary France, held at Keele University in 1995 and co-hosted by the Goethe Institute Manchester. Since then a number of new papers have been added and others substantially revised.

As well as acknowledging the particular generosity of the Goethe Institute, Manchester and the assistance of the aforementioned societies and institutes, the editors would like to thank the following bodies for generous support: the Service Culturel of the French embassy, London; the British Academy; the British Council, Rome; and the Royal Historical Society. We would also like to thank Palgrave for their patience and support.

Finally, we would like to record our debt to our original co-organizer, Peter Morris, whose enthusiasm, intelligence and good humour contributed so much to the success of the Keele conference. His unexpected and untimely death was a deep shock; the academic community is the poorer for his loss.

Notes on Contributors

David Ellwood is an Associate Professor in Contemporary International History, University of Bologna.

Niall Ferguson is a Professor of Political and Financial History, Jesus College, Oxford.

Paul Furlong is Professor of European Studies and the Head of School of European Studies, Cardiff University.

Stephen Gundle is a Senior Lecturer and Head of the Department of Italian, Royal Holloway College, University of London.

Douglas Johnson is an Emeritus Professor of French History, Department of Hisory, University College London.

Carl Levy is a Senior Lecturer in European Politics, Department of Social Policy and Politics, Goldsmiths College, University of London.

Robert Lumley is a Reader in Italian Cultural History, Department of Italian, University College London.

Charles Maier is the Director of the Minda de Gunzburg Center for European Studies and Krupp Foundation Professor of Europea Studies, University of Harvard.

Paolo Pombeni is Professor and Chair of the Department of History, Public Law and Political Science, Unviersity of Bologna.

Mark Roseman is a Professor of Modern History, Department of History, University of Southampton.

Carola Sachse is the Research Director, Max Planck Institute, Berlin.

Christopher Seton-Watson is an Emeritus Fellow of Oriel College, Oxford.

Chris Warne is a Lecturer in French, School of European Studies, University of Sussex.

1
1918–1945–1989: The Making and Unmaking of Stable Societies in Western Europe

Carl Levy

I. The end of the Cold War and the challenge of historical periodization

There is much to suggest that the world wars and the postwar settlements marked major turning points in the ability to establish stable and successful societies in Western Europe. World War One was followed by a period of great instability, culminating in many cases in the overthrow of democracy, the rise of fascism and eventually further war. After World War Two most Western European countries enjoyed a lengthy period of unparalleled stability and prosperity. Now there is a growing feeling that the end of the Cold War marks another turning point. This book is about the turning points of 1918, 1945 and 1989 and their relationship to the stability and prosperity of Western European societies.

The rapid dismantling of Cold War Europe between 1989 and 1992 undermined the accepted wisdom of a thousand history survey courses, namely, that 'Yalta' Europe was as inevitable as death and taxes. How many historians predicted the imminent collapse of the Soviet Union in 1985? The Russian dissident, Andrei Amalrik's, *Will the Soviet Union Survive Until 1984?* (1980), was considered a brave piece of political science fiction. Zdeněk Mlynář's *Night Frost in Prague: The End of Humane Socialism* (1980) was read as the sad epitaph to a failed experiment in reformism. When the social scientist Randall Collins, employing geopolitical Weberian sociology, suggested to a gathering of distinguished Swedish academics in Uppsala in the middle 1980s that the Soviet Union was about to collapse, his views were received politely; privately, though, Professor Collins' ideas were probably thought incredible.[1]

To a historian or political analyst in 1985, possibly even in the summer of 1989, a map of Europe as it was in the year 2000 would have seemed utterly fanciful. Who in 1985 predicted, for example, the early arrival of Slovenia, Macedonia, Slovakia and Georgia to the community of sovereign nation-states?

In some senses 1989 changed everything, adding a new postwar turning point to a twentieth-century European history with its fair share of them. But at the same time it is not clear what its impact was – if any – on the way historians interpreted the earlier turning points of 1918 and 1945. As historians began publishing major modern and contemporary histories of Europe in the wake of the events of 1989 to 1992, by and large they did not abandon the intellectual framework of the 'interwar' and 'postwar' eras. Eric Hobsbawm's *Age of Extremes* (1994)[2] and Mark Mazower's *Dark Continent* (1998)[3] are organized around the two talismanic dates 1914 and 1989 (or 1991). *The Pity of War*, Niall Ferguson's stimulating and controversial study, focuses on World War One, but it too invokes the logic of the three postwar eras.[4] Richard Vinen's new study, true enough, is critical of the perspectives of the older generations of historians. Histories of twentieth-century Europe have been warped by the generational experiences of their authors, he argues. Thus Vinen (born 1963) finds the 'Age of Extremes' approach, the obsession with the interwar period as unbalanced and misleading. Even so he still must wrestle with 1918–1945–1989 in order to advance his revisionist cause. And in fact, the periodization that he advances in his text ends up rather conventional. His book is divided into parts that follow the logic of pre-1914, interwar period, Cold War and post-1989.

The new vistas opened up by 1989 have of course encouraged some reevaluation of the respective significance of the postwar eras. Many now see the period 1918–89 in some form or other as a unity; for Mazower or Hobsbawm, for example, an age of ideological extremes flowed from the unintended effects of the guns of August 1914. From this kind of perspective, it is not clear if the 1989/91 era has ushered in an uncharted new era of globalization, or whether it in some senses represents a return to the pre-1914 conditions. There are certainly some similarities, for example, between the new global economy, one the one hand, and the gold standard and sound money phase that characterized the last 40 or so years of the so-called Long Nineteenth Century (1789–1914) up to World War One.[5]

For Niall Ferguson, 1918 and 1945, the inter-war period and the Cold War were a horrible and avoidable parenthesis in the history of Europe. If the British Expeditionary Force had not intervened in continental

Europe late in the summer of 1914, and the French had been defeated by German armies as quickly as in 1870–71, Imperial Germany might well have created its version of the EEC/EU decades earlier. Without four years of enormous bloodshed, economic dislocation and social collapse, the 'Age of Extremes' might not have happened. Hitler would have lived out his life as an obscure painter in a German dominated *Mitteleuropa* and Lenin ended his days in Swiss exile as a frustrated but politically impotent ideologue. There would have been no Auschwitz and no Gulags; perhaps the British Empire or Commonwealth might have survived as a global power in this counterfactual parallel universe.[6]

Richard Vinen will have no truck with the view that the 1914–89 period is a kind of horrible aberration. He is dismissive of historians who view the *Belle Epoque* before 1914 through rose-tinted glasses. For Vinen there have been two transformative experiences in the twentieth century: one is the unique era of peace and prosperity that most West Europeans have experienced since the 1950s. The other is the negative example of totalitarianism: the history of Europe in the second half of the twentieth century can be understood as the aftershocks of the intended and unintended effects of the Hitlerian and Stalinist regimes. Indeed, as Richard Vinen asserts, the entire political culture of Europe after 1945 is a long meditation on the politics of Adolf Hitler. The value system embodied in Nazism is the opposite of what Europe has promoted since its demise. And even early in the twenty-first century the threats posed by biotechnology or new waves of racial intolerance and xenophobia always refer to Nazism as the exemplar of a possible nightmare alternative Europe.[7]

But whatever the particular weightings and evaluations, the interwar/postwar schema still holds its grip on the historians. This is most strikingly apparent in Norman Davies's history of Europe, a magisterial work that spans the millennia, not only Plato to Nato but prehistoric Europe to Daniel Cohn-Bendit.[8] But in Davies's introductory methodological chapter the periodization under discussion in this volume is prominent. Thus Davies's criticism of the Allied Scheme of History rests on the assumption that a certain reading of 1918–1945–1989 will affect the writing of grander histories of Europe. Davies is critical – arguing that the Allied Scheme of History induces a geographical blindness in its practitioners to all things East. Furthermore, the Allied Scheme of History is suffused with the naïve assumption that Anglo-Saxon liberalism is the logical and inevitable outcome of Europe's history.[9] What is salient for our purposes, however, is that the author of a massive history of Europe that stretches back to prehistory should still be guided by the dates 1918–1945–1989.

II. A brief overview of the arguments

On one level, clearly, the question posed here is a descriptive or phenomenological one about periodization. In looking at the creation of stable orders in Western European societies we want to know whether 1918, 1945 and 1989 are the key points of change or discontinuity. Or, to ask it another way, are the periods 1918–1939/45, and then 1945–1989 coherent eras, retaining their own distinctive character from beginning to end and clearly distinct from the eras following or preceding them?

At a deeper level, the attempt to arrive at a clear periodization is at the same time a search to define the underlying processes of change and continuity. Those who see the postwar eras as being decisive turning points tend implicitly or explicitly to be advancing one or more of the following propositions. One is that the conduct or experience of war (or of victory or defeat) was a transformative experience, setting the terms that frame a whole postwar era. Some analysts emphasize the new economic or technological conditions ushered in by war, others war's social and demographic consequences; more recently, by contrast, there has been a growing tendency to talk about the cultural resonances and public memorialization of war. A second proposition is that the ends of wars provided unique and decisive opportunities to create new settlements. This was true both at the domestic level and at the same time in the international sphere. Lessons gained over longer periods could be implemented with particular force and consistency in linked national and international postwar reconstructions. A third proposition, closely related to the second, is that the outcomes of wars gave rise to new and lasting international power constellations – ushering in victorious alliances and displacing some kinds of regimes altogether.

But are wars such turning points? The trend in recent social histories of the world wars has been to emphasize the continuities, rather than the discontinuities. Where postwar governments innovated, they often merely articulated intellectual or social trends that had long predated the war. And if we use stabilization in Charles Maier's sense, as a comprehensive term to describe the way the capitalist democracies learned to accommodate their different élites and integrate the less-well off members of society, might this not be seen as a long-term process, that would have taken place with or without the major wars?

The question that forms the background to this volume is thus whether the experience of war, and the various postwar re-orderings and settlements, were as innovative or influential as they appeared, or whether they were shaped or overshadowed by trends and changes that had other origins and conjunctures. The aim of the volume cannot be to offer *comprehensive* answers to what are enormous subjects of enquiry. Instead, one of its guiding principles has been to invite historians from different generations and with very different methodologies to think about the processes of change and stabilization across the epochs in question. Diversity, not comprehensiveness, is its aim.

A second principle that has guided this collection relates to the balance drawn between examining international settlements and domestic stability. One of the central questions about the postwar moments, after all, is whether their significance derives from the international peace settlements, or from domestic reconstruction, – or precisely from the fact that *both* domestic reconstruction and the forging of international settlement were taking place at the same time. This volume opens with a number of essays on the international scene and these form Part I. Overall, though, we devote more space to *domestic* processes of stabilization, in Part II. This balance of emphasis does not reflect any assumption here about the 'primacy of domestic politics' but simply our desire to capture the wide range of important new work that has been taking place on social and cultural change in modern capitalist societies.

A third principle adopted was that of focusing the national contributions on just three societies – France, Germany and Italy. The decision to restrict contributions to the three principal continental players in Western Europe was taken to facilitate comparison – both cross-national comparisons and comparisons across the dividing lines of 1918, 1945 and 1989. Thus the first two papers in the national section (Ferguson, Furlong) offer comparisons on economic stabilization in Germany and Italy after all three postwar eras. The next two (Gundle, Sachse) allow comparisons of social change across the 1918–45 periods, again in Germany and Italy, while the last two essays in this section (Lumley, Warne) approach the political culture of Italy and France 1945–1989. The third and final section in the book presents a longer overview of the political settlements in the three postwar eras in France, Germany and Italy.

III. The international context for national stabilization: 1918–1945–1989

It is in the context of the international framework that we find the most radical challenge posed to the accepted periodization. In exploring the applicability of the concept of empire to understanding European history in the twentieth century, Charles Maier's chapter introduces a different chronology and a different set of turning points. Early in his career Maier wrote a magisterial account of the recreation of a stable bourgeois Europe in the 1920s.[10] Later on he investigated the comparisons between the outcomes of settlements of 1918 and 1945 in Western Europe.[11] A decade ago, he compared and contrasted the trajectories of Western and Eastern Europe from the middle of the 1960s to 1989.[12] In the present volume, however, Maier offers another periodization to understand the intersection of the European domestic settlements of 1918–1945–1989 with international economic, political and military factors. In earlier work Maier contrasted the different policies and effects of the American interventions in the first two postwar eras of 1918 and 1945. American hegemony after 1945 is now understood within a broader sociological history that stretches from the 1860s to the 1970s.

Maier argues that the modern nation-state itself may be conceptualized as an empire. Thus in the 1860s railways, telegraphs and military might allowed Piedmont, Prussia, Meiji Japan or the Northern Federal government of the USA to triumph over challengers from the peripheries. From the 1860s to the 1940s nation-states became the engines for new or revitalized formal overseas empires, while Nazi Germany created its imperial New Order in Europe itself. After 1945 an informal American empire guaranteed the prosperity and stability of the western half of Europe. (Though one might modify this latter point by reference to the growing literature arguing that the British held the ring in Western Europe from 1945 to 1947 and that the sterling bloc was still an extremely important player until the late 1950s.)[13]

Thus domestic stability in Western Europe was achieved through the American informal empire. The Marshall Plan represented the clearest example of domestic arrangements in society and economy and an international alliance system being forged in parallel. As Patricia Clavin has recently noted, the 'lessons of 1931'[14] were never far from the Americans. Protectionist regionalism was to be avoided and the world trade system sustained not least to defend the newly created global interest of the war-mobilized American industrial and agricultural industries of 1945. The post-1945 achievement rested on the creation of global financial and trading regimes (Bretton Woods, GATT and so on) that ensured prosperity and stability in Western Europe. And the Marshall Plan, as we will see in greater detail when we discuss David Ellwood's contribution, nurtured a new form of European regionalism (EEC) very receptive to the further liberalization of the GATT regime in the 1960s.

In contrast to the post-World War One situation, the perceived Soviet threat after 1947 meant that American economic intervention in Europe was designed to support the collective security of Western Europe. Indeed, American economic and financial intervention may have been more successful after 1945 just because the weakest and most problematic economies of Eastern Europe were forbidden by Stalin to join the Marshall Plan.[15]

The American Empire was informal in the sense that it assumed that American hegemony in Europe would be won through consensual acceptance of American leadership in NATO. In Europe the Americans relied upon informal pressures and occasionally dirty tricks to marginalize their left-wing opponents; in Asia, Africa or Latin America military intervention was a constant alternative throughout the Cold War. The Soviet Empire of course placed little reliance on consensus; when it tried to do so – in 1956, 1968, 1980 or 1985 – it always faltered.[16] When all else failed unquestioned hierarchy, force or the threat of force kept this Eurasian Empire together, even if the leadership of the Soviet Union thought very carefully before it used its own troops in Eastern Europe.

For Charles Maier the collapse of the Soviet Union's Eastern European empire in 1989 was little more than a coda. The turning point for Eastern Europe and the Soviet Union occurred in the 1970s. The economic and political success of the American Empire spurred on changes associated with the loosely drawn term, globalization. The turning points were the dual challenges of the oil shocks of the 1970s and the variety of industrial and technological changes identified with robotization and digitization. At first the events of the 1970s seemed to undermine the basis of the American informal empire, as two decades or more of unparalleled growth were threatened in Europe by the oil price shocks.

But even during the height of the debate about US decline in the late 1980s, a weakened American empire was still far superior to the comatose economies and political systems of Eastern Europe and the Soviet Union. The Soviet Empire was the absolute loser in this contest; oil revenues concealed its decline, and the command economy could not respond to the challenge of the new post-industrial economy. Gorbachev's incoherent reforms of the Soviet economy after 1985 merely made the crisis terminal.[17] The separation of Eastern Europe from the West after 1947 may have assisted the reconstruction and ensuing boom in the 1950s and 1960s, reintegration of Eastern Europe and the Soviet Union in the Western debt markets in the 1970s and 1980s limited their options after 1985 as the crisis deepened.

Thus for Maier the 1970s signalled the beginning of the end of the last great traditional empire in Europe: the Soviet Union. But for Maier the 1970s also signalled the beginnings of a truly global economy and the de-territorialization of power away from even the greatest sovereign nation-states, albeit he would be cautious about how far this process will be allowed to proceed. After all he is a sociological historian not a historical sociologist.

David Ellwood pursues the concept of the informal American Empire by probing the dual effects of Americanization and European integration in Western Europe after 1945 and 1989. Ellwood's essay thus returns us to the more familiar postwar framework, reviving the sense of 1945–89 as a clear epoch. But his approach here is not necessarily incompatible with Maier's. Maier is looking at the origins and broader context of the imperial system that triumphed after World War Two; Ellwood is looking at its application in the postwar period. There would after all be no doubt for Maier, too, that in terms of *international political settlement* 1945 did represent the opportunity to create new European alliances.

Ellwood's argument is that in the late 1940s a compromise was struck between the Europeans and the Americans that lasted until the late 1980s. Unlike Alan Milward[18] (who tends to see the form in which European integration emerged in the 1950s as a flat rejection of US proposals for greater federal integration), but like Michael Hogan,[19] Ellwood describes a delicate dialogue across the Atlantic. West Europeans attempted to develop their own means to cope with America's presence as a European power. Security matters were firmly in the hands of Nato, even if the French became semi-detached until the 1980s and 1990s.

In business, trade and money the Europeans had far greater autonomy, but this led to ambiguities. While American policy makers may have been consistent advocates of deeper European integration in the 1940s and 1950s, in the last two decades of the twentieth century the drive to deepen the single market or institute a single currency provoked American fears of a 'Fortress Europe'. By the 1990s there was open speculation about the connection between European strategic power, the US dollar and the Euro in the twenty-first century. Trade disputes between Europe and the USA, which had been a fact of life since the 1960s, seemed in the late 1990s to be spinning out of control.[20] Trade disputes and possible future friction between dollar and Euro blocs indicated that the informal empire was populated by far from docile clients.

Nevertheless in one respect, the USA still acted as imperial guardian. American involvement in the wars of Yugoslav succession generated barely concealed condescension towards the USA's NATO partners.

On the other hand, the interventions in Bosnia and Kosovo demonstrated that the European attitude towards the formal military relationship with the USA remained remarkably consistent throughout the century. Since 1916, Ellwood argues, America's potential European partners or subordinates have always wanted to mobilize as much or as little US power needed to secure national objectives. But the end of the Cold War exposed these conflicting objectives, since the needs of both sides began to diverge in dramatic ways, because national interests were now no longer harmonized by a common threat from the East.

Ellwood, like Maier, argues that the recent period has seen major challenges to the US–European alliance. For Maier, though, the real turning point was not the end of the Cold War but technological and economic changes in the 1970s. Again, this difference reflects Maier's search for the underlying explanation for changes and Ellwood's concern with their political consequences. In one respect, however, Ellwood's analysis offers a major complement to Maier's – by reminding us of Stanley Hoffmann's observations that the European powers' convergence has actually encouraged them to heighten their idiosyncrasies. The paradoxical concomitant of Maier's de-territorialization of power may thus be the growing emphasis by nation-state leaders on their separate interests, even as, and precisely because, their separate ability to control their prosperity and well-being diminishes.

The American responses to the new post-Cold War realities of her allies in Europe were ambiguous. James Baker said that many of America's European partners 'scattered like birds' in the face of the Gulf War and the Yugoslav emergency. Other American diplomats were frustrated that Europe did not speak as one voice on defence and international affairs, even if they were members of a European Union. But these same diplomats grew nervous when a European defence identity potentially threatened Nato's hegemony. Nato's expansion eastwards was also seen a way of generating a new sense of solidarity, even if the Americans were frustrated by the slow pace of a parallel expansion of the EU.[21] Meanwhile American foreign aid packages had shrunk. The US always supported joint aid action with its European partners. Outside of its military commitments, the US in the 1990s had become a 'superpower on the cheap'.[22] On the other hand the Americans refused to risk their soldiers on the ground, they preferred the chimerical pursuit of high technology warfare, which was harder to fight in the mountains of the Balkans than the deserts of Iraq.[23]

Ellwood's and Maier's intuition that the third postwar era may inaugurate an era of greater turbulence between the USA and Europe was thus confirmed on occasion during the wars in the former Yugoslavia in the 1990s. But the wars of the Yugoslav succession not only threatened to place the relationship between the US and Europe under greater strain, for a brief moment Franco-German friendship was unhinged by their respective patronage for Serbia and Croatia. And with it disturbing memories from 1914 and the 1940s were recalled.

This brings us to Christopher Seton-Watson's chapter. Although this volume focuses on Western Europe, the settlements in Eastern Europe after 1918–1945–1989 had a profound effect on the internal affairs of France, Germany and Italy. Comparisons between the three postwar eras in Western and Eastern Europe also produce some fascinating variations on the theme of periodization that we have discussed so far.

After 1989, the unresolved issues of the Paris Peace Treaties appeared to return to the European agenda. Niall Ferguson noted on the eightieth anniversary of the Versailles Peace Conference, that three issues had undermined the peace after 1919: Franco–German mistrust and hatred, American isolationism and the intractable issue of the Wilsonian concept of the self-determination of nationalities. The first two were solved after 1945, yet the third has revived to threaten the post-Cold War era.[24] Seton-Watson, for example, draws parallels between the Macedonian question in 1913 and a possible Macedonian question today. However, parallels between eras can be overdrawn, and Kosovo may not be followed by the bogeyman of 1913, Macedonia.[25] Indeed the intervention in Kosovo in 1999 and swift return of Albanian Kosovars to Kosovo was intended to prevent the destabilization of Macedonia. History is rarely that hideously symmetrical. If Serbia completes its democratization, the recent conflict in Kosovo may draw the present cycle of bloodletting to a close. But this may also be dependent on different behaviour by the Great Powers and a break with a historical cycle that stretches back to the late nineteenth century.

In his recent history of the Balkans, Misha Glenny suggests a periodization for war and instability in the Balkans that fits rather nicely with Maier's previously discussed relationship between empire and periphery.[26] Foreign observers of Balkans' conflicts of the nineteenth and twentieth centuries have usually thrown their hands up in frustration and horror and suggested that the causes of local interstate and civil wars were ancient hatreds and traditions of vendetta. In contrast Glenny discerns a correlation between Great Power intervention and the ensuing deepening of violence in the region. The first round of intervention occurred after the Congress of Berlin in 1878 when the Great Powers agreed that Ottoman power would be replaced by a series of competing alliances in the Balkan Peninsula which led to regional and then world war. The second round was initiated by Austria's ultimatum to Serbia in July 1914 and was completed in 1923 with the great population exchanges between Bulgaria, Greece and Turkey and the Treaty of Lausanne. The third round of intervention occurred when the Italians attacked Greece in 1940 and ended with the division of the area into contesting Cold War blocs and the neutrality of Yugoslavia by the early 1950s. The final round happened when the EU recognized the independence of Slovenia and Croatia in 1991 and may have been completed with the Kosovo intervention in 1999. These interventions, Glenny concludes, were 'so destructive that they guaranteed the Balkans' relative economic backwardness, compared to the rest of Europe'.[27] At the beginning of the twentieth-first century it can be hoped that the cycle may have been broken. Nevertheless the relationship between imperial centre and periphery has been maintained. Kosovo and Bosnia are essentially protectorates of the UN, the EU and the informal American Empire. Perhaps this time the area will be assured stability and economic development through international and European integration, nevertheless one older pattern discussed by Seton-Watson is still evident and this still has the potential to undermine the fragile Balkan peace.

In this regard 1918–1945–1989 presents a hideous unity. Each postwar era saw the defeat (until now, sadly only temporarily) of authoritarian methods of organizing the state system of Europe. But each era also saw the stability assured within or between the borders of nation-states of Europe by population transfer (pioneered in the first period), genocide (a term coined just before 1945) and ethnic cleansing (a term known in the second period but made infamous after 1989). How much of the current stability of prosperous, tolerant, liberal Europe relies on these ghastly aspects of 1918–1945–1989?[28] Is postcommunist Poland more stable and therefore a leading candidate for entry into the European Union because it is no longer the multinational state like before 1945? Did the extermination of the Jews by the Nazis, the expulsion of the Germans and the transfer of the Ukrainians purchase this prized stability? How many Serbs will return to Croatia and how many Serbs will stay in Kosovo? Will Bosnia ever be more than a loose confederation of ethnic statelets? And do not the Great Powers and the international organizations secretly hope that stability will be maintained in the years to come by not being too insistent about undoing ethnic cleansing? Or perhaps they would be secretly satisfied with Greater Serbia, Greater Croatia, Greater Albania and an internationally guaranteed shrunken Muslim Bosnia?

In 1989, as Seton-Watson argues, Germany was the ghost at this banquet. Except for a brief wobble, a postnational unified Germany under Kohl recognized the borders of its eastern neighbours. However the relationship between the nation-state, its citizens, third country nationals, refugees and illegal immigrants in Western Europe meant that events in Eastern Europe impinged directly upon the domestic politics of Western Europe in a way they did not in 1918 or 1945. After 1918, there was a refugee problem and the Nansen passport system paved the way for the postwar international refugee regime, but the refugee issue was overshadowed by other pressing postwar problems.[29] After 1945 and especially by the 1960s the flow of refugees from the East was assimilated into the demand for labour to fuel the European boom. Furthermore, the Cold War made refugees from the East (after the failed rising in Budapest in 1956 or the crushing of the Prague spring in 1968) into prized guests of their hosts.[30] Indeed the national identity of the Federal Republic of Germany was built on waves of German-speaking refugees from the East from its inception to reunification. The rise of the political salience of refugees and asylum-seekers after 1989 can be tied to a new surge of migration to Europe that began around 1985. The massive flows of refugees fleeing ethnic cleansing in the former Yugoslavia from 1991 onwards revealed a larger issue that affected the stability of West European democracies.

The relationship between citizen, third country national, refugee, asylum-seeker, illegal immigrant consumed the politics of all of Western Europe in the 1990s in a way it did not after 1945.[31] The very bases of liberal democracy and citizenship were at stake in Western Europe. To what extent would the citizenship of Europeans find its basis in *jus soli* or *jus sanguinis*? Certainly, the rise of the far right has been linked to the real or imagined growth of immigration, though the enduring lessons of 1945 reduced its electoral presence in unified Germany compared with Austria, France, Belgium or Italy. By the late 1990s politicians and policy makers feared for the stability of Western Europe. International law would have to be modified to limit the flow of would-be asylum seekers, even if the limited opening of labour migration (closed after 1973) seemed necessary to supply booming economies. International law would have to be amended to limit the flow of asylum seekers into Western Europe. This, it was argued, would therefore limit the appeal of the new type of far right that mixed the fascist tradition of the first postwar era with the endorsement of the trappings of democratic practice that was the product of the post-1945 era.[32] But with the dilution of the Geneva Convention of 1951 one of the finest legacies of the second postwar era would be undermined.[33]

Beyond Seton-Watson's own contribution, we might point to yet another basis for comparing the periodizations of Western and Eastern Europe, and one which again echoes Maier's theme of centre and periphery; empire and nation-state. In a recent impressive survey of the political economy of Central and Eastern Europe Ivan Berend has argued for a three-pronged periodization.[34] During the first period from the 1870s to the 1930s the region was largely an agricultural periphery of Western Europe. The major technological changes of the second industrial revolution were not successfully integrated into the economies of the Habsburg and Russian empires. A stratum of the native middle classes (especially in the Czech lands, Hungary and Poland) attempted unsuccessfully to drive for fuller organic growth before and after 1914–18. By the 1930s most of the region had succumbed to Nazi Germany's economic imperialism before direct or indirect physical control was imposed. From the 1940s to the 1960s the area was modernized and industrialized through the Stalinist command economy. Despite being largely isolated from Western Europe, Eastern Europe was closer to Western levels in the 1960s than at any time before or since. However, growing trade and financial linkages with the West and cheap subsidized oil from the Soviet Union from the 1960s to the 1980s did not prevent the East from failing to meet the challenges of the third industrial revolution (digitization and robotization). After 1989 the region has been gradually reintegrated into the Western European and global markets. But the decades' long linkage with the primitive market of the Soviet Union and the crises of the 1980s and 1990s meant, as Berend wrote in 1996, that a wide gap between the economies of Western and Eastern Europe was still to be bridged. By the year 2000 the star performers of East Europe had barely exceeded the output they had in the year the old regime collapsed.[35]

The challenges of transition confronting the Eastern European states in the 1990s – privatization, marketization, the creation of a transparent legal system that guarantees civil and property rights – liberal democracy – were similar to ones confronting the successor states after 1918, this avenue was blocked by Stalin after 1947. But after 1989, a new Marshall Plan was not available for the region, although the former lands of the GDR received enormous fiscal transfers from the Federal government that were a localized functional equivalent.

In the 1980s there had been much talk by dissident intellectuals about the rediscovery of Central Europe, but once the Soviet Union collapsed most citizens of Eastern Europe wanted rapid integration into Nato and the EU.[36] Entering the EU has taken longer than many thought possible and recently there have been increasing fears by citizens of post-communist Eastern Europe of surrendering part of their newly won sovereignty to the EU. Nevertheless the alternatives were few: formal or informal empires have been the usual two choices for the region during the first two postwar eras: the European Union offered a more consensual confederal alternative. Failure to integrate Western and Eastern Europe in the early twenty-first century may be the greatest threat to the internal stability of Eastern Europe and – history has taught us – as a result to the internal stability of the domestic settlements in the West.

IV. The economics of stabilization 1918–1945–1989

The next section of this introduction turns to the management of the economies of two important European states, namely, Germany, the leading player in Europe in all three postwar eras, and Italy, in some respects Western Europe's greatest economic success story.

Both Niall Ferguson and Paul Furlong are very conscious of the contribution to German and Italian stability made by the international developments described by Maier, Ellwood and Seton Watson. The Allies' decisions at Versailles created massive problems for the interwar German economy, for example, while the US presence after 1945 radically transformed the environment in which (West) Germany made its economic policy choices. US presence, Marshall Plan and Cold War offered new opportunities and removed old temptations for Italian decision-makers too. Yet both authors believe that the varying ability of the two states to achieve economic stability was shaped as much by domestic factors as by global economic changes or the international political settlement.

In his contribution, Niall Ferguson compares the Weimar Republic's miserable economic performance with the spectacular growth in the Federal Republic of Germany. He is among the forefront of those authors who have shown that the severity of the slump in Germany, and the ineffectiveness of democratic politicians' response, had a great deal to do with the institutional and psychological legacy of the disastrous inflation of the early 1920s. The question Ferguson poses, therefore, is how, after 1945, West Germany managed to avoid this see-saw between inflation and over-restrictive deflationary policies. At the same time, he uses the issue of public finance as the essential focus for a comparison spanning all three postwar eras – 1918, 1945 and 1989. War reparations after 1918 and the pressures of reunification after 1989 both placed great pressures on German finances.

Here, as in *The Pity of War*, Ferguson argues that the reparations schedule given to the Germans after 1919 was manageable. Ferguson believes that the corporatist bargain that re-established stability in Germany in the middle of the 1920s prevented governments from addressing the deeper causes of the economic malaise: the unsatisfactory state of German public finances since World War One. In the early 1920s the German government refused to raise interest rates or cut budgets to solve the problem of indebtedness. But in the first postwar era while employers and trade unions may have controlled prices and wages, they did not control government budgets and interest rates. Ferguson insists that the descent into hyperinflation in the early 1920s cannot be explained employing sociological political economy. By the 1920s the holding of government bonds had become a major spectator sport for all social classes, therefore, he contends that there were no discernible class interests at stake. The problem in the 1920s was not social constraints but the lack of political will of individual politicians and the poor management of the institutions of public finance.

In the aftermath of the other two postwar eras, German governments have behaved differently. In Ferguson's view, the reasons for their success are not to be found in some magic synthesis of economics and social policy as implied in the label of the 'social market economy'. Instead, a political will and a new mindset were present in policy makers and politicians when public finance policy was set in Bizonia between 1945 and 1947. After 1989, he concludes, when the inflationary pressures and public indebtedness of reunification threatened the German economy, interest rates were raised, with indebtedness offset to some extent on to Germany's partners.

Though not primarily concerned with fiscal matters, Mark Roseman's chapter draws on Ferguson's conclusions, emphasizing the importance of the fact that after 1945, German authorities in the western zone and in the FRG could carry out a massive exercise in monetarism and risk widespread unemployment and unpopularity for longer-term benefits. But whereas Ferguson argues that early Weimar governments were in principle free to make better decisions, and in the end attributes their failure to do so to lack of political will, Roseman's explanation for the difference between public finance policy in the 1920s and 1950s is more structural in character. The combined impact of Nazism, war and Allied occupation transformed the relationship between the federal authorities responsible for monetary and fiscal policy on the one hand (the Bank deutscher Länder and the economic ministries) and regional authorities, business and labour, on the other.

Ferguson's and Roseman's different approaches to explaining government behaviour also have implications for uses of periodization. Ferguson's essay implies that the better performance of Bonn governments on the stability issue was essentially the result of a learning experience; the traumatic experience of hyperinflation was enough to cure German governments of being casual with price stability. The lessons learned did not alleviate hyperinflation's disastrous legacy in 1929 but they did mean that future postwar reconstructions would not make the same mistakes. Roseman, by contrast, places more emphasis on the new structural conditions after 1945, in particular, the effects of Nazi rule on the German power-élites, the experience of total defeat and occupation and the new relationships established between Allied occupiers and German élites.

In a companion to the chapter by Ferguson, Paul Furlong analyses the question of economic management in Italy. Although the fulcrum of his argument rests on the post-1945 period, Furlong looks back to Liberal and Fascist Italy and forward to events leading to the so-called Second Republic, claimed by some commentators to have arrived with the collapse of Christian Democratic hegemony after 1992. Mussolini's dictatorship instituted the monetarist polices not pursued by the democratic politicians of the Weimar Republic. The reduction of the debt and financial stability were secured by the physical coercion of the working class. In the post-1945 period monetarist policies dominated government policy until the middle of the 1950s. A certain degree of consensus for this policy was present but it also was dependent on the isolation from power of the Communist and Socialist parties and associated trade unions. The opening to the Socialists in the 1950s and the 1960s, the vastly increased power of the trade unions after 1969 and a cautious opening to the Communists in the 1970s saw the implantation of a form of 'bargained Keynesianism'.

Thus, after 1945 the reorganization of public finances along German lines was never acceptable to the left. But neither did the Christian Democrats support such reforms in the 1970s or 1980s. Serious inflation in the 1970s and 1980s undermined the remarkable economic progress of the small and medium sized enterprises of the 'Third Italy'. Furthermore, attempts at using planning in the 1960s and 1970s had also been a failure. If public industry was rather successful in assisting the economic miracle of the 1950s and 1960s, it threatened the viability of the private sector in the 1970s and 1980s.[37] In the 1980s Italian Keynesianism was assimilated into the clientelistic political system of the Christian Democrats and their allies, the Socialists.

In terms of periodization, Furlong paints a complex picture composed of three overlapping patterns. The first, as in Germany, is of a strong contrast between the interwar and postwar periods, with the Italian economy growing much more quickly in the post-World War Two era – though its 'miracle' kicked in somewhat later than the German one. The second is one of continuity: throughout the period from the pre-World War One period to the present day, Furlong sees a continuing weakness in the ability of the Italian state to act as decision-maker and leader, a weakness resulting in – and then further exacerbated by – clientelistic relationships between the administration and a variety of social groups clamouring for special treatment. The third is a cyclical pattern. In contrast to the German case, where the lessons learned after the hyperinflation of the early 1920s provide a clear watershed, Italy had no single such defining moment. Instead in response to perceived failures in the prevailing line or to changing world conditions, governments cycled through a recurring sequence of deflationary and then expansionist phases. Mussolini's early monetarism of the 1920s was succeeded by the clientelism of corporative public industry during the financial emergency of the 1930s. In the 1940s and early 1950s the Christian Democrats carried out a renewed policy of monetarism under the guidance of the Liberal Luigi Einaudi. Afterwards, and particularly in the 1970s and 1980s, the politics of clientelist entitlements and the political usage of the public sector had more than a few parallels with the Mussolinian regime of the 1930s. Monetarist polices were thus carried out by Italian governments during the first two postwar eras. In the first case a dictatorship carried out monetarist policies through fiat. In the second case the Christian Democrats executed deflationary policies within the context of the early Cold War and against the will of the left.

Furlong follows Maier in seeing the post-1945 system beginning to unravel not as a result of the end of the Cold War, but already before 1989 because of global economic challenges since the 1970s. These challenged the Keynesian and growth-based policies of the preceding decade or more. Though Furlong ends his chapter on the cusp of the 1990s, it is worthwhile pursuing the argument through that decade to see how far the logic of 'bargained Keynesianism' was eroded. Italians had never created the efficient fiscal system of the Federal Republic of Germany, but the Bank of Italy served an equivalent source of probity and efficiency to the German Federal Bank. In the 1990s the *tangentopoli* scandals and the pressures on Italy to meet the Maastricht criteria and join the single currency by 1999 forced major reforms of the old regime. But successful economic policy was either carried out by governments of 'technicians' usually economists or bankers with connections to the Bank of Italy, or governments of the centre-left whose economic policy was essentially dictated by the Bank of Italy. The only government of the right, led for seven months in 1994 by Silvio Berlusconi, worried domestic and international bankers. In a reversal of historical roles, in the 1990s the post-Communist left became the champions of technocratic monetarist governments and after 1996 when in power followed the suggestions of the Bank of Italy. While the left had become the party of sound money the Christian Democrat centre-right until 1992 and the new right in the 1990s represented the party of easy money.

Privatization of public industry, the efficient collection of taxes and the blunt and traditional instrument of interest rates raised by the Bank of Italy seemed to signal a break with a form of political economy linked to the Christian Democratic republic.[38] However even the reformists of the 1990s could not break completely with the past. The entitlements of the system of 'bargained Keynesianism' (state pensions, especially the generous conditions for drawing civil service pensions, to name the most glaring example) remained largely untouched. To that extent, the underlying continuities may prove the stronger pattern.

Creating the consumer society 1920s–1950s

In discussions of the stabilization of capitalist societies, the position of labour has always enjoyed a central place. The institutional evolution of the labour movement and of the socialist parties is a well-researched story and one that requires no further elaboration here. In the last few years, historians' interest has turned more to changes in the character of the family, in consumer and leisure behaviour, and in their implications for class identities and social relations. Recent work on the Great Boom in postwar Western Europe, for example, has drawn attention to the role of the nuclear family in the development of the consumer society.[39]

In the present volume Stephen Gundle and Carola Sachse, take up this theme, but challenge both the established chronology and the idea that it was the Americans who brought the consumer society to Italy and Germany.[40] Instead, they argue that the basis for the mass consumer societies of the economic miracles of the late 1950s and early 1960s was the result of social and cultural innovations developed during the Fascist and National Socialist regimes and in some cases dating back to World War One.

As Gundle shows in the chapter devoted to Italy, with their programmes of leisure and entertainment, the Fascists had hoped to combat the increase in private materialism, reinforce the communal spirit and promote their ideological programme of autarchy. In fact the programmes produced the reverse, offering means of escape from the exhortations of the official regime. But they were not without consequences; the emergence of consumer and leisure industries after 1945, associated with the economic miracle, had a noticeable Italian flavour to them and built on developments from the interwar period. Gundle's argument here is corroborated by recent work on the 1950s. Italians adopted aspects of American production techniques and marketing but geared them to specific Italian traditions of artisanal craft and design.[41] The motor scooter, furniture, kitchen appliances or ready-to-wear fashions[42] are merely a few examples of this synthesis.

Carola Sachse investigates the evolution of the German family from the interwar years to the post-1945 period. Sachse shows how the 'social rationalization' movement of the Weimar period originally promoted greater comradeship between the sexes and more equal partnership within the family. But the Nazis harnessed this movement for the modernization of the family to their own racist ends. The social engineering of the so-called Aryan family was intended to see-off the 'threat' of racial and biological degeneration.

National Socialist family policy was full of contradictions. While the Nazis extolled the family, their policies sought to draw all family members into different public and party organizations. But as in the Italian case, the Nazi policies had unintended results. The creation of organized leisure opportunities encouraged the flight into private consumerism. And the discrediting of racial engineering produced its post-war reaction in a new public commitment to the sanctity of the private sphere.

In the aftermath of total collapse in 1945 the German family took on a very special significance. In a time of total breakdown in society, of bombed out families, of mass expulsions, the nuclear family and the extended family were essential for survival. But these were nuclear and extended families in which women were placed in a commanding position. Within a decade, true enough, a new domesticity occurred in Germany. Normality was equated with the return of men to the family or to the formation of new ones led by men. Yet there is some indication that the 1920s search to engineer a more 'rational' relationship between the sexes had had some enduring influence on changing roles within the family.

The Italian and German cases differed in significant respects. Although the industrial triangle of Italy suffered heavy bombing and northern society was ripped apart by civil war after 1943, the pressures on the Italian family were less because Mussolini's regime failed to inspire absolute defiance to the bitter end. The roles of some women were changed by their participation in the Resistance, but this was a minority affair.[43] The racial radicalism of Nazism was not present to the same degree in Italy. The low level of industrialization in Italy compared to Germany, and the ineffectual mobilization of rural Southern Italy meant that Fascist modernization or any sort of modernization were ineffective. Nevertheless in terms of chronology the pairing of the Italian and German cases are illuminating. The family as the centre of the new consumer society of the economic miracles is rooted in events predating 1945. Thus the periodization in the Italian and German cases, 1920s–1950s, makes much more sense than the simple assumption that consumerism began only after 1945 and only in American format.

Between post-materialism and the end of the Cold War

A number of the contributions considered thus far – notably from Maier, Ellwood and Furlong – argue that in some way or other the settlements that emerged after World War Two have been shaken by the new challenges – be it since the 1970s, in Maier's model, or since 1989, in Ellwood's. In this section, Robert Lumley and Chris Warne pursue the theme by analysing the evolution of Italian and French political culture in recent decades. Although the two essays adopt very different perspectives, both the Italian and the French cases raised a common question, namely whether the political convulsions of the late 1960s do not, in fact, represent a more significant turning point than the fall-out of the end of the Cold War.

For both Italy and France, liberation in 1944–5 and the Resistance had a profound and lasting influence on their political cultures – an influence that lasted until the 1990s.[44] In both cases strong communist parties dominated much of the working class and a good deal of the intelligentsia until the 1970s and 1980s. While France had its explosive, short-lived May 1968, Italy had a 'creeping May' that lasted for much of the 1970s. In both cases the rediscovery of various forms of unorthodox Marxism by students and their teachers in the 1960s led within a decade to the discrediting of all varieties of Marxism for the intelligentsia and the educated middle classes.[45] But there are also notable differences between France of the Fifth Republic and the Italian 'First Republic'. Although France after 1989 confronted the challenge of a united Germany (discussed by Douglas Johnson in his chapter), it did not experience the same domestic crisis that Italy (*tangentopoli* and the Mafia threat) experienced between 1992 and 1994.[46]

In comparisons of American and European societies Arthur Marwick has argued for a coherent era, the '1960s', dating from approximately 1958 to 1974,[47] from the economic miracles to the first oil shock. Other origins of the 'Sixties' are interwoven into his narrative. The liberalization of politics and culture from above and below also created its own momentum. The younger generations were more educated and affluent and created new political subjects and cultural identities. The (flawed) products of liberal reform and the welfare state, greatly expanded high schools and universities, were the centres of revolt. However, the excluded also were mobilized: African Americans and for our purposes, factory workers in France and Italy. Exogenous events such as the nuclear arms race, Algeria and especially the war in Vietnam gave these movements brief moments of international cohesion.

Nevertheless the tempo and nature of each national 'Sixties' was quite different. Italian and French youngsters only incorporated the American politics of 'Woodstock Nation' after it was effectively over. And in any case this largely Anglo-American alternative lifestyle culture did not readily translate into the youth politics of Italy or France in the late 1960s or early 1970s. Warne argues that the divide in generations in France happened with the panic about teenage delinquency and pop music of the early 1960s. Although it was directly influenced by Anglo-American exemplars, they seem to have a flavour of the 'Fifties' rather than the entirely different context of the more chronologically relevant Californian 'Summer of Love' in 1967. German too also had its unique path to the Sixties. In the conclusion to her chapter in this volume, Carola Sachse emphasizes the effects of radically different experiences of two generations of Germans. The unspoken experiences of the generation of the 1940s (Nazism, total defeat, expulsion, mass rapes) made the German family an uncomfortable place for the generation of the 1960s. And it helped generate a vigorous youth revolt spurred on by the need to come to terms with their own personal, unmentionable German national past.

By comparing the effects of 1968/9 and 1989 in Italy and France, the two chapters in this book place the effects of the Sixties within a different context than Marwick has done. The social liberalism or post-materialism of the past 30 years grew out of the legacies of the 1960s. The Green movements and parties and other new social movements of the past 30 years can be traced back to the veterans of the 1960s.[48] Nevertheless the subcultures and social movements dealt with by Lumley and Warne in their chapters involve participants who were not present in the 1960s. In this respect there is little or no continuity between 1968 and 1989.

Robert Lumley considers social movements in Italy in relation to 1968/9 and 1989. From 1968 left-inspired movements questioned the very stuff of modern society: the routinization of politics, the institutionalization of knowledge; and the idea of technocratic progress. The democratization of civil society was promoted within schools, neighbourhoods and factories. Although forces within the centre-left governments of the 1960s laid the basis for this renovation of civil society, the Christian Democratic dominated governments were unable to institute effective reform their attempts merely stoking the flames of protest.[49] The explosion of industrial militancy in 1969 followed by a legally binding charter of workers' rights revitalized the trade unions, which gained greater strength as interunion Cold War tensions eased.[50] With the conventional routes blocked, the great reforms in social life in the 1970s (the legalization of divorce and abortion, to name two) were initiated by social movements found outside the ineffectual party system.

However by the early 1980s this period of mobilization was over. The political system had withstood the challenges of right-wing subversion and left-wing terrorism through the flawed 'historic compromise' between the Communists and the Christian Democrats. From the 1970s vantage point, the years 1968 and 1969 had seemed to break with the bi-polar Cold War world of Italian politics and simultaneously extend ideological mobilization and confrontation in civil society; by the 1980s, the generation of 1968 had been demobilized or incorporated within a revived centrist coalition, led by anti-Communist Socialists and Christian Democrats.[51]

After 1989 the Northern League accelerated the decline and fall of the so-called First Republic. In their infancy the various leagues in the North adapted the unconventional methods of political mobilization associated with the new social movements of the 1960s for their own ends. However, once the Northern League gained electoral success, it combined old-fashioned party organization with the charismatic, near Leninist-style leadership of Umberto Bossi. Like the movements of the 1960s, the leagues attacked the dead hand of a corrupt Italian state, but the comparison ends there. Right-wing regionalist populism replaced the rhetoric the unorthodox grassroots left.[52] Besides the rather bizarre cases of certain prominent members of the Northern League who began their political lives as sixties radicals there were other unintended effects of 1968. Italian politics had become secularized over the past 30 years. Catholic and Communist subcultures were gradually weakened which in turn opened political space for new players like Bossi's Northern League, Silvio Berlusconi's *Forza Italia!* and the 'post' Fascists.[53]

In many other respects the politics of the Northern League represent a break with the traditions of the sixties. Unlike the internationalism of 1968, Lumley notes, these new politics were parochial. In their most unique form the populist politics of the locality was celebrated. Indeed the Northern League threatened the very unity of Italy. Furthermore the activists and voters behind the Northern League's meteoric rise, the owners of small and medium sized-family businesses in provincial Lombardy or Veneto, were alien to the educational and cultural outlook of the students of 1968 or even the Southern workers of the northern industrial triangle of 1969. Finally the differences in the unorthodox politics of the 1960s and the 1990s is revealed in attitudes towards 1945. In the elections of 1994 the victorious if fractious partnership of Berlusconi, Bossi and the 'post-Fascists' turned their backs on the history of the Republic.[54] The end of the Cold War, the post-1989 era, undermined the coalition of forces that endorsed the post-1945 settlement. It now became clearer that the students of 1968 and workers of 1969, though challenging the system, had in fact been demanding a fulfilment of the radical promises of 1945. Now they found themselves in unexpected partnership with more conservative groups seeking to preserve the unity of the nation-state.

Chris Warne's account of the effects in France of 1968 and 1989 posits a more enduring continuity from the 1960s, while simultaneously challenging the specific importance of 1968. The first thing that should be recalled is the different context of the French and Italian domestic settlements by the early 1960s. The end of the Algerian War in 1962 and the constitution of the Fifth Republic created a firmer framework than that present in Italy for responding to the events of 1968. In the long run, the Fifth Republic permitted the rotation of power between right and left in a way the Italian system did not. If Italy had its 'creeping May' after 1968, France had its two 'Mays': the extra-parliamentary 1968 and the electoral 1981. The triumph of the Socialist opposition and their Communist allies using the rules of de Gaulle's constitution deepened the legitimacy of the political system in France, (although it did not prevent corrosive political corruption that began to undermine this settlement in the 1990s).

Warne argues that 1945 had not really been a point of rupture with the politics of the prewar Third Republic as was once believed. But the social transformations of the 1950s and early 1960s led to the formation of a modern youth culture. He shows that this emergent youth clashed with the paternalism of older generations well before the riots of 1968 – a process that can be observed in the popular musical culture of the late 1950s and early 1960s and adult reactions to it. In fact, 1968 saw the culmination of a series of generational collisions.

Contrasting the Italian with the French cases, it is clear that the in the decades after 1968, the Gaullist state proved successful at responding to and integrating the protesting educated young. One can discern flash points in the middle 1970s and 1980s where students protested against reforms of the educational system,[55] but Warne believes that in the fall-out of 1968 the French state learned to abandon the paternalism that had characterized it in the 1960s.

Warne is thus reasonably optimistic about the French state's ability to respond to the challenge raised by a new social actor: the unemployed displaced children of immigrant workers (the *beurs*) who with 'native' French youth created a new hybrid anti-racist youth culture. This had no equivalent in Italy, which experienced significant inward migration only from the late 1980s.[56] The movement against racism that the *beurs* spearheaded in the 1980s was successively assimilated in a revived post-Keynesian Socialist Party. Even so, the post-1989 era has posed greater challenges to the first principles of Gaullist, liberal and traditional left-wing politics, as a younger generation in the 1990s challenged the assumption that immigrants shared a common French culture founded on the principles of secular republicanism. Particularly worrying to France's intelligentsia and policy makers have been those who refused to recognize the logic of assimilation and either forged new hybrid transcultural spaces around hip-hop or embraced Islamic culture.

In this respect superficially, at least, after 1989 the Italian and French cases seem to be moving closer together. Many commentators in both countries noted a parallel between the emergence of ethnic separatism in the aftermath of the disintegration of the Soviet Union and Yugoslavia and the rise of multicultural France and regionalist Italy. But the differences are also quite striking. The functional equivalent of Italy's Umberto Bossi may have been Le Pen. But the French FN had greater continuities with the traditional neo-fascist far right than the Northern League's odd mixture of neo-liberalism and regionalist populism. In Italy the traditional neo-fascist right, the MSI and its successor 'post-Fascist' Alleanza Nazionale, were less willing to play the race card.[57] Moreover, the social actors of these movements of contention or culture in each case could not be more different: prosperous Brescian businessmen and unemployed *beurs* in the *banlieux* of Paris are unlikely bedfellows.

V. Political frameworks across the three postwar eras

The final section of the book examines the effects of political settlements in France, Germany and Italy over the three postwar eras. Although the importance of economic and financial management and the processes of social modernization raised in the preceding sections is not slighted, the international balance of power in Western Europe, on the one hand, and the effects of domestic constitutional settlements, on the other, are given greater emphasis here.

One of the crucial factors for each postwar era was the territorial, economic and political re-arrangement of Germany. From the French point of view this was just as significant as the changing role of the United States. As Douglas Johnson notes in his chapter on France, policy makers and politicians were fixated on France's position as a world power. Certainly in order to be a first order power, France needed allies outside Western Europe, but France also had to decide how to cope with its German neighbour. The settlement after 1945 and the Cold War solved a dilemma faced by the French in the 1920s and 1990s. After 1945 France could retain the trappings of a big player on the global stage through Europeanism. French-led European integration served to ward off threats from the Soviet Union but it also incorporated the Federal Republic of Germany in an alliance where France was the dominant partner.[58] After 1989 German reunification was disquieting for François Mitterand and the French political classes. Even in an era of European integration and Friendship Treaties, Johnson notes, the French were still obsessed with older demographic fears. And when Germany was reunified the notion of 80 million Germans somehow overwhelming 58 French citizens was never far from the minds of newspaper editors or for that matter Mitterand.

But in 1990 Mitterand had few cards to play. Russia was dependent on German aid and investment, George Bush was keen to facilitate German unification and the British were Eurosceptics. Similarly in the early 1920s France found few powerful allies to support a policy of German isolation. Britain and the United States were not interested and the French governments were hostile to the Soviet Union that was increasingly friendly to Germany. But in 1990 Mitterand had a tried and tested option that had failed his predecessors in the 1920s. Deeper European integration, meaning deeper foreign and security policy and the pillarization of the EC into a European Union was proposed. German policy objectives were given far greater weight in the European Union of the 1990s. France acceded to the recognition of Slovenia and Croatia, accepted the Maastricht criteria for the single currency and agreed to have the new European Central Bank located in Frankfurt.

The dilemma the Germans had confronted since 1918 had been solved, but within the overarching architecture of the informal American empire and the European Union. A unified and economically powerful Germany was permitted to take the leading role in the affairs of the continent without resorting to war. For more sober German observers the limits of German power were already clear by 1916, and that was because Germany would never match the global power of the USA or the potential and real power of nearby Russia. Max Weber fought against unrestricted submarine warfare in 1916 and 1917 precisely because he wanted, as he put it in a letter, to keep 500,000 American sharpshooters out of the European continent.[59] In 1918 when defeat loomed, the disillusioned but still fiercely nationalist liberal Max Weber saw little alternative but a future Germany being a junior partner in an Anglo-American alliance.[60] Although he would have winced, Weber probably would have endorsed a German diplomat's belief in the 1950s that West Germany would have to be satisfied at being a 'greater Belgium'.[61]

Germany accumulated immense 'soft power' based on its economic success after 1945. In his chapter Mark Roseman examines how West Germany succeeded in achieving economic success and democratic political stability unlike the Weimar Republic after 1918. There is little doubt as to the crucial difference between post-1918 and 1945. The territorial settlement within Germany between the victorious and conquering allies was crucial. The western allies limited the political space for revanchist right-wing movements to flourish through the licensing of parties. In any case, the rapid construction of an anti-Communist alliance in the west after 1947 incorporated forces that might have turned against a democratic settlement in different circumstances. The emergence of the first mass party of the centre right in German history that unreservedly endorsed liberal democracy and a welfare state, the bi-confessional Christian Democrats, was an enormously significant factor in any explanation for the stability of West German democracy after 1945. But the conclusion one must draw from Roseman's chapter is that the 'x' factor in 1945 was the Anglo-American presence on German territory that was lacking in 1918.

Roseman has previously written on the relationship between the legacies of the National Socialist regime and the modernization of liberal democratic West Germany.[62] Both there and in the contribution to the present volume, he in some respects echoes an earlier and famous analysis by Ralf Dahrendorf.[63] Dahrendorf argued that a flattening and transformation of the social class structure of postwar West Germany created a different structural framework to carry out policy in this new postwar era. Thus, for example, the massacre of Junker families after the failed assassination attempt on Hitler in 1944 opened a vacuum on the top. Roseman is less convinced of such directly sociological changes, but certainly argues strongly that there was no automatic access to power for a military–agrarian élite in the postwar years. Their absence, and the changed relationship of the former Weimar non-Nazi political and labour élites to the Allies were essential elements of the new settlement.

Continuing the sociological theme, other authors have argued that the working class was transformed. At the end of the war mass refugee migration undermined local proletarian subcultures, while mass mobilization for total war had also had its effects. Hitler feared another 1918 Revolution and thus attempted to integrate workers into the regime through social welfare provisions, leisure activities and forms of consultation on the shop floor based on a meritocracy of the skilled.[64] Albeit this was also a meritocracy of a so-called racially superior Aryan workforce: the skilled workers managed a force of millions of slave labourers.[65] Here too Roseman is more cautious; it was the Nazi separation of the working class into a leadership in exile (or concentration camp) and a rank and file in factory or on the battlefield that was arguably more important in shaping labour politics in the early postwar years.

If Roseman is sceptical that a sociological revolution had taken place by 1945, he is even more critical of the view that Germany's postwar stability can be attributed to institutional innovation. Positive though the Basic Law's contribution has undoubtedly been, it was not the key to the FRG's success. The CDU's clear ascendancy emerged in 1953 even before the 5 per cent electoral threshold was fully implemented (in the elections of 1957). The Basic Law became the basis of West German's constitutional patriotism in the 1960s not because it reshaped German society. Rather, the political and psychological impact caused by the experiences of Nazism, war and total defeat and the postwar conditions of Occupation and Cold War created the space and time for a stable and democratic settlement to succeed and made the Basic Law a success.

Thus, unlike the early years of the Weimar Republic, there was no question of cartels of trade unions, big business and civil servants being able to hold the government to ransom in the FRG's early years. The army of course, long a key player in German politics, was revived only gradually and within the context of treaties with Western allies. As we have already noted in discussing Ferguson's chapter, the politics of public finance that bedevilled the early Weimar Republic did not trouble West Germany in the 1940s and 1950s. If in 1923–24 the French and Belgians intervened in the Ruhr to force a sovereign German government to pay its reparations, currency reform was carried out by German local authorities in conjunction with their western occupiers. Indeed the Federal Republic of Germany emerged from the reaction of the Russians to this policy. Sovereignty was therefore born out of the consequences of radical monetarist reform guided by the occupiers of the western zones; in the 1920s German governments tried to undermine the reparations payment schedule, undermine the Paris Peace treaty and thereby gain greater autonomy on the international stage against the victorious West. After 1945 the Basic Law and the mighty D-Mark became sources for Western German identity and 'post-national' patriotic pride. But both sources of German identity after 1945 had been fashioned under the guidance of occupying powers.

Paolo Pombeni's survey of the Italian political settlement over the three postwar eras focuses more on the relationship between the constitutional arrangements and the degree of long-term stability in Italy. Roseman's chapter suggests that the post-1945 settlement in West Germany enabled a unified Germany to meet the serious challenges of the 1990s relatively successfully. Italy in the 1990s was still in search of institutional reform to escape from constitutional problems that stretched back to the establishment of the modern Italian state under Piedmontese hegemony in 1861.[66] Indeed the monarchical constitution was based on the Piedmontese *Statuto* of 1848 and functioned under all regimes until 1946. The periodization and themes in Pombeni's chapter therefore bring to mind Maier's earlier discussions about empire and periphery, with in this case the Italian nation-state playing the role of ramshackle centre. The legitimacy of the Italian state has therefore been tested by the periodical crises between the centre (Piedmont or Rome) and the regions that have erupted in the wake of each of the three postwar eras.[67] The 'Southern Question' was a key factor after 1918. The settlement after 1945 had to see off the regionalist threat in Sicily and the particular problems of German and French border regions, while after 1989 northern regionalism threatened the post-1945 consensus.[68]

Pombeni takes a domestic approach to the effects of 1989. The collapse of the old party system after 1989 cannot be attributed to events abroad. Neither is 1989 in itself a particularly important milestone for the crisis of the 'First Republic'. Instead, he insists that confidence in the political parties had been declining since the 1960s. After the threats of subversion and terrorism were overcome, the traditional political parties lost their last claim to deep support, namely as defenders of the Republican constitutional order against the threats from the extreme left and right. The constitutional issue of the 1980s was the reform of the legislative and executive branches of government, and therefore creating a stable, efficient and transparent liberal democracy. But the reform of the constitutional order was entrusted to the old political parties, the very players who had much to lose if their efforts had been effective. Thus the collapse of the old party system in the wake of the *tangentopoli* scandals was already foreshadowed by the failures of constitutional reform in the 1980s.

The traditional political parties were also becoming sociologically outmoded. Pombeni, echoing Lumley, argues that party politics based on class, religion and ideology had gradually become less salient to voters as Italian politics became secularized. Therefore, Communism and Christian Democracy were less appealing even before the framework of Cold War tensions disappeared with the Soviet Union's demise.[69] The new dispensation of the 1990s seemed to open vistas for constitutional reform. But Pombemi exhibits caution about the likely long-term effects, a caution borne out by events in the 1990s. The regionalist populism of the Northern League, the 'virtuous minorities' of anti-Mafia groupings, magistrates and other transitory reform alliances set the pace of change between 1992 and 1994.[70] However, looking back in the year 2000, the vicious circle that Pombeni argued stopped reform in the 1980s was re-enacted in the late 1990s by new or recycled political players.

Certainly there has been change from the post-1945 settlement as we have argued in the context of our earlier discussion of Furlong's chapter. Governments of technocrats and the centre-left have privatized the vast majority of the old holding companies and introduced Italy to a more transparent form of capitalism. Welfare entitlements have become less open to political manipulation and the deficit has been tackled in order to allow Italy to enter the single currency in 1999. Older patterns of clientelism associated with the 'First Republic' have been undermined. However, just like their predecessors early in the 1980s, the new political parties of the late 1990s were unable to reform the constitutional structures precisely because it hurt their own or their allies closest interests. The parties of the 'First Republic', of the post-1945 settlement, were replaced by newcomers or at least parties sporting new names. But the First Republic never gave birth to a Second Republic.[71] If the post-1989 era seemed to prove the robust nature of Germany's so-called temporary Basic Law, the flawed Italian constitutional settlement of post-1945 (or post-1861) survived the political earthquakes of post-1989.

Unlike Johnson or Roseman, Pombeni does not believe that international relations were important for setting the pace of change after 1989. Pombeni suggests that the collapse of Soviet hegemony in Eastern Europe and the collapse of the Soviet Union itself showed Italians that things could change, but otherwise they do not form an important part of his argument. The underlying assumption therefore is that once the Christian Democrats were established in power after 1948, foreign policy was of little importance because it was done by others: the USA, Nato or the EU. And this in turn helped stabilize Italy after 1945. In contrast, one could argue, the instability of Italy after 1918 was related to the hostile attitudes of Liberalism, the monarchy, the armed forces to the emergence of mass democracy on the one hand, and the prevalence among the political élite of geo-political expansionist imperialism, on the other.[72] The king did not prevent Mussolini from marching on Rome in 1922 and allowed him to seize dictatorial power in 1926. He endorsed Mussolini's wars in the 1930s and 1940s because not only did the king fear that unilateral action might sacrifice the last formal powers of the monarchy to the *Duce*, the king also saw Mussolini as a defender of Italy's interests as an imperial and great power. In 1943 when the king approved the removal of Mussolini from power, he failed to defend his own capital from the Germans and thus undermined the credibility of the old regime after 1945.

The new political ruling class in Italy, like its counterpart in West Germany, accepted the intervention of the Americans and excluded the Communists from key roles in domestic and particularly foreign policy. But at least in the late 1940s and early 1950s hard bargaining concerning the Peace Treaty, the fate of Italian colonies and the issue of Trieste gave lie to the idea that the Italians had already earned their later title of the 'Bulgarians' of the West.[73]

The international conditions described by Roseman in his chapter on Germany do not mirror those found in Italy. Unlike Germany, Italy did not experience the same sort of absolute total defeat. Indeed, it was the Resistance, which had been led by a now pariah left, that paradoxically gave the new political ruling class a degree of legitimacy that the Germans of the western zone lacked. Nor was the Italian constitution written under western supervision nor were the Italian political parties licensed, nor for that matter was Italy partitioned into two states representing different ideologies. Italy was free to deal with its own past and its future destiny, even if the US always had informal and at times dubious ways to push events in its favour. From the late 1950s Italy became a republican partyocracy in which the Christian Democrat leadership was consumed in internal party struggles that took pride of place over international affairs and not infrequently also over domestic policy making. The executive branch of government withered on the vine and as we have noted constitutional reform met with constant delay. The settlements of post 1945 shaped German and Italian responses' to realities after 1989: the experience of occupation in Germany and the more complex relationship between victor and defeated in the case of Italy set both on divergent paths when 'Yalta Europe' disappeared.

Thus for the Germans the end of the Cold War and reunification meant a final reckoning with the legacies of 1945 and a questioning by certain intellectuals and academics of a national identity shaped by foreign occupation.[74] For the Italians the end of the Cold War opened to question the entire history of the nation since 1861.

VI. Conclusion

Perhaps the biggest lesson of the contributions in this volume is that there are many different ways to approach the issues of stability and stabilization. From the evolution of international relationships, through the management of currency stability or changing policies towards the family, to the transmutation of political discourse and imagery – all these processes are explored here to help interpret patterns of cohesion and stability in European societies. Manifest in this diversity is a range of different understandings both of what stability and stabilization are, and of how they are engendered and disrupted.

Stability is, of course, a vexed and elusive concept. So far this introduction has preferred to use debates concerning historical periodization to approach the subject indirectly. That is because though all of our contributors in one way or other operate with a sense of it, they have largely sensibly refrained from the defining the term; like most puddings, it tends to disintegrate when nailed too firmly to the wall. So it was appropriate to have the historical case studies firmly in the minds of the readers of this volume before trying to tackle stabilization head on at the end of this chapter.

At its simplest it denotes the absence of violent disruptions, conflicts or challenges to a given system over a given period of time. But this is not a very useful definition. For one thing, the stable equilibrium of a system that has learned to live with a certain measure of change and disorder may well be more robust than a precarious equilibrium of a society, currently at peace, but flinching at every minor sign of conflict or disruption. In this latter sense it is clear that stability can coexist with some conflict and may well need to coexist with change. One of the decisive characteristics of the 1950s in Germany and in the 1960s in many parts of western Europe, was 'dynamic stability' – the striking co-existence of dynamic change and a widespread sense of cohesion.

A second feature of stability is that even those political systems that we can all agree to be robust and adaptable will construe the nature of and origins of their own stability in very variable ways. If industrialists in the Ruhr had employed gun thugs to shoot at strikers in postwar West Germany (as the mine owners of Harlan County did in 1960s West Virginia), for example, the resulting crisis for the whole West German political system would have been profound. What may be an acute sign of instability in one country may well be tolerable in another. Stability, to use Anthony Giddens' term, is a reflexive phenomenon, in which participants' perceptions and understandings form an important part of thing itself. In any given social context stability is co-defined by contemporaries' expectations and indeed also by the value they place on it. In Germany after World War Two, as Sachse reminds us in her chapter, there was an overwhelming desire for peace. But as a number of the contributors to this volume demonstrate, for many Europeans in the generation coming of age in the 1960s and 1970s, the pressing social problem more was a surfeit of stability than its absence. The interpretation a number of scholars have put on 1968 – there is a hint of it from Warne in this collection – is that an increase in conflict actually satisfied expectations and rendered society paradoxically more stable!

Because it is such a subtle, complex and highly reflexive phenomenon, stability *per se* is not so easily distinguished from the preconditions of stability. In the case of a clearly defined social phenomenon such as war, it is fairly easy to distinguish between the phenomenon itself and its causes. The origins of World War One may remain a contentious subject, but at least they are clearly separable from the war itself. But in relation to stability analysts are likely to adopt a very diverse range of approaches and chronologies, reflecting their different understanding of where stability is located.

Amidst the diversity, however, in terms of periodization, some common themes emerge, that both affirm and challenge our sense of 1918, 1945 and 1989 as the major turning points of European history. On the one hand, it is clear they remain compelling milestones. The ends of wars brought major changes to the international scene – the emergence onto the European stage of the victorious USA and the division of Europe after 1945, the disappearance of the Soviet Union after 1989–91. After the wars, western European nations either had to, or were inspired to, produce new constitutions or seek major internal reforms. The two world wars presented all the combatant nations with major economic challenges, the successful or unsuccessful resolution which would have a lasting influence on the stability and character of the postwar states. In these and other ways, the ends of wars and the construction of the postwar orders shaped the character of the ensuing epochs. The post-1945 era was so successful not least because so many lessons had been learned after 1918 about how not to construct the postwar framework.

But in other respects, when we talk about the differences between the interwar, postwar eras, and the post-1989 era, it is clear we are referring to phenomena only indirectly related to war and peace-making. In such cases 1945 or 1989 are merely convenient markers to distinguish between the effects of processes that are in fact more continuous and follow different timetables. This is evident, for example, in the changes in leisure behaviour and families described by Gundle and Sachse in this volume. What makes the post-1945 period seem so different, in fact, is precisely the complementary interaction between a new international framework after 1945 and an evolution of European capitalist economies already underway since the 1920s. As Maier points out, 1945 thus proved to be a positive turning-point, because the new relationship of Western Europe and the USA in the shadow of the Cold War was reinforced by economic and social change ongoing since the 1920s.

Similarly, the openness and uncertainty of the post-1989 era is only partially the result of the international uncertainties generated by the end of the Cold War. Instead, as Charles Maier, Paul Furlong and Robert Lumley show in different ways, the political and economic foundations of the post-1945 settlement had been increasingly tested since the 1970s. The Keynesian consensus was undermined by the new challenges of globalization and the information revolution. At the same time, the established political parties found themselves having to respond to the changing social and cultural bases of politics in affluent societies. In these ways, as Charles Maier would argue, the economic and political bases of the 'American empire' were being undermined even before the end of the Cold War threw the whole international order into question.

Although this mixture of trends has thrown much into question, there is little sign that 1989 signals a return to the disorder and rivalries of the 1920s and 1930s. A 'post-national' unified Germany, a relatively stable French Fifth Republic and an Italian Republic painfully advancing towards a reform of its constitution demonstrates the enduring strength of the post-1945 settlement. Something fundamental changed in Western Europe between the 1950s and 1970s. The powers of Western Europe ceased to be the coordinating metropolitan centres of overseas empires and finally became nation-states who simultaneously embarked on the construction of a new type of confederation now known as the European Union.

Western Europe is thus far stronger in the post-1989 era than in the aftermath of 1918 or 1945. Recent histories of Europe place the interwar crisis and the Great Boom of the 1950s to the 1970s in a new perspective when they assess the stability of Western Europe during the period of slow growth and long-term unemployment that affected France, Germany or Italy at times in the 1980s and 1990s. Richard Vinen refuses even to consider a comparison between the economic misery of the 1930s and the problems of the 1980s or 1990s.[75] Between the 1950s and the 1970s, Mark Mazower argues, Western Europe underwent a fundamental shift in its economy and its national systems of social welfare. In Western Europe, peasant society, a source of enormous economic and social instability in interwar Europe, almost completely vanished.[76] The cumulative effects of national economic growth and the expansion of the welfare state make it hard to draw parallels between the situation since 1989 and that in 1918 or 1945.

Yet, as Christopher Seton-Watson reminds us, for all the enduring changes, there have been some ominously recurrent patterns. The end of the Cold War visited its causalities on the Balkans and the former Soviet Union, as previously the post-1918 and post-1945 eras were touched off bloody civil war and chaos in Eastern Europe. In the year 2000, with the democratization of Serbia[77] and the halting but unstoppable expansion of the EU into Eastern Europe, the settlement fashioned in Western Europe after 1945 promises to bring a happier history to the eastern half of the continent. Yet the unresolved political dilemmas of European integration, the debates over the boundaries of citizenship, migration and asylum and the future of the welfare states of Western Europe demonstrate that stability, in the very different western half of the continent, always evolves through a dynamic equilibrium.

If the eras after 1945 and 1989 were fundamentally different from 1918, this was not least because of the massive presence of the Americans in Europe. The Old Continent adapted Americanization after 1945. Western Europeans incorporated into their economies, societies and culture certain congenial aspects of American civilization. But neither Coca-Cola in the 1950s nor the Internet[78] in the 1990s have or will homogenize important differences between both the civilizations on both sides of the Atlantic. The West European model of social welfare was significantly different from the American model 30 years ago and has diverged since the decline of big state liberalism in the USA.[79] American attitudes towards capital punishment, guns, abortion and organized religion differ significantly from those of a goodly number of the citizens of Western Europe. After 1989 the politics of trade and money and the question of a European defence identity became sources of tensions within the informal American Empire. These questions will be major determinants of stability or turbulence in the years to come.

Notes

1. For a discussion of the literature in the 1980s predicting the fall of the Soviet Union, see R. Vinen, *A History in Fragments. Europe in the Twentieth Century*. (London: Little, Brown and Company, 2000) pp. 656–7. For Randall Collins, see *Weberian Sociological Theory*. (Cambridge: Cambridge University Press, 1986). The encounter in Sweden was related to me by one of the members of the audience present at a paper read by Professor Collins at the University of Uppsala's Institute of Advanced Study.
2. E. Hobsbawm, *Age of Extremes*. (London: Michael Joseph, 1994).
3. M. Mazower, *Dark Continent*. (Harmondsworth: Allen Lane, 1998).
4. N. Ferguson, *The Pity of War*. (Harmondsworth: Allen Lane, 1998).
5. Beginning in the 1980s, sociologists in a largely uncritical fashion began to call this period an era of postmodernity and investigate the political, economic and cultural effects of globalization. Naturally there are exceptions to the rule. Paul Hirst and Grahame Thompson have been the most merciless critics of their colleagues' infatuation with globalization. They argue that the era before 1914 witnessed far greater globalization than the last decades of the twentieth century, see P. Hirst and G. Thompson, *Globalization in Question*. (Cambridge: Polity Press, 1996). From another angle Richard Vinen criticizes the nostalgia for this era of sound money. For many Europeans the *Belle Epoque* was experienced as a time of poverty or mass migration induced by wretched living conditions at home, see Vinen, pp. 17–37.
6. Ferguson, see 'Conclusion: Alternatives to Armageddon'.
7. Vinen, pp. 636–7.
8. N. Davies, *Europe. A History*. (Oxford: Oxford University Press, 1996).
9. Davies, pp. 39–42.
10. C. Maier, *Recasting Bourgeois Europe. Stabilisation in France, Germany and Italy in the Decade After WWI*. (Princeton NJ: Princeton University Press, 1975).
11. C. Maier, 'The Two Post-war Eras and the Conditions for Stability in Twentieth Century Western Europe', *American Historical Review*, 86, 2 (1981), pp. 527–52.
12. C. Maier, 'The Collapse of Communism: Approaches for a Future History', *History Workshop Journal*, 31, Spring, (1991) 34–59.
13. P. Clavin, *The Great Depression in Europe, 1929–1939*. (Basingstoke: Macmillan now Palgrave, 2000) pp. 213–14.
14. Clavin, 198–215; T. Geiger, '*Pax Americana* and European Integration, 1945–58', in T. Geiger and P. Kennedy (eds), *Regional Trade Blocs, Multilateralism and the GATT: Complementary Paths to Free Trade?* (London: Pinter, 1996) pp. 56–78.
15. Clavin, p. 200, p. 210.
16. R. Service, *A History of Twentieth-Century Russia*. (Harmondsworth: Penguin, 1998) p. 313; Vinen, pp. 296–7, 303–4

17. There is a vast literature on the collapse of the economies of Eastern Europe and the Soviet Union, see especially I.T. Berend, *Central and Eastern Europe 1944–1993. Detour from Periphery to Periphery.* (Cambridge: Cambridge University Press, 1996); Service, pp. 428–553; Vinen, pp. 475–517.
18. A. Milward, *The Reconstruction of Western Europe 1945–51.* (London: Metheun, 1984); A. Milward (with the assistance of George Brenner and Frederico Romero), *The European Rescue of the Nation-State.* (London: Routledge, 1992).
19. M. J. Hogan, *The Marshall Plan. America, Britain and the Reconstruction of Western Europe.* (Cambridge, Cambridge University Press, 1987).
20. J. Peterson and E. Bomberg, *Decision-Making in the European Union.* (Basingstoke: Macmillan now Palgrave, 1999) pp. 250–1.
21. J. Peterson, *Europe and America. The Prospects for Participation*, 2nd edition. (London: Routledge, 1996); J. Sperling (ed.), *Europe in Change. Two Tiers or Two Speeds? The European Security Order and the Enlargement of the European Union and Nato.* (Manchester, Manchester University Press, 1999).
22. Peterson and Blomberg, p. 251.
23. M. Ignatieff, 'The New American Way of War', *New York Review of Books*, 20 July 2000, pp. 42–6.
24. N. Ferguson, 'The Truce that Lied', *Financial Times Weekend*, 17–18 July 1999, p. 1. An interesting edited collection appeared several years ago that systematically evaluated the legacies of the Paris Peace Treaties in light of the ethnic conflicts after 1989, see S. Dunn and T. G. Fraser, *Europe and Ethnicity. World War I and Contemporary Ethnic Conflict.* (London, Routledge, 1996).
25. It has recently be argued that the ethnonationalism of earlier Macedonian nationalists of the 1910s has been replaced by a civic nationalism forged when the Republic of Macedonia was created in postwar Yugoslavia, see J. Baer, 'Balkan Tales: Macedonia – a Nation Lacking Nationalism?', *The Asen Bulletin*, 18, Winter (2000) 3–13. Unfortunately, this may be too optimistic.
26. M. Glenny, *The Balkans 1804–1999. Nationalism, War and the Great Powers.* (London: Granta Books, 1999).
27. Glenny , p. 661.
28. This has not escaped the notice of the recent historians of twentieth-century Europe, see Davies, pp. 897–1055; Mazower, pp. 40–76, 213–32.
29. M. R. Marrus, *The Unwanted: European Refugees in the Twentieth Century.* (Oxford, Oxford University Press, 1985); C. M. Skran, *Refugees in Inter-War Europe: the Emergence of a Regime.* (Oxford: Clarendon Press, 1994).
30. The most recent review can be found in, UNHCR, *The State of the World's Refugees. Fifty Years of Humanitarian Action.* (Oxford: Oxford University Press, 2000), chaps. 1,7.
31. A. Bloch and C. Levy (eds.), *Refugees, Citizenship and Social Policy in Europe.* (Basingstoke: Macmillan now Palgrave, 1999).
32. C. Levy, 'Fascism, National Socialism and Conservatives in Europe, 1914–1945: Issues for Comparativists', *Contemporary European History*, 8, 1 (1999) 97–126.
33. C. Levy, 'The Geneva Convention and the EU: a Fraught Relationship', 'The Refugee Convention at 50', International Association for the Study of Forced Migration and University of the Witwatersrand, 7th International Research and Advisory Panel, Eskom Conference Centre, Midrand, South Africa, 8–11 January 2001.
34. Berend.

35. M. Wolfe, 'Avoiding the trap of transition', *Financial Times*, 11 October 2000, p. 25.
36. C. Levy, 'Max Weber and European Integration', in R. Schroeder (ed.), *Max Weber, Democracy and Modernization.* (Basingstoke: Macmillan now Palgrave, 1998) pp. 124–5.
37. The most recent survey of the Italian economy since 1945 is Vera Zamagni's, 'Evolution of the Economy', in P. McCarthy (ed.), *Italy since 1945.* (Oxford: Oxford University Press, 2000) pp. 42–68. For the economic vitality of the 'Third Italy', see P. Ginsborg, *L'Italia del tempo presente. Famiglia, società civile, Stato 1980–1996.* (Turin: Einaudi, 1998) pp. 27–59.
38. C. Levy,'From Fascism to 'Post-Fascists': Italian Roads to Modernity', in R. Bessel (ed.), *Fascist Italy and Nazi Germany: Comparisons and Contrasts.* (Cambridge: Cambridge University Press, 1996) pp. 165–96.
39. For a recent interesting summary of these arguments see, Vinen, pp. 440–57.
40. S. Strasser, C. McGovern and M. Judt (eds), *Getting and Spending. European and American Consumer Societies in the Twentieth Century.* (Cambridge: Cambridge University Press, 1998).
41. C. Duggan and C. Wagstaff (eds.), *Italy in the Cold War: Politics, Culture, Society 1948–1958.* (Oxford: Berg, 1995).
42. N. White, *Reconstructing Italian Fashion. American and the Development of the Italian Fashion Industry.* (Oxford: Berg, 2000).
43. V. De Grazia, *How Fascism Ruled Women. Italy, 1922–1945.* (Berkeley : University of California Press, 1992) pp. 272–88.
44. S. Berger, M. Donovan and K. Passmore (eds), *Writing National Histories. Western Europe Since 1800.* (London, Routledge, 1999) Part VII.
45. For the French case see, S. Khilnani, *Arguing Revolution: the Intellectual Left in Postwar France.* (New Haven and London: Yale University Press, 1992). For Italy see, R. S. Gordon, '*Impegno* and the encounter with modernity: "high" culture in post-war Italy', in P. McCarthy (ed.), *Italy Since 1945*, pp. 197–213.
46. Ginsborg, pp. 471–564.
47. A. Marwick, *The Sixties. Cultural Revolution in Britain, France, Italy and the United States c. 1958–1974.* (Oxford: Oxford University Press, 1998).
48. D. Richardson and C. A. Rootes (eds), *The Green Challenge. The Development of Green Parties in Europe.* (London: Routledge, 1995).
49. S. Tarrow, *Democracy and Disorder. Protest and Politics in Italy, 1965–1975.* (Oxford, Clarendon Press, 1989). I. Favretto, '1956 and the PSI: the end of "Ten Winters"', *Modern Italy*, 5, 1 (2000) 25–45.
50. G. Bedani, *Politics and Ideology in the Italian Workers' Movement.* (Oxford, Berg, 1995) pp. 139–94.
51. Ginsborg, pp. 257–337.
52. J. Farrell and C. Levy, 'The Northern League: Conservative Revolution?', in C. Levy (ed.), *Italian Regionalism. History, Identity, Politics.* (Oxford: Berg, 1996) pp. 131–50.
53. S. Gundle and S. Parker (eds), *The New Italian Republic. From the Fall of the Berlin Wall to Berlusconi.* (London: Routledge, 1996).
54. Levy, 'Historians and the "First Republic"', in *Writing National Histories*, pp. 265–78.
55. C. A. Rootes, 'Student Activism in France: 1968 and After', in P. Cerny (ed.), *Social Movements and Protest in France.* (London: Pinter, 1982).

56. R. King (ed.), 'Special Issue. The Italian Experience of Immigration', *Modern Italy*, 4, 2 (1999) .
57. L. Cheles *et al.* (eds), *Neo-Fascism in Western and Eastern Europe*, 2nd edition. (London: Longman, 1995); P. Taggart, *Populism.* (Buckingham: Open University Press, 2000) pp. 73–88.
58. A. Cole, *Franco-German Relations*. (London: Longman, 2001).
59. Levy, 'Max Weber', p. 122.
60. Levy, 'Max Weber', p. 123.
61. Levy, 'Max Weber'. p. 117.
62. M. Roseman, 'National Socialism and Modernization', in Bessel, *Fascist Italy*, pp. 197–229.
63. R. Dahrendorf, *Society and Democracy in Germany*. (London: Weidenfeld and Nicolson, 1967).
64. For the linkages between the postwar concept of codetermination and these policies see, J. Gillingham, *Coal, Steel and the Rebirth of Europe 1945–1955. The Germans and the French from Ruhr Conflict to European Community*. (Cambridge: Cambridge University Press, 1991).
65. U. Herbert, *Hitler's Foreign Workers: Enforced Foreign Labour in Germany under the Third Reich*. (Cambridge, Cambridge University Press, 1997).
66. For a recent survey of the Italian settlement since 1945, see G. Pasquino, 'Political Development', in P. McCarthy (ed.), pp. 69–94.
67. C. Levy (ed.), *Italian Regionalism. History Identity Politics*. (Oxford: Berg, 1996).
68. C. Levy, 'Italian Regionalism in Context', in *Italian Regionalism*, pp. 1–30.
69. Ginsborg, pp. 293–304.
70. Ginsborg, pp. 471–564.
71. G. Pasquino, 'Political Development', in P. McCarthy (ed.), *Italy since 1945*, pp. 87–94.
72. A. A. Kallis, *Fascist Ideology. Territory and Expansionism in Italy and Germany, 1922–45*. (London: Routledge, 2000) pp. 11–26; M. Knox, *Common Destiny. Dictatorship, Foreign Policy and War in Fascist Italy and Nazi Germany*. (Cambridge, Cambridge University Press, 2000).
73. J. L. Harper, 'Italy and the World since 1945', in P. McCarthy (ed.), *Italy*, pp. 95–106.
74. S. Berger, 'Historians and Nation-Building after Reunification', *Past & Present*, 148 (1995) 187–222.
75. Vinen, pp. 518–51.
76. Mazower, pp. 290–331.
77. T. Garton Ash, 'The Last Revolution', *New York Review of Books*, 16 November 2000, pp. 8, 10–14.
78. C. Levy, 'The European Road to the Information Superhighway', in V. Symes, C. Levy and J. Littlewood (eds), *The Future of Europe. Policies and Issues for the Twenty-First Century*. (Basingstoke, Macmillan now Palgrave, 1997), pp, 175–205; C. Levy, 'After Liberalisation: Is There Still a European Road to the Information Superhighway?', 50th Annual Conference of the Political Studies Association, London School of Economics, London, 12–15 April 2000.
79. G. Esping-Andersen, *The Three Worlds of Welfare Capitalism*. (Cambridge, Polity Press, 1990).

Part I

The International Context for National Stabilization: 1918–1945–1989

2
Empires or Nations? 1918, 1945, 1989...

Charles Maier

> Nella vita degli imperatori c' è un momento, che segue all'orgoglio per l'ampiezza sterminata dei territori che abbiamo conquistato, alla malinconia e al sollievo di sapere che presto riunceremo a conoscerli e a comprenderli; ... è il momento disperato in cui si scopre che quest' impero che ci era sembra la somma di tutte le meraviglie è uno sfacelo senza fine ne forma, che la sua corruzione è troppo incancrenita perché il nostro scretto possa metterevi riparo, che il trionfo sui sovrani avversari ci ha fatto eredi della loro lunga rovina.
>
> In the lives of emperors there is a moment that follows upon the pride in the unbounded breadth of the territories that we have conquered, upon the melancholy and the relief of knowing that we shall soon renounce learning about them and understanding them; this is the desperate moment in which we discover that this empire which seemed to us the sum of all wonders is a defeat without end or form, that the rot is already too gangrenous for our sceptre to be able to repair it, that our triumph over our enemy sovereigns has made us heirs to their long ruination.
>
> Italo Calvino, *Le città invisibili*

I

It is with a certain sense of foreboding that I propose to address the issue of international settlements in the twentieth century.[1] The foreboding is not about the intellectual challenges inherent in the topic, although these are formidable. Rather it is unease about where the world is actually heading. In 1989 we all greeted the triumph of democratization – a decade underway in the Iberian and Latin American regions, just taking place among the Communist states – as a final resolution of twentieth-century ills. The events from 1989 to 1991 appeared to be the delayed promise of Woodrow Wilson's international order of 1918–19 or the Anglo-American coalition of anti-fascist allies of 1945. Whether as Western onlookers or as European participants we could share in those rare exalted moments when the new order of the ages, a great collective breakthrough seemed about to emerge. Recall the crowds that greeted Woodrow Wilson when he arrived in Europe aboard the 'George Washington' in January 1919, or the relief and euphoria when the killing ceased in May and then August 1945, or the dancing atop the Berlin Wall and the crowds in Wenceslas Square in November 1989. Of course, such collective ebullience had to ebb; the liminal flux was fated to congeal again into quotidian transactions.[2] But in fact the disillusion and problematic viscosity of public life reemerged as greater than one might have expected. And we were not sure what order of public problems we were discovering.

Were we coming face to face with the renewed ethnic and national conflicts of 1914 that were resumed in the late 1920s after the interlude of post-1918 state-building, but were suppressed finally by the Communist organization of Eastern Europe? We might chalk up such a reemergence to the revenge of history; at least we could comfort ourselves with the feeling of dreary familiarity. If this was the case, we could say, we have passed this way before; we have witnessed these tired quarrels: earlier Balkan wars, earlier Irish troubles, earlier nationalist agitation in the Muslim world. Such movements are not fun, but they need not spell international catastrophe if the large powers were not themselves embroiled in these quarrels. But perhaps the renewed brush fires of ethnicity were not a reprise of earlier quarrels, perhaps they signalled a new sort of international composition, not amenable to the present precarious agreements brokered by the great powers one finds in the Balkans at the end of the twentieth century. In that case we can take no reassurance from their unpleasant familiarity.

Alone, this question makes it urgent to reflect on the nature of the historical transition through which we are now living. In conventional terms we can cast the inquiry in terms of international settlements, and logically compare the passage now underway with the settlement after 1918 and that after 1945. Of course one might quarrel with the concept of settlement after 1918: the Versailles system offered no durable equilibrium. Nearly 20 years ago I argued in fact, that 1918 and 1945 had to be understood as part of a single cumulative settlement: it took two postwar efforts to institute the equilibria that allowed for a peaceful international order and a tranquil domestic accommodation.[3] But I do not wish to take up that particular argument in this chapter. For the present inquiry it does not matter particularly whether we construe 1918 and 1945 as two separate settlements or part of a transaction reached piecemeal and *seriatim*. What is crucial is the prospect for domestic and international equilibrium today. I hope that this analysis helps furnish some conceptual tools for addressing that issue.

What do we mean by a settlement? We think in terms of a set of international transactions, whether consensual or imposed by force, that keeps interstate conflict short of war, or in terms of a balance of power that guarantees a sort of peaceful equilibrium. But we also think of a series of domestic group compromises that allow for the generally peaceful conduct of politics and economic life at home. When historians and political scientists refer to the post-World War Two settlement, they do not mean just the Soviet–American balance or the upshot of Yalta. They refer to the negotiations between representatives of labour and capital, or between social democrats and liberals or even conservatives that had been impossible to secure in the interwar era. They refer to the acceptance of managerial capitalism on the part of labour's delegates and the acceptance of a welfare state and full-employment policies on the part of business representatives. The post-1945 settlement bridged social classes and interests as well as nation-states.

II

The question follows naturally, to what extent must internal and international settlements reinforce each other? Can we establish the proposition that no international settlement is really durable unless it coincides with a general ideological consensus; and no domestic pacification is likely unless these is a high degree of international equilibrium? Does peace at home require peace abroad? Is it true conversely that peace in the international arena will fray if there is no shared ideological consensus?

To approach an answer, consider first the conditions conducive to maintaining international equilibrium. The most venerable analysis has emphasized the balance of power, a concept developed by statesmen themselves in the eighteenth century, which suggested that the comity of great powers tended to preserve itself by coalescing against any hegemonic threat from among its own number. The concept was, in a sense, Newtonian; it looked at great powers as uniform bodies and did not pay attention to their internal composition. Once revolutionary France appeared, of course, statesmen changed their analysis to take account of the internal constitution of states. States that were revolutionary at home, conservatives now argued in Austria, Britain, and Prussia were impelled by their internal dynamic to seek conquest and upset the status quo. From Burke and Pitt, Gentz and Metternich, to Henry Kissinger's analysis of the Vienna settlement written more than four decades ago, students of international equilibrium included the domestic constitution of states in their calculations. Similarly, Kissinger's *Nuclear Weapons and Foreign Policy* took up again the Vienna statesmen's implicit distinction between revolutionary and non-revolutionary powers.[4] The former were not merely out to aggrandize their power or their territory but to smash through the implicit international rules of the game. Kissinger cited Nazi Germany and Soviet Russia. If such powers did not arise, international systems remained stable.

I would propose a different emphasis: The Vienna settlement preserved the peace so long as two different interests might reinforce each other. At the outset, as historians usually emphasize, stability depended upon the calculation of Metternich and Castlereagh that it would be prudent to reinstate France, safely restored as an unadventurous monarchy, in the concert of Europe. Underlying this policy, and continuing after 1815, lay a shared French, British and Austrian interest in offsetting Russia (and its possible Prussian partner) geopolitically, while at the same time there was a shared Austrian and Russian interest in offsetting any western tendencies toward liberalism or revolution. Austria thus reinforced one coalition to counterbalance Russian strategically, but simultaneously constructed an ideological coalition with Russia to suppress democratic trends. Vienna organized a transnational regime safe for landowners and an alignment conducive to the balance of power – but they were not one and the same. The principles of geopolitics and ideology overlapped but were not congruent. It was the crosscutting international alignments that made the settlement relatively robust. Ideological conformity was only one factor.[5]

The Vienna settlement, of course, does not allow us to test the revived claim that democratic states do not make war upon each other.[6] No matter how great an ideological consensus might have briefly prevailed, it was not a democratic one. Nonetheless, Immanuel Kant had argued that the first requisite of 'perpetual peace' was a commitment on the part of states to preserve republican institutions. Richard Cobden and Mill proposed that countries involved in extensive trade and committed to maintaining what today might be called market democracies (or at least liberal market oligarchies) were unlikely to resort to force. In 1917–19 Woodrow Wilson argued that authoritarian states whose foreign and military policy lay beyond parliamentary scrutiny would be aggressive actors; his Second Armistice note to Germany in October 1918 made the theory explicit and provoked an abdication crisis in the Reich. Recent political theorists have sought to test the theory, although they can draw on only a small subset of potentially valid cases in which two democracies might have conflicts of interest. In any case the theory proposes that there is a domestic basis to international equilibria. But what is the nature of this basis, if it at all exists?

Insofar as the Vienna settlement preserved peace from 1815 until the wars of 1853 to 1870, it rested upon a consensus among agrarian élites, represented by British Tories, Austrian, French, Russian and Prussian statesmen, who took it for granted that traditional aristocracies were the natural governors of society. Vienna tended to break down precisely when these élites differed on the right role to take toward revolutionary challenges to the landlord order. The British opted out of counter-revolutionary enforcement, at least abroad. Peterloo was not to be matched by an expeditionary force to Madrid, and certainly not by sanctioning a Franco–Spanish expeditionary force to Mexico or Bogota. The Vienna settlement suggests that it was not democracy or liberal regimes *per se* that preserved peace, but just any sort of consensus on regimes and domestic social hierarchies that was important. Yet we cannot accept even this relatively weak correlation without examination of counter-arguments.

Despite the example of the Vienna settlement we cannot be certain that shared commitments on domestic institutions, in this case on aristocratic government, acted as an efficacious force for peace. If this were the case, it would be difficult to explain eighteenth-century warfare. The great wars of religion, or even of Louis XIV, might be attributed to ideological conflicts, but eighteenth-century societies after the Peace of Utrecht were evolving compatibly toward aristocratic-monarchical syntheses. The differences in their internal institutions were not so grating that they produced revolutionary challenges. Instead the powers (to use the Newtonian black-box terminology of the time) fought over colonial empires on their periphery and the resources of Central and Eastern Europe, from Italy to the Baltic, and the upper Rhine to the Dnieper. These two vast areas of unsettled control meant that the Western colonial contenders and the Eastern empires interlocked in major coalitions. The shared institutions of the *ancien régime* could not assure peace when the stakes were so potentially great.

Furthermore we can adduce the negative case: there are periods when despite major institutional differences, international equilibrium can still be maintained. It is not clear that we should consider the period from 1870 to 1914, even less the years from 1890 to 1914, as just an era of peace. The years witnessed an arms race and they were increasingly punctuated by crises that threatened general war. Nonetheless, to the degree that peace was preserved, the international order did not require ideological conformity. Indeed the European international balance rested upon the fact that the most ideologically advanced democracy and the most insistent autocracy could strike an agreement. The balance of power (although it was internally hardening into a dangerous bipolar deadlock)[7] rested upon the capacity for major states to disregard their domestic differences. Alexander III had to be feted in Paris, Raymond Poincaré had to be toasted in St Petersburg. Cold War bipolarity suggests a similar conclusion. Insofar as we wish to construe the Cold War, as John Gaddis proposed, as a long peace,[8] then that peace could not have rested upon shared ideological premises. Two blocs confronted each other and stayed out of major war except in Asia despite their differences. In short, given the long record from 1713 to 1989, is it possible to make any persuasive correlation between the structure of domestic regimes and the preservation of peace between states?

I would take recourse in a different sort of argument. Stable international structures, I believe, do reveal characteristic regimes, but not all states in such a structure (whether concert, alliance, bipolar or multilateral framework) need share the same regime. What seems critical to me is that a certain domestic series of arrangements be sufficiently established within *each* major country such that its own regime (or political and socioeconomic institutions) is stable enough so that it provides no impetus for sudden aggression outward or intervention from abroad. Countries with differing political arrangements or economic institutions can co-exist compatibly provided that each is relatively stable at home. On the other hand, no country in internal upheaval is an island. Revolutionary transformations are always international events although the magnitude of their disturbance may be small if they are small or isolated. The Cold War remained cold in part, I believe, because of the danger of nuclear weapons. But it also remained cold because each society evolved or had forced upon itself a domestic arrangement that was well defined. In the West these domestic arrangements rested upon the class settlements reached between 1944 and 1948. In the East they rested upon Soviet *force majeur*. At several instances in the postwar decades there were serious challenges: in the GDR in 1953, in Hungary in 1956, in Czechoslovakia in 1968, in Poland from 1981 to 1983 – and then of course the general breakdown after 1987. The early ones, however, which did not originate in the centre of the bloc, could be suppressed by force and the West was not prepared to intervene. The political and economic regimes were quickly brought back to the norm that was compatible within the bloc. Relations within blocs remained stable because the West decided not to intervene. Had the uprisings been more protracted or more generalized, that is, had the Soviet forces not been relatively quick and resolute, and had the atomic arsenals not set new deterrent limits on intervention, wider conflict might not have been averted.

To summarize up to this point, I think there are important corollaries between international stability and domestic arrangements. But at the most general level, they rest not on the nature of particular domestic regimes, but on the stability of whatever domestic institutions participant nations may already possess. Since Western nations have tended to develop within a common overarching system of ideas about politics and have rubbed elbows for many centuries it is not surprising that the evolution of institutions has been similar, but not always. Political theorists and social scientists may find this preliminary argument too trivial to be interesting. It does not predict how particular regimes behave. It certainly does not assert that democracies behave well; indeed it does not even claim that democracies at least behave well with each other (although the claim may be true). It just argues that internal instability is a major provocation of internationally destabilizing behaviour, whether the latter originates from outside the state in upheaval, or within one or another of the groups contending for power within the society in turmoil. It does not furnish any maxims for statesmen, such as Henry Kissinger would like, because even if the lesson might be to encourage any state in turmoil to overcome its domestic troubles, onlookers differ on how to overcome a revolutionary challenge. Some prefer suppression, others concession and reforms.

III

Switch the focus from ideological systems to the institutional architecture of the international system. Consider two highly abstract ideal types of collective institutional agents – nations and empires. Nations are autonomous and sovereign political communities ostensibly constructed upon a shared linguistic or ethnic uniformity or at least ethnic coexistence. Their architects and defenders usually claim that the political institutions of modern nation-states are based upon the representation of individuals according to civic ground rules. The concept of citizenship upon which they rest posits civic equality and shared participatory rights (at least for the dominant ethnic community).

Empires are different. By empire I refer to a form of territorial organization that groups different nations or ethnic communities around a sovereign centre which possesses preponderant resources of power and/or wealth. Whereas a nation usually claims to represent its citizens according to principles of equality, an empire is hierarchic. It frankly envisages that one political community must remain the major initiator of policies and coordinator of economic activity. At the same time, each constituent territory of an empire, including the metropole, tends to reproduce the hierarchical organization of communities that marks its overall structure. It replicates within the imperial centre some of the disparities of influence and income that characterize the centre's relationship to the periphery. Empires have losers as well as winners, victims as well as beneficiaries. The winners, naturally enough, make their peace with empire more easily, and they justify the outcome as the result of inevitability or rationality or historical necessity. The losers often engage in a guerrilla war that seems pointless, sacrificial, and deviant to the winners. Empires thus impose the dialectic of pacification and violence. The key to successful imperial control or coordination rests upon the shared stake of leadership for the élites in each territorial component. Empires are projects of rule in which a provincial élite feels it comprises part of the ruling class of the structure as a whole. Empires, in a sense, are efforts at transnational linkage within a hierarchy of peoples.[9]

As a framework for economic activity, a nation can occupy a particular rung of development – predominately agricultural, or industrial or late capitalist, and so on – or it can include different levels of development simultaneously. Once liberal tenets displaced mercantilist policies, the political framework of nations has determined no particular relationship among the agricultural, industrial, financial and service-oriented activities that take place on their territory.[10] They can be highly interdependent or relatively segmented.

Again, empire is different: whether inside its metropolitan territory or between home country and dependencies, economic activity is both integrated and differentiated. High value-added production takes place at the 'centre'; low value-added production takes place at the 'periphery'; the imperial organization tends to throw a political bridge over the flows of products, investments, profits and labour. This 'imperial' pattern thus tends to undermine the national bases of productive processes and legal jurisdiction. Multinationals, of course, are old news, but the multinationals of the 1960s or even the early twentieth century tended to disperse complete units of production in different countries. Today's dispersion often involves different activities; the firm will seek different product components in plants across the globe or assemble them in a different country. At the same time firms also seek production or marketing alliances outside their national territory without renouncing their corporate identity. The observer must be careful here. Although a hierarchical differentiation of supranational financial and productive processes accompanies empire, the economic process has its own momentum. So-called globalization undermines national control of economic activity, but not always to realign finance and production within any imperial framework. Instead it can disconnect political from economic space entirely.[11]

Both nations and empires can be democratic, but the democracy of the empire is confined to the metropole, and it tends towards more plebiscitarian forms: a focus on presidential politics, a preoccupation with the transmission and registration of momentary opinion through the media and the poll. So far as society is concerned, nations value equality; empires come to terms with stratification. They can be opulent for some and rewarding for many even as they impose subjection on others. In return for encroaching inequality they allow wider choices of life style and limit the stigmata of deviance. They are cultivated and cosmopolitan; they offer splendid opportunities for bureaucrats and those who can lend their rhetoric to the hierarchic project. Virgil remains the pre-eminent master of this gorgeous apologetic – but even he knew enough to end his *Aeneid* with a founding act of murderous violence.

The thesis of this chapter is that despite public rhetoric and ideology, empires or imperial systems have proven indispensable at each critical effort at twentieth century stabilization. Our statesmen repeatedly appeal to nations, but fall back on empires. In those intervals when imperial coordination has collapsed – for example, the 1920s and perhaps the first half of the 1990s – stabilization has proven precarious and ephemeral. The interplay between affirmation of the nation and persistence in empire provides an analytical tool for comparing the settlements of 1918, 1945, and perhaps post-1989.

A few important qualifications are necessary. It must be understood that the patterns of empire, which have proved so recurrently compelling, were not the formalized colonial domains that were divested after 1945. Rather they were structures of informal hierarchy and exchange. Empire, as used here, refers to the differentiation and hierarchization of the world economy and cultural systems – not just the frameworks of formal rule. In the sense meant here, the United States has been an imperial power, albeit one that in the developed world, at least, did not have to rely upon coercive domination.

Moreover, the effect of imperial settlements (at least in the West) was not to suppress nation-states but to preserve them. As the Scholastics once said about grace: *imperium non tollit sed perfecit*. Nationality clearly thrived in many respects during the postwar period; the resistance to Nazism rehabilitated some national commitments. Without the structures provided by supranational authorities, postwar nations would have slipped into nasty civil strife and communal quarrels. Modern empire thus helped reinvigorate national appeals and allowed them to recover another lease on life.

The open question at the end concerns the nature of developments since 1989. Do they adumbrate another twentieth-century 'settlement' that ostensibly rests on nationality but in fact consolidates empire? Or are they tending towards a qualitatively new linkage of economic and social organization, which at one and the same time would integrate global or regional economic units without recourse to imperial political hierarchy? Such an outcome would substitute, in effect, regional market organization for international politics, a development consonant with the nineteenth-century Saint Simonian dream of a transition from the governance of men to the administration of things or what in the 1970s enthusiasts celebrated about multinational corporations. Alternatively, might we actually be witnessing a successful effort to dismantle integrative tendencies, whether imperial or national and reinvigorate political representation and economic control at the local level? If so, will this effort be marked by a churlish territorial populism and xenophobia, or a real communitarian and democratic breakthrough? And would such an effort accomplish a durable rollback, or just an interruption of trends for a decade or two?

Obviously the polarized typology between nation and empire hardly does justice to the variety of sovereign states in modern times; in some major respects it actually falsifies experience. First of all, even imperial nations usually order their domestic affairs as if they approximated nations: their internal ground rules posit a national and not imperial identity for those inside their home territory. At the same time, every nation is to some degree an empire. No nation is devoid of political inequality or a distinction between centre and periphery. Every nation collectively privileges some of its citizens more than others and subordinates regional or ethnic communities. Every nation sets up its own unequal trading system within its own borders and depends upon regional inequalities of income to move labour and resources. States like to claim that they are nations even when they govern far-flung imperial domains. Nations encapsulate imperial relationships even within very circumscribed territories. Still, the distinction may serve the cause of historical and political analysis.

IV

Let us reflect on the phases in which *modern* nations and *modern* empires emerged on the world scene. By modern nations I refer to sovereign states as they were almost all reconfigured in the decisive decades from 1850 to 1880. Whereas British and French nationality might be attributable to an earlier era, most national states were recast in the three decades after mid-century. Now this is a strong claim since most historians of modern nationalism and nation-states trace their emergence to the emerging civic consciousness of the Enlightenment and the age of American and French revolutions.[12] But the decisive foundations, I propose, were not completed until the generation after the revolutionary upheavals of 1848. In the next three decades the following processes took place:

1. Nations opted not for confederal but national territorial organization.[13] The advocates of an older quasi-federal organization of land lost out to the advocates of strong centrally governed nations. The organization of Italy and Germany, the American Civil War, the victory of the Mexican liberals, of the outer Daimyo over the Shogunate, and so on – all testified to the same world-historical controversy over nationalism and confederalism, and nationalism won.
2. A new class coalition emerged behind these victories: a melding of landed aristocrats, hitherto dominant in national government, with 'bourgeois' representatives of industry, of the bureaucracy and the learned professions. This was the new coalition within the modern Conservative and Liberal parties in Britain. It comprised the social elements that Cavour and Bismarck built upon within Piedmont and Prussia and later Italy and Germany. It was the coalition that put an end to Reconstruction in the United States and that organized Mexico after the French effort at conquest, that Canovas engineered in Restoration Spain, or that the Meiji oligarchs soldered together. The men who made the reenergized nation-states of the latter nineteenth century collectively represented wealth, technology, expansive energy as well as ancestry.
3. A new dominant technology made possible the rationalization of territory.[14] The emergence of large-scale iron and steel manufacture

> with the bridges, ships and above all, railroad development that accompanied it, made possible the physical mastery of national territory. Completion of the Union Pacific, the Canadian Pacific, of the Freycinet plan for the linkage of the French republican interior, the Italian north–south lines, later the Mexican lines and the Trans-Siberian railroad meant more than a mere transportation revolution. The promoters of rail transportation were key actors in the new political coalitions of the second half of the century; rail lines served military occupation and strategy and the exploitation of territorial wealth. In effect the railroad (and the telegraph) changed the national interior from a spatial void to an energized territory. Contemporary science furnished analogues for the national enterprise, whether the post-Darwinian doctrines of biological competition, or the new physics of fields which identified an underlying energy level to all points in a space that no longer seemed empty. Hence, within a fateful generation a decisive set of interlocking transformations reconfigured the territorial frameworks of collective life. This generation experienced the contested victorious imposition of more centralized government over 'feudal' localism and the amalgam of entrepreneurial, technical and military élites with older landed magnates. The mastery of national space as virtual field of energy inscribed by lines of force as well as railroad and telegraph lines; indeed the drawing of new lines in all domains, between bourgeois and proletarian, private and public, male and female, hygienic and pathological, developed and under-developed.

For the larger and most vigorous territorial units, the acceleration to empire after 1880 was already inherent in their national development. Consolidating the national state meant reworking *de facto* subjection within their frontiers, even as the new national school systems inculcated the alleged equality of citizenship. Peasant communities at the edge had usually been poor. But now these peripheral peoples – Celts to coloureds, Sicilians, Poles, western Slavs – were pulled into the national vortex, taught the national language, bred to serve as domestic servants, or recruited to forge the heavy metal which their rulers were using to become united, rich and powerful. Those mobilized, we finally deigned to recognize, formed counter-communities, preserving customs, faith, ethnic identity to the degree possible. Every large nation thus verged on being an implicit empire.

No surprise, then, that empires seemed a natural outgrowth of nations. National monarchs liked to call themselves emperors: Louis Napoleon had revived the title in 1852. With respect to her South Asian territories the British queen was an empress after 1885; the sovereign of unified Germany reclaimed the designation; the Habsburgs, Romanovs, the heads of state of China and Japan and Brazil were already styled emperors. Some of this was just venerable usage. The 'old empires' of Eastern Europe were genuinely imperial, but in contrast to the new overseas empires they extended the boundaries of their national states to include contiguous peoples. Some of these contiguous peoples possessed special collective and territorial status inside their respective imperial frontier – Finland, Poland, Alsace-Lorraine, the diverse Austro-Hungarian crown lands, diverse part of the Ottoman Empire. Others were simply treated as parts of the core domain. The dominant people usually ended up trying to achieve incompatible objectives; they often hoped to impose concepts of cross-ethnic national loyalty and preserve their own hegemonic status. Austro-German liberals tried to run Cisleithania but parliamentary life became paralysed by the contention among its ethnic claimants. The Magyars ran Transleithania by exploiting disparities of electoral representation; they dominated a large territory by keeping other peoples far from influence and power. (In this respect, though, common techniques of *Herrschaft* and hegemony united landlord-dominated territories whether they were within old empires or new nations. In the great territories of subject peasantry – Russian, Hungary, Romania, the Italian *Mezzogiorno*, East Prussia, Ireland, Andalusia, the deep south of the United States, Yucatan, and so on – forms of landlord control ran the gamut from manipulated electoral systems to harsh vagrancy laws, to the hiring of local gangsters and lynching.)

The construction of overseas empires added new elements less to the arsenal of subjugation than to the organization of world political and economic space. Although the Spanish and Portuguese still retained some of their imperial territories acquired in the early modern era, the new colonial empires were run by modernized nations: the British, the French, Dutch, Americans, Germans, then the Italians and Japanese, and in its later format the Belgians. As noted at the outset, the ideology of domination could not be civic equality, although the British envisaged an evolution toward cloned parliaments and the French developed a concept of assimilation. The empire was frankly a structure built around concepts of differentiated economic and social functions. It was to provide material and later human resources for the strategic competition of the colonizing nation. It posited an evolutionary view of human development, such that the projects of the colonizers could be eminently justified in terms of tutelage.

But the new empires did not rest upon or require a major break with the non-ideological characteristics underlying the reconfiguration of nation states. Whereas railroad development was central to the mid-century concept of national space, now the role of ships became crucial. The development of the steel-clad ship, the rotary turbine (rather than the vertical steam cylinder), gunnery control, eventually the oil-fired engine provided technological advances but were hardly technological ruptures. Whether rail lines, shipping lines, and from the 1930s on, airlines, the sinews of empire remained devices for linear movement of goods and people. So too, the preoccupation with the construction of a bounded and exclusive territory was extended to overseas empire. Since the rules and ideologues of empire were simultaneously political leaders and opinion leaders at home, they shared the same fixation with territorial space as an index of vitality. Deep into the interwar period, the intellectual conceptualization of empire was a natural outgrowth of the project of nation-states. Empires and nations were complementary organizations of world territory: mutually exclusive indeed necessarily competitive, modern, expressions of vital collective interests, indices of sophisticated development and vigour alike. Both empires and nations were to die for.

V

But they were not the same, and the differences could appear, crucial. Subject peoples within the borders of empires (or at least their élites) claimed to be national communities and they aspired to national statehood. Nations, too, subscribed to ideologies of uniform civic identity and equality (with caveats for women, children, people of colour, the property-less, the illiterate and the feeble-minded). Empires did not. Imperial rivalries, moreover, appeared more dangerous to world peace after 1898 than mere national rivalries, although these were troublesome enough. Indeed we might best envisage World War One as a result of concentric imperial contests. The struggle that was localized in southeastern Europe over the disintegration of the Ottoman and Habsburg 'old' imperial domains became caught up in the larger Anglo–German and German–Russian rivalries. Each might have been settled, albeit messily, by a series of *ad hoc* compromises. Intertwined they were likely to prove far more difficult to resolve without large-scale war.

The two major ideological analyses of the 1914–18 catastrophe, moreover, each underlined the imperial attributes of world politics as the factor more disruptive of peace. Napoleon III had declared, 'L'empire, c'est la paix.' 'L'empire c'est la guerre', Lenin wrote in effect in 1916, as

Rosa Luxembourg had already declared a decade earlier. Not only that, capitalism tended toward empire. Lenin's influence, however, remained confined to the rulers and supporters of a Bolshevik experiment quarantined by the major exponents of world opinion. But Woodrow Wilson, who controlled the decisive military and economic resources at the end of World War One, could not be ignored. He did not explicitly condemn empire – some of his best allies ran empires – but he did explicitly condemn the unlimited prerogatives of executive control that empires retained. He also envisaged that nations, not empires, should be the constituent units of world socicty. Empires, the balance of power, and the 'old diplomacy', had produced the Great War; democratic nations met aspirations for self-determination and their peoples had an interest in world peace and collective security. The League of Nations and the postwar treaties were designed in theory to construct a new world order based upon these principles. The allies' empires, the United States' own colonial holdings were justified as a transitional framework mandated by the League to prepare their peoples for self-governance. The Geneva order was intended to usher in a world of pluralist nations, united in collective self-interest, but not super- or subordinated to imperial centres.

The Wilsonian settlement and the Geneva order did not work very well, and we all know many reasons for its failure. The issue of German power was not resolved; the Soviets remained in quarantine; and the United States withdrew from the postwar international institutions. National self-determination was less benign and peaceable a force in a situation, which, as in postwar Eastern Europe, left many newly mobilized ethnic groups living as irredenta in other nations. Germans in Poland and Czechoslovakia, White Russian in Poland, Croats unhappy with Yugoslavia, among other groups, ransomed the politics of the new nations to aggrieved nationalist elements. The separate nationalities looked precisely to outside powers for financial and political support.

It might be argued that the national programme did not work because it was not consistently applied. Had the nation-states of 1918–19 enjoyed the ethnic uniformity that they would have in somewhat altered borders after 1945, the principle of national self-determination might have involved less conflict. The Czechs would have been freed of the Sudeten Germans, and Poland would have been ethnically homogenous. But the existence of irredenta (up to twenty-five million of the one hundred million inhabitants in East Central Europe) was not only a source of instability in Eastern Europe. Neither was the revisionism of nationalist Germans and Hungarians who were angered at the strictures of Versailles and Trianon respectively.

VI

But it was not just the ethnic inconsistencies of nation-state formation that undermined the Geneva order. Nation-states as such also proved inadequate to the economic tasks of postwar reconstruction. This proved to be the case even when their economic policy makers shared common ground rules for economic stabilization. Indeed it was precisely because they did share common ground rules as sovereign units that they were plunged into depression. A pluralist system of formally equal sovereign states could not stabilize a high-employment economy that normally responded to transnational parameters and signals. The prewar economy had become increasingly international. It depended upon several patterns of exchange among the developed (and underdeveloped) world that had emerged in the era from the mid-nineteenth century until its rupture in 1914. These international patterns or systems of 'regulation' (in the French sense) involved trade, finance, that is, transfers of capital and labour. We have to consider the fate of them all.

Each centre of empire had served as a major source of capital, an important producer of industrial exports, and a significant importer of raw materials. Britain funded development in the Western Hemisphere (South America, the United States, and Canada) as well as in its Asian dominions. France invested heavily in Russian securities (that in turn funded railroad development), while Germany likewise served as a major investor in Eastern Europe and a consumer of East European agricultural products. More modestly, the Habsburg domains provided a territory for regional exchange and the flow of industrial goods and capital from Austria and Bohemia into the Kingdom of Hungary, while Italy played a similar role in the Balkans. The bulk of world trade and investment, it is well known, did not flow between metropole and colonial domains, but from Western states to Eastern Europe.

Nonetheless, these patterns had produced the classic differentiation of function that we can define as imperial. Indeed when Lenin analysed imperialism, it was the Western economic hegemony in Eastern Europe, not in Africa or Asia, which was his major source of data. And in each case these flows of trade and investment were disrupted: the Habsburg domains were severed, Russia was removed for almost a decade from the world economy, the Western powers had few resources. To be sure, exchange and investment began to recover in the last 1920s, only to be cut short by the world depression.[15]

The disruption of *de facto* imperial economic exchange was not the only source of economic distress. Nation-states involved, as noted, prevalent ideas and orientations of genuine and spurious ethnic equality. For Eastern Europe the imagined communities were often peasant communities, now confronting dwarf plots and an over-saturated commodities market. Their outlet for migration, moreover, had been closed off – in part by the economic distress in the cities of Central Europe (urban populations stabilized or stagnated between the wars), and above all by the United States' restriction of immigration in 1924. Imperial powers, or those claiming to be organizers of an international order, must be willing to absorb distressed labour as well as distressed goods; and this became impossible during and after World War One.

But the lack of an imperial hierarchy affected labour in another way. Hobson had suggested, with some acuteness, that the 'taproot' of imperial projects involved income inequality at home. Income inequality allowed élites to accumulate savings for which they sought safe and profitable overseas outlets. Conversely, though, imperial organization helped employers to stabilize income inequality within their home territories, not so much perhaps by developing low-wage competition offshore (for example, Indian cotton workers), as by making the gold convertibility of international currencies the criterion of economic maturity. But how could economies in which wage levels did (in good neoclassical fashion) determine the equilibrium employment level price actually restrain labour costs? Employers might exhort their workers at home to heed the price of labour in competitor nations; but if labour costs were rising simultaneously abroad, the warning lost its urgency. After World War Two and the establishing of United States economic preeminence, keying wages to productivity provided a new and effective instrument for wage restraint. Between the wars, productivity indices were more rudimentary. Taylorism, Fordism and similar approaches in effect proposed keying increases in wages to output. They involved productivity guidelines, *avant la lettre*. They justified management's control of the productive process but did not durably control wage pressure. Instead capital responded to real wage rises in line with neoclassical predictions, by firing labour. By 1930, preserving the restored ground rules of the pre-1914 imperial system of financial exchange in the new world of sovereign nation states required labour redundancy on a world scale. Both before 1914 and after 1945, imperial structures in effect rendered it easier to make neo-classical adjustments; they could keep international wage levels relatively lower and employment levels higher.

Finally, the Wilsonian architecture of the world harboured contradictory pressures: it encouraged the self-sufficiency of national units, but insisted on the substantial settlement of accumulated international payments, including war debts (and indirectly reparations). As the newly emergent creditor nation par excellence, the United States could enforce (or forgive) the flow of international payments. Washington forgave about half the *de facto* burden of international debt arising from World War One but clung to repayment of the rest. This pressure fell upon Western countries as a deflationary charge. In effect, the structure of international payments became a pressure for restricting investment not a source for expanding them. As Charles Kindleberger pointed out most trenchantly, British capital was no longer a sufficient source for financing world debt and consumption, while American capital remained the hostage of inconstant politics.[16] No imperial source of capital or purchasing power stood ready to assist, as it would after 1945. At best the international bankers who periodically came together to help arrange currency stabilization served as a transnational centre of coordination, although they acted to reinforce deflationary pressures.

But transnational coordination is different from imperial coordination: it is polycentric and not hegemonic. It traps bankers or policy makers into prisoner–dilemma choices between sacrificial cooperation and unilateral defection from common policy (for example devaluation). The central bankers and policy makers who imposed deflationary policies on their respective states between 1930 and 1933–36 were no longer responding to the regulations and incentives of a financial metropole. At best they shared a gentlemanly ethos that they had inherited from the pre-1914 period when indeed there had been a partially coordinated financial system. They were members of a club, but not agents of an empire.

VII

The settlement after 1945 was different. The nations of 1919 were reestablished with the exception of the Baltic states. In fact, however, there was to be no extended period in which nations attempted to cope with postwar problems on their own. Within a couple of years two quasi-imperial frameworks had emerged. In Eastern Europe, the Communist Parties imposed a transnational form of single-party control oriented upon Soviet leadership. They used political enthusiasm and terror alike to encourage common policies. In Western Europe, the United States hesitated, but then stepped in to provide political and economic leadership. American policy worked precisely to prevent the deflationary spiral of international claims among nations that had reached such a destructive and destabilizing effect after 1929. From the imperial centre emanated a flow of credits designed to stimulate recovery and growth and preserve democratic coalitions.

The American empire[17] (call it perhaps more neutrally the Atlantic system of imperial coordination) also resolved the dilemma of wage regulation in a way that remained compatible with high employment – a solution that had eluded national economic policy makers after 1918. As noted, United States policy makers convinced employers and employees in the Marshall Plan countries and later in the OECD more generally to accept the basic linkage of wage to productivity increases. This decisive rule emanated from the imperial centre and was fostered by productivity missions, trips to the US for compliant labour leaders – and of course by the results for growth and employment. Switching over to productivity guidelines took place between 1947 and the early 1950s. In the first two postwar years, wage restraint either depended upon solidarity pacts and wage freezes concluded as the war closed, or it disintegrated in wage–price spirals that were monetized by governments seeking to preserve national consensus. The ejection of the Communist Party representatives from governments in Belgium, France and Italy permitted stabilization policies. The process remains visible to the historian by virtue of the documented controversies concerning incentive payments, speed-ups, and the dismantling of 'COLAS' or escalator clauses. The American empire, to put it somewhat tendentiously, rested on piecework. Such a result could not have been achieved within the Wilsonian or Genevan system, for it required one country to foot the bills of transition. Until 1971, Washington at least paid for the results it wanted; Moscow did not have to bother. Thereafter, however, Washington used its financial hegemony to draw subsidies from its allies, among other reasons to subsidize American energy purchases, while the Soviet Union used its own energy resources to help sustain satellites whose restiveness it wished to suppress,

The American imperial framework was not just the product of credit creation. A new Atlantic élite emerged, earning its credentials by missions to Washington and to New York. Trans-Atlantic trips, common foreign policy forums, a network of clubby associations for talk and mutual self-regard created in effect a transnational ruling group. Their glossy bulletins featured group photographs in which prestigious Americans and Europeans communicated with each other at seminar tables or over drink and food. If Soviet rule was based on *Kto kogo*, the American principle was *Kto c kem*. The most prominent members of the Atlantic élite achieved a semi-sacral status: Marshall, McCloy, Lovett, Spaak, Monnet, and other 'wise men' who exhorted to common effort and cooperation. Below this summit, a cadre of international civil servants served in Washington, Paris and elsewhere. Within two decades subsidiary networks arose around think tanks, banks, unions, and so on. This new imperial culture served those nations that were small and likely to be submerged on their own, such as the Benelux countries. It also served those who sought rapid development or rehabilitation: in Europe, Germany and Italy, and in Asia, Japan. The most self-sufficient states sought to cut special deals within the imperial framework: the French resisting full integration and the British seeking preferential access to the Washington centre. The latter, of course, had the advantage of sharing the new lingua franca of the empire: indeed mastery of English would become the cultural passport for every claimant to élite status. By the late 1960s sustained affluence extended Americanization deep into the middle classes and the new expanded ranks of university students to the degree that pop culture and rock began to undermine the very imperial structures that abetted their diffusion.

VIII

It is time to ask some hard questions. First, was the postwar structure of Western affluence and stability really imperial – even in the sense this chapter defines imperial? Did it require a hierarchical array of national societies and peoples and a differentiation between centre and periphery? Did it live upon the discrepancy between the high value added labour or managerial and symbolic tasks performed at the centre and less valued tasks performed in the periphery or by migrants from the periphery? Did cultural modes and styles emanate from the centre, or emerge diffusely from different locations? If not the pre-1914 system, should not, the post-1945 international structure in the West be specified more accurately as being post-imperial? (In which case the Soviet collapse can be interpreted as just a final stage of decolonization.) Second, was the choice between empire and nation really so polarized after 1945, or at least after the 1950s? Could we not tell a different story of benevolent 'integration' (whether or not we accept Alan Milward's paradoxical claim that integration was designed to permit an enhancement of national power)?[18] Have not the European Union, or other collective institutions such as the IMF, decisively contributed to prosperity and stabilization in recent decades? By extension, could we not argue that a consensually forged alliance structure allowed a durable international settlement? Has the only choice been between empires and nations?

One alternative model of the post-1945 settlement would doubtless focus on the voluntary delegations of economic sovereignty as represented by the European Community and Union. It would contrast the consensual delegation of functions in the West to the obedience imposed in Eastern Europe. But it is not at all clear that without an overarching security and financial framework largely financed from across the Atlantic, West Europeans could themselves have successfully entered their own cooperative frameworks. My own suspicion is that the exercise of Washington's leadership in the decade after 1947 created the preconditions for the Community that consolidated itself after 1957. A second alternative model would focus on the cooperative potential within each country and on the self-regulatory capacity of civil society, including markets. The key to affluence and stability after 1945 could be sought, not in the maintenance of a hierarchical system and the cooptation of élites, but just in the progressively wider institutionalization of market activity – and perhaps associational life more generally. In such a view, the decomposition of the Communist system during the 1980s followed upon a robust assertion of civil society and what Weber would have termed 'non-imperative' associations.

In such an analysis, market outcomes are indifferent to scale. The size of sovereign political units remains irrelevant so long as they permit free trade and capital movements. Moreover, if markets and the spread of market regulation do tend toward optimal economic activity, then only the most minimal political enforcement of market frameworks is required for stability. Such a view is in line with a long tradition of analysis from Smith to Cobden and Mill and thence to most contemporary neo-classical international economists. But it has encountered powerful opposition from theorists who emphasize the differential power relations institutionalized in production and exchange, whether Marx, Polanyi, or the diverse analysts of imperialism. I cannot claim the theoretical training to evaluate the claims, but it may be that different conclusions imply differing premises with respect to spatiality. Just as post-Keynesian economists have claimed that temporality is critical to their analysis (and indeed social science in general has come to focus on historicity and path analysis), it may be that territoriality can be shown to play a critical role in the analysis of unequal exchange. Space is no more a neutral medium than time with respect to political and economic activity. It is important to develop a historically informed theory of territoriality.[19]

IX

The consequences of the alternatives raised above are fundamental to any reasoned assessment of the period of post-Cold War turbulence during the 1990s and our likely future. We do not know, of course, whether the world since 1989 or 1991 is groping toward a new settlement comparable to that negotiated within and between countries after 1945, or whether it is skidding into an era of diffuse violence and turmoil. While the Communist world was shaken to the roots of its existence at the end of the twentieth century, Western societies may have been afflicted just by a normal bit of institutional wear and tear. And obviously if economic or market forces alone can assure a transnational stability, prospects in the West are more cheering than if they cannot. But can the market reproduce the conditions for its own success? Comparison of the interwar outcomes with those before 1914 and those after 1945 suggests rather that stability and growth depended critically on a political framework and indeed on what I have stipulated as empire. Now the historian might be correct in the interpretation of the past, but very misguided about the current situation. Markets might indeed have been too weak to regenerate war-ravaged societies, but the enhanced capitalism of the late twentieth and early twenty-first centuries may be more self-regulating. Speaking personally, I am doubtful. I do believe that we relied on something 'very like' an empire in the postwar period, that it provided an undergirding of 'peace and prosperity', and that we shall need some equivalent territorial ordering to emerge successfully in the era that has followed 1989. It is difficult not to think that such a process will eventually take place in the territories of former Soviet space that do not find some regional anchorage in the West. Perhaps the most likely scenario elsewhere is the intensification of trends towards economic regionalism, with each region built around a potentially hegemonic empire: Japan on the Pacific rim, Germany in the enlarged European Union, the United States in the western hemisphere, India in South Asia, and China in southeast Asia.

Whether or not such a trend continues, political leaders cannot simply remount the territorial approaches that prevailed before 1970. For the generation after 1945 the organization of political jurisdictions and economic activity remained based on the territorial units reorganized after 1860. The architects of nationality in the late nineteenth century were obsessively territorial in their concepts of political and economic control. Nineteenth century state builders, entrepreneurs, social scientists and intellectuals were preoccupied by lines of all sorts – frontier lines, telegraph and telephone lines, blood lines, colour lines, and lines of force – and by the spaces they connected and enclosed. Technological advance from the railroad lines of the mid-nineteenth century until the assembly lines of the mid-twentieth likewise focused on the capacity to move people, goods, and information across these bounded spaces; economic development stressed the conversion and application of physical energy. Over the past generation, however, these motifs have changed; our technical imagination focuses on the movement of ideas and photons; our spatial metaphors have gone from boundaries designed to enclose or exclude to non-hierarchical networks: lines and spaces to networks. The real presence of territoriality has faded, but the nostalgia for territoriality remains.

This deconstruction of territorial orientation, I believe, dates from the economic and political crises of the 1970s – less overtly dramatic perhaps than those of the 1930s, but unsettling to governments, economic interests, and individuals alike, and comprising the institutional cusp of the late twentieth century. The economic difficulties associated with stagflation did not yield to neo-Keynesian solutions, for they involved less a cyclical phenomenon than a painful and still unfinished transition to new industries, unfamiliar principles of labour stratification, and new geographical distributions of economic power. The impact of gender issues and the political mobilization of once acquiescent students and workers (not to mention Third World guerrillas) augmented the dislocation. From one perspective, these years, above all the quinquennium 1968–73, formed the major *caesura* of the postwar era. From another perspective the 1970s began to close one century. It had begun with the reconfiguration of nation states in the 1860s. It had progressed into the age of empire, the spread of Fordist production, and the clash of socialism and fascism. It was ending with the exhaustion of the Left, incapable of inventing a new project after the completion of its welfarist agenda in the 1960s, the attrition of its working-class base, and its incomplete analyses of the transformations underway. The collapse of Soviet and East European Communism was just part of that general exhaustion, neither its cause, nor the cause of the political turmoil in the 1990s elsewhere. Even as it closed the century of empires and nations, the 1970s simultaneously opened a postmodern era whose contours are only slowly discernible. What Gertrude Stein once said about Oakland applies increasingly to a world that diffuses shopping malls, fast food outlets, and CNN reports: 'There's no there "there".' Perhaps more appropriately, our 'there' is everywhere. We live in the twilight of territoriality whether as children in cyberspace or jaded travellers in the airport archipelago. So it is not clear how principles of territorial organization can or shall be reconnected with political and economic regulation. The earlier grand settlements following on 1860, 1918 and 1945 matched claims about the ordering of political space with transactions among new classes, exploiting new technologies. All we can say now is that to judge from earlier outcomes – negative as well as positive – it would be shortsighted to deny the role of imperial coordination as an underpinning of economic growth and even of the so-called market democracy. Civil society and markets alone did not assure the stabilization of Western democratic societies after 1945. Nor did self-sufficient nation-states. They seem increasingly unlikely to do so after 1989.

Notes

1. This essay was written in 1995.
2. For models that imply the inevitability of relapse into everyday institutional life see, V. Turner, *Dramas, Fields and Metaphors: Symbolic Action in Human Society*. (Ithaca: Cornell University Press, 1974) pp. 32–59, 231–99 and V. Turner, *The Ritual Process*. (Chicago: Aldine, 1969). Also see Albert O. Hirschman's alternation of public spirit and private fulfillment in *Shifting Involvements: Private Interest and Public Action*. (Princeton: Princeton University Press, 1982). It is consonant with most of our experience, but does not allow for the fact that 'everyday experience' may have been rendered less constraining and more open by the efforts of the anti-structural interlude. Cf. C. S. Maier, *In Search of Stability: Explorations in Historical Political Economy*. (Cambridge: Cambridge University Press, 1987) pp. 271–3.
3. 'The Two Postwar Eras and the Conditions for Political Stability in Western Europe', *American Historical Review*, 86, 2 (1981), pp. 259–93.
4. H. Kissinger, *A World Restored: Metternich, Castlereagh, and the Problems of Peace, 1812–1822*. (Boston: Houghton Mifflin, 1957); H. Kissinger, *Nuclear Weapons and Foreign Policy*. (New York: Council on Foreign Relations, 1957). The literature on the balance of power is large see, Craig and George, cited below; also see F. H. Hinsley, *Power and the Pursuit of Peace: Theory and Practice in the History of Relations between States*. (Cambridge: Cambridge University Press, 1963); and E. V. Gulick, *Europe's Classical Balance of Power*. (Ithaca, NY: Cornell University Press, 1955).
5. See Paul Schroeder's superb synthesis, *The Transformation of European Politics 1763–1848*. (Oxford: Clarendon, 1994) pp. 517–636, esp. 537–8.
6. M. Doyle, 'Liberal Institutions and International Ethics', in K. Kipnis and D. T. Meyers (eds), *Political Realism and International Morality*. (Boulder CO: Westview Press, 1987); and M. Doyle, 'Liberalism and World Politics', *American Political Science Review*, 80 (December 1986) 1151–70.

7. See G. A. Craig and A. L. George, *Force and Statecraft: Diplomatic Problems of out Time*. 2nd edn. (Oxford and New York: Oxford University Press, 1990) pp. 35–47, for the inner transformation of the so-called balance of power after 1879.
8. J. L. Gaddis, *The Long Peace: Inquiries into the History of the Cold War*. (New York: Oxford University Press, 1987).
9. See M. Doyle, *Empires*. (Ithaca NY: Cornell University Press, 1986) for similar features of empires.
10. For distinctions between market-oriented and territorial- (or state-) oriented concepts of economic orientation see: R. Gilpin, *The Political Economy of International Relations*. (Princeton: Princeton University Press, 1987); R. Rosecrance, *The Rise of the Trading State: Commerce and Conquest in the Modern World*. (New York: Basic Books, 1986); S. Krasner, *Structural Conflict: The Third World against Global Capitalism*. (Berkeley and Los Angeles: University of California Press, 1985); M. Mann, *The Sources of Social Power*, vol. II: *The Rise of Classes and Nation-States, 1760–1914*. (Cambridge and New York: Cambridge University Press, 1993) pp. 33–4, 254–96.
11. David Harvey's, *The Condition of Postmodernity: An Enquiry into the Origins of Cultural Change*. (Oxford: Basil Blackwell, 1989), is a book above all (in its rather breathless sweep) about the unmooring of space and time in the transition from Fordism to flexible accumulation. Obviously, I am indebted to Immanuel Wallerstein's concepts of core and periphery (although I would contest the notion of a world economic system). Also see for the conjunction of postmodern life with the unmooring of territoriality John Ruggie's, 'Territoriality and Beyond: Problematizing Modernity in International Relations', *International Organization*, 47, 1 (1993) 139–74.
12. See Mann's summary of the literature on nationalism, *Sources of Social Power*, pp. 214–53.
13. R. C. Binckley, *Realism and Nationalism, 1852–1870*. (New York: Harper, 1935), neglected today, astutely emphasized this global choice. Mann also points to it, apparently independently, see *Sources of Social Power*, pp. 353–4.
14. By dominant technology I do not mean the methods of production that made preponderant quantitative contributions to national income, but the sector that integrated recent innovation and helped to transform productive activity by virtue of its backward and forward linkages, and captured the public imagination.
15. A. Teichova, *An Economic Background to Munich: International Business and Czechoslovakia*. (Cambridge: Cambridge University Press, 1974); Royal Institute of International Affairs, *The Problem of International Investment*. (London, New York, Toronto: Royal Institute of International Affairs, 1937).
16. C. Kindleberger, *The World Depression*. (Berkeley and Los Angles: University of California Press, 1973). On the burden of international payments see B. Eichengreen, *Golden Fetters: The Gold Standard and the Great Depression*. (New York: Oxford University Press, 1992), esp. ch. 7.
17. I have discussed postwar American policy as imperial in 'Alliance and Autonomy: European Identity and U.S. Foreign Policy Objectives in the Truman Years', in M. J. Lacey (ed.), *The Truman Presidency*. (Cambridge and New York: Cambridge University Press and Woodrow Wilson International Center for Scholars, 1989) pp. 273–98; and in R. Ahmann, A. M. Birke and M. Howard

(eds), *The Quest for Stability: Problems of West European Security 1918–1957* (Oxford: Oxford University Press and German Historical Institute, 1993) pp. 389–434.
18. A. S. Milward with the assistance of G. Brennan and F. Romero, *The European Rescue of the Nation-State*. (London: Routledge, 1992).
19. John Ruggie has made a start in 'Territoriality and Beyond'.

3
America as a European Power: Four Dimensions of the Transatlantic Relationship: 1945 to the Late 1990s

David Ellwood

Introduction: the lessons of last time

As an alternative to the familiar view of the post-1945 years in the West, dominated by the confrontation with the Soviets and the efforts of the Atlantic nations to face up to it, the following pages suggest something of the attempt made by the Americans and the west Europeans to reconcile aims in their foreign and domestic policies identified well *before* that conflict broke out, with the demands of the new situation. They highlight the parallels as well as the contrasts between the various sets of national priorities, and in the world-views which lay behind them. They demonstrate how 'an uneasy but highly successful trans-Atlantic compromise'[1] finally emerged over the grand strategic questions of interdependence among the Western allies.

Whatever its costs, this compromise took European societies well beyond the postwar urgencies of stabilization, towards an era of development, whose benefits included the greatest boom the industrial world has ever known and a radical change in its modes of social evolution. A new balance had of course to be struck when the Cold War eventually ended, but the uneasy compromise was not renegotiated. Instead West Europeans attempted to develop their own means for coping with the many dimensions of America's presence 'as a European power' (James Baker), while defending their own historical priorities and identities. In security matters they often failed; in business, trade and money they did much better; in the clash of models of modernity across the Atlantic a complex pattern of dependence and appropriation prevailed.

When World War Two was over, everyone sought to avoid the mistakes made last time and provide their version of liberal capitalism with a new lease of life. However it soon emerged that no power had done more to reflect on the nature of the world it wanted to see built than the United States. While individual seers after World War One, such as Henry Ford or Herbert Hoover, had already pointed to the tasks of social and economic modernization awaiting a half-ruined Europe if peaceful development was to be guaranteed, the crisis of totalitarian war gave their arguments far more force, bringing them general recognition. Now they were embraced and elaborated by a wide coalition of political, business and intellectual interests, and when coupled to the power of a transformed Federal machine, became the standard analysis justifying the benevolent hegemony the US now set out to create.[2] But there was a missing element in this vast process of mental adjustment. What these calculations left out was the possibility that the liberated Europeans might have views of their own on the future of the world, and on their own place in it.

In any event, while American wartime visions of a modernized world economic and security order inevitably clashed with Cold War realities from the Potsdam conference of July 1945 onwards – in particular the overwhelming force of the German question – they were not thrown radically off course by them. Although scaled down, in some ways they were strengthened, becoming functional plans. Meanwhile, whatever their national circumstances, all the West Europeans nations (outside Germany), sought to renew their economies and their sovereignties, and they all set out to construct a version of the 'welfare state', in fulfilment of the promises made to their long-suffering citizens before and during the years of war.

The Cold War clearly increased the weight of American hegemony and in the early years intensified West European dependence on US strategic and economic strength, as embodied in the North Atlantic Treaty of 1949. But it also made more urgent tasks of national reconstruction and modernization as defined locally. Then the speed of the recovery and the discovery of the interconnectedness of the European economies once West Germany began to function industrially, raised issues of prospect which went well beyond the boundaries of the NATO relationship. While the *ad hoc* political culture of Atlanticism was useful in managing the consequent difficulties in public, west European assertiveness grew during the 1950s and 1960s, eventually provoking a challenge to the entire basis of American hegemony, in the shape of Gaullism.

By this time, though, the success of European reconstruction and integration was beyond doubt, and the balance of power and responsibility in the trans-Atlantic condominium had shifted. No longer desperate for security against Germany or the Soviet Union, all concerned could see that in general terms, 'the clash and mutual accomodation of... different trans-Atlantic ideals [had] produced a remarkably creative period of Western politics and economics.'[3] A radically revitalized West had appeared on the scene, based on a patchwork amalgamation of American and European ideas of 'the good life', and driven forward by a new, American-invented form of political and economic energy: *growth.*

Yet even in the heyday of American hegemony, in the 1950s, each European society had put in place its own mechanisms for taking what it wanted from the American inspiration and rejecting the rest, for reconciling production and consumption, collective and individual spending, traditional ways and rising living standards. The outcome, said an admiring American observer later, was the reinvention of 'those quirks [that] make Europe something more than just a "market"... the traits that make Europe European'.[4]

America's prescriptions for Europe's reconstruction

After World War Two the conviction of the Americans that they knew 'Europe's' interests much better then the Europeans did gradually harden into a set of policies whose substance changed little between the late 1940s and the late 1960s. John Foster Dulles believed that the United States possessed in Europe 'both moral rights and political power', acquired through the sacrifices of two World Wars and by all the aid money poured in to the Old World thereafter.[5] Dulles was only the most prominent among the multitude of American commentators who never hesitated to use these rights and powers to project into the European sphere the vision and the judgements they had built up from America's twentieth-century experience of the world it had tried so hard to leave behind.

What were these judgements? Simply that the planet in general and America in particular must be saved from the never-ending follies of European history. Europe itself might yet be saved from the same follies but only by actively incorporating in its future the lessons of America's historical development, in particular those regarding the connection between economic progress and political stability. President Roosevelt's view was only the most extreme version of what by 1945 had become a general outlook. The American historian John Harper has written:

> While couched in benign, universalist rhetoric, Franklin Roosevelt's solution was brutally simple and comprehensive. Through forced decolonisation, disarmament, and (in the case of Germany) deindustrialization, Europe from Brest to Brest-Litovsk was to be effectively retired from the international political scene. Like Jefferson and Wilson, Roosevelt believed that the European state system was fundamentally wicked and rotten; left to their own devices, the Europeans would once again bring misfortune to the world. Arrangements were therefore designed to facilitate a strategy of *divide et impera* toward Europe . . . [while limiting] America's entanglement . . . [6]

Yet America's public message for the postwar world was of course a positive, constructive one, and even before hostilities ended it had found concrete expression in new institutions like the United Nations and the Bretton Woods system, in which the Europeans were expected to be present. The message itself was articulated according to the audience: international statesmen were offered Wilsonism reorchestrated in an economic key; the starving masses were promised the export model of the American Dream.

The Four Freedoms Declaration, the Lend-Lease Act and the Atlantic Charter – all promulgated in 1941 before the US had even entered the conflict – each announced in its own way the three great American themes for world reform and reconstruction: *collective security*, *free trade* and *raising living standards* everywhere. These were promises fashioned to revitalize capitalist democracy wherever its survival was at stake, and to make the global sacrifices of wartime seem worthwhile. Born out of America's modern economic history, matured through the years of dealing with the financial mess left by World War One, they also owed much to the prescriptions of the New Deal. By the end of the war specific recipes had been drawn up to apply them to each of the European countries and even to particular problems within them.[7]

It was taken for granted that American money and methods would be necessary to lead the Europeans in the right direction, and with the arrival of the Marshall Plan the effort was finally made. Behind the European Recovery Program was not simply the urge to fight Communism on as many fronts as possible, but the firm conviction that all the worst prognoses of the wartime phase had been confirmed, and that America could not possibly be content with simply bailing out the Europeans for the third time in 30 years. Now US help would only be administered on condition that radical reform be undertaken to tackle the roots of totalitarianism and war as Washington understood them. This meant modernization as before, but accompanying this demand there now appeared a specific, explicit American drive to conquer finally all the old forms of nationalism and particularism seen as persisting in Europe, setting in motion in their place a grand sweep of 'unification', first economic then political. As a prestigious New York economist and banker, and senior Marshall Plan administrator, later explained, Americans were all agreed: 'Union was needed to imprison Europe's evil genie, nationalism, in a solid federal cage'.[8]

The Marshall Plan recognized that whatever the earlier intentions, Europe could not be 'retired' from the international scene, if only because the most basic political problem of all – the future of Germany between France and the Soviet Union – remained unresolved, and because so many European statesmen were now pressing the US to save them from Communism just as eight years previously they had cried out for salvation from Nazism. Tired of these pleas, the designers of the new world system saw the Old World in the grip of an overwhelming 'spiritual crisis', a product not simply of the war, the struggle for reconstruction and the fight against communism, but what to them seemed like the political and cultural bankruptcy of a civilization.[9]

Hence the ERP was always intended to have long- and short-term effects which would go well beyond the neutralization of Communism. To substitute the fear-based security systems which had dragged Europe into the abyss in 1914 and 1939, the Marshall Plan offered individual Europeans and their families the promise of ever-greater prosperity. An 'economic United States of Europe' would emerge, in which the American Dream could be dreamt without leaving home: 'You Too Can Be Like Us!', that was the promise of the Marshall Plan.[10] In a famous speech of October 1949, the Marshall Plan Administrator, the businessman Paul Hoffman, called for the creation of 'a single large market' in Western Europe.[11] Foreseeing the creation of a huge free trade area in Europe with a single currency and a harmonized banking system, one of Hoffman's deputies argued how in one vast market 'mass production for mass consumption and intensive internal competition [would] restore the dynamic of enterprise and economic growth'. The results, in the space of 10 to 25 years, would 'transform the economic face of Europe, European productivity and European living standards'.[12]

When Eisenhower came to power in 1953, the new president likewise had no doubt about the scope of Europe's problem seen from the security point of view. The correct formula for dealing with it was 'a US of Europe – to include all countries now in NATO and ... Sweden, Spain and Yugoslavia, with Greece definitely in if Yugoslavia [were]'.

This was a private judgement written down in June 1951 in Eisenhower's time as the first Supreme Allied Commander in Europe, but his convictions became if anything firmer in his years as president.[13] In spite of all the set-backs ascribable to nationalism in the workings of the Marshall Plan, in rearmament, in the European Defense Community saga, and in the disappointing performance of the European Coal and Steel Community, Eisenhower still saw Western Europe in late 1955 as a potential 'third power bloc', built on a strong form of federalism which would guarantee that 'every one would profit by the union of all them and none would lose'.[14] It was on this basis that Eisenhower and Dulles eventually gave such strong political backing to the EEC design incorporated in the Treaty of Rome, and turned their backs on the model of loose inter-governmental cooperation under the OEEC, or in EFTA, favoured by the British.

The Grand Design of the Kennedy years was intended to merge the heritage of the ERP integrationists with that of the security-oriented builders of NATO in a partnership of mutually respecting equals. The economic 'miracles' in the western European countries starting from 1954–55 onwards seemed to justify everything the economic Wilsonites had always believed in. And yet no-one could pretend that a 'third power bloc' had emerged, much less a partnership of equals. Under the impact of Charles de Gaulle's challenge to American prescriptions, the years from Kennedy's election to the mid-1960s witnessed intense debate and reappraisal over the previous 20 years of trans-Atlantic experience.

The Europeans' need for America

If the American vision of western Europe's requirements was so clear and sustained, what of the nature of the link seen from the other side of the water? Did common features in fact unite the situations and the needs of France, Britain, Italy etc. in the postwar period? How disposed were they to realize that the United States might know best what was good for them?

With the Cold War well under way the editor of the *Economist*, Geoffrey Crowther, on a lecture tour in the United States in early 1948, made as clear as possible why the basic definitions of security had by now broadened, and why men like him looked westward for their salvation:

> Unless we in Europe thought that we could rely on receiving from America moral support at all times, economic support for the moment, and armed support if ever again we are assailed by the hordes of barbarism – if we could not believe that the new world would continue to be called in to redress the balance of the old – then our outlook would . . . be black indeed.[15]

In spite of all the forms of American reassurance built in to the Truman Doctrine, the Marshall Plan and the North Atlantic Treaty, European dependence on the US became ever more fervently and pessimistically expressed after the Korean outbreak in 1950, especially by groups of anti-Communist intellectuals. In a 1951 collection of essays on *America and the Mind of Europe*, the Swiss philosopher Denis De Rougemont sounded a characteristic note:

> Compared with what it was in 1900 the Europe of today appears to be very sick indeed. It has been amputated of one-third of its territory on the East. City after city is still a mass of ruins. Blood-clots at the national frontiers impede the vital circulation of men, money and goods. And, pehaps, worst of all the European capacity for formulating ideas of progress and social justice seems to have drained away to other continents, leaving behind on the one side apathy and on the other cynicism . . .[16]

By 1954, notwithstanding the signs of recovery all around in Europe's physical and social fabric, Raymond Aron remained eloquent on the collapse of the Old World and the need for America's sustenance. Declaring that World War One had destroyed traditional European society, while World War Two had finally 'exhausted the vitality of a civilization', Aron denied that the Marshall Plan or NATO had significantly strengthened the security of western Europe. Instead only the construction of a fully integrated Atlantic community under confident American leadership would suffice to avoid the worst.[17]

So a general pattern of political action and reaction across the Atlantic quickly became clear over the first postwar decade. While official talk was all of interdependence and shared destinies, the reality was dependence and fear of abandonment as much as fear of war. It was the western Europeans who pressed the Americans to stay in Germany after 1946; when the American army finally left Italy at the end of 1947, it was over the loud protests of the local conservative forces; in Greece and Turkey too precarious ruling groups directed ever-louder pleas for deliverance to Washington. It was they and their peers elsewhere who mounted the campaign for instant military aid that produced the Truman Doctrine, the security guarantee of the North Atlantic Treaty and – supreme fulfilment – the return of operational US forces to Europe in 1951. But these were waves of persuasion 'to which the Americans finally succumbed with great reluctance and then only half-heartedly', writes the German historian Wilfried Loth.[18]

The impulse to look to America first was evident across a variety of issues. The British expected massive, unconditional support for their currency from dollar funds and were only turned down on the third of their applications, in 1953.[19] The French pleaded for support for their colonial empire in South East Asia and felt betrayed by the outcome of Dien Bien Phu. The West German opposition wanted the Americans to create the premisses for reunification, which they would then manage themselves. The dismay of the British and the French at American behaviour during the Suez crisis was of course enormous, and led to a portentous rupture: while the British scuttled back under the American umbrella, the French set out on a daring path of self-sufficiency and challenge.[20] Even while the European communities were being created – nominally to reinforce European independence – it was taken for granted that American money and technology would be indispensable in the running of the ECSC and Euratom.

Whenever the American side attempted to impose serious conditions on its support, there were huge protests from the beneficiaries. In the Marshall Plan, against the explicit instructions of Washington, the European participants 'refused to engage in joint programming [or] adapt national production plans to European needs'; instead they sought to 'preserve the greatest degree of national self-sufficiency and autonomy', writes Michael Hogan in his great history of the conflict in Anglo-American relations set off by the Plan.[21] None of the European nations were willing to give anything but the smallest concessions to the maximalist demands for integration, even unification, which started in the ERP era, and it is Alan Milward's thesis that the the limited degree of integration which did eventually emerge owes part of its origins to accumulated resistance in the face of American pressures.[22]

In fact all of the west Europeans needed and wanted the money, the protection and the extraordinary capacity of the Americans to improvise ways of projecting their power in the world exemplified by the Berlin airlift, but they desired these benefits to be attuned to their own priorities and aspirations. The subsequent tensions exploded at the time of the Korean conflict, when in public the greatest trans-Atlantic unity was being proclaimed. The resulting general military escalation led to massive re-armament everywhere. Yet if the threat was as grave as everyone seemed to agree it was, the actual organization of defence in the West remained incoherent, ineffectual, and contentious.

While all the West Europeans made significant sacrifices for re-armament, none matched up to the objectives set for them by the Americans, and all resented the pressures to do so which accompanied Washington's vast military aid in their favour. The Council on Foreign Relations commented in 1951:

> European governments were more interested in preserving their recent economic gains and keeping domestic tax rates and living standards within politically tolerable limits; thus they tended to expect more from the United States and proportionately less from their own peoples.[23]

The NATO arguments over 'burden-sharing' which continued throughout the Cold War, and which have simply taken different form today, find their origins in this post-Korean situation.

Managing the Cold War: the European search for alternatives

By their behaviour in the Korean crisis, the Europeans showed, among other things, that they did not in fact believe the Soviet menace to be as serious as the Americans insisted it was. But this was a difficult position to express in public since they had been the ones insisting on the military danger when Washington was offering only psychological and economic support. The result was ambivalence and resentment.

It was partly to dispel sentiments of this sort that a network of 'Atlanticists' emerged on both sides of the Atlantic Ocean during the 1950s, reflecting a shift in emphasis in communicating America's purposes away from the one-sided, mass 'information' efforts of the Marshall Plan era and towards the more delicate, long-term tasks of alliance-building, thought best left to cooperative efforts managed by local leaders.

Yet in spite of the successes of Atlanticism, various forms of political and intellectual doubt over the new dependence on the United States flourished in the Europe of the 1950s, even mirroring at times the prejudicial anti-Americanism of the Communist left. Such sentiments owed much to the continuing militarization of the Cold War, stimulated by the first Soviet H-Bomb explosion in 1953. Even before then the military correspondent of the *New York Times* was reporting that 'Europe simply does not take the threat of imminent war as seriously as the United States does', and that resentment was growing against the strain of maintaining preparedness as defined exclusively by Washington. There was the suspicion, comments the historian Wilfried Loth that, '(b)oth sides preferred to deal with their security problems through preventive accumulation of power rather than through reliance on measures to develop mutual trust.'[24]

The advance towards an arms race was one which European governments were unable either to resist or to accept. In spite of the force of their link with America, the West Germans suffered particularly from the constraints of their destiny as 'a half-nation . . . both the product and prime victim of the Cold War', as one of its leading political commentators described it in 1987.[25] Yet many years would pass by before a credibly different approach to the Cold War appeared from any of the west Europeans, specifically a viable *political* alternative to militarized East–West confrontation. Churchill's plaintive demands for summitry met with no response;[26] the various plans put forward under the names of Van Zeeland (1953), Heusinger/Blankenhorn (1953, 1955), Eden (1955), Globke (1959) all fell by the wayside.[27] Only in the *Ostpolitik* era beginning in the late 1960s did this impulse, long-nourished in Bonn, find mature expression, meeting of course intense American suspicion.[28]

In the previous decade Charles de Gaulle's challenge had touched on every aspect of the political and strategic falsehoods which he saw underlying the Atlantic system, but his rebellion, while starting out from premisses which many European governments might have shared, went well beyond the bounds of the *modus vivendi* in force at that time. By then most of the Europeans powers appeared to have settled for a marriage contract with the US whose terms could be elegantly described as conditional dependence but which in practice often seemed to reflect an attitude of: 'we want to be dominated, but on our terms . . .'

As de Gaulle's challenge proceeded beyond military affairs to economic and monetary fields, to the organization of technology and even – in Servan-Schreiber's *Le défi americain* (1967) – to the presence of US investment in Europe, so the whole existence of the trans-Atlantic relationship became dominated by the confrontation. In reality by the mid-1960s such assertiveness reflected trends going well beyond the designs of de Gaulle. An American commentator wrote in 1964:

> The real cause of disarray is that Atlantic institutions are . . . technologically obsolete because NATO was not built to deal with nuclear and missile weapons systems, and archaic because the postwar structure

> of leadership failed to keep pace with the buoyant European economies and a miraculous re-birth of the continent's self-confidence.[29]

The transformation of the OEEC into the OECD, the Trade Expansion Act of 1962 and the 'Grand Design' based on it, these were the most prominent of the efforts made to counteract the unexpected success of the Common Market and the effects of de Gaulle, as well as to offset the pivotal role of Germany in European security. But they were also attempts to bring European responsibilities into line with the realities of power in the Atlantic system as the Americans saw them.

Lucid commentators on the spot warned the Kennedy Europeanists that times had changed and their efforts would not succeed. Ronald Steel's *End of Alliance* of 1964 was particularly prescient:

> In the sense that it seizes upon the new kind of loyalty being created in Europe, and upon the desire to be both separate and different from America, Gaullism is far stronger than de Gaulle and is likely to outlive its chief exponent just as Bonapartism survived the demise of Napoleon.[30]

From stabilization to growth: the renewal of the 'West'

In 1960 the OEEC, the Organization for European Economic Cooperation set up in 1948 to organize the European response to the Marshall Plan, was refounded, with the US and Canada now entering as full members, to become the OECD, the Organization for Economic Cooperation and Development. Article 1 of its founding convention states the agency's purpose as:

> to achieve the highest sustainable economic growth and employment and a rising standard of living in Member countries, while maintaining financial stability, and thus to contribute to the development of the world economy.

Ten years earlier almost all of these objectives would have been familiar to European statesmen and their advisers. But the arrival from America of the concept of economic growth as a supreme goal of policy, well beyond security or welfare, brought a significant evolution in the idea of progress itself to the Europe and the West. With the unprecedented success of the European economies in the 1950s and 1960s came the canonization of the growth idea and its propagation as a full-scale model of society.[31]

In reality, with a change of generation and the arrival of the economic 'miracles' in Europe had come a new complexity in the Euro–American relationship. Seen in longer-term perspective the era outwardly dominated by the Cold War is just as likely to be remembered for the encounter, in the postwar reconstruction process, of what were to become the two dominant models of progress in the West, two different approaches to the problem of bringing the new possibilities of expanding production and economic management to the salvation of capitalist democracy.

In a hundred different ways – most explicitly in the Marshall Plan – the Americans offered their experience of a prosperity which was economic, private, consumerist, limitless and available for emulation. Personalities, products, magazines, advertising, films, television, fashions, 'lifestyles' – all served to project abroad the American Dream's 'promise of an ever-increasing prosperity for an ever-increasing majority', and revolutionize in the process the impact of American power.[32]

But the recent experience of the West Europeans made them much more interested in release from the nightmares of two World Wars and the intervening depression, and so they built systems which were socially oriented, collective and welfarist. There was, writes Alan Milward, 'a strong common identity of thought between Spaak, Schuman, Adenauer, De Gasperi and Monnet:

> It is to be found in their understanding of the search for security by the western European population after 1945 and in the very wide interpretation which they, like the population, gave to it. Going far beyond the problems of military defence and physical protection, they interpreted it to mean an economic security in daily life of a more comprehensive and assured kind than before the war . . . We are not dealing with social reformers, nor, except in the case of Monnet, with economic innovators, but merely with statesmen well attuned to the themes of fear, of the need of reassurance, and of the fundamentally conservative yearning for a more certain personal and political order which shaped democratic politics in those years.[33]

From the middle of the 1950s on, the terms of the subsequent confrontation of models were becoming clear. Visceral fear began to gave way to a climate of peace and optimism, fostered by 'the steady diffusion of growth's economic and social benefits', as a French commentator explained. The Fourth Republic's politicians were learning that 'for the bulk of the population sharing the fruits of expansion and economic modernization, with better standards of living, improved amenities, and more social services, counted for more than questions over the Atlantic Alliance, Germany, and colonial wars', wrote J. P. Rioux 30 years later.[34]

At the same time renewed arguments about 'Americanization' reflected an awareness that the ability of the Americans to project their system of life expressed powers more challenging than the variety bought by their dollars or manipulated by their national security state, creative energies far more dynamic and appealing than those that had built the welfare state. What the US now deployed to greater effect than ever before was its capacity to invent and distribute mass culture, a potential then almost wholly lacking in the Old World and one which brought back old worries to its governing élites, but now with a new intensity. In 1954 the Swiss philosopher Jeanne Hersch, expressed concerns which would return in cycles throughout the rest of the century:

> The Americans make us uneasy because, without wishing us ill, they put things before us for our taking, things which are so ready to hand and so convenient that we accept them, finding perhaps that they satisfy our fundamental temptations... Masses of American products are forced upon us by artificial means, especially where films are concerned... Even when we can make a choice between products, we are influenced by a sort of force within ourselves, which we fear because it is indeterminate and indefinable... the threat we feel hanging over us is not something evil; it is a vacuum, such as is produced by rapid movement.[35]

One of the factors in Konrad Adenauer's preference for Bonn over Frankfurt as the capital of the Federal Republic was reportedly the 'totally Americanized' nature of the latter as he saw it: 'As much as I like working with the Americans, I did not want us to become Americanized,' he told the London *Times* in 1961. His successor as Chancellor, Ludwig Erhard, would provoke his fellow citizens by telling them that their passion for the market economy was making them 'more American than the Americans'.[36] In France the left-wing political scientist Maurice Duverger dissociated himself from what he called the fashionable idiotic anti-Americanism of the time in a 1964 interview with *Le Monde*, but he insisted:

> It must be said, it must be written. There is only one immediate danger for Europe, and that is American civilization. There will be no Stalinism or communism in France. They are scarecrows that frighten only sparrows now... Today all that belongs to the past. On the

> other hand, the domination of the American economy, the invasion of the American mentality – all that is very dangerous.[37]

Thirty years later the same worries were to reappear, this time on the lips of conservative critics such as Norman Stone and Ernst Nolte. Deploring the crisis of post-Cold War political legitimacy in the West and attributing it to the 'decline of class differences, [the] role of the mass media in politics, [the] spread of hedonistic culture', Professor Stone explained that the roots of the phenomena are all to be found in the postwar experience of 'Americanisation':

> It goes back very obviously to the 1950s, but you can take it back to Hollywood in the 1930s. Democracy, Reader's Digest, rock music and the easy prosperity of 'gadgets' spread. Sensible people saw that this changed the nature of politics . . . Prosperity and democracy create their own social problems because the old disciplines become relaxed . . .[38]

The more radical Nolte has defined his cultural project as an attempt to 'liberate [the Germans] from their sense of collective guilt' in order that they can 'throw off the American civilization of the world and reclaim their identity and their difference.' The reunited Germans are to be exhorted to 'recover a national consciousness founded on values other than those of civilization as Americans understand it.'[39]

In historical terms Americanization appears as an expression useful for characterizing a particularly distinctive form of modernization, superimposed with great political, economic and cultural force, but more or less randomly, on each European country's own variant. The Marshall Plan and its productivity drive together represented only elements in this process, exceptional and temporary interventions when the US attempted deliberately to remake the old world in the image of the new. For the most part west European societies were free to resist the projection of American power in all its forms, to take what they wanted from the American model and to cultivate their own versions of neo-capitalism.[40]

Entirely free they were not: the imperatives of the Cold War and generalized anti-communism remained dominant themes in European politics all the way through the postwar period and caused continuous tension between the defence and welfare priorities in national budgets. It was the reality of expansion of course, which served to make these tensions politically manageable, thereby fostering the spread of the growth consensus.

So in the sphere of ideals as well as practical politics and economics, the institutionalization and success of those three great, specific themes the United States brought to the postwar world – collective security, free trade, and rising living standards – had turned out to be the forces which effectively guaranteed the transition from stabilization and recovery to modernization in western Europe. The 'revolution of rising expectations', which its peoples had expressed ever since the first postwar era,[41] had been fulfilled by consumption, whatever the misgivings of traditional authorities at the outcome. When developed in western Europe and added to the European welfare state's capacity in its heyday to 'combine economic efficiency with human dignity',[42] these were the themes which laid the basis for the unprecedented, unimaginable success of 'the West' in the 45 years following the end of Hitler's war.

After 1989: America as a European power

In the course of the *annus mirabilis* 1989 both President Bush and Secretary Baker had stated as unequivocally as possible: 'the United States is and will remain a European power.'[43] The absurdity of imagining the converse made it clear to all that the underlying balance of force between the sides had changed less than might have been imagined in more than three decades. The old NATO faith in *collective security* could not hide the fact that this was not a relationship of equals, or even a fully functioning partnership, in spite of various attempts between 1962 and 1990 – all American-inspired – to make it appear so.[44] What the Europeans wanted from the formal Atlantic relationship was what they had so earnestly sought in so many different ways ever since 1916: if not domination at least defence *on their terms*. In other words they worked for the mobilization of as much or as little US power as they deemed desirable, in order to ensure the realisation of the security goals which they defined – singly or together – on their own behalf.

Europe's unmatched capacity to involve the United States in its conflicts in this way stretched back to the Great War era and was amply confirmed by the Bosnian war. Even the smallest dispute seemed to contain this potential, a reality clearly open to manipulation and requiring the most strenous efforts on the part of America's governments to explain to their domestic constituencies. Wishing no longer to hegemonize or to reform the Old World by 1997, the US was still unable to wean the West Europeans from this form of dependence upon America, 'and its consequent, and psychologically inevitable, resentment of Washington', as the commentator William Pfaff saw it.[45]

At the same time, all concerned realized that on the economic front the trans-Atlantic relationship was in very different condition compared to the previous decades. The US appreciated Europe's ability to speak with one voice on the key issue of trade liberalization, and the successful conclusion of the GATT process in 1993 seemed to justify the decades of effort American trade negotiators had dedicated to the grand Wilsonian–Rooseveltian vision of *free trade* 'everywhere in the world' (FDR's refrain in the Four Freedoms speech of 1941). Even the nascent World Trade Organization appeared to confirm the rightness of the post-World War Two design of an International Trade Organization, abandoned in the unpromising atmosphere of 1949 and now resurrected. At GATT's concluding ceremonies the US representatives used language which could easily have been taken from a speech by the New Deal Secretary of State Cordell Hull. An ever more open world trade system, said Vice President Gore would bring 'mutual prosperity, growth and partnership', thereby creating jobs and fostering social progress. The vision of the US Trade Representative Michael Kantor completed the virtuous circle:

> The key for maintaining growth is to build up the middle class throughout the countries of the world. Enabling people to move from poverty to the middle class is a process which assures them the ability to buy our products as well as those from their own countries. It reinforces democracy and stability in those countries. Finally it reinforces the world trade system and is essential for its future success.[46]

Hence the third panel in the great World War Two tryptych, *raising living standards everywhere*, had become the supreme definition of progress in the latter half of the twentieth century. Asking himself who would go on to 'own' the twenty-first century, – Japan, Europe or America – the MIT economist Lester Thurow declaimed: 'The 19th century belonged to Great Britain. The 20th century belongs to the United States; we generate the world's highest per capita overall standard of living'.[47] But it was not the physical facts of production and consumption which gave the US its hegemony, rather its proven ideological, political and cultural ability to transform the history of its success in a recipe for others.[48]

Beyond the obvious questions of security, trade and prosperity, there was always a fourth dimension of American power at work conditioning and colouring the transatlantic relationship in the twentieth century. The urge of US mass culture to project its presence into Europe, in an endlessly changing variety of forms and directions, represented a force for change which Europeans had always been obliged to come to terms with. By the end of the century, to measure the penetrative power of the industries and cultures bringing EuroDisney and *Jurassic Park*, Internet, Windows '98 and all the rest – meant discovering just how Europe's characteristic twentieth-century impulse to respond to America as myth and model of modernity had evolved by the 1990s.

Indeed, with the old worries of the Cold War gone, America's role as creator and seller of uniquely appealing examples and life-styles became more prominent. No longer held up as a comprehensive model of society, American products, fashions, stars, symbols, icons and languages (including the computer versions) remained ubiquitous and compelling, available for appropriation, adaptation – and rejection – by everyone.

But the outcomes were not comforting to those who believed in a common destiny for the members of the European union. Just as the old Washington technique of *divide et impera* so often gave the US the last word among its squabbling allies in the Cold War, so by the late 1990s the new American challenge was provoking (though unwittingly) a hardening of attitudes, a striking of defensive, protectionist postures which seemed likely to increase divisions among the Europeans rather than unite them. While Hollywood, Microsoft and McDonald's marched onwards, explicit resistance to America took the form not so much of rejection of whatever the United States stood for, produced or did, but of struggle against the *inevitability* of the destiny of convergence and homogenization on the American pattern. Stanley Hoffmann's 1964 intuition that '(t)he more European societies become alike in their social structures and economic makeup, the more each national society seems to heighten its idiosyncracies,'[49] had become, 30 years later, the focal point of a vast confrontation over identity, diversity and convergence in which a part-real, part-imaginary United States served as the supreme counter-point against which each society sought to define its sense of itself and its future. Was this then to be the true legacy of Europe's American century?[50]

Notes

1. David P. Calleo, 'For Europe, New Walls to Integration', *International Herald Tribune*, 9 May 1994.
2. The best guide to it remains, Robert A. Divine, *Second Chance. The Triumph of Internationalism in America During World War II.* (New York: Atheneum, 1967); cf. C. M. Santoro, *Diffidence and Ambition. The Intellectual Sources of United States Foreign Policy*. (Boulder, CO: Westview Press, 1992).
3. Calleo.
4. James Fallows, 'The Information Revolution: New Strains for Europe, America and Asia', *International Herald Tribune*, 16 May 1994.

5. Pascaline Winand, *Eisenhower, Kennedy and the United States of Europe.* (New York: St Martin's Press, 1993), p. 34.
6. John Harper in S. Romano (ed.), *L'Impero riluttante,* (Bologna: ISPI, 1992); cf. Harper, *American Visions. Franklin D.Roosevelt, George F. Kennan, and Dean G. Acheson.* (New York: Cambridge University Press, 1994).
7. D. W. Ellwood, *Rebuilding Europe. Western Europe, America and Post-war Reconstruction.* (London: Longman, 1992), pp. 19–24.
8. H. Van B. Cleveland, *The Atlantic Idea and its European Rivals.* (New York: Council on Foreign Relations, McGraw-Hill, 1966), p. 105.
9. Cf. remarks by George Kennan and H. Fish Armstrong, editor of *Foreign Affairs,* cit. in Ellwood, p. 92.
10. Ellwood, pp. 88–9.
11. Ellwood, p. 159.
12. Ellwood, pp. 154–5.
13. Winand, p. 37.
14. Winand, p. 81.
15. G. Crowther, *The Economic Reconstruction of Europe.* (Claremont: Claremont College, 1948), p. 76.
16. H. Hamilton, *America and the Mind of Europe.* (London, 1951), p. 30.
17. R. Aron-Doubleday, *The Century of Total War.* (New York: Garden City, NY, 1954), pp. 83, 173–4, 312.
18. W. Loth, 'The East-West Conflict in Historical Perspective – An Attempt at a Balanced View', *Contemporary European History,* 3, 2, (1994) 193–202, here p. 196.
19. Alan Milward, *The European Rescue of the Nation State.* (London: Routledge, 1992), pp. 358–63.
20. Henry Kissinger now asks whether 'the United States' national interest [was] really served by bringing home in so ruthless a fashion to two of America's most indispensable allies that they had lost all capacity for autonomous action'; H. Kissinger, *Diplomacy,* (London: Simon & Schuster, 1995), p. 544.
21. M. J. Hogan, *The Marshall Plan: America, Britain and the Reconstruction of Western Europe, 1947–1952,* (Cambridge: Cambridge University Press, 1987), p. 87.
22. A. J. Milward, *The Reconstruction of Western Europe,* (London: Methuen, 1984).
23. Cited. in Ellwood, p. 178.
24. Loth, p. 199.
25. J. Joffe cited. in Gustav Schmidt, 'Divided Europe – Divided Germany (1950–1963)', *Contemporary European History,* 3, 2 (1994) 155–92, here, p. 173.
26. They are eloquently discussed in H. Kissinger, pp. 466–7.
27. Schmidt, pp. 165–6, 180.
28. Cf. Kissinger, p. 735.
29. Frank Munk, *Atlantic Dilemma: Partnership or Comunity?,* (Dobbs Ferry, NY: Oceana Publications, 1964), cited. in R. Wolfe, 'Atlanticism Without the Wall: Transatlantic Cooperation and the Transformation of Europe', *International Journal,* XLVI, 1 (Winter 1990), 137–63, here pp. 144–5.
30. R. Steel, *End of Alliance.* (New York: Viking Press, 1964), pp. 79–81.
31. I have discussed this development further in *Rebuilding Europe,* ch. 12.
32. Ellwood, chs 9, 12; phrase on American Dream by E. N. Luttwak in the *Times Literary Supplement,* 10 June 1994; specific experiences of this process are examined in R. Kroes, *et al.* (eds), *Cultural Transmissions and Receptions. American Mass Culture in Europe.* (Amsterdam: VU University Press, 1993); the French

case is examined in depth in R. Kuisel, *Seducing the French. The Dilemma of Americanization.* (Berkeley: University of California Press, 1993).
33. Milward, *The European Rescue*, p. 337.
34. J. P. Rioux, *The Fourth Republic 1944–1958.* (Cambridge: Cambridge University Press, 1987), p. 243.
35. UNESCO, *The Old World and the New: their Cultural and Moral Relations, International Forums of San Paolo and Geneva, 1954, 1956*, cited in R. Kuisel (Paris: UNESCO), p. 114.
36. Both citations discussed and placed in historical context by Michael Ermarth, 'The German Talks Back: Heinrich Hauser and German Attitudes toward Americanization after World War II', in M. Ermarth (ed.), *America and the Shaping of German Society 1945–1955.* (Providence/Oxford: Berg, 1993), p. 102.
37. Cited in R. Kuisel, p. 191.
38. *Sunday Times*, 25 July 1993.
39. *La Stampa*, 19 May 1993.
40. 'Questions of Cultural Exchange: the NIAS Statement on the European reception of American Mass Culture', in Kroes, pp. 321–33.
41. The phrase was coined by the Marshall Plan Deputy Administrator Harlan Cleveland in July 1950; on its earliest manifestations cf. E. H. Carr, *Nationalism and After.* (London: Macmillan – now Palgrave, 1945).
42. Calleo.
43. 'Address by Secretary of State Baker Before the Berlin Press Club, Berlin, 12 Dec 1989', *American Foreign Policy. Current Documents 1989*, (Washington DC: Department of State) Doc. 126. The concept was later elaborated by the Democrat-appointed Under Secretary of State for European Affairs, Richard Holbrooke in 'America, a European Power', *Foreign Affairs*, (March/April 1995).
44. In the same speech Baker went as far as to suggest that a new bi-lateral treaty might be contemplated. These hopes dwindled into the Joint Declaration of the Madrid summit, 1995.
45. Pfaff, 'Western Europe Missed Its Chance to Take Charge', *International Herald Tribune*, 5 December 1995.
46. Gore speech, Marrakesh, 14 April 1994 reproduced courtesy of United States Information Service, Rome; Kantor speech in *La Voce*, Rome, 15 April 1994.
47. *Washington Post/Guardian Weekly*, 26 April 1992.
48. cf. Jorge Castaneda, 'La revanche des pauvres', *Le Nuovel Observateur*, 6–12 Feb 1992.
49. Hoffmann, 'Europe's Identity Crisis: Beteween the Past and America' (1964), reproduced in Hoffmann, *The European Sisyphus. Essays on Europe 1964–1994*, (Boulder, CO: Westview Press, 1995), p. 18.
50. But the American people, said conservative and liberal critics alike, had from the beginning of the century been led by their prophets to expect more, much more: the benevolent triumph of their values and ideals. Frustrated and disappointed, they were by now deeply alienated from the outside world; cf. John B. Judis, *Grand Illusion. Critics and Champions of the American Century.* (New York: Farrar, Strauss & Giroux, 1992); Wm. Pfaff, *Barbarian Sentiments. How the American Century Ends.* (New York: Hill and Wang, 1989). I have examined these issues in more depth in 'The American Challenge Renewed. U.S. Cultural Power and Europe's Identity Debates', *The Brown Journal of World Affairs*, Winter/Spring 1997.

4
The Nationalist Challenge to Stability in Eastern and Central Europe: 1918–1945–1989

Christopher Seton-Watson

The settlement after 1918

On 28 June 1914 in Sarajevo the heir to the Austro-Hungarian throne, Franz Ferdinand, was assassinated by a Bosnian Serb student, sponsored by a secret sect of the Serbian general staff known as the Black Hand. Its aim was the creation of a Greater Serbia at the expense of Austria-Hungary. Serbian nationalism had been inflamed by victory over the Turks in 1912–13, and had spread to the Serbs, Croats and Slovenes under Austro-Hungarian rule. The growing Southern Slav (or Yugoslav) threat to the integrity of the Empire led to its decision to crush, and eventually absorb, Serbia. Germany backed Austria-Hungary, while the Russians backed their fellow Slavs, the Serbs. The war that followed had by 1917 escalated into a world war. This is a classic example of the consequence of a mixture of local frustrated nationalism and the ambitions of external great powers.

The stable European system by 1918, which had survived numerous crises since 1870, had been shattered. Germany was prostrate in military defeat, and two multinational empires, Austria-Hungary and Russia, pillars of the pre-1914 system, had disintegrated. The task of the peacemakers who assembled in Paris in January 1919 was therefore to build a new stable European order. Their main concern, inevitably, was 'the German question': how to control the nation whose geographical position, rising population and industrial strength made it, even at the moment of defeat, a potentially hegemonic power. The Treaty of Versailles, signed on 28 June 1919, imposed on Germany minor amputations of territory, disarmament and the payment of substantial reparations. It did not destroy Germany's capacity for revival, but did create a very widespread feeling of national humiliation. One of the most humiliating items in the peace treaty was the cession to Poland (on economic grounds) of a corridor to the sea, separating Germany from East Prussia. Hitler's promise to tear up the 1919 peace settlement was one of the main reasons for his advent to power in 1933.

Determining the fate of Germany was much less complex than settling the problems of the successor states to Austria-Hungary and Russia. By the time the peacemakers met, the hitherto subordinate nationalities had already realized their pent-up nationalist ambitions; but the new frontiers remained to be determined. This involved adjudicating between innumerable conflicting claims often marked by violence. In reaching their decisions the peacemakers were mainly influenced by the doctrine of self-determination, as preached above all by President Wilson. But historic, economic and strategic considerations were not entirely ruled out, as a result of which there were many compromises and inconsistencies. The main features of the 1919–21 settlement were: restoration to Poland of the independence which had been destroyed by the partitions of the eighteenth century; the creation of two new multinational states, Czechoslovakia and the Kingdom of the Serbs, Croats and Slovenes (later renamed Yugoslavia) in East-Central Europe; and a string of new states on Russia's western border, Finland, Estonia, Latvia and Lithuania. (Armenia, Azerbaijan and Georgia, which won a precarious independence in 1917, were forcibly reunited with Russia in 1920–21 by the Bolshevik Red Army.) Within the new frontiers the pre-1914 problems of frustrated nationalities re-emerged as a problem of frustrated minorities. These constituted 34 per cent of the population in Czechoslovakia, 30 per cent in Poland, 25 per cent in Romania and 17 per cent in Yugoslavia. Nevertheless after 1919 more people than ever before were living under governments of their own nationality.

The architects of the New Europe hoped that its imperfections would in time be lessened through the League of Nations, whose charter contained an Article (no. 19) providing for peaceful change. They also imposed upon the small powers (Czechoslovakia, Bulgaria, Hungary, Poland, Romania and Yugoslavia) obligations to treat their national minorities fairly by guaranteeing to them what we would now call 'human rights'. But in the event only Czechoslovakia complied substantially with its obligations, and the League of Nations, as the guarantor of the peace settlement, had no power of enforcement. (The worst record was that of Italy, who as a great power undertook no obligation, and ruthlessly persecuted its German and South Slav minorities, which it had acquired solely on strategic grounds.) For the same reason Article 19 remained a dead letter. In fact the geographical distribution of the national minorities was so complex that any attempt to make 'clean cuts' between ethnic groups, by detailed revision of frontiers, would probably have diminished their total number by no more than 5 per cent.

The New Europe remained after 1919 divided between victors and vanquished, between 'haves' and 'have-nots' in contemporary parlance. For the first ten years it seemed that stability had been attained. Democratic Germany accepted the settlement in Western Europe, and though it never accepted the eastern settlement, it implicitly renounced any attempt to alter it by force. But its fragility became apparent with the resurgence of aggressive German nationalism under Hitler in 1933. Prominent in his programme was the incorporation of all Germans within the border of the Third Reich. In March 1938 he annexed Austria, whose union with Germany had been vetoed in the Treaty of Versailles, on strategic grounds and in violation of the principle of self-determination. The annexation of the German areas of Czechoslovakia followed quickly, and in 1939 Hitler demanded the return of Danzig and the Polish Corridor in the name of self-determination. This was a pretext for the pursuit of far greater ambitions. Nevertheless there is a similarity between 1919 and 1939: once again frustrated nationalism, combined with the support of Poland by external great powers (Britain and France), provided the spark which led to a second world war.

The second most important 'have-not' was Hungary. After 1920 one-third of the Hungarian nation lived under alien rule, and in Slovakia and Romania the ruling majority had become a minority ('top dog' had become 'bottom dog', and vice versa). Hungary's frontiers with Slovakia and Romania had certainly been drawn with a certain anti-Hungarian bias, on economic and strategic grounds. But no minor frontier revisions could have solved the problem of 600,000 Hungarians (the so-called Śźekelys) who were totally surrounded by Romanians. Hungarian grievances were fanned by Fascist Italian sponsorship, which made any local settlement more difficult.

The third 'have-not' was Bulgaria. The Treaty of Neuilly of December 1919 confirmed the settlement of 1913, which ended the Balkan Wars, in which, to the exclusion of Bulgaria, Serbia and Greece partitioned Macedonia, and Bulgaria was cut off from the Aegean by Greece. The consequent grievances were a continuous source of Balkan instability between the wars.

Italy's position was ambiguous. On the one hand it was a victor, and completed its unity by the acquisition from Austria-Hungary of the

Trentino and Trieste, the historic targets of Italian irredentism since 1866. On the other hand, a large section of the Italian people regarded the outcome as a 'mutilated victory', in that Italy had been cheated, by her allies' support for the creation of Yugoslavia, of her aspirations to hegemony in the Adriatic and the Balkans. After 1922 the Fascist government deliberately cultivated this temperament of a 'have-not'. By itself Italy could not alter the peace settlement, but Hitler's advent to power gave Mussolini his opportunity. In the meantime Italy promoted Macedonian and Croat terrorism, and turned Albania into an Italian protectorate.

Russia must also be included among the 'have-nots'. It was the great absentee from the Paris Peace Conference, not because of deliberate exclusion by the peacemakers, but rather as a consequence of the fragmentation of the Russian Empire by revolution, civil war and the explosion of non-Russian nationalism along its borders. In 1919–21 war between Poland and Russia ended with the Treaty of Riga, by which Russia was forced to agree to the independence of Estonia, Latvia and Lithuania, and to the incorporation of millions of Ukrainians and Belorussians in Poland. It had already been forced to cede Bessarabia, largely inhabited by Romanians, to Romania. The USSR, which was formed in 1923, never recognized the 1919–21 Peace Settlement. An uneasy stability was established through bilateral pacts of non-aggression between the USSR and its European neighbours, and after the advent of Hitler to power, by the USSR joining the League of Nations and concluding defensive alliances against Germany with France and Czechoslovakia. But on 23 August 1939 the Ribbentrop–Molotov Pact gave the USSR its opportunity, in conjunction with Germany, to tear-up the 1919–21 settlement to its advantage.

The USSR was originally composed of the Union Republics, Russia, Belorussia, Ukraine and Transcaucasus (a temporary amalgam of Armenia, Azerbaijan and Georgia). Within Russia 17 non-Russian autonomous republics and regions were formed. But behind this appearance of federalism and decentralization, political power was monopolized by a centralized All-Union Communist Party, controlled by Moscow. Nevertheless a large degree of cultural autonomy was tolerated, and even encouraged. Non-Russian languages were taught in schools and non-Russian literature was published, provided it conformed to the Party line. 'National deviation' was severely punished, but the survival of national and ethnic identities provided one basis for the explosion of anti-Russian nationalism in 1989.

In the light of events after 1989 two countries which came into existence in 1918–20 deserve further consideration: Czechoslovakia and

Yugoslavia. Both contributed to the destabilization of East-Central Europe in 1938–41. In the 1920s Czechoslovakia seemed the most stable, and best governed state, of the area. Its large German and Hungarian minorities enjoyed political freedom and representation in parliament, and there seemed to be a fair prospect of their peaceful integration in the Czechoslovak state, so contributing to the stability of Europe. But that prospect vanished with Hitler's advent to power, which inflamed the national grievances of the Sudeten Germans. Czechoslovakia was amputated by the Munich pact of 1938, and in March 1939 divided between a German protectorate over the Czech lands, and a Slovak state nominally independent but in fact wholly dependent on Germany. This situation lasted until 1945. Even in the 1920s relations between Czechs and Slovaks had not always been harmonious. They spoke very similar languages, and were both Slavs: but their histories and cultures and social structures were very different, and about one-third of the Slovaks remained disaffected, accusing the Czechs of breaking the promises of autonomy made to them during World War One. In 1938–9, Slovak disaffection was skillfully exploited by Hitler to achieve one of his earliest objectives, the destruction of the Czechoslovak state.

The destruction of Yugoslavia is in certain respects similar. As with the Czechs and Slovaks, the Serbs and Croats spoke the same language (though using different alphabets) and were both Slavs: but their histories and cultures were very different. The Croats had failed in 1918–22 to obtain their Yugoslav ideal of a federal state in which they and the Slovenes would have equal status with the Serbs. The Kingdom of the Serbs, Croats and Slovenes (as it was known up to 1929) was in fact dominated by the Serbs, ruled by a Serbian king, and inspired more by the ideal of a Greater Serbia. Italian support for Croatian separatism (and terrorism) helped to maintain Serb-Croat antagonism. In June 1928 a Serbian deputy shot and fatally wounded the leading Croat statesman in parliament. King Alexander reacted by establishing a royal dictatorship, renamed his country Yugoslavia, and tried to strengthen a Yugoslav national consciousness. In 1934 he was assassinated by a Croat terrorist trained clandestinely in Italy. In September 1939 agreement was reached for granting substantial autonomy to Croatia: but war prevented its validity being tested.

In view of the tensions in the Balkans in the last half of the 1990s and the beginning of the twenty-first century, Albania also deserves special mention. Albania had been freed from Turkish rule by the Balkan wars of 1912–13: but from the first the fragile Albanian state was threatened by its two neighbours, Serbia (and later Yugoslavia) and Greece. The new frontiers left 440,000 Albanians in Yugoslavia and 200,000 in Greece. Between the wars small-scale violence often broke out along Albania's frontiers, but it remained intact owing to the protection of Italy. In April 1939 Italy destroyed its independence by invasion and annexation.

The settlement after 1945

Between 1938 and 1941 Hitler and Stalin wiped the 1919 settlement off the map. All the 'have-nots' had their national grievances at least in part resolved. Hungary was awarded much of the territory it had lost in 1919: a large slice of Slovakia, half of Transylvania (from Romania) and Ruthenia, the eastern tip of Czechoslovakia inhabited mainly by Ukrainians. Bulgaria obtained most of Macedonia (from Yugoslavia), access to the Aegean (from Greece) and the Southern Dobrudja (from Yugoslavia). Yugoslavia was partitioned: Slovenia was divided between Germany and Italy, which also acquired the Dalmatian littoral; Macedonia was given to Bulgaria, the Voivodina, with its large Hungarian minority, was restored to Hungary; and a fascist Croatian state was created which included Bosnia. The USSR, with German collusion, annexed the Baltic states, Bessarabia (from Romania) and the Belorussian and Ukrainian districts which Poland had seized in 1919–21. Between 1941 and 1943, all these border territories were conquered by Germany. In 1941 the German armies were greeted as liberators in many non-Russian areas, but Hitler threw away a historic opportunity by applying his racial policies, which treated especially Slavs as inferior races and had the ultimate objective of forcibly settling one million Germans on Russian soil. As a result national frustrations were intensified, and most non-Russians were as fiercely determined as the Russians to liberate themselves from German rule.

At the end of the war in May 1945 Germany was far more prostrate than in 1918, and, unlike 1918, under military occupation by its enemies. Unlike 1918, when Russia was in chaos, the USSR was the dominant power in East-Central Europe. In 1949 the military demarcation line between the Western and Soviet armies became the political boundary partitioning Germany into two states. The new European order was determined by the Yalta and Potsdam Conferences, which ratified the territorial gains the USSR had made in 1939–41. Poland was compensated for the loss of her non-Polish territories by the acquisition of a large area of eastern Germany up to the Oder-Neisse line. About eight million Germans were expelled, and their places taken by Poles. This process of what now would be called 'ethnic cleansing' solved the interwar problem of the German, Ukrainian and Belorussian minorities of Poland by a method which the peacemakers of 1919, had, to their credit, not even contemplated. Czechoslovakia was restored within its pre-1938 frontiers, except for the cession of Ruthenia to the USSR. Its interwar problem of a German minority was solved as in Poland, by the expulsion of over three million Sudeten Germans. Otherwise there were few changes in the 1919 frontiers: Italy lost the Istrian peninsula to Yugoslavia, which expelled its Italian minority; and Romania lost the Southern Dobrudja to Bulgaria and Bessarabia to the USSR, where it became the Moldavian SSR. The frontiers of Austria, Hungary, Yugoslavia and Greece remained unchanged. The greatest beneficiaries, from a nationalist point of view, were the Ukrainians, who between the wars had been divided between the USSR, Poland, Czechoslovakia and Romania, and were now for the first time politically united.

Between 1945 and 1948 Communist regimes subservient to the USSR had been established in East Germany and in the whole of East-Central Europe east of Austria and Italy, with the exception of Greece. This gave the area a stability that it had not enjoyed since 1914. That stability was formalized, economically and militarily, by Comecon and the Warsaw Pact. Most of the communist parties were purged of their veteran leaders, accused of 'national deviations'. Within the USSR the political and professional élites of the Baltic republics were systematically deported to Siberia for collaboration with the Germans, and two minor nationalities, the Chechens and Tatars, were deported *en masse,* and their autonomous republics abolished. With the exception of Yugoslavia, all attempts to throw off Soviet domination were repressed: in East Germany in 1953, in Poland and Hungary in 1956, in Czechoslovakia in 1968, in Poland again in 1970 and 1982. Yugoslavia asserted its national independence in 1948 by breaking with the USSR and later becoming a leading member of the 'non-aligned' bloc. One consequence was a further purging of other communist parties, in order to root out the 'Titoist deviation'. In the 1960s Romania became another exception, by challenging Soviet plans for closer economic integration and launching a revival of Romanian cultural nationalism of a strictly communist character. In 1968 Čeauşescu refused to participate in the Warsaw Pact's invasion of Czechoslovakia. This can now be seen as a straw in the wind. The Soviet attempt to destroy national feeling had proved in the end unsuccessful. It in fact kept national consciousness and resentment alive and vigorous, and as soon as the Soviet political and military grip weakened in the 1980s, frustrated nationalism erupted throughout East-Central Europe and within the USSR itself.

Once again the Yugoslav case requires special consideration. Its suffering in World War Two was appalling. Partition in 1941 was followed by internecine conflicts between Serbs and Croats. The massacre of Serbs (and Jews) by Croat fascist Ustashi bands was surpassed in atrocity only by Germany's extermination camps. Bulgaria carried out a denationalization policy in Macedonia. Resistance to Germany and Italy was divided between Mihailović's Chetniks and Tito's partisans, who fought each other as fiercely as they fought the enemy occupiers. Mihailović was a Serbian chauvinist, his Chetniks were all Serbs, and his ultimate aim was a Greater Serbia. Tito was a communist, half Croat half Slovene, and whose partisan forces were truly Yugoslav and fought for the restoration of Yugoslavia. Tito's forces emerged victorious in 1945. The constitution of the new Yugoslavia was modelled on that of the Soviet Union, comprising six republics: Slovenia, Croatia, Bosnia, Serbia, Montenegro and Macedonia. Yugoslavia was now proclaimed a state of four nations (Serbs, Croats, Slovenes and Muslims) living in harmony together. The Albanian and Hungarian minorities were granted autonomous status within Serbia (Kosovo and Voivodina). Between 1945 and 1948 the Yugoslav communist regime was as repressive as the Soviet, and remained repressive, but less imitative of the Soviet model, after the break in 1948. Nationalism did not disappear, and manifestations of Croat dissent in the 1960s and the 1970s were firmly dealt with. In Serbia there was dissatisfaction over the diminished weight it exercised within the four-nation state. In Bosnia a distinct Muslim national identity developed. But genuine attempts were made by the communist rulers to reconcile nationalities; and in retrospect it seems almost a miracle that, after the experiences of the war, Tito was able to recreate a Yugoslav state and give it stability for 35 years.

The settlement after 1989

The weakening of the communist grip over both the USSR and East-Central Europe led in 1989–93 to an explosion of repressed nationalism, the disintegration of the USSR, the reunification of Germany and the disappearance of Soviet-style communism. Neither Nazism nor communism had been able to destroy the national identities of the peoples of East-Central Europe, nor their aspirations to political freedom. During the late 1980s not only did the Estonians, Latvians and Lithuanians, Ukrainians, Armenians, Azeris and Georgians begin speaking again the language of 1919, but the infection spread to nationalities of whom the outside world knew virtually nothing: the Chechens, Tatars, Abkhazians and Ossetians, to mention only a few. The Balkan and Caucasian states regained their independence: the Chechens have fought two wars for theirs. In all these states there are Russian minorities of varying sizes, caused by the influx of Russian administrators, industrialists and workers, and armed forces during the period of Soviet rule. After 1989 the borderlands of the old Russian Empire seemed to relapse into the near-anarchy of 1918–23. A fundamental difference, however, between 1918 (and 1945) and 1989 is that the nationalist explosion occurred not as a result of war nor of foreign instigation, but from internal causes. The local wars and tensions between, for example, Russians and Latvians, Armenians and Azeris, Georgians and Ossetians, remained local and did not threaten the stability of the rest of Europe.

In time no doubt a stable settlement will emerge, as it did after 1918. But outside the former USSR the frontiers of 1918, as modified in 1945, remained unchanged, and minority problems remained a potential cause of instability. For a good deal of the 1990s Hungarian–Slovak and Hungarian–Romanian relations were disturbed by the old nationalist rhetoric in all three countries. Romania hoped to recover Bessarabia, but this has been frustrated by the development of a Moldavian identity and language and the growing desire in the 1990s to maintain independence from both Romania and Ukraine. In Italy, the formation of a right-wing government that held power for seven months in 1994 saw some nationalist voices calling for the recovery of Istria, and even Dalmatia, from Slovenia and Croatia.

The two new multinational states of 1918 also disintegrated. After 1948 the Czechoslovak communists pursued a policy of centralization, based on the Soviet model, which in its indifference to Slovak national aspirations differed little from the policy of their democratic predecessors between the wars. Slovak nationalism had been strengthened by the experience of independence, however limited, between 1939 and 1945, and it was significant that when the Czechs rebelled in 1968 Slovakia remained passive. After 1989 the Czechs repeated the error of 1918, in not tackling the Slovak question at once, and in indulging in protracted negotiations. On 1 January 1993 Slovak independence was declared. This rupture, however, did not affect European stability in the 1990s.

The opposite was true for Yugoslavia. Tito's death in 1980 was one major cause of its disintegration. It is also true that though Yugoslavia was not the 'artificial' creation depicted in much of contemporary comment, it owed its origins and its survival in part to external threats: from Italy and Hungary between the wars, from the USSR after 1948. Once the Soviet threat disappeared, centrifugal forces eclipsed the centripetal.

Throughout the 1990s external forces threatened to convert Yugoslav instability into European instability. German support for Slovene and Croat independence, a revival of Russia's historical sympathy with the Serbs, and international Muslim sympathy with the Bosnian Moslems were restrained through the channels of the UN, the EU and NATO. The threat that a nationalist revisionist regime in Russia might undermine cooperation during the wars of the Yugoslav succession did not materialize.

At the turn of the century the main threat in East-Central Europe to European stability still lies in Albania, Kosovo and Macedonia. During the communist years the Albanian minority in Yugoslavia benefited by the establishment of an autonomous Kosovo republic, which allowed the use of the Albanian language in schools, the press and public administration (and on road signs). And while Albania was ruled by the most ruthless of communist dictators, Enver Hoxha, there was little incentive for the Kosovo and Macedonian minorities to seek union; the collapse of Albanian communism, and the abolition of Kosovo's autonomy within Serbia by Milŏsević, a promoter of a Greater Serbian programme, made union more desirable. With the collapse of the post-communist government in Albania in 1997, Albanian nationalists were able to obtain arms to counter the repressive measures of the Serbian government that had been carried since 1989. This led to the crisis in 1998–9, the temporary massive ethnic cleansing of the majority Albanian Kosovar population in 1999, its reversal, and the occupation of Kosovo by UN and NATO forces. Since then Kosovo has been effectively an international protectorate even if legally it is still part of the Serbian Republic of Yugoslavia. In Macedonia a national identity had developed under Tito, and in 1991 it declared its independence. This action aroused suspicion and anger in Serbia, which has always regarded Macedonians as 'South Slavs'; in Bulgaria, which had historic claims to the area; and in Greece, which accused the new republic of territorial designs on Greek Macedonia. In the 1990s these frustrated or conflicting nationalisms were seen as potential sources of destabilization, and even of a third Balkan war. But the pressure eased in the 1990s. Macedonian civic nationalism seemed to withstand the pressures of the Kosovo crisis and the democratization of Serbia boded well for the future peaceful resolution of tensions. However, very recently Macedonia has entered a phase of near civil war between Slavs and Albanians.

I have left to the last what many observers in Eastern Europe, and some in Western, considered as the greatest potential threat to stability: the reappearance of a 'German question' as a result of reunification. The differences between 1989 and 1918 were of course enormous. A stable West German democracy had established itself over 40 years, in contrast to the unstable democracy of the Weimar Republic, which lasted for only 15. And despite a territorial amputation in 1945 that was far harsher than that of 1918, very few voices were raised after 1989 to demand a reversal of the 1945 settlement, except from the rapidly dwindling numbers of expellees from Czechoslovakia and Poland. After 1989 Germany signed a treaty with Czechoslovakia, recognizing its 1939 frontiers, and with Poland, recognizing the Oder-Neisse boundary. Throughout the 1990s Germany played a major role in the economic reconstruction of East-Central Europe, the Russian Federation and the other independent republics of the former Soviet Union. With Poland, Hungary and the Czech Republic as members of NATO and the German government as a patron of candidate members in East-Central Europe to the EU, the position of Germany is not comparable to the revisionism of the interwar era. German economic influence in East Central Europe is immense, and in the early 1990s the Czech Republic was being described as Germany's economic satellite. But for potential economic hegemony to be translated into political dominion would require an upheaval equivalent to that of 1914–18 or 1939–45, which is mercifully inconceivable in the foreseeable future, despite the tragic events that afflicted the Balkans in the 1990s.

Select Bibliography

R. Crampton, *Eastern Europe in the Twentieth Century*, 2nd edn. (London: Routledge, 1997).

S. Dunn and T. G. Fraser (eds), *Europe and Ethnicity: World War I and Contemporary Ethnic Conflict.* (London: Routledge, 1996).

M. Glenny, *The Balkans 1804–1999. Nationalism, War and the Great Powers.* (London: Granta Books, 1999).

P. G. Lewis, *Central Europe since 1945.* (London: Longman, 1994).

J. Rothschild and N. M. Wingfield, *Return to Diversity. A Political History of East Central Europe since World War II*, 3rd edn. (Oxford: Oxford University Press, 2000).

Part II

The Domestic Processes of Stabilization

A. The Economics of Stabilization: 1918–1945–1989

5

Public Debt as a Postwar Problem: The German Experience after 1918 in Comparative Perspective

Niall Ferguson

I

Wars nearly always increase state debts; perhaps the most common of all postwar problems is what to do about those debts. The theoretical literature on this subject tends to distinguish between the *international* distributional conflicts which arise, usually described as the victors seeking to shift part of their debt burden onto the shoulders of the losers,[1] and the domestic distributional conflicts, which are frequently portrayed in terms of class. Thus Alberto Alesina has argued that 'the choice of how to manage [a large public debt] is the result of a redistributive struggle between economic agents...over income and wealth distribution.'[2] Following Ricardian practice, Alesina's 'political theory of debt' distinguishes between three economic 'groups': rentiers, businessmen (profit-earners) and workers (wage earners):

> The 'rentiers' oppose explicit default or inflation and favour various forms of tax increases; and since, they, in general, belong to the upper middle class, they tend to be averse to progressive taxation. The 'businessmen' favour inflation, debt default and eventually non-progressive income taxes, or a combination of these three measures. They benefit from inflation as a means of reducing the debt burden, possibly as a means of reducing real wages and of stimulating exports via exchange depreciation. They oppose taxes on wealth and physical capital. The 'workers' favour taxes on wealth and on capital, progressive income taxes and debt default; they are hurt by inflation if real wages fall but they gain from it if employment increases. The 'workers'

oppose proportional income taxes and indirect taxes on necessary goods.[3]

In the historical literature, a special place is occupied by the German experience between 1919 and 1923: the classic case, it is often said, of a postwar economy plunged into hyperinflation by just such international and domestic distributional conflicts. For Alesina, inflation is the 'residual outcome' of a stalemate between these three groups, each of which has 'enough power to block taxes on itself, but not enough political influence to impose explicit taxes on others'.[4]

This chapter begins by summarizing the literature on the German inflation. It then offers a critique of those arguments that portray the inflation as the inevitable (and even justifiable) consequence of excessive public indebtedness. In the third section, the German debt problem is set in a comparative perspective. The fourth section reconsiders the causes and consequences of the inflation. In the fifth, an alternative to the sociological or class-based model is suggested. Finally, some contemporary parallels are drawn.

II

On 27 April 1921, after much haggling and prevarication, Britain, France, Belgium and Italy agreed a total for the reparations due from Germany under the Versailles Treaty. The 'headline' figure was 132 billion goldmarks;[5] and the demand was backed by the threat that the Ruhr industrial region would be occupied if the Germans did not pay up. The modalities of payment were also specified. Beginning at the end of May 1921, Germany was to pay interest and amortization on so-called 'A' and 'B' bonds totalling 50 billion goldmarks in the form of a 2 billion goldmarks annuity. In addition, from November of that year the Germans were to hand over a sum equivalent to 26 per cent of the value of German exports. This implied a total annual payment of around 3 billion goldmarks. When German exports had reached a level sufficient to pay off the 'A' and 'B' bonds, non-interest-bearing 'C' bonds with a face value of 82 billion goldmarks would be issued.[6]

'Would the whips and scorpions of any government recorded in history,' John Maynard Keynes indignantly asked readers of the *Sunday Times*, 'have been potent enough to extract nearly half their income from a people so situated?'[7] In Keynes's view, 21 billion goldmarks was the most which could be paid.[8] Ever since, it has repeatedly been argued that the debt burden imposed in the form of reparations was the principal reason why Germany suffered hyperinflation in the early 1920s.[9] True, the German budget was already badly out of kilter before 1921, Heinz Haller argued, but the Allies' demand for cash reparations made matters much worse.[10] Because of a structural balance of payments deficit, according to Frank Graham, Germany had no option but to buy hard currency by selling papermarks, thus driving down the exchange rate, pushing up import prices and hence the domestic price level.[11] Barry Eichengreen has put it bluntly: reparations were 'ultimately responsible for the inflation' because without reparations there would have been no budget deficit.[12] In the words of Gerald Feldman, the Allied peace terms 'made impossible demands and promoted intolerable choices' and the reparations were 'a disincentive to stabilize'.[13] As that suggests, a frequently drawn conclusion is that German governments – expected by the Allies to raise taxes to pay for reparations which were almost universally unpopular – had no alternative but to seek to avoid paying. The most obvious way to do this was to allow inflation to continue, for, in Graham's words, the view was 'by no means without justification that improvement in the public finances would lead to still more severe exactions'.[14] It also supposedly made political sense to allow currency depreciation to continue unchecked, since that had the effect of boosting German exports.[15] This should have put pressure on the Allied economies, forcing them to accept that reparations could only be paid at the expense of Allied industry. According to Steven Schuker, the depreciation of the mark had a second advantage: because so much of the money lent to Germany in the period was never repaid, one historian has gone so far as to speak of 'American "Reparations" to Germany'.[16] Depreciation was therefore, according to Holtfrerich, 'in the national interest' – the most effective way of 'persuading the rest of the world of the need for a reduction of the reparations burden'.[17]

The inflation has also been seen as the inevitable and even justifiable consequence of domestic distributional conflicts. In his *Tract on Monetary Reform*, Keynes presented the choice between inflation and deflation – the course adopted by Britain after 1919 – as more or less straightforward: a government which balanced its budget and restored its currency to pre-war parity ran the risk of reducing aggregate economic output and employment; a government which continued deficit finance and therefore inflation, on the other hand, would boost output and employment levels, albeit at the expense of bondholders and other savers with paper assets. Thus in Britain the war was paid for – and more, in that the real value of the war debt actually rose – by imposing deflation and hence unemployment on the working class; while in Germany (and of course in Russia) it was the bondholders who paid. Though inflation was 'worse' than deflation 'in altering the *distribution* of wealth', Keynes suggested that deflation was 'more injurious' in 'retarding the *production* of wealth'. Though he expressed sympathy for the middle class, 'out of which most good things have sprung', he therefore favoured the former, 'because it is worse in an impoverished world to provoke unemployment than to disappoint the rentier'.[18]

In fact, Keynes explicitly identified as an exception to this rule 'exaggerated inflations such as that of Germany'; however, this important qualification has tended to be forgotten.[19] In the words of Graham, for example, 'the balance of material gains and losses' of the German inflation was 'on the side of gains'.[20] This line of argument was developed in the 1960s by Karsten Laursen and Jørgen Pedersen, among others. Not only did German output increase in 1920, 1921 and 1922, they argued, but so did investment, creating a potential for sustained growth which only the depressed conditions of the post-1924 period prevented from being put to use.[21] A vital piece of evidence in this case is the fact that German employment levels were unusually high by international standards in the years 1920–22[22] – this was what Graham principally had in mind when he wrote that 'Germany accomplished the actual process of transition from the war to a stable post-war monetary structure at a lower real cost' than Britain and the US.[23] Economic history textbooks also stress the distributional advantages of inflation, at least for the pre-hyperinflation period.[24] By implication, an alternative policy would have led to lower growth, lower investment and higher unemployment; Britain is the obvious worse case.

To explain the different policy choices in each country, historians have invoked a mixture of sociology and political culture. Thus it has been suggested by Ross McKibbin that in Britain some social groups whose material interests were actually harmed by deflation nevertheless supported the 'conventional wisdom' of sound money for economically irrational reasons, equating Gladstonian orthodoxy with moral rectitude.[25] In France a middle course was adopted, which moderately devalued the national debt – a recognition of the relative but not absolute power of the *rentier* in French society. In Italy the distributional conflict proved impossible to resolve within a parliamentary system, so that the stabilization of the currency had to be undertaken by Mussolini's dictatorship. In Germany, by contrast, a crucial section of the bourgeoisie – entrepreneurs and the managerial business élite – defected to the side of the working class, supporting inflationary policies in the pursuit of a rapid physical expansion of Germany industry, but at the expense of shareholders, bondholders and banks.[26] Whereas earlier accounts portrayed big business as the sole beneficiaries of the inflation, reaping the benefits of low real interest rates, low taxation and a weak exchange rate, it is now argued that workers also did relatively well.[27] The inflation was thus the unplanned outcome of a tacit 'inflationary consensus' between industry, organized labour and other social groups averse to deflation.[28] The loser was the rentier; but the overall effect was to make society as a whole better off and more equal than it would have been if deflation had been attempted.[29]

This line of argument has political implications. Haller estimated that tax levels would have needed to exceed 35 per cent of national income to balance the budget without further government borrowing; a level of taxation modest by contemporary European standards but which, according to Haller, would have been politically intolerable in the early 1920s. Inflation is thus said to have 'secured the parliamentary form of government for the period of the Weimar Republic', since any attempt to have stabilized fiscal and monetary policy would have led to a political crisis.[30] One inference the reader may draw from Charles Maier's pioneering comparative study, *Recasting Bourgeois Europe*, is that a corporatist 'inflationary consensus' in Germany postponed – if only for a decade – the descent into fascism; though Maier also suggests that Nazism differed from Italian fascism in being partly a reaction against corporatism:

> If Italy had earlier developed a liberal corporatism to replace her antique parliamentary and party structure, fascism might well have appeared unnecessary for bourgeois defence. On the other hand, if Germany had not passed through the crucible of capitalist corporatism, Nazism might have seemed unnecessary for middle-class viability.[31]

III

When viewed in a comparative perspective, however, Germany's debt burden in 1921 was not so large as to make hyperinflation inevitable. In fact, 82 of the 132 billion gold marks were to some extent 'notional', in that the 'C' bonds to that value would only be issued at some unspecified future date when German economic recovery was sufficiently advanced.[32] This cast a shadow over the future and to some extent limited the Reich's ability to borrow on the international market, but it meant that Germany's immediate obligations in 1921 were less than 50 billion gold marks – as little, in fact as, 41 billion (taking account of what had been paid after 1919). That had been the sum regarded by Keynes himself as payable in *The Economic Consequences of the Peace*. Moreover, inflation had already substantially reduced the real value of the Reich's internal debt by mid-1921 to around 24 billion gold marks so, as a proportion of national income, the Reich's total liabilities including the A and B bonds amounted to around 160 per cent.[33]

This was undoubtedly a higher debt burden than Germany had previously experienced. The average ratio of total public sector debt to net national product between 1890 and 1913 had been just over 50 per cent.[34] It is also a higher debt burden than the present Federal Republic has ever had to endure (it reached its maximum of 61 per cent in 1997).[35] It was also a higher debt burden than France had faced after the Franco-Prussian War. If one adds together the indemnity demanded by Bismarck (5,000 million francs) and the existing French national debt (11,179 million francs), the total liability is equivalent to around 84 per cent of 1871 net national product.[36] However, the German debt burden in 1921 including reparations was more or less exactly what it had been at the end of 1918 (160 per cent).[37] It was also slightly *less* than the ratio of the total British national debt (internal and external) to gross national product in the same year (165 per cent). Yet in Britain the cost of living peaked at just under treble its pre-war level in November 1920, and the annualized inflation rate never exceeded 22 per cent.[38] The ratio of debt to GNP had been even higher for Britain in 1815: close to 200 per cent.[39] Yet Britain had become the nineteenth century's most successful economy – and its most stable polity – despite that burden. The debt-to-GNP ratio also exceeded 200 per cent after World War Two without triggering hyperinflation.[40] France too was able to cope with post-war debt-to-NNP ratio which reached a peak of over 185 per cent in 1922 without resorting to hyperinflation (see Figure 5.1).[41] It is also worth adding that the ratio of debt to NNP under Hitler reached 150 per cent in 1942: it rose to a peak of more than 268 per cent before the German currency once again collapsed in 1945–7.[42]

Nor was the annual payment being demanded from Germany in 1921 exceptionally high. As we have seen, annual reparations as scheduled by the London Ultimatum implied a total annuity of around 3 billion goldmarks. At least 8 billion gold marks and perhaps as much as 13 billion goldmarks were actually handed over in the period 1920–23: between 4 and 7 per cent of total national income. In the hardest year, 1921, the figure was 8.3 per cent. This was far less than Keynes's wild guess of between 25 and 50 per cent of national income.[43] To be sure, this was certainly a bigger proportion of national income than that subsequently paid under the Dawes Plan (at peak, around 3 per cent).

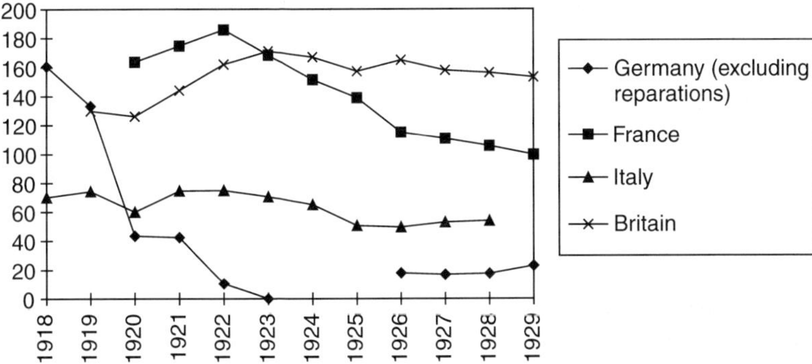

Figure 5.1 Public debts as a proportion of net/gross national product, 1918–1929
Sources: Germany: Hoffmann *et al.*, *Wachstum*; James, *German Slump*, pp. 52, 375. Balderston, 'War Finance'; Webb, *Hyperinflation*, p. 49; Witt, 'Finanzpolitik und sozialer Wandel', p. 424; Mitchell, *European Historical Statistics*, p. 390. Others: Alesina, 'End of large public debts', pp. 49, 61, 65.
Note: Figures for Italy and Britain are expressed as a proportion of GNP; for Germany and France as a proportion of NNP.

But it compares favourably with the French reparations burden half a century before. Between June 1871 and September 1873, France paid Germany 4,993 million francs: around 9 per cent of net national product in the first year, and 16 per cent in the second. Chile, Mexico and Argentina all had external debt-servicing burdens in excess of 7 per cent of national output in 1985; in the case of Chile, the figure was 14 per cent.[44]

Finally, it was not wholly fantastic to expect Germany to pay a lower annual burden over a longer period than had been the case in the 1870s. The Young Committee's report of 1929 is often ridiculed for proposing that Germany continue to pay reparations until 1988. But between 1958 and 1992 Germany paid more than 163 billion marks to the rest of Europe in the form of net contributions to the European Economic Community/European Union budget. In addition, a further 379.8 billion marks has been paid as 'unrequited transfers' to other countries (17.4 per cent of which was accounted for by official reparations payments such as payments to Israel and compensation to individual victims of Nazism).[45] Of course, the annual sums involved have represented a modest proportion of national income; but the final total is rather more in nominal terms than was asked for in post-Versailles reparations; this was precisely the long, scarcely perceptible transfer the Young Plan aimed at.

IV

The real problem with the Versailles Treaty, of course, was not that it was too harsh, but that the Allies failed to enforce it. In 1870–3 the Germans had occupied large tracts of Northern France and linked the payment of the indemnity to their withdrawal: the faster the French paid, the sooner the Germans left. In 1919, by contrast, the Allies imposed the reparations total in 1921 after they had lifted the naval blockade, and with only a minimal force on the ground in the Rhineland. Rather than using occupation as an incentive to encourage reparation-payment, the Allies – or rather the French – sought to use the threat of a larger occupation as a sanction to discourage default. This was psychologically misconceived, as it encouraged the Germans to gamble that the French were bluffing. The alternative course of action was, in effect, voluntarily to pay reparations; not surprisingly, democratically elected politicians were reluctant to approve taxes for this purpose. The difficulty facing Weimar politicians – even those few who sincerely believed that Germany must fulfil the peace terms – was simple: they had to reconcile competing claims on the Reich budget from, on the one hand, their own electors, and on the other, Germany's former enemies. To put it simply: the Allies might want reparations for the damage done to them by the war; but German voters also felt entitled to 'reparations' for the hardship they had endured since 1914.[46]

According to German budgetary figures, total real expenditure under the terms of the Versailles treaty in the years 1920 to 1923 amounted to between 6.54 and 7.63 billion goldmarks. This accounted for around 20 per cent of total Reich spending and 10 per cent of total public spending. Put another way, reparations accounted for a fifth of the Reich deficit in 1920, and more than two-thirds in 1921.[47] But even if one subtracts reparations payments, total public spending was still running at around 33 per cent of net national product, compared with around 18 per cent before the war.[48] And although without reparations inflation might have been lower and revenues therefore higher, it is still likely that there would have been deficits, as with lower inflation the costs of domestic debt service would not have been so sharply reduced. It cannot be assumed that domestic spending would not have risen had reparations magically been abolished.

In addition to the costs of servicing the funded debt, German reparations to Germans included higher spending on public sector pay, doles for the unemployed, of which the Reich paid half, subsidies for housing construction and subsidies to keep down the costs of food.[49] There was also the cost of paying pensions to over 800,000 war wounded, 533,000 war widows and 1.2 million war orphans.[50] The most notorious 'hole' in the budget, however, was the deficit run by the rail and postal systems: the deficit on the Reichsbahn accounted for around a quarter of the total Reich deficit between 1920 and 1923. In part, this was a consequence of purchases of new rolling stock and a failure to maintain the real value of fares and freight rates.[51] But it was also partly due to the government's concern to maintain employment levels, which led to chronic overmanning.[52] The situation was similar in the postal, telegraph and telephone system.[53] In addition, the cost of reconstructing the German merchant marine (aimed at maintaining employment in the ship-building industry) accounted for as much as 6 per cent of total Reich expenditures in 1919 and 1920.[54] Such 'domestic reparations' were more important than actual reparations in generating the German fiscal deficit.

And it was the deficit, not the debt burden, which was excessive (especially at a time of rapid economic growth and falling unemployment) and was disproportionately financed by money creation. As a proportion of estimated net national product, the deficit fell from around 18 per cent in 1919, to 16 per cent in 1920, to 12 per cent in 1921 and 9.4 per cent in 1922; but this was still far too high, and it rose again to more than 22 per cent in the nightmare year 1923.[55] At the same time, a rising proportion of government borrowing was financed by mere money creation (44 per cent of the debt was short-term in 1918; by 1922 virtually all of it was). It was here – in the inability of Weimar governments to reduce domestic expenditure in order to service the external debt, and in the readiness of the Reichsbank to print money on demand – that the proximate causes of the descent into hyperinflation lay.

Nearly all the former combatants faced the same problem, of course: a debt burden so high that paying the interest on it precluded generous expenditures of welfare of the sort which had been dangled, carrot-like, before voters during the war. Britain too had its hopes of 'homes fit for heroes'. The difference was that in Britain the proponents of debt-service and amortization won; whereas in Germany the proponents of welfare spending did. That was why inflation gave way to deflation in Britain in 1921, while in Germany the printing presses kept rolling until the currency's final collapse.

As early as 1922 the German national debt (excluding reparations) had been reduced by inflation so much that in dollar terms it was almost exactly what it had been in 1914 ($1.3 billion compared with $1.2 billion on the eve of the war). By contrast, Britain's was almost ten times its pre-war level and America's more than a hundred times larger (see Table 5.1). In 1923 the German internal debt all but disappeared: it was equivalent to less than one per cent of NNP (Table 5.2). In February 1924, despite the protests of advocates of full 'revaluation' in Germany, the Finance Minister Hans Luther effectively cancelled Germany's war debt. In drawing up the third Emergency Tax Decree of February 1924, which promised modest (10–15 per cent) revaluation of private mortgages and debentures, he explicitly ruled out similar treatment for the 60 million marks worth of war bonds still in circulation (until reparations had been paid – meaning never).[56] The combined debts of the Reich and states

Table 5.1 National debts in dollar terms, 1914 and 1922

	1914	*1922*	*1922 as a percentage of 1914*
USA	1,338	23,407	1,749
Britain	3,440	34,251	996
France	6,492	27,758	428
Italy	3,034	8,689	286
Germany (Reich)	1,228	1,303	106

Source: Bankers Trust Company, *French Public Finance*, p. 137.

Table 5.2 German public debt and net national product, 1914–1923

	Total debt (Reich and states) end of calendar year	*Nominal NNP*	*Debt as a percentage of NNP*
1914	22,043	46,000	47.9
1915	34,323	55,520	61.8
1916	57,477	58,586	98.1
1917	87,119	67,568	128.9
1918	125,523	78,259	160.4
1919	179,050	134,489	133.1
1920	230,000	529,838	43.4
1921	310,000	730,476	42.4
1922	1,403,000	13,612,523	10.3
1923	5,119,160,061,000	5,958,494,594,594,590	0.1

Note: Nominal NNP figures arrived at by multiplying Witt's figures by wholesale price index.
Sources: Balderston, 'War finance'; Webb, *Hyperinflation*, p. 49; Witt, 'Finanzpolitik und sozialer Wandel', p. 424; Mitchell, *European Historical Statistics*, p. 390; Holtfrerich, *Inflation*, pp. 67f.

had been equivalent to around 40 per cent of GNP in 1913. In 1928 the figure was a mere 8.4 per cent. By contrast, as a result of the return to the pre-war dollar exchange rate and the resulting deflation, Britain's national debt continue to increase, reaching a crushing 178 per cent of GNP in 1928.[57]

V

The inflation, and its subsequent legal ratification, had far more serious consequences than Keynesians like Graham or Laursen and Pedersen appreciated. The Italian economist Costantino Bresciani-Turroni, who wrote one of the first serious studies of the subject in 1931, listed them as follows: falling productivity; a misallocation of resources; 'profound disequilibrium in the economic organism'; 'the vastest expropriation of some classes of society that has ever been effected in time of peace'; and declines in public health and morality:

> It annihilated thrift [he went on] ... It destroyed ... moral and intellectual values ... It poisoned the German people by spreading among all classes the spirit of speculation and by diverting them from proper and regular work, and it was the cause of incessant political and moral disturbance ... [It] encouraged the political reaction against democracy.[58]

Although he had come down on the side of inflation, Keynes himself had in fact expressed similar views in his *Economic Consequences*, which famously endorsed the view (attributed to Lenin) that 'the best way to destroy the Capitalist System was to debauch the currency':

> By a continuing process of inflation, governments can confiscate, secretly and unobserved, an important part of the wealth of their citizens. By this method, they not only confiscate, but they confiscate *arbitrarily*; and, while the process impoverishes many, it actually enriches some. The sight of this arbitrary rearrangement of riches strikes not only at security, but at confidence in the equity of the existing distribution of wealth. Those to whom the system brings windfalls ... become 'profiteers', who are the object of the hatred of the bourgeoisie, whom the inflationism has impoverished not less than of the proletariat. As the inflation proceeds ... all permanent relations between debtors and creditors, which form the ultimate foundation of capitalism, become so utterly disordered as to be

> almost meaningless . . . There is no subtler, no surer means of overturning the existing basis of society . . . In Russia and Austria–Hungary this process has reached a point where for the purposes of foreign trade the currency is practically valueless . . . There the miseries of life and the disintegration of society are too notorious to require analysis; and these countries are already experiencing the actuality of what for the rest of Europe is still in the realm of prediction.[59]

The most modern research provides ample support for these arguments of a *generalized* crisis, rather than one in which particular classes won or lost. In particular, the claim that the inflation stimulated investment has been called into question by the work of Dieter Lindenlaub, whose detailed study of engineering firms suggests that rising prices (or to be precise, uncertainty about future prices) actually discouraged investment.

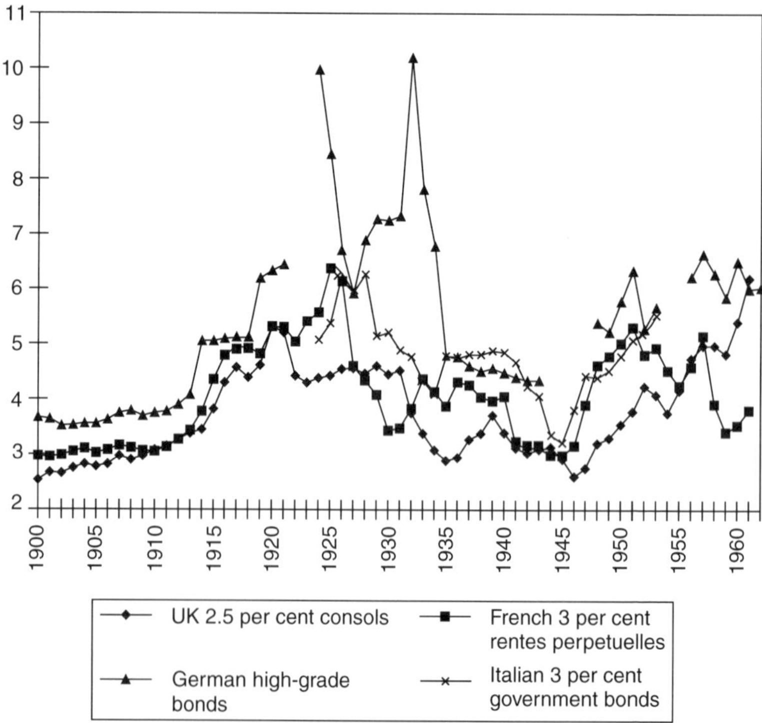

Figure 5.2 European bond yields, 1900–1962
Source: *Sidney Homer, A History of Interest Rates*

1920 – the year of stable prices – was when firms undertook new capital projects, and many of these had to be abandoned when inflation resumed in 1921.[60] More generally, it seems hard to deny that whatever benefits the inflation conferred in 1921 and 1922 were compensated for by the sharp falls in production and employment after hyperinflation set in. It has been persuasively argued by Theo Balderston that, because of its damaging effects on the banking system and the capital market, the inflation was indirectly responsible for the onset and peculiar severity of the slump in Germany; in particular, Balderston emphasizes the way high bond yields made it increasingly hard for the public sector (including local authorities) to maintain housing investment levels in the 1920s.[61] The extent to which, over the long-term, the memory of inflation led to a substantial risk-premium on German bond yields is shown in Figure 5.2. Interestingly, even before World War One, there was a yield gap or spread between Germany, on the one hand, and Britain and France on the other, which partly reflected the perception that German public finances were less sound than those of her western neighbours.[62] But the war and inflation substantially widened that; and the second currency collapse of 1944–6 ensured that the differential persisted into the 1960s.

VI

Sociological explanations of the German descent into hyperinflation tend to overlook the fact that, in fiscal terms, the conflict that really mattered was between holders of government debt and tax-payers; and that these were far from being distinct groups approximating to the bourgeoisie and working class, or even occupational subdivisions thereof.

Everywhere the number of bondholders had been greatly increased by the war. If one adds together the total number of subscriptions to the nine German war loans, just under half were for amounts of just 200 marks or less; for the last four war loans, the proportion of such small subscriptions averaged 59 per cent.[63] In 1924 around 12 per cent of the internal British national debt was held by small savers.[64] It is also sometimes forgotten that many of the biggest holders of war bonds were institutional rather than individual investors – insurance companies, savings banks and so on – whose large wartime purchases were effectively made on behalf of small savers. For example, 5.5 per cent of the British debt in 1924 was held by insurance companies and 8.9 per cent by the clearing banks.[65]

At the same time, there was an increase in the number of people paying direct tax. In Britain the number of income tax-payers more than trebled from 1,130,000 in 1913/14 to 3,547,000 in 1918/19, while the proportion of wage-earners rose from zero to 58 per cent. To be sure, wage-earners only accounted for around 2.5 per cent of the net revenue from the income tax; but they could hardly be indifferent to the £3.72 each of them on average paid in 1918/19.[66] In Germany tax deducted from wages at source accounted for a steadily rising share of total direct tax revenue as middle-class tax-payers delayed payment of their tax bills, leaving inflation to reduce them in real terms.[67] German working class tax-payers were therefore even more concerned about direct tax. It is also vital to remember the postwar changes to electoral franchises, which had previously been restricted by wealth or income qualifications in most countries: democratization might have been expected to increase the political representation of voters who were neither bondholders nor direct tax-payers. In Britain, however, the ratio of voters to income tax-payers actually fell from 6.8:1 before the war to 6:1 in 1918 – the number of tax-payers had increased more than the number of voters (by 214 per cent compared with 177 per cent).

Class analysis of the sort favoured by sociology therefore simply will not work because the crucial groups – bondholders, tax-payers and voters – had been too much altered by the war and to a large extent overlapped. Winners in one respect could simultaneously be losers in another: in this, German peasants were no exception.[68] The choice for a great many voters – not all of them necessarily 'bourgeois' – was between receiving income in the form of interest on war bonds, but losing it in higher taxation, or avoiding the taxation but losing the war bonds to inflation. But this was not a choice with which they were presented by politicians.

The combination of fiscal and monetary laxity which characterized German economic policy between 1919 and 1923 therefore cannot be explained in terms of class conflict or 'corporatism'. Corporatist collaboration of bosses and unions there certainly was when it came to wages and prices. But budgets and interest rates were never directly controlled by organized capital and labour. Rather, the complexity of creditor–debtor relationships, cutting across class and party lines as they did, precluded a straightforward politics of economic interest around the Cabinet table, on the Reichstag Budget Committee or within the Reichsbank. Under those circumstances, individual decision-makers had more room for manoeuvre than historians have generally recognized. This is why it is no mere counterfactual fantasy to suggest that they could have acted differently.[69]

VII

All this has some important implications for contemporary policy-makers and, indeed, for any general theory of public debt. It supports the hypothesis that absolute levels of debt (or rather, ratios of absolute debt to GDP) are not useful indicators of inflation risk: what matters is the size of annual deficits (or rather, the rate of growth of debt) and the way they are financed. This has considerable relevance to current debates on European finance, in which the question of public debt plays an important role.

The end of another war – the Cold War – and the absorption of the German Democratic Republic by the western Federal Republic in 1990 led (as a few commentators, including the author, predicted at the time)[70] to a substantial increase in German public borrowing. To be precise, German public debt rose from 42 per cent of GDP in 1991 to just over 60 per cent in 1996, almost twice the figure for 1980. This was due to increased deficits at the federal, *Land* and local levels: the average public sector deficit for the years 1991–96 was 5.5 per cent. Yet these deficits did not have the inflationary consequences feared by some because of the prompt monetary tightening by the independent Bundesbank. Instead, the cost of unification led to an influx of foreign capital and an appreciation of the deutschmark against other currencies. One side-effect of this was to place enormous strain on the Exchange Rate Mechanism linking the German currency to those of other European Union Members. Indeed, the knock-on effects of higher European-wide interest rates can be seen in the public debt figures for a number of other countries. Between 1991 and 1997 the French public debt rose from 36 per cent to 58 per cent of GDP; the Italian from 102 to 122 per cent; the Spanish from 46 to 69 per cent and the Swedish from 53 to 77 per cent.[71] The British debt also rose from 36 per cent to 53 per cent, though how much of this increase was due to 'structural' (recession-related) factors and how much to discretionary increases in public expenditure by a government sliding towards electoral disaster remains a matter for debate.

At the time of writing, German public debt has been stabilized at around 60 per cent of GDP. Nevertheless, in the absence of radical reform of the state pensions system, further fiscal 'overstretch' seems inevitable in the coming decades. This is a problem which nearly all continental states face. According to OECD figures, the present value of unfunded pension liabilities amounts to 98 per cent of GDP in France, 113 per cent in Italy and 139 per cent in Germany. That gives total public liabilities of 155 per cent for France, 201 per cent for Germany and 236 per cent for Italy. These figures imply debt burdens of the sort only previously caused by major wars. The only European state which does not face this difficulty is Britain. In the past 17 years, British public debt has grown far less than those of the major continental states (from around 54 to 56 per cent of GDP), while its unfunded pension liabilities amount to just 5 per cent of GDP, due to the Thatcher government's decision in the 1980s to break the link between the state pension and average earnings.[72]

As if oblivious to the fiscal problems of the members states, the authors of the Maastricht Treaty included among their 'convergence criteria' governing eligibility for EMU two which specifically related to fiscal policy. It was agreed that, in order to be eligible to participate in EMU, a country's 1997/8 ratio of debt to GDP should be no more than 60 per cent, and its deficit should not exceed 3 per cent of GDP. However, not only have these criteria been honoured in the breach by a number of countries, whose treasuries have resorted to ingenious accounting expedients; it is also far from clear how far EMU members will be obliged to abide by these rules in future years. The maximum deficit criterion is now notionally permanent under the 'stability and growth pact' of December 1996: after EMU, any member state which runs a deficit of 3 per cent or more will have to have a good excuse (like a recession or a natural disaster), or it will be liable to a fine of between 0.2 and 0.5 per cent of GDP. But quite how such fines will assist with balancing the budget in future is obscure. Even more obscure in the light of the evidence presented in this chapter is what, if anything, such crude fiscal rules can contribute to the stability of the euro as a currency.

The other contemporary case of interest, which much more closely resembles that of Weimar Germany, is post-Communist Russia.[73] Thanks to high inflation in the early 1990s, the total Russian debt is relatively modest in relation to GDP. However, the failure of successive governments under President Yeltsin to reform the system of taxation has meant that annual deficits have continued to run at relatively high levels. The funding of these through the sale of relatively short-run bonds created a situation very like that of 1921–22 in Germany, when a loss of confidence in the rouble led to a sudden crisis, with foreign investors refusing to 'roll over' their holdings of debt and the cost of debt service rocketing. Although it is widely believed that Russia was merely a victim of a financial panic – a domino effect or 'contagion' – which originated in South Asia in 1997, the underlying state of Russian public finance in itself gave good grounds for a loss of confidence, regardless of the absolute level of state indebtedness.

The problem of state indebtedness is thus a complex one. Clearly, any major 'shock' like a war or revolution is likely to cause an increase in public indebtedness. This need not always be inflationary, however; or at least, it need not lead to an inflationary spiral. The determining factor is not the size of a country's debt relative to its domestic product, but the expectations of investors and traders on the bond market as to the scale of future deficits – in other words, the projected rate of growth of debt – and the ability of the market to finance these. These expectations, though expressed as forecasts of the future, are in large part reflections of the past. The question is therefore how past deficits are explained; for forecasts plainly stand little chance of being accurate unless they are based on a good explanatory model.

The suggestion advanced here is that the sociological explanation of inflation is, for all its appealing simplicity, too crude. The case of Weimar Germany shows that fiscal deficits cannot be understood simply as the outcome of domestic class conflict, but depend on the complex interaction of bondholders, tax-payers and voters, all overlapping groups, as well as the sometimes autonomous actions of politicians and central bankers. A state can sustain a large public debt and recurrent deficits without succumbing to inflation, provided the bond market believes that the political will exists to service debt and maintain relative exchange rate stability. Despite the relatively high public debt levels of European Union states – only four of whom in fact met the Maastricht criteria for EMU membership – falling bond yields attest to the confidence of investors and traders that this is the case. Any intimation of a failure of political will, however – as happened in Germany in 1921–23 and as may yet happen in Russia – can lead to rapidly accelerating inflation as the state is forced to resort to money creation.[74]

Notes

1. See Albrecht Ritschl, 'Sustainability of High Public Debt: What the Historical Record Shows', Centre for Economic Policy Research Discussion Paper 1357 (1996).
2. Alberto Alesina, 'The End of Large Public Debts', in F. Giavazzi and L. Spaventa (eds), *High Public Debt: The Italian Experience*. (Cambridge: Cambridge University Press, 1988), p. 34.
3. *Ibid.*, pp. 38f.
4. *Ibid.*, pp. 35 and 41–9.
5. 'Goldmarks' was contemporary shorthand for marks adjusted for inflation since 1914; in US dollars the total was around $31.4 billion.
6. C. S. Maier, *Recasting Bourgeois Europe: Stabilization in France, Germany and Italy in the Decade after World War I*. (Princeton: Princeton University Press, 1975),

pp. 241f.; Bruce Kent, *The Spoils of War: The Politics, Economics and Diplomacy of Reparations, 1918–1932.* (Oxford: Clarendon, 1989), pp. 132–8. The 12 billion goldmarks still outstanding from the 20 billion goldmarks demanded at Versailles was tacitly included in this total, while sums due to Belgium were not, so that the final sum outstanding was between 123 and 126.5 billion goldmarks.

7. John Maynard Keynes, *The Collected Writings of John Maynard Keynes*, vol. XVII: *Activities, 1920–22, Treaty Revision and Reconstruction*, ed. E. Johnson. (London: Macmillan for the Royal Economics Societies, 1977), pp. 242–9.
8. John Maynard Keynes, *A Revision of the Treaty*. (London, 1921). Cf. Niall Ferguson, 'Keynes and the German inflation', *English Historical Review*, (1995) 368–91.
9. At the nadir in December 1923, the cost of living index reached 1.25 trillion times its pre-war level (1,247,000,000,000). Though most combatant countries experienced some measure of inflation and few were able to return to their pre-war gold standard parity, this was the worst case. Poland did better despite having to fight a war: its price level rose by a factor of 1.8 million; even Russian prices went no higher than 50 billion times the pre-war level before the currency was reformed: Costantino Bresciani-Turroni, *The Economics of Inflation: A Study of Currency Depreciation in Post-war Germany*. (London: Allen & Unwin, 1937), pp. 23f., 161–5.
10. Heinz Haller, 'Die Rolle der Staatsfinanzen für den Inflationsprozeß', in Deutsche Bundesbank (ed.), *Währung und Wirtschaft in Deutschland, 1876–1975* (Frankfurt am Main: F. Knapp, 1976), pp. 137f. See also Carl-Ludwig Holtfrerich, *The German Inflation, 1914–1923*. (Berlin/New York: De Gruyter, 1986), pp. 137–55.
11. F. D. Graham, *Exchange, Prices and Production in Hyperinflation Germany, 1920–1923*. (Princeton: Princeton University Press, 1930), pp. 134, 117–49, 153–73.
12. Barry Eichengreen, *Golden Fetters: The Gold Standard and the Great Depression, 1919–1939*. (New York/Oxford: Oxford University Press, 1992), p. 141.
13. Gerald D. Feldman, *The Great Disorder: Politics, Economics and Society in the German Inflation*. (New York/Oxford: Oxford University Press, 1993), pp. 255–72.
14. Graham, *Exchange, Prices and Production*, pp. 4, 7–9, 11, 30–5, 248, 321.
15. *Ibid.*, pp. 174–97, 209, 214–38, 248.
16. S. Schuker, 'American "Reparations" to Germany, 1919–1933', in G. D. Feldman and E. Müller-Luckner (eds), *Die Nachwirkungen der Inflation auf die deutsche Geschichte, 1924–1933*. (Munich: R. Oldenbourg, 1985), pp. 335–83.
17. Carl-Ludwig Holtfrerich, 'Die deutsche Inflation 1918 bis 1923 in internationaler Perspektive. Entscheidungsrahmen und Verteilungsfolgen', in Otto Büsch and Gerald D. Feldman (eds), *Historische Prozesse der deutschen Inflation 1914 bis 1924. Ein Tagungsbericht* [*Einzelveröffentlichungen der historischen Kommission zu Berlin, Bd. 21*]. (Berlin: Colloquium – Verlag, 1978), p. 327.
18. John Maynard Keynes, *A Tract on Monetary Reform*. (London: Macmillan – now Palgrave, 1923), reprinted in *Collected Writings*, vol. IV (Cambridge: Cambridge University Press, 1971), pp. 3, 29, 36.
19. Though not in Barry Eichengreen, 'Understanding 1921–1927: Inflation and economic recovery in the 1920s', in B. Eichengreen, *Elusive Stability: Essays in the History of International Finance, 1919–1939*. (Cambridge: Cambridge University Press, 1990), pp. 24–56.

20. Graham, *Exchange, Prices and Production*, esp. pp. 321, 324.
21. K. Laursen and J. Pedersen, *The German Inflation, 1918–1923*. (Amsterdam: North-Holland Pub. Co., 1964), pp. 95–8, 124ff.
22. Graham, *Exchange, Prices and Production*, pp. 278f., 317f.; Laursen and Pedersen, *German Inflation*, pp. 77, 123.
23. Graham, *Exchange, Prices and Production*, pp. 289; 318–21.
24. See, for example, F.-W. Henning, *Das industrialisierte Deutschland, 1914 bis 1972*. (Paderborn: Schoningh, 1974), pp. 63–83.
25. Ross McKibbin, 'Class and Conventional Wisdom: The Conservative Party and the "Public" in Inter-war Britain', in R. McKibbin *The Ideologies of Class: Social Relations in Britain, 1880–1950* (Oxford: Clarendon, 1990), pp. 259–93.
26. Alesina, 'End of Big Public Debts', pp. 50–68.
27. Holtfrerich, *Inflation*, pp. 227–62.
28. Maier, *Recasting Bourgeois Europe*, pp. 114, 228–31.
29. Holtfrerich, *Inflation*, pp. 265–78. See also J. Fleming, C.-D. Krohn and P.-C. Witt, 'Sozialverhalten und politische Reaktionen von Gruppen und Institutionen im Inflationsprozeß. Anmerkungen zum Forschungsstand', in Büsch and Feldman (eds.), *Historische Prozesse*. For a useful survey see Charles P. Kindleberger, 'A Structural View of the German Inflation', in Gerald D. Feldman *et al.* (eds), *Die Erfahrung der Inflation, [Beiträge zu Inflation und Wiederaufbau in Deutschland und Europa 1914–1924*, Bd. 2]. (Berlin/New York: De Gruyter, 1984), pp. 10–33.
30. Haller, 'Rolle der Staatsfinanzen', p. 151.
31. Maier, *Recasting Bourgeois Europe*, p. 592.
32. Sally Marks, 'Reparations Reconsidered: A Reminder', *Central European History* (1969), 356–65.
33. Niall Ferguson, 'Constraints and Room for Manoeuvre in the German Inflation of the early 1920s', *Economic History Review* (1996), pp. 635–66.
34. W. G. Hoffmann, F. Grumbach and H. Hesse, *Das Wachstum der deutschen Wirtschaft seit der Mitte des 19. Jahrhunderts*. (Berlin: Springer-Verlag, 1965), p. 788.
35. Statistisches Bundesamt, *Statistisches Jahrbuch 1997*. (Wiesbaden: Metzler-Poeshd, 1997), tables 24.3, 20.5; Deutsche Bundesbank, *Monatsbericht*. (August 1998), p. 56.
36. This is pursued in greater detail in Niall Ferguson, *The World's Banker: A History of the House of Rothschild* (London: Weidenfeld & Nicholson, 1998).
37. Calculated from figures in Theo Balderston, 'War Finance and Inflation in Britain and Germany', *Economic History Review*, 42 (1989) 222f.; Peter-Christian Witt, 'Finanzpolitik und sozialer Wandel in Krieg und Inflation 1918–1924', in Hans Mommsen, Dietmar Petzina and Bernd Weisbrod (eds), *Industrielles System und politische Entwicklung in der Weimarer Republik*. (Konigstein: Athenaum Verlag, 1977), vol. I, p. 424; B. R. Mitchell, *European Historical Statistics, 1750–1975*. (London: Macmillan – now Palgrave, 1981), p. 390; Webb, *Hyperinflation*, p. 49.
38. J. A. Dowie, '1919–20 is in Need of Attention', *Economic History Review*, (1975), 429–50.
39. Calculated from figures in B. R. Mitchell and P. Deane, *Abstract of British Historical Statistics* (Cambridge: Cambridge University Press, 1976).
40. Ritschl, 'Sustainability'.

41. Alesina, 'End of Large Public Debts', p. 49.
42. H.-J. Braun, *The German Economy in the Twentieth Century: The German Reich and the Federal Republic*. (London/New York: Routledge, 1990), pp. 112, 115.
43. Holtfrerich, *Inflation*, pp. 148f.; Webb, *Hyperinflation*, pp. 54, 104; Eichengreen, *Golden Fetters*, pp. 129f. Cf. Charles S. Maier, 'The Truth About the Treaties', *Journal of Modern History*, (1979), 56–67.
44. Webb, *Hyperinflation*, pp. 107f.
45. Niall Ferguson, 'The Cash Fountains of Versailles', *The Spectator*, 14 Aug 1993, 14–16.
46. Niall Ferguson, 'The German Inter-war Economy: Political Choice Versus Economic Determinism', in Mary Fulbrook (ed.), *German History since 1800*. (London: Arnold, 1997), pp. 258–78.
47. See the estimates in Bresciani, *Inflation*, pp. 437f.; Graham, *Hyperinflation*, pp. 44f.; Holtfrerich, *Inflation*, p. 148.
48. Calculated from figures in Webb, *Hyperinflation*, p. 37; Witt, 'Finanzpolitik und sozialer Wandel', pp. 424f.
49. Feldman, *Great Disorder*, pp. 214–39.
50. Richard Bessel, *Germany after the First World War*. (Oxford: Clarendon, 1993), pp. 73, 79.
51. Norbert Paddags, 'The Weimar Inflation: Possibilities of Stabilization before 1923?' (unpublished MSc dissertation, Oxford, 1995), pp. 20–4. See also Bresciani, *Economics of Inflation*, p. 71n.; Webb, *Hyperinflation*, pp. 33, 37.
52. Paddags, 'Weimar Inflation', p. 38.
53. Figures in *Deutschlands Wirtschaft, Währung und Finanzen. Im Auftrage der Reichsregierung den von der Reparationskommission eingesetzten Sachverständigenausschüssen übergeben*, pp. 107–10.
54. See Niall Ferguson, *Paper and Iron: Hamburg Business and German Politics in the Era of Inflation 1897–1927*. (Cambridge: Cambridge University Press, 1995) pp. 280ff.
55. Ferguson, 'Constraints and room for manoeuvre', pp. 653–66.
56. Feldman, *Great Disorder*, pp. 46f., 816–9.
57. Calculated from figures from Hoffmann *et al.*, *Wachstum*, pp. 789f.; Mitchell and Deane, *British Historical Statistics*, pp. 401f.
58. Bresciani, *Inflation*, pp. 183, 215, 261f., 275, 286, 314f., 330ff., 404.
59. John Maynard Keynes, *The Economic Consequences of the Peace*. (London: Macmillan – now Palgrave, 1919), pp. 220–33.
60. Dieter Lindenlaub, *Machinebauunternehmen in der Inflation 1919 bis 1923: Unternehmenshistorische Untersuchungen zu einigen Inflationstheorien*. (Berlin/New York: De Gruyter, 1985).
61. Theo Balderston, *The German Economic Crisis, 1923–1932*. (Berlin: Haude & Spener, 1993), *passim*.
62. Niall Ferguson, 'Public Finance and National Security: The Domestic Origins of the First World War Revisited', *Past & Present*, (1994) 141–68.
63. K. Roesler, *Die Finanzpolitik des Deutschen Reiches im Ersten Weltkrieg*. (Berlin: Duncker and Humblot, 1967), p. 207.
64. E. V. Morgan, *Studies in British Financial Policy, 1914–1925* (London: Macmillan, 1952), p. 136.
65. *Ibid*.
66. Balderston, 'War Finance', p. 236.

67. P.-C. Witt, 'Tax Policies, Tax Assessment and Inflation: Towards a Sociology of Public Finances in the German Inflation, 1914 to 1923', in P.-C. Witt (ed.), *Wealth and Taxation in Central Europe: The History and Sociology of Public Finance.* (Leamington Spa/Hamburg/New York: Berg, 1987), pp. 137–160.
68. Robert G. Moeller, 'Winners as Losers in the German Inflation: Peasant Protest over the Controlled Economy', in G. D. Feldman, C.-L. Holtfrerich, G. A. Ritter and P.-C. Witt (eds), *Die deutsche Inflation. Eine Zwischenbilanz.* (Berlin/New York: De Gruyter, 1982), pp. 263–75.
69. See Ferguson, 'Constraints and Room for Manoeuvre'.
70. Niall Ferguson, 'Über the hill: Why the new Germany's a Weakling', *The New Republic*, (1991) 24–7.
71. Deutsche Bundesbank, *Opinion of the Central Bank Council Concerning Convergence in the European Union in View of Stage Three of Economic and Monetary Union*, (Frankfurt, 1998), table 4.
72. Gabriel Stein, 'Mounting Debts: The Coming European Pensions Crisis', *Politeia* (1997).
73. See Niall Ferguson and Brigitte Granville, 'Weimar Germany and Contemporary Russia: High Inflation and Political Crisis in Comparative Perspective', *Voprosii Ekonomiki* (Moscow, 1997).
74. This explains the close correlation observed by Capie between episodes of hyperinflations and civil unrest: see Forrest Capie, 'Conditions in which very rapid inflation has appeared', *Carnegie-Rochester Conference Series on Public Policy*, 24 (1986) 115–68.

6
Stabilizing Italy: 1945–1989

Paul Furlong

Introduction

In the study of settlement and stabilization, what is Italy's claim on our attention? By stereotype, it may appear to be so politically unstable and unpredictable as to merit puzzlement rather than serious comparative analysis. All theories have to acknowledge outliers, but that should not be a licence thereafter to ignore them. A proper understanding of this issue should include the difficult cases as well as those held to be mainstream. This chapter contends among other things that though its friends and its critics alike have argued to the contrary, Italy is not an exception, but has been and remains part of Western Europe in its politics as in so much else. Within that context, Italy is not a small or peripheral nation in economic terms. Here again, exceptionalism raises its head. Though it is the fourth largest economy in the EU, and a member of the G8 group of leading world economies, Italy's voice is not a strong one in international circles. It is often argued that Italy punches below its weight in international and European affairs, and hence there is a tendency for it to be neglected as an international actor by academics. Domestic political factors, including the government's instability and the lack of alternation among the governing parties, certainly encouraged commentators to treat it as an aberrant case in comparative political studies. Yet appearances and predictions to the contrary, Italy's liberal democracy has survived since 1945. If the overall political stability and economic success match those of its comparators, and if Italy itself is closely integrated into Western economic and political systems, to exclude it from the family because of some inconvenient idiosyncrasies is facile and intellectually unsatisfactory. If, as is also the case, Italy's successes are claimed on behalf of the Western European model, it cannot be disowned for its less appealing features.

In terms of our understanding of how the Western European model of stabilization works, Italy poses some important questions. In the immediate aftermath of World War Two, Italy had neither the strategic significance of Germany nor the political influence of France, but had economic and political problems as serious as either. Both the economic and the political problems were long term, and had been exacerbated rather than created by the appalling experience of war. A further factor was the lengthy period of Fascist dictatorship from 1922 to 1943, whose already obvious decrepitude had been accelerated by military failure and by the domestic discontent that followed it. Yet Italy prospered for a period of over 40 years after 1945, despite its initial internal weaknesses and its lack of international weight. Its economic growth rates matched those of its European partners, standards of living rose rapidly though unevenly throughout the country, and a comprehensive welfare and social security system was gradually established. On the other hand, the constitutional political system functioned around a much criticized and counterproductive paradox, in that it combined exaggerated governmental instability with unusual electoral stability. A further associated oddity was that though governments fell frequently, the ministerial élites changed little. The same party, the Christian Democrats, remained in government from 1945 to 1993, and provided every Prime Minister from December 1945 to July 1981. There was therefore a lack of genuine alternation of parties in government, and as is often the case in dominant one party systems, the strength of the governing parties was not matched by their competence in government or by their integrity. This phenomenon, the striking disparity between the economic success and the political problems, which is perhaps at the core of dismissive judgements of Italy's status, was referred to by political scientists in the 1970s as 'political lag' and in the 1980s as the 'stalled system'.[1]

Since 1989, some of this has changed. To a perhaps greater extent than other Western European countries, Italy has undergone fundamental party-political reform. Though the relative health of the economy should not be in serious doubt, the political system has undergone important practical changes, with the sweeping away of a ruling party coalition that in various formats had governed Italy since 1947. This has been associated with an apparent breakthrough in the long-running debates on constitutional change. After many years of argument these may produce genuine reform to the postwar institutional framework in the early twenty-first century. Italy therefore provides an example of a stable and in many respects successful postwar settlement, followed now by what appears to be a period of major political readjustment. This chapter will examine how the political settlement of 1945 came under increasing strain before 1989. It will focus on the growing contradictions in the political economy of the settlement of 1945 present in the 1970s and 1980s. The political economy of the settlement of 1945 was already under strain due to domestic and international pressures on governmental policy before the dramatic events of the early 1990s. Therefore this chapter concludes at the cusp of the 1990s. It will examine long-standing contradictions in Italy's political economy and will not venture into subsequent developments, such as the growth of the Northern League or the dramatic series of scandals known as *tangentopoli* that swept away the political parties of post-1945. As a political scientist I will engage in the literature of my discipline but I will place the arguments concerning the case of post-1945 Italy within a dynamic historical framework.

The postwar settlement

The foundations of the postwar system in Italy can be summarized using categories similar to those used for other major countries of Western Europe. A liberal democratic constitutional agreement provided the formal framework for the relatively rapid development of mass political parties. Both the mass parties and the constitutional consensus within which they worked were unprecedented in Italian politics. With a more limited and evolving political consensus about the proper distribution of collective resources, a select few of the political parties provided stable government and operated the proper constitutional forms for over four decades. In political economy, Italy found the logic of Keynesianism as compelling as did other countries, and in its own way successfully applied the instruments of economic management to the objectives of long-term growth, moderate income redistribution, and secure employment. Internationally, Italy found remedies for its traditional anxieties about its nineteenth-century status as 'the least of the great powers' in European integration and in the US military umbrella.

One of the question marks about Italy's European status, and one closely involved in understanding the Italian political settlement, has been whether Italy should be included in the group of states considered to have a fully modern political system. This question is implicit in the categories referred to earlier, political lag and stalled system.

The process of political modernization in Italy did not begin with a clean slate in 1945. Italy's Liberal state lasted from 1870 to 1922. It never properly succeeded in establishing modern political institutions, if by that we mean the more or less autonomous institutions of liberal democracy including independent democratic political parties accountable to the electorate, and a government that derives its authority in some sense from their parliamentary voice. Associated with the lack of autonomous political parties was the weakness of civil society, especially the failure to develop an appropriate capacity for association and interest representation. Before World War One public administration came to be used extensively for the purposes of patronage, so that electoral support particularly in the South depended on the distribution of state benefits to clienteles, usually in the form of licences, exemptions, employment and eventually pensions. The political base for the Liberal state remained narrow, and its collapse was at least partly due to its incapacity to integrate the emerging mass political movements, especially the Socialists and the Catholics, after World War One. Its main objectives from its early years were the maintenance of public order, the consolidation of a unitary political authority, and the integration of Italy into the prevailing alliances as an equal and active partner. Because of internal weaknesses, it suffered from a series of imbalances and incongruities, which included unresolved religious questions (the status of the Vatican, the role of Catholics in public life, the condition of the Catholic peasantry), economic disparities between North and South, and an inefficient and élitist bureaucracy. Under the Liberal regime, the state itself was limited in its scope and regulatory in its methods. Its main economic function was to provide a stable legal framework within which the economic activity of individuals and enterprises could take place, and to guarantee the separation of state and civil society through the protection of the independent rights of each. This was a typical nineteenth century liberal state, in that it combined limited economic functions with a powerful array of resources for the control and suppression of internal dissent. Within its own sphere, the power of the state was absolute, reflecting the liberal inheritance of traditional views about the nature of sovereign political authority. Only secondarily and incrementally did the state come to develop wider and more welfare-oriented powers of intervention in the economy and society, and this happened without fundamental change in the constitutional or administrative framework.

The Fascist regime did not resolve these long-term issues, though it was associated with the development of mass political propaganda and a considerable increase in state involvement in the economy. Overall, from this point of view Fascism has to be seen as a step back from political modernization, an attempt to resolve issues of stabilization by the imposition of autocratic central authority. In their different ways, the Liberal state and the Fascist regime can be seen as exercises in state-building which developed and retained the structures of the regulatory state and had only very limited success in finding more sophisticated ways of resolving the state–civil society relationship.

The more complex forms associated with pluralistic state-building only began to develop with the postwar Republican system. The new Republican constitution of 1948 represented a major advance on what had gone before. Whatever their divisions, the new mass parties (the Christian Democrats and the Communists, mainly) were united in their concern to put the authoritarianism and anti-liberalism of the Fascist regime behind them. An unprecedented opportunity for political development was offered by the opening up of civil society, the granting of new freedoms of association, of the press, of opinion, and the constitutional safeguards against abuse of political power. This offered the hope that this could occur in such a way as to resolve the traditional profound conflicts in the relationship between civil society and the state. But the new polity inherited some of the weaknesses of the past, particularly the anachronistic state apparatus and the divisive representative relationships associated with clientelism. Public administration continued to be ruled by internal norms and structures that dated from the de Stefani reforms of 1923. These, though introduced by the Fascist government, were characteristically Liberal in principle and practice. They continued to provide the framework within which patronage could flourish. In the postwar Republic, the massive extension of state involvement in the economy and the development of state-funded welfare provided new opportunities for this. In electoral politics, the introduction of universal suffrage and the emergence of the new mass political parties did not sweep away the older forms of representation. Patronage continued in modified form, and had to subsist with the more modern forms of representation based on issues, interest and allegiance. Though the political parties were new, the state within which they operated was still largely that inherited from the previous regimes. The Fascist penal code, the *Codice Rocco*, continued to provide the framework for the routine administration of justice. Even the standing orders of the new Republican parliament were inherited without major reform from the last Liberal parliament of 1921. One of the main consequences of this was that though political parties had explicit mention in the new constitution (Article 49) they were not recognized as such in parliament. Parliament's structures continued for some time to apply more individualistic concepts of representation, with negative consequences for the relationship between executive and legislature. Thus the postwar settlement brought a radical constitution, universal suffrage, a complex party structure, and rapid socioeconomic growth, but its failure to grapple with the historical issues at the core of political authority led to a state-form which is a hybrid of modern pluralism and traditional élitism.

The impact of potentially positive innovations was also limited by the terms of the settlement itself. The institutional pluralism of the 1948 constitution was constrained by a variety of factors that showed themselves as the constitution was implemented. First, the exclusion of the second largest party, the Communists, from government after May 1947 undermined the enthusiasm for the more radical elements in the new constitution. Granted an open and pluralist framework, the governing parties after 1948 adopted a defensive strategy. To implement measures such as regional devolution or the referendum procedure was to risk handing powerful political weapons to the potentially subversive and de-legitimized Communists. Even the provisions for establishing a Constitutional Court suffered; this did not become functional until 1955, and the other two provisions (regional government and referendum) had to wait until 1968 and 1970 respectively. The failure properly to reform the Fascist penal code until the 1980s, though not attributable to precisely the same tactical objective, was nevertheless indicative of the same general priorities. Second, the concern to keep control over the administrative levers led to the practice of *partitocrazia*, literally 'partyocracy'. This meant that the governing parties distributed management posts in the expanding public sector to party appointees, in accordance with party weights in the governing coalition. This practice further encouraged the development of state-managed patronage throughout the public sector, and ensured that party-political involvement in policymaking was felt everywhere. Eventually the distribution of public sector posts, especially at regional level, came to include the Communists, in implicit recognition of their political strength, even though they remained excluded from central government. Difficulties in maintaining party discipline within the governing parties and problems of absenteeism in parliament resulted in a similar though rather more legitimate involvement of the Communists in ensuring the day-to-day management of parliamentary business. These practices, which developed slowly but became increasingly obvious after the difficult years of the 1970s, were not formalized or openly acknowledged. There thus developed a dual mode of government, involving a conventional separation between the 'constitutional arc' and the 'institutional arc'. The constitutional arc comprised all those parties who had contributed to the overthrow of Fascism and who had been involved in drafting the 1948 constitution, and whose support for the postwar settlement could be assumed. The institutional arc comprised the more limited group of those parties who were also deemed acceptable as full members of the governing coalition. The Communists were recognized to be part of the 'constitutional arc', but the formal business of government, including ministerial posts, being limited to the parties of the narrower 'institutional arc', was not within their reach.

At the core of the system was the lack of an alternative to the ruling Christian Democrat party (DC). The electoral support of the Christian Democrats remained remarkably steady over four decades, based on a mix of social conservatism, anti-Communism, support for the welfare state, and initially strong support from the Catholic Church. The DC dominated the business of coalition formation. The stability of their support ensured that they could impose long-term patterns of behaviour favourable to their concerns. And their unchallenged position as the largest party in the coalition meant they could claim the major share of posts in any government, including those governments in which they did not provide the prime minister.

This dual mode developed its own conventions and procedures, the detail of which was especially intricate on matters relating to the formation and stability of the governing coalition, since it was this which governed the distribution of resources around the system. Formal politics in and outside parliament was dominated by the confrontation between the governing and non-governing parties, especially between the DC and the PCI. Informal politics was much more flexible and positive, and this took place mainly in private in the permanent committees of parliament and in the meetings between ministers, senior party officials and senior civil servants. But the division between the two impeded balanced political growth, and distorted the ways the state responds to political and civil society. The practical and routine reliance on the opposition to ensure the passage of government business and to help maintain social peace was undermined by the constant need to remind the electorate of the suspect legitimacy of the second largest party. The political system circumvented this 'roadblock' only by dint of some potentially hazardous manoeuvres.

Summarizing, no doubt with rude simplification, we can regard these issues in the state–civil society relationship as concentrated round a set of dichotomies, as shown in Table 6.1.

Table 6.1 Italian policy-making styles

Policy process	*State*	*Civil society*
Location of activity	Central ministries, peripheral offices	National and local trade associations, interest groups, churches
Historical origins	Traditional, Liberal	Modern, postwar
Framework of operations	Public, impersonal formal norms	Private, personalized informal conventions
Pace of development, adaptability	Low, rigid	High, flexible
Scope of access for individuals	Limited	Open

Between these two spheres lay a hybrid world, comprising not only the political organizations in the narrow sense but also those elements of the state which operated outside the traditional ministerial framework – particularly the autonomous agencies, the public bodies and the public sector in industry. We should also include in this intermediate sphere the new instruments of local government, particularly the regional governments. In the process of managing the boundaries between the two arenas, the political parties especially had a pivotal role. Political parties formed the main link between the apparatus of the state and the organization of civil society. They determined which route issues were to follow in the intricate paths that made up the varied modes of policy-making. It was the governing parties who exercised discretion over access to public resources, whether these were material, moral, legal or hierarchical. It is they who controlled the gates between the formal and the informal, who mediated between the rigidity of the bureaucracy and the dynamism of an active and expanding economy, who maintained and developed the conventions by which the political system operated.

There were, as we have seen, a number of reasons why it was not possible for the governing parties to manage without recourse to the compromise and short-circuits of the party-political world which lay between state and civil society, the *partitocrazia*. The unacknowledged reliance on the official opposition was a practical necessity imposed by the internal divisions of the ruling parties, which compelled them to moderate their public inflexibility in private. But this was a relatively late development, and before the involvement of the opposition there were other factors in play for longer. First, the process can be interpreted as an attempt by politicians to escape the stultifying constraints of the central public administration in order genuinely to achieve the reforms needed to rebuild Italy after 1945. Second, a similar but less worthy motivation was the need to circumvent the rigid lines of central control so as to maintain and enhance the patronage networks with which ministerial office was so closely connected. Third, in the absence of any unifying authority within the Christian Democrats, the exchange of public resources was the means by which a semblance of internal coherence and order was maintained within the governing party itself. Finally, the process provided a convenient if rather arbitrary way of keeping access to policy flexible and open without threatening the long-term survival needs of the governing parties. The role of ministers in those departments that had a large patronage role (such as Agriculture, Education and Posts) directly reflected these contrasts and constraints. There tended to be an implicit pact between ministers in these departments and their senior officials, in which ministers dealt with the limited range of policies and legislation that was of interest to them for whatever reason, and left the routine administration entirely untouched. One simple statistic illustrates how important ministerial control was for the DC. In the 45 governments between 1947 and 1992, the Agriculture ministry was always held by a Christian Democrat, Education was held 42 times out of 45, and the Postal ministry 41 times. Particularly in these areas, but throughout the executive branch as a whole, the routine of the system was maintained and dominated by the governing party.

The contrast and interaction between the formal and the informal, between the public and the private, between legal norms and practical short cuts, between the traditional and the modern, gave shape and meaning to the entire policy process. These contrasts were most visible in the central political institutions. Political decision-making entailed a complex process of exchange between conflicting groups mediated by the political parties, especially the DC, who used public resources as currency to contain and to reduce societal conflict. Contrasts permeated the way politics worked, and served an important function, that of stabilizing and enforcing the rules for the distribution of public spoils among conflictual sectional interests. They could serve this purpose because they gave *de facto* legitimacy to the disjunctures and irrationalities inherent in them, against which there was no appeal. They were needed above all to maintain the conventional balance among parties and among interest groups, by enforcing the disparity of treatment to be expected for particular interests, and by providing a sanction against excessive opportunism on the part of those most favoured.

An Italian model?

This approach enables us to understand the Italian political system as a specific variant within the family of Western European policy processes, with their emphasis on structured interaction among a number of groups, bounded by institutional continuities, with routine exchange of political goods at the core of political decision-making. In general terms, this interaction is determined by differing levels of resources, by variations in forms of dependence, and by the different impact of strategies, rules and processes of exchange. These are the key features of Western European pluralism. In Italy this complex interaction

- followed a pattern of distribution of resources broadly established in earlier regimes;
- was sanctioned by a constitutional system which emphasizes formal law and representational pluralism;
- was mediated through a public administration which separated routine patronage from substantial policy; and
- depended on the permanence in office of the governing parties to maintain the stability of the exchange values and to determine the outcomes of the barter in an orderly manner.

These descriptive elements may be relatively easy to identify individually, but it is more of a challenge to characterize this synthetically. Conventional models of European pluralism have increasingly shifted attention towards interest-group/bureaucracy interaction, implicitly downgrading the influence of parliament and even of the formal organization of the political parties. The predominance of parties in Italy normally discouraged this emphasis on organized interest groups. When they were the objects of study, the research usually was permeated by reference to the pervasive control of the governing parties, the weakness of the bureaucracy and the dependence of interest groups on association with party representatives.

An alternative attempt to explain the postwar settlement was found for a while in the 1970s and 1980s in neo-corporatism. This also has no great purchase in the Italian case. Despite or because of the rhetoric of Italy's corporatist past, it did not appear to have developed neo-corporatist structures in its postwar government. At least until 1989, periodic sightings of emerging patterns of corporatist intermediation (for instance, with the wages policy agreement of 1983) proved premature, perhaps because Italy lacked the core state structures to guide such a strong form of representation.[2] The term 'consociational' was widely used in a pejorative sense by critics of the Italian mode of policy-making in the 1970s and early 1980s. The problems with this term are several.[3] Consociationalism has not been convincingly applied as an explanatory model outside its original homeland, the Netherlands, partly because of the difficulty of finding the equivalent degree of élite consensus over major policy within an agreed constitutional framework. In Italy the consensus was limited to a stalemate supported by a restricted range of parties, and conventionally relied on a single dominant party to enforce the rules by which negotiation is conducted. Consociationalism was used in Italy as a generic term of abuse to refer to the secrecy with which deals were struck and their failure to achieve substantive policy change. This altered the original content of the term, which originally applied to the capacity of the system to make genuine progress using rules accepted by all, in which no one party is predominant. As we have seen, these qualities did not apply in Italy.

The competitive pluralist model of representation was implicit in parts of the constitution, in parliamentary regulations handed down from the Liberal state and in the practices and conventions of the state apparatus. It therefore had the undoubted advantage that it had descriptive plausibility when applied to the normative framework, even if it failed to explain fully the real distribution of power within the system. Also it vied with other forms of representation, particularly with class-based representation through the mass parties and the clientelism of the traditional administration. In all the governing parties, the distinctions between parties, interest groups and factions were blurred, so that it was not at all obvious what type of politics is going on – individualistic support, issue-based representation, class-based representation, associational support, clientelism. Because of the factionalized party structures at regional or provincial level the associational networks might have actually functioned as electoral machines for the politician whose patronage network dominated in the area – not for the association membership nor even for the party as a whole. In some areas, again particularly in the south, preference voting sustained the local patronage strategies of notables, who also relied on their membership of modern mass parties to give them access to office. Issue, class, association and client-group combined to put cross-pressures on the elected representatives and to confuse the political input into the policy-making process. The party-dominated pluralism succeeded in guaranteeing a modicum of stability for the ordinary processes of government, but could do little to stimulate élite consensus over the substance of collective public interest, and rested on a very low level of public satisfaction with the way democracy worked in Italy. The competitive and highly pluralist pattern of representation did determine how coalitions were formed and how proposed legislation was ranked. But it did so on the basis of criteria which related to factional objectives, not on criteria related to national aims about the stuff of modern politics elsewhere – inflation, unemployment, trade balance, social security and welfare. Its capacity to aggregate and identify the collective public interest was not strong, and the legitimacy of the representative system suffered accordingly.

While accepting the quantitative predominance of party élites in formal decision-making processes, research in the 1980s led to the conclusion that there was a fundamental distinction between partisan policy-making and substantial policy-making. Partisan policy-making means processes in which a political grouping uses formal procedures to express coalitional preferences; substantial policy-making refers to preferences of the various actors (usually having a party-political link) for specific action in a sector of public policy – pensions, taxes, energy and so on. Research by Dente and Regini found that preferences expressed in the partisan arena rarely showed the same pattern as those expressed in the substantial arena – allies and antagonists in the one were not necessarily allies and antagonists in the other. Furthermore, the pattern of alliance and antagonism within the substantial arena varied from issue to issue. The implication of this is that coalitions formed at the partisan level were not necessarily paid for directly in the currency of substantial policy. This also suggested that, within the variety of configurations available, substantial policy arenas might be characterized by sectoral rather than comprehensive decision-making, with considerable cooperation across groups who were antagonistic in the partisan arena, and by openness to the specific preferences of other actors. The comparative model based on the difference between substantive and partisan policy-making had clear affinities with the policy community and issue network literature. And it helped explain some of the paradoxes of Italian policy-making – such as particularly the apparent 'politicization' of decision-making, in the party-political sense, together with the lack of obvious pattern connecting the various sectors and issues.

The policy community approach had the advantage that it was intuitively plausible because it began with the recognition of the first paradox of Italian politics: the domination of the political system by the same group of parties for over 40 years, and the apparent lack of any significant overall patterns or strategies in policy making during this period. Notions of political lag generally failed to address this issue, while clientelism and immobilism signified[4] the lack of an overall national pattern, not the existence of one. Policy community and issue or policy network studies began by accepting this superficially patternless phenomenon, and identifying the mechanisms within it which actually structured the way decisions were made – in particular, resources, processes of exchange, constraints, objectives and rules. Like the pluralist theories from which they derived, policy community approaches concentrated attention on intermediate élites, on non-dominant organizations which either by selection or by their own initiative came between formal political office-holders in central government and the diverse policy interests of particular sectors.

Analysis within this framework did not presuppose any one overall pattern – it was possible to argue in different cases for different models, ranging from unregulated sectoral competition between élites, through issue networks, to incorporation into policy communities by administrative élites. In Italy, the individual explanations in specific cases of substantial policy showed some areas of 'community' behaviour, but were overlaid with partisan policy-making. The partisan policy-making was much less structured than the substantial policy-making and was closer to the issue network model than to community pattern (see Table 6.2):

In the Italian case, the 'rules of the game' within which strategies were played out were characterized by the reliance on rapid switches between the formal and informal, described above, which was a defining characteristic of Italian policy-making. Though individual policy communities might have subsisted in some areas where there were dominant groups able to structure the exchange, in the majority the

Table 6.2 Varieties of policy-making models

	Policy community ideal type	*Partisan policy in Italy*
Group resources	Even across restricted range of non-party groups	Skewed to parties
Relations with bureaucracy	Dominated by professional associations	Professional associations weak
State leadership capacity	Authoritative	Lacking authority
Preferred strategy	Consensual integration, cooperative	Selective exchange, clientelist
Objectives	Group-specific	System maintenance
Value-system	Interest-based, flexible	Given, non-negotiable
Élite strategies	Technocratic, dirigiste	Populist, distributive

system was one of sub-dominant players using the informal rules so as to maintain the relative imbalance of resources. This was particularly the case in employment, health care and fiscal policies. The awkwardness of formal procedures led the players in the game to seek informal arrangements, so as to get around the formalities. This made them subordinate in specific cases to those who had the authority to waive the application of regulations, such as individual ministers, individual *assessori* in local government, or those who acted for them. Power in this context was predominantly but not exclusively discretion over the application of written formal rules.

The informal rules of the game, which governed the actual process of exchange, appeared to place a high premium on contract-type issues typical of the market-place. The market-place to which these rules referred however was structured and closed, and the rules reflected this. While any attempt to identify informal unstructured and flexible guides to behaviour must be extremely approximate, observation suggest that the following constituted the basic rules of the games before the 1990s:

- *Confidentiality of agreements* – contracts reached between parties could not be minuted in official records of any sort, and if necessary structures were developed within formal institutions to allow contracting parties to adjourn into restricted non-recorded committees.
- *Reciprocity of relationships* – trust was essential between the contracting parties, particularly since the exchange might amount to no more than agreement to support now in return for unspecified support later.
- *Conflict avoidance* – the societal basis was highly conflictual, but the policy rules excluded the possibility of zero-sum conflicts. Irreconcilable conflict between contracting parties would disturb the policy market and would threaten the integrity of the other rules. Orderly exchange required the acceptance of the procedures by all those involved and complete commitment to the process of exchange.

But the lack of electoral or other sanctions against errant behaviour made the confidentiality, reciprocity and commitment difficult to sustain. Outside the informal and private arena of agreement, other factors intervened. Further rules were required which recognized the need for adaptability.

- *Arbitrariness of values* – the exchange was based on subjective assessments of worth, and might change radically and rapidly.
- *Temporary nature of alliances* – the fluidity of values and the lack of external pressure to the contrary ensured that alliances between

players were rarely of long duration, and in any case were not expected to be so. It follows from this that it was difficult to reach agreement about policy changes that might be likely to have long-term or structural effects much beyond the duration of the alliance.
- *Flexibility of membership* – exclusion from one sectoral exchange network did not entail exclusion from all others. Despite repeated efforts by one party or another to impose complete consistency of alliances, parties did in fact achieve different sectoral and territorial arrangements.[5]

Explaining Italian stability in the post-1945 era: the uses of models from political science

The previous discussion enables us to explain how clientelism subsisted in what was otherwise a modern pluralist system, with its own conformation of resources, dependency, strategies and exchanges. Clientelism was a set of informal bilateral relationships between the patron and a varying number of individuals. This should not be seen as a set of strict dyadic relationships separated from one another, but rather as a loose network of such relationships, in which individuals might have been both patron and client. Power, meaning control of resources, followed formal office-holding, and dependency was lack of access to office. The resources were usually material, relating to state financial benefits such as pensions and allowances, or to contracts for public procurement, but might also be facilitative – as for instance when the patron waived a particularly irksome regulation to the benefit of a client. In return the client provided political support of a variety of types including voting. Little need be said of the strategies of the client since the client had very few options available: exit or loyalty, but no voice. This was not a free-market exchange. The client could not affect public policy, since public policy was largely incidental to the exchange. The objectives of the patron were to maximize the extent of the clientelist support and to deploy it as a resource in the range of political relationships undertaken. The strategies employed by the patron were vote-maximizing, where the vote depended not on perceived competence, ideological affinity or sociological affiliation but on an instrumental relationship. Clientelism as a theory of the substantial policy process was highly unspecific as to outcome. By definition it presupposed very limited resources and strategies on the part of societal interests, and suggested a general lack of concern for the effects of the outcome on the collective interest. But it may cover action in the partisan policy arena, where it explained at least partially the determination of policy outcomes in their effects on specific interest groups in Italian society such as public employees, professional associations, and pension groups.

The approach employing the concept of policy communities on the other hand is characterized by a more equal sharing of resources, a more consensual style of management, and a high degree of institutional coordination. There was little evidence of these in partisan policy-making in Italy, where the exchange of political goods was at its most complex and most fluid.

Most contemporary non-Italian research using this analysis emphasized the crucial role played by public administration in the processes of marshalling the interests, selecting the intermediary groups, and regulating the competitive elements. Indeed, the conformation and the processes internal to government apparatus determined to a large extent how successfully governments achieved their objectives in interest-group management. In Italy, the interests of public administration were primarily the preservation of their corporate structure, its job security, the ease of working conditions, and particularly the rigid protection against political interference provided by the statutory procedural requirements. Interest-group regulation was not part of the territory of public administration except under relatively rigid conditions. Such regulation was normally carried out within a bureaucratic market-place, in which professional bureaucrats acted as market makers, exercised some autonomous control over resources, and were able to play a pivotal role in substantial policy making. But in Italy, the political parties were the market makers. After 1945 public administration was the missing actor, silent in the debate, usually lacking any sense of its own preferences in individual sectors, and restricted by the formality and awkwardness of its procedures from entering genuine negotiations with politicians and interested groups. Italian public administration was one of the main reasons why the structured market predicted by the pluralist approach could be fully applied. The above analysis would suggest that the professionalization of public administration in Italy was a necessary condition of progress to an orderly system of interest-group regulation and this has certainly been one of the key themes of government policy in the post-1989 era.

Historical development of policy: towards 1989

The use of a static framework derived from political science modelling suggests that an analysis of Italy's processes of partisan and substantial decision-making clearly fit into the post-1945 West European pattern of pluralist intermediation. (Of course, one must note the particular Italian variations based on the longevity of the dominant coalition, the persistence of patronage-based exchange, and the anomalous role of an unreformed public administration.) What this framework does not tell us is how to look at the chronological development of policy and, in particular, how the postwar settlement developed and why it came under pressure in the 1980s. We can now apply the same kind of analysis to the historical development of public policy, beginning with general observations about some common features, and identifying the Italian variant.

Macro-economic policy lay at the heart of public policy decisions after 1945, because it determined the scope and direction of government spending and because it affected the framework of prices, labour relations, social mobility and welfare needs within which other policy operates. In comparative terms, the historical objectives of economic policy in post-1945 Western Europe are usually identified as follows (not necessarily in this order of priority):[6]

1. self-sustaining and balanced growth of national income (gross and per capita);
2. stable prices, or at least levels of inflation in line with competitors;
3. balance of payments equilibrium; and
4. full employment, or as close as is compatible with the proper functioning of the labour market.

These objectives were an integral part of the Keynesian postwar consensus, formed out of the experience of the depression, the war, and the rapid rebuilding of the economies of continental Europe. They implied an activist government role in the economy, and the belief that within limits the state could actually manipulate the demand side of the economy so as to correct imbalances and to mitigate the worst effects of cyclical trends. They also imply the use of what Heidenheimer refers to as the 'big levers' – monetary instruments, tax policy, government spending.[7]

In Italy, only monetary policy was a reliable tool, the other two being ruled out as either ineffective or uncontrollable. As elsewhere in Western Europe the objectives of macroeconomic policy were also instruments through which the benefits of economic development could be shared throughout the population through the development of welfare policies, improved education and health, and rising real wages for the entire workforce. Social policy in postwar Western Europe was characterized by the adoption in principle of universalism, even if different routes were used to achieve it and sometimes very imperfectly and very late. The benefits of economic growth were considered entitlements for the entire population to share, if necessary through direct state intervention.[8] The adoption of these aims and of the instruments they entailed put economic policy at the pivot of government activity, so that choices of economic policy had direct consequences for all other aspects of policy – social security, employment, education, health, defence, industry. All of these policies entailed redistributive effects both from the direct consequences of the policies themselves (particularly if they involve transfer payments) and because of the tax and government borrowing implications. Hence even when budget balances were not giving cause for concern the question of levels of deficit or surplus was not only financial and macroeconomic it was also a social and political question.

With these objectives and with these tools, governments in Western Europe were therefore committed to economic management. This applied whether they wished it or not. In more industrially developed countries, even when governments (usually led by conservative parties) attempted to disengage from one or other of the objectives, their own actions had an unavoidable impact, because of the size and scope of government economic activity. In some countries – Italy included – governments at times took on direct responsibility for growth through indicative planning and through state ownership or support of key sectors. The Italian experience of national planning lasted only from 1964 to 1972, but regional and sectoral plans were a constant feature of government thinking, and public sector ownership had been a powerful weapon throughout the postwar until the 1980s.

As in the rest of Western Europe, in Italy throughout the post-1945 era there was an implicit tension in the medium term between anti-inflationary objectives and the goal of near-full employment. Until the early 1970s, this was kept within manageable proportions by the sustained high growth rates and by the effectiveness of the Philips curve relationship, the trade-off between wage inflation and unemployment. But even then, governments had to make difficult choices about their priorities and about the kinds of instruments they were willing to use to achieve them. The most difficult choices tended to be over incomes policies, which in the later years of the Keynesian period became an increasingly important means of keeping the relationship between wages and growth within tolerable dimensions. It follows from these points that government policies had a further re-distributive impact on income, because of the different impact of inflation or unemployment burdens on different sectors of the economy – savers or consumers, wage-earners or unwaged, users of collective services or of private services. This was particularly important in Italy, where the failure to bring government revenue and spending into balance resulted in high interest rates for government debt, which when sustained over a number of years had structural effects on capital investment and on forms of saving.

In Italy as elsewhere, development of the strategic choices underwent a profound change in the early 1970s following the collapse of the Bretton Woods exchange rate system in 1971 and the oil price rises of 1973–4. The inflation and recession that followed brought into question the economic assumptions on which the postwar Keynesian consensus had been founded. They revealed the difficulties of increasing or even of maintaining established levels of welfare in times of wage inflation and declining real growth rates, and led to an increasing polarization over issues of income distribution and economic growth.

The Keynesian consensus relied on the government's direction of the 'big levers' to deliver optimal resource allocation for the economy as a whole. This connection had the important political effect of promising a genuine reduction or even elimination of the bitter social conflict that had characterized economic development in Europe from the middle nineteenth century onwards. When it failed, or was superseded by new and unfavourable relationships between unemployment and inflation, the business of optimal resource allocation was no longer compatible in any relatively simple way with the reduction of social conflict. In Italy as elsewhere, the state had to find a new role and to alter its objectives on strategic issues.

Italy's historical variation

Most of the specific differences in Italy have already been described, and there is no need to repeat the detail here. Italy had a late and uneven industrial development that left the country deeply divided; it had bitter political divisions left unresolved and a public administration that identified itself with nineteenth century models of the state. Its application of the Keynesian consensus was therefore incomplete, mainly because its control of the instruments of demand management was limited and because the political intentions behind social policy never fully adopted the universalistic principles typical (in various ways) of modern European welfare states.

The limited objectives of Italian public policy were sometimes camouflaged with the rhetoric and even some of the instruments of technocratic social democracy, for example during the planning phase in the 1960s, but this never achieved the effectiveness of the French *dirigisme* on which it was modelled. In part, as Tarrow argued, this was because of the way in which state organization was structured, with a highly diffuse distribution of authority ill-suited to the uniform implementation of central objectives.[9] In part also, it resulted from the deliberate choices of successive generations of Christian Democrat and lay politicians to use the public sector for populist, distributive purposes. In Italy, the break-up of the postwar managerialist alliances, such as they were, occurred rather earlier than elsewhere, with the outbreak of serious labour unrest in the 'hot autumn' of 1969, which coincided with Italy's first major postwar recession. From this point on, the function of the state had to change radically. The conflict between worker and employer could no longer be managed with the promise of distributive welfare funded by increased growth and mediated by the ubiquitous and accommodating majority party. A graphic indication of the failure of the state in the 1970s came with the *scala mobile* wage indexing agreement between employers and trade unions in 1975, which was settled in bilateral negotiations between the two in defiance of the government's attempt to impose a classically Keynesian incomes policy.

In the 1970s and 1980s the pretensions of the state to manage the conflicts engendered by economic change were severely constrained, and increasingly the state was in practice if not in rhetoric limited to maintaining the equilibrium between independent social groups through its distributive policies. The function of public spending was to guarantee as far as possible the relative position of the competing groups, without any real capacity for altering the equilibrium or directing its development. Political exchange was therefore characterized by an unstable combination of conflict and dependency.

A consequence of these changes, in dramatic contrast with the unstable equilibrium of the 1950s and 1960s, was the increasing divergence between what groups demanded of the state and what the state could deliver. Underlying this was the replacement of the bipolar conflict of organized labour and relatively compact interests of the industrial owners with a multiple conflict, sometimes referred to as polycentric conflict.[10] This conflict was between individual groups over the distribution of public resources. But it was also between the state and sectoral and regional groups, over the availability of resources and over the scope and content of reform. The state was therefore an important actor in this conflict, not only because of the pressure on public spending but also because of the widespread consensus within the political and administrative élites of the need for radical change to existing structures of control and of delivery of policy. This is turn resulted at least partly from the awareness of the process described above, the development of financial and practical constraints in managing the ever-expanding functions of the post-Keynesian state.

These developments can be presented in diagrammatic form. Figure 6.1 provides a chronological view of the changes in the roles of the state and its interaction with the international and domestic conditions. The approach is that adopted earlier in this chapter, based on the assumption that Italy had a specific variant of general patterns of state intervention. It therefore shared with other similar countries the predominance of Keynesian objectives and instruments, their break-up and the emergence of more conflictual policy processes. In the Italian case these were exacerbated by the variety of historically specific factors: in particular the regional imbalances, the unreformed state structure and the governmental predominance of a single party. Figures 6.2 and 6.3 together with Table 6.3 provide a brief outline of the main features of the policy process that resulted from this development.

These processes undermined the traditional functions of state intervention as rational manager of the macroeconomic constraints within which the economy operated. The consequences of the state's failure were at first the development of a vicious circle of erratic growth, persistent inflation and increasingly inequitable distribution of resources within society. This overlapped to some extent with the attempted reform of the state during the historic compromise period, from 1976 to 1979, when Communists and Christian Democrats were briefly in

Table 6.3 A model for the 1980s

Policy process in Italy: polycentric conflict and dependence
1. Increasing societal division
2. Exclusion of weakest groups
3. Permanence of party oligopoly
4. Interdependence of parties
5. Weakness of state coordination
6. Urgency and complexity of reform
7. Public spending as currency of compromise with strongest groups
8. Exchange of political resources between parties to establish ranking of parties and clients

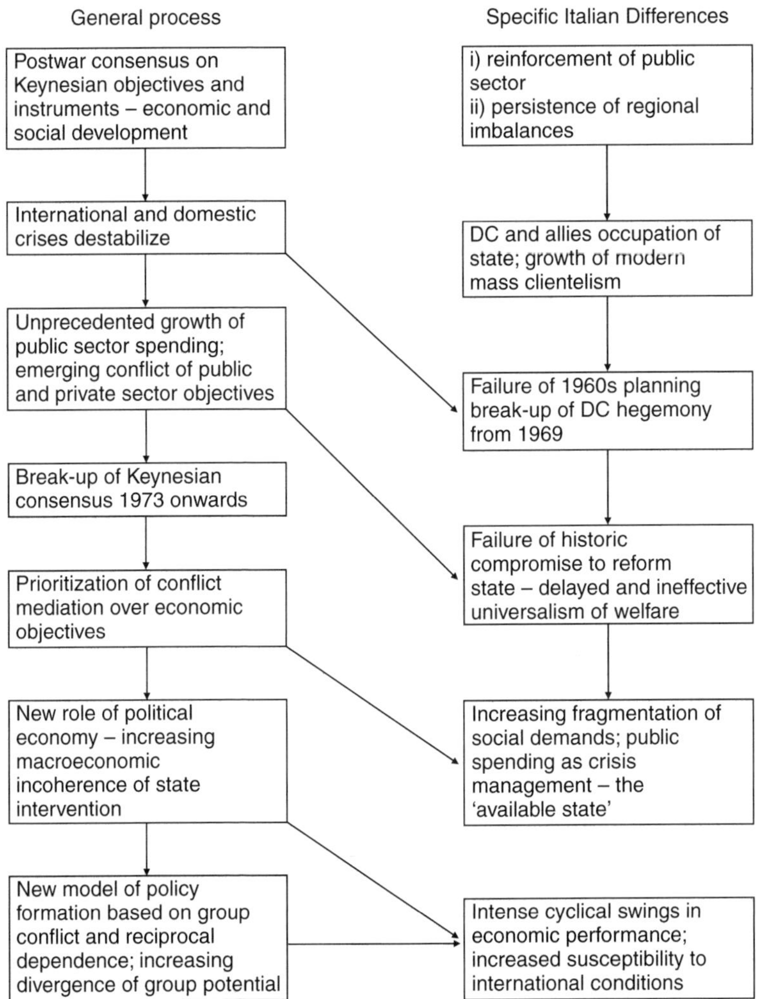

Figure 6.1 The conflict /dependency/exchange model – Italian variant

coalition together. This helps explain why the neo-corporatist restructuring attempted from 1976 to 1979 failed. The attempt to break out from the cycle was led by the state, with austerity programmes and state-directed industrial restructuring backed up by attempts to reform the public administration, and (more successfully) radical changes to the health services and the pensions system.

The anti-inflationary objectives of the period were however impeded by two main factors. The first of these was the usefulness of the *scala mobile* to both sides of industry. For the employers it removed a major workplace irritant from the negotiating agenda, by ensuring that wages were subject to automatic procedures. Inflation allowed them to maintain their profit margins, though at the cost of loss of international competitiveness and increasing exchange-rate instability. For the unions, it was a highly favourable deal that seemed to enhance further

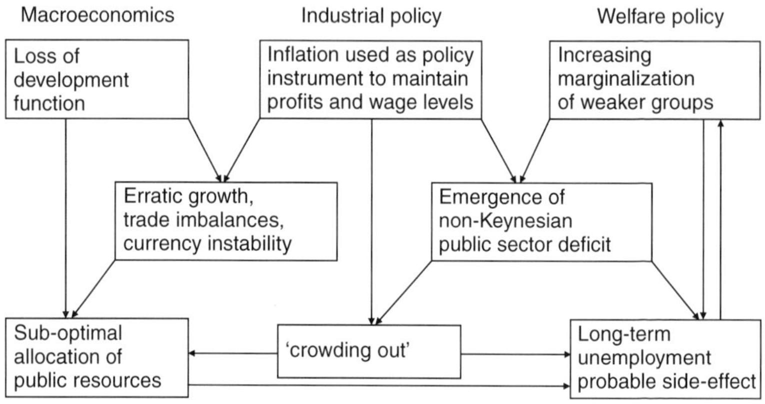

Figure 6.2 Sectoral consequences to 1983/4

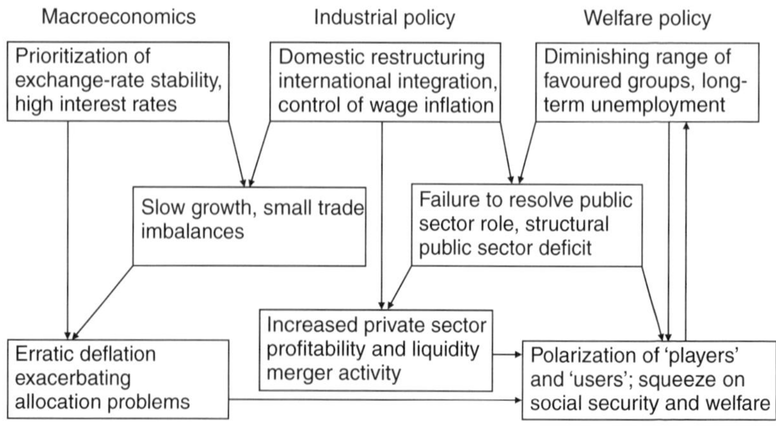

Figure 6.3 Sectoral consequences after 1984

their weight in national policy-making. The second difficulty was the unwillingness of all the governing parties, including those who loudly proclaimed their fiscal virtue, to desist from using the public sector as an employment exchange for patronage purposes. Factors such as the *scala mobile*, the reform of pensions and the use of the Integration Fund (*Cassa Integrazione*) as a form of employment subsidy reinforced the differences between the formal labour market and the increasingly widespread informal black and grey markets. Thus the emerging integration of employers and unions into government-led structures for national economic direction was stifled by the fragmentation of the labour and patronage markets, and by political differences over the scope and purpose of state intervention.

The advent of the Craxi government in 1983 was followed by an unprecedented shift in political strategy on the part of the governing parties. Within the constraints fixed mainly by the need to maintain the employment functions of public sector ownership, the new government found itself the point of convergence of several trends. One was the extraordinary increase in the size of the public sector deficit. The second was the renewed confidence of Italy's private sector entrepreneurs, who had been able to shake out labour in the formal industrial sector during the recession of the early 1980s. There was also the confidence that the apparent decay and defeat of the Red Brigade terrorists would bring an end to the sporadic violence and sabotage which had been affecting many larger enterprises during the late 1970s at the height of the terrorist violence. To this was added the prospect for the Socialist Party, of which Craxi was leader, of profiting from the loss of votes of the Communists and Christian Democrats at the 1983 elections. A further stimulus to change was the increasing impact of the exchange rate mechanism of the European monetary system, appearing to enforce monetary prudence and certainly preventing any easy recourse to the weapon of devaluation to maintain competitiveness. Perhaps surprisingly, granted Craxi's political origins, the shift after 1983 was away from state-led solutions towards restructuring led by the market – but always within the limits set by the political processes on which the governing parties relied. Craxi's major successes in this context were the renegotiation and reduction of the *scala mobile* in 1983 and 1984. Also, the tax reforms of 1983, and the reform of the Milan stock market in 1984, which resulted in a considerable increase in the inflow of funds and the value of assets quoted. There was also a partial restructuring of the state participation system that resulted in a return to profitability. The pressures for reform were added to by the prospect of the Single European

Market, enforcing further international integration on Italy's private and public sector traders.

But in other sectors Craxi's government was less successful. The emergence of persistently high levels of long-term unemployment, particularly among younger entrants to the labour market, contributed to an increasingly sharp difference in pay and prospects between those who are part of the formal employment system and those who have to survive at its margins. Also, the public sector deficit remained extremely difficult to control. Public spending was difficult to control in any case because of the impact of inflation and the interest-rate implications of the ERM. Its use as the currency of political compromise to mediate the increasing numbers of political claims added to the constraints on government and reduced their control over the key levers and over policy in general.

This showed itself in three specific ways. First, rapid technological progress and unprecedented social mobility took their toll on the previously compact mass organizations that articulated diverse interests in relatively consistent forms. In their different ways, both the DC and the PCI felt the force of these social changes that fragmented and undermined their social support. In retrospect, the historic compromise period when they were in coalition represents a late and unexploited opportunity for the two mass political parties to reform the state into a modern instrument of political organization. Instead the colonization of the state by the governing parties in the 1980s further undermined the state's effectiveness and eventually destroyed the old party system in the 1990s.

Second, it is not just the state that was at the mercy of a multitude of sectoral interests. Employers, trade union confederations and the major pillars of civil society that provided their power of social mobilization had increasing difficulty in guaranteeing any but the most short-term of political bargains, whether over government coalition strategy or over substantial policy reform. In the 1980s, none of the major interest groups or their political agents were representative enough to make the political exchanges work beyond the immediate political horizon. It was in the face of this increasing crisis of representation that the 'new social movements' of the 1970s fragmented into a variety of competing special interests. In the process, established political parties came under challenge from environmental, civil liberties, and regional organized groups who were able to mount significant electoral challenges that bore fruit in the 1990s.[11]

Third, the gradual loss of control by the established groups shows itself in the effective relinquishing of state authority to the more compact and powerful of the economic interests, particularly the big multinational conglomerates – a re-emergence of the tradition of 'sub-government'. In mediating the competing demands of the FIAT group and other conglomerates including Berlusconi, the Italian state had to deal with successful modern commercial enterprises whose cultural and administrative resources were much superior in quality to its own.[12] The loss of control also shows itself in the way in which organized illegality was confronted. In the 1970s the state had to face widespread political terrorism, which it eventually defeated by giving controversial and unprecedented powers to a special police organization. In rather different ways, the struggle against the Sicilian mafia and the Neapolitan camorra demonstrated the same constraints and the same strategy of circumventing the rigours of the law through special mandate.[13]

The central organization of the state was increasingly in conflict with the professional and client groups involved in its major welfare and service functions, but it lacked the organizational, revenue or moral autonomy to ensure its predominance. It was not only that the fragmented interest groups were in conflict with one another and dependent on the state; the state itself was internally divided, and was dependent on particular groups within and outside its own structures. Some of these divisions were ideologically based, and related to the long-standing disagreements within political élites dealt with earlier. But other divisions result from the peculiar position of the public administration and enlarged public sector, which made them both deliverer and recipient of resources. When the state was itself a client, engaged in the market for employment and corporate privileges, reform of the structures achieved an intimidating complexity. The more responsive political leaders realized the need for reform, but they had to bargain with the managers, administrators and clerical staff of the state sector. They had to exchange limitations on reform in return for cooperation in reducing demand, collaboration in managing supply of services more rationally, partial reductions in employee privileges, and in some cases in return simply for better information and more adequate reporting of results.[14] Increasingly the state directed its resources in favour of the strongest sectoral and regional groups, that is, those groups who had most to exchange in the new market of public policy.

This process was challenged however by the threat of international competition and integration. It also had to contend with the fractious and newly confident interests of large private sector capital, and by the divisions between what Maurizio Ferrera referred to as the 'welfare' and 'producer' constituency – between those who were net recipients of social security and welfare, and those who were net contributors.[15] Thus in managing the inherent tensions between anti-inflation and anti-unemployment policy, the state's scope for choice was ever more restricted by the incoherence and irrationality of its own intervention. Just as the postwar settlement was the product of complex interaction between international and domestic processes, so also was the break-up after 1989. Looking back to the post-1945 settlement, it is possible to argue that had it not been for international pressures, the stabilization would not have been so inflexible, and may have been able to adapt more readily and more rationally. But such a line of argument would also have to acknowledge that without the international pressures, the stabilization might have been radically different in character and might not have shown the same capacity for long-term survival.[16]

Notes

1. R. Zariski, *Italy, the Politics of Uneven Development.* (Hinsdale, IL: Dryden Press, 1972); G. Sartori, *Teoria dei partiti e casi italiano.* (Milano: Sugarco, 1982)
2. M. Dal Co and P. Perulli, 'The Trilateral Agreement of 1983: Social Pact or Political Truce?', in O. Jacobi *et al.* (eds), *Economic Crisis, Trade Unions and the State.* (London: Croom Helm, 1986), pp. 157–70; M. Regini, 'Social Pacts in Italy', in I. Scholten (ed.), *Political Stability and Neo-corporatism* (London: Sage, 1987); M. Regini, 'The Crisis of Representation in Class-oriented Unions', in S. Clegg *et al.* (eds), *The State, Class and the Recession.* (London: Croom Helm, 1983).
3. A. Lijphart, *The Politics of Accommodation.* (Berkeley: University of California Press, 1975, 2nd edn)
4. See for example P. Lange and M. Regini, 'Regolazione sociale e politiche pubbliche: schemi analitici per lo studio del caso italiano', *Stato e mercato*, 19 (April 1987) 97–121.
5. Persistent examples of this were the attempts by one of the major governing parties, usually the DC, to enforce the coalition arrangement operative in the national government as a formula for all possible local governments. In this they were generally supported by the minor governing parties, particularly the PSDI (Social Democrats), who tended to lose office locally when heterogeneity of alliances was allowed to flourish.
6. A. J. Heidenheimer, H. Heclo and C. T. Adam, *Comparative Public Policy: the Politics of Social Change in Europe and America.* (Basingstoke: Macmillan now Palgrave, 1983), pp. 122–67.
7. *Ibid.* pp. 125ff.
8. P. Flora and A. J. Heidenheimer (eds), *The Development of Welfare States in Europe and America.* (New Brunswick, NJ: Transaction Books, 1981); also P. Flora (ed.), *Growth to Limits: the Western European Welfare States since World War II*, 5 Vols. (Berlin: W de Gruyter, 1986)
9. S. Tarrow, *Between Center and Periphery: Grassroots Politicians in Italy and France.* (New Haven: Yale University Press, 1977).

10. R. Brunetta, *Spesa Pubblica e Conflitto* (Bologna : Il Mulino, 1987).
11. D. Pinto, *Contemporary Italian Society: A Reader*. (Cambridge: Cambridge University Press, 1981).
12. Little detailed information is available on the workings of the major conglomerates, but a thorough account of the Montedison empire is A. Marchi and E. Marchionetti, *Montedison 1966–1989* (Milano: Franco Angeli, 1992); see also A. Friedman, *Agnelli and the Network of Power*. (London: Harrap, 1988); C. Peruzzi, *Il caso Ferruzzi* (Milano: Edizioni del Sole – 24 Ore, 1987).
13. On the Mafia, see P. Arlacchi, *Mafia Peasants and Great Estates*. (Cambridge: Cambridge University Press, 1983); *Mafia e Potere Politico – relazione di minoranza e proposte unitarie della commissione parlamentare d'inchiesta sulla mafia* (Roma: Editori Riuniti, 1976); J. Chubb, *Patronage, Power and Poverty in Southern Italy: A Tale of Two Cities*. (Cambridge: Cambridge University Press, 1982).
14. An example from the Health Service is described in M. Ferrera, 'Reforming the Reform – the Italian Servizio Sanitario Nazionale in the 1980s', *Centro de Estudios Avanzados en Ciencias Sociales, Instituto Juan March Madrid, Estudios Working Papers* January 1991, no.13.
15. M. Ferrera, *Il Welfare State in Italia: Sviluppo e crisi in prospettiva comparativa* (Bologna: Il Mulino, 1984).
16. A fuller version of this argument may be found in P. Furlong, *Modern Italy – Representation and Reform*. (London: Routledge, 1994).

B. Creating the Consumer Society: 1920s–1950s

7

Visions of Prosperity: Consumerism and Popular Culture in Italy from the 1920s to the 1950s

Stephen Gundle

It is widely recognized that important changes took place in the economy and in society in Italy in the 1950s. The postwar republican constitution was broadly accepted. The country's alignment with the West was settled, and the most pressing problems arising from the impact of war on infrastructures resolved, Italy began the conversion to consumerism that would finally consolidate its institutions and provide a common texture of aspirations and lifestyles to the country as a whole. Italy would continue in some respects to be an abnormal democracy (without alternation of parties in government) and a variety of political and social crises in the 1960s and 1970s would test the capabilities of the country's leaders to the utmost. However, it is broadly accepted that the main steps towards stabilization on the basis of liberal democracy and consumer capitalism occurred in the 1950s. In that decade, television broadcasts started. Mass production began to get underway, domestic electrical appliances came within the reach of the middle classes and within the purview of poorer sectors of the population, and cities, especially in the North, experienced an unprecedented influx of people from the countryside and the South. The great collective passions that had sustained the Resistance and the clashes of the late 1940s began to give way to individual and familial strategies for material betterment.

In most accounts of this process, great importance is given to the United States. America is credited with having secured, by its intervention in the 1948 election, the dominant position of the Christian Democrats (DC) in power. And, largely through the Marshall Plan, with providing Italy (as the rest of Western Europe) with a new development strategy based on a future of mass production and widespread prosperity. The extraordinary proliferation of images of America and ideas of American derivation in Italy in the 1940s and 1950s apparently confirms the view that the United States was not only an ideal society but also a model for the future. To achieve prosperity, it seemed to be suggested, all Italians had to do was to model themselves on Americans, or at least on the images of American life that were fed to them through magazines, advertisements and the movies.[1]

This chapter will seek to offer a somewhat different perspective on the development of Italian consumerism. First, it will suggest that modern forms of consumption took shape in parts of the country from the 1920s. Second, that these drew inspiration not only from America but also from France and Germany. Third, that the national cultures of consumption that took shape in the interwar years carried over with remarkably few alterations into the postwar period. Fourth, that political forces, through the social and cultural networks they sustained, while they opposed some aspects of private consumption, also contributed to the diffusion of consumerist practices and aspirations among the lower classes. As a consequence of this shift of perspective, the development of consumer culture should not be seen purely or even largely the result of Americanization, but rather as the fruit of interaction of a variety of domestic and international motivations.

Many of the issues examined in this chapter may be approached from a variety of disciplinary perspectives: economic history, social history and political science, to name but three. If not all of these are fully developed here, it is not because they are not held to be important. But because it has been decided to focus particularly on cultural and aesthetic aspects of Italy's conversion to consumerism, in the belief that differences between models of consumption may most easily be distinguished in these fields. Following a brief general discussion, sections will be devoted in turn to the role of political and cultural forces, motorized transport, advertising and cinema.

Consumerism and Americanization

In two widely cited and positively received books and a number of articles, Victoria De Grazia has explored the way in which American models of modernity penetrated Fascist Italy and were sometimes used by enlightened Fascists to forge institutions and strategies to reduce conflict and integrate the population.[2] She attributes the formation of the *Dopolavoro* organization in the 1920s to such influences and also relates the development of a commercial peer culture among teenage girls in the 1930s to the presence of American movies. De Grazia's work is important because it presents a quite dynamic, modern picture of life especially in Italian cities in the 1930s, in marked contrast to the vision of pauperism held out for example by Gianfranco Vené.[3] As a historian whose work is largely, if not entirely, confined to the pre-1945 period, she avoids the pitfall of always judging Italian customs and lifestyles of the interwar years against the standards of those of the 1950s. Thus she portrays a burgeoning commercial culture, in which fashion, illustrated magazines and film-going were part of the texture of life. From De Grazia more than any other historian, we have an impression of Italy in the Fascist period as a society in which forms of consumerism were taking shape and occurring.

In one respect at least this picture should not be surprising. Similar trends were happening everywhere in Europe in this period. Moreover, Fascism was primarily concerned, at least as far as the bourgeoisie was concerned, with stabilizing a society ridden with class conflict and irreconcilable differences. To achieve this, it could not only use a stick, even if this was necessary in the early stages and remained a vital tool; it also had to offer a carrot in the form of some material benefits and rewards. In the final pages of his *Recasting Bourgeois Europe*, Charles Maier pointed to the forging in the 1920s of techniques of social integration and control, on the one hand, and the creation of common experiences and communities of consumption, on the other, in a way that prefigured the social armistice of the post-1945 period and paved the way to stabilization.[4]

De Grazia's writings highlight the way in which America pioneered ways of reducing industrial conflict and offered possible solutions to European élites seeking to overcome threats of revolution. She argues that the formation of mass consumer cultures in continental Europe was a direct consequence of the global role that America took on from the 1890s. As the world market expanded massively under American leadership, American civic mores, consumer styles and mass cultural models shaped the institutions and outlooks of other societies that were themselves engaged in the process of becoming modern. America's success, she asserts, was due to its economic and cultural power and also, perhaps more significantly, to its role in pioneering a new type of modernity in which class-based political conflicts ceased to be a serious source of social instability.[5]

There is clearly a good measure of truth in this and the importance of the American model in European modernization in the twentieth century is undeniable. But De Grazia's analysis does present a number of problems.

First, it may be argued that it is methodologically wrong to conceptualize local cultural patterns and political configurations as temporary obstacles to Americanization or as the sources of minor variants on a pattern of development that had been established in the United States by the turn of the century. Second, it is historically erroneous to suggest, in the Italian case, a defective or insufficient model of modernity gradually replaced by a more integrated American one. At no point in the period under discussion was America the only foreign reference point; in the interwar years Germany was influential and so was France in both the interwar and post-1945 periods. Indigenous visions and pressures always played a crucial part in the way Italy became a consumer society. In contrast to the assumption that there was essentially only one route to consumerism, an American one, it can be argued that in fact there were several. Every West European country developed a variant of its own, involving a mixture of American ideas, inputs from other European societies at acomparable or higher level of development, and domestic innovations.[6]

These points are not made simply for the sake of polemic, but rather because it is important to understand the limits as well as the extent of American influence on European development.[7] It is also important, if it is to be appreciated how and why Europeans embraced consumerism after the privations of the war years, to understand that they did not perceive it solely as something new and American, no matter how popular America and American images of prosperity might have been. Rather it was something that had a familiar face and which also grew out of established commercial cultures. Shifting the emphasis to the domestic arena and highlighting the importance of conflict and exchange between different models makes it possible to give proper place to the often contradictory interplay of market and non-market activities and incorporate the clash of different political cultures into the explanation of Italian modernization.

The role of political forces

Consumerism eventually undercut the sources of some of Italy's political divisions; but, over the period under consideration here, it also furnished opportunities to political forces to supply goods and services cheaply or free of charge to less well-off sections of the population. In this way these forces reinforced their support, put down roots in community life and made themselves an integral part of the process of modernization. Typically, political subcultures and the non-market leisure activities they sponsor have been seen as characteristic of an early phase of mass society;[8] the hostility they almost always showed towards individual consumption demonstrated their fundamental backwardness. In fact, it may be argued that the rejection of consumption was only one aspect of political leisure. In Italy, organized, non-market leisure activities did not precede the emergence of consumerism and commercial leisure but developed *in conjunction* with them. Political forces sought to condition and shape the way the population encountered new forms of communication and leisure and in this they succeeded to some extent. Because of their intrinsic value, or because of state support or as a result of continuing political conflict, some subcultural practices actually acquired a long-term foothold in popular culture. In most cases though, they simply served to introduce wider strata to pleasures and practices that would later be enjoyed more freely outside the rather masculine and paternalistic contexts of politicized leisure.

Each of the three politico-cultural forces that structured and organized social life in Italy between the 1920s and the 1960s was distinctive in some respects; but they all shared some common features and the competition between them helped expand the range of their activities. In addition to their specific ideological appeal, each sought to elaborate a vision of the nation that involved necessarily an ongoing engagement with modernity.

The Fascists' attitude towards consumption was contradictory. At one level they adopted a hostile approach. They were intermittently anti-bourgeois, they ran campaigns against luxury and in favour of frugality and they tried to discourage women from taking an interest in fashion and beauty. Passivity and individual self-indulgence were rejected in favour of physical fitness and uniformed collective activities. 'Masculine' values, such as adventure, daring and courage, were preferred to 'feminine' interests in comfort, love and escapist entertainment. However, Fascist policies were not consistent or unidirectional. In some ways they blocked the development of consumerism (most significantly, the involvement of Italy in wars in Ethiopia, Spain and then World War Two retarded economic growth considerably). Elsewhere, they sought to harness or promote it. The activities of the after-work clubs organized by the *Opera Nazionale Dopolavoro* (OND) were important in this sense. These were organized to replace left-wing leisure associations, de-politicize workers and provide them with some reasons to be grateful to the regime. They often possessed radio sets, organized film shows, and made available goods at discount prices.[9] In short, they provided contexts in which lower class people of limited economic means encountered commercial cultural products and developed a taste for them. The Fascists also used the clubs to promote basic tourism (in the form of day trips) and sport. They hoped that these would neutralize any untoward consequences of the former innovations by encouraging patriotic sentiments (love of Italy's past and its natural beauty) and by toughening people up in readiness for war. In fact, as Cross has shown, outings fed desires for holidays, while sport fuelled the consumerist cult of the body and the self.[10]

After 1945, the OND continued to exist under the new acronym ENAL (*Ente Nazionale Assistenza Lavoratori*). But its importance diminished as Catholics and Communists set up a plethora of associations designed to consolidate their support. The Catholics had in fact established networks from the 1880s and, within strict limits, they had been able to extend these under Fascism. But after 1945 these resources took on a more general political significance as lay Catholic activists sought to resist left-wing competition and complement the Church's bid to extend clerical influence. The Communists, for their part, aimed to compensate for their ejection from government in 1947 and the electoral defeat of the left the following year by seeking to extend their influence in society.[11]

Neither the Catholics, despite the dominant position of the Christian Democrats in government, nor the Communists could shape economic policy to the extent that the Fascists did, but they made strenuous efforts to shape society and culture. Both preferred organized to private leisure, although family life found a more explicit recognition in Catholic thinking. They disliked much commercial culture and were suspicious of pleasure. They preferred simplicity to luxury and work to entertainment or comfort. Yet, despite this resistance, and in part because of the rivalry between them, they proved quite adept at harnessing novelty or conditioning the way people encountered cinema, popular publishing, holidays and television. Their impact, it is almost certainly true to say, was much more marked among the lower middle and lower classes in the North and Centre of the country, that is to say, among those living in some proximity to modernity unable to afford the higher entry-level costs of commercial culture. But this does not mean that, once their role in introducing poorer people to the pleasures of film going or the seaside was exhausted, they went into terminal decline. Political divisions and community bonds gave them a lasting resonance.[12]

The rise of popular motoring

Although the very origins of consumption are sometimes assumed to have been American,[13] in fact throughout Europe the period between the 1880s and the 1920s saw the city become a site of bourgeois consumption and display. In response to the crisis of overproduction of the late nineteenth century, a variety of strategies were developed to plan and organize consumption. In Italy, developments in the direction of consumerism occurred late and in a partial way. But by the early years of the century goods were being displayed in Milan and Turin in a manner that approximated to Paris and London. Department stores and galleries had appeared, including Milan's Galleria Vittorio Emanuele, tram systems had opened and electric street lighting had begun. Although the country remained predominantly poor and agricultural, the bourgeoisie filled its homes with Liberty-style furnishings and founded Alpine walking, football and cricket clubs. Consumerism was associated with ease, leisure and wealth. It did not present itself with an accessible face, rather it forged associations with élitism and snobbery. The posters that Marcello Dudovich produced for the La Rinascente stores in the 1910s and 1920s, for example, evoked high society elegance and decorum.[14]

The motor car provides an example of the élitism of early Italian consumerism. Cars were taken by the Futurists as symbols of a brash machine age, and indeed, to the horror of traditionalists, some city walls were pulled down to make way for motorized transport. But cars were in fact made in a fairly traditional way and, far from being functional necessities, they were viewed as playthings of the rich. The car was born out of the craft traditions of coach building made by small manufacturers, mostly concentrated in Milan and Turin. Advertisements did not highlight speed or even movement; rather, they suggested that a motor vehicle could add tone to an upper class lifestyle. Typically, they featured stylish, wealthy ladies and mountain resorts.[15]

With production organized in this way, it is not surprising that even by 1932 there were still only 188,000 cars on the road in Italy, less than a third of the number in France and Britain.[16] Yet in the course of the 1930s ownership was widened to include sectors of the middle class and the idea of ownership as an aspiration just trickled down to the lower middle class. How did this modest but significant transformation occur? Unquestionably, the American model was an influence. Fordism and scientific management appealed both to leftists like Gramsci, who contrasted Americanism with the stagnation and complacency of European capitalism, and to modern-minded industrialists. In 1923 Fiat, one of the foremost Italian companies, adopted some American manufacturing techniques in its new Lingotto plant, and the company's Mirafiori factory, which opened in 1938, included assembly-line production for the first time. The coach builder, Pininfarina, visited the Ford factories in 1921 and some influence of the streamlining pioneered by Chrysler could be seen in a number of Lancia and Fiat vehicles by the 1930s. The Fiat 1500 (Aprilia) saloon of 1935 is a particular example of a car with an American look.[17]

Yet it would be quite wrong to imagine that Fordism found a pure application in Italy. What occurred was a certain modernization of coach building and car manufacture with reference to the United States, not the replacement of an Italian model by an American model. As Penny Sparke observes, 'The collaboration between the body-makers and the car manufacturers remained a constant through this period and beyond, showing how the acceptance of modernity was, in Italy, tempered at all times by the retention of craft skills and the aesthetic values represented by them.'[18]

The real fruit of the shift to larger scale production in this period occurred with the Fiat 500 'Topolino'. Over 100,000 of these were sold before the war, many of which were exported. Was this, at least, a result of the application of a Fordist philosophy? It has sometimes been claimed that this was so, but in fact the car was put into production largely as a result of the policy pressures of the Fascist regime. Fascism sought to undermine the image of motoring as a status symbol and instead to harness cars and all other machines to its project for imperial expansion. As a consequence of this pursuit of a 'metallic modernity', Fiat saloons were turned into political symbols and given names like Ardita and Balilla.[19] Patterns of production were also directly and indirectly affected.

The Fascists adopted a number of unrelated policies that created a favourable climate for the production of a cheaper car that some middle class people could afford. The regime invested heavily in roads, albeit for public needs including the movement of troops. It also poured money into Fiat by commissioning lorries and aeroplanes. The latter pushed the company towards volume production and assisted technical development. In addition, the regime introduced a sharply progressive vehicle tax in the 1930s, which produced a certain move away from larger, more expensive cars. Moreover, by virtue of its rivalry with Nazi Germany, the regime exhorted Italian companies to match the example of the Volkswagen 'Beetle' when the latter was personally launched by Hitler. Finally, companies like Fiat were put under pressure to produce cheaper cars in the later 1930s, to show that retail prices were not increasing. In fact Fiat had hoped that rising living standards would carry more people towards its 995cc Balilla model (which, at Lit.110,000, was twice what the Topolino would cost). The failure of this to happen resulted in commercial as well as political pressure to go in the opposite direction and cut costs and reduce dimensions.

No substantial democratization of car ownership occurred in the 1930s. Even the Topolino sold at a cost roughly equivalent to the annual salary of a white-collar worker. Thus, it was driven mainly by smart ladies, doctors and the sons of well-off parents.[20] But the advent of the Topolino did take the *idea* of the family car to the middle classes. As a nearly economical vehicle that renounced all connections with luxury cars, it turned private ownership into a tangible aspiration. As people began to travel, taking day trips to the mountains or the seaside, courtesy of the regime's popular train excursions, the appeal of a potentially privatized leisure took shape.

There were two other ways in which Fascist policies helped spread the cult of the car and contributed to what might, with the benefit of hindsight, be termed a proto-culture of mass mobility. First, it provided much support for motor racing. In the 1930s the Mille Miglia became a national passion to an extent that would not be equalled after the war, and the duels between Tazio Nuvolari and Achille Varzi, and between both and the German drivers of the time, were widely followed.[21] Mussolini took a personal interest in motor racing and Nuvolari, on account of his dashing style and disregard for personal safety, was held up as a Fascist symbol.[22] Second, a significant boost was given to motorcycle production. Advertisements for Moto Guzzi bikes appeared in Fascist party periodicals and the regime deemed that this form of transport was the most appropriate for local Fascist officials.[23] Pictures of the *Duce* on motorcycles (although his real preference was for Alfa Romeo cars), in addition to the abolition of all taxes on them in 1933, helped spread their popularity among better-off workers, factory foremen and artisans.

Motoring actually declined after the war. There were in fact some 20,000 fewer cars on the road in the early 1950s than in the late 1930s.[24] Given the economic situation, car ownership was no longer a tangible aspiration for many and manufacturers simply sought to keep production going. The Topolino remained the most popular vehicle in circulation. In consequence, little occurred beyond depoliticization of existing models. Quintavalle notes that advertising images, sometimes provided by artists of the stature of De Chirico and Sironi (who, however, offered rather ordinary, literal representations of Fiat models), went in two directions. In place of the bourgeois luxury of the 1920s, the idea of the family car took shape. The Fascist emphasis on speed, on the other hand, was replaced by a youthful, sporty attitude.[25] Only the appearance of the Fiat 600 in 1953 and, most significantly, the launch of the Fiat 500 in 1957, a full 12 years after the war, brought the car once more within the reach of the lower middle classes. The Fiat 500 was the first genuinely mass-produced car in Italy; it was not merely a reduced version of a larger model (as the 600 was), it was an original product conceived specifically for a new market and for new times. With its rounded, appealing shape and youthful look, it encapsulated a lifestyle that reflected a new mental outlook based on privatized mobility.[26]

There can be little doubt that Fiat's decision to invest in the production of these models was influenced by American ideas about productivity and growth. But it was also, indeed primarily, a decision influenced by the company's experience in the 1930s and its assessment of likely increased market potential in the 1950s and 1960s. Although, like most companies, Fiat sought to rebuild mainly on the basis of traditional structures and markets, it did not reject innovation. The company's managing director, Vittorio Valletta saw that, while the country was still poor, there were domestic pressures to pursue wider consumption which arose from the democratic climate of the postwar years and the stimulus of the entry of the masses on to the national stage. Broadly speaking, Fiat's strategy grew out a combination of these impulses.

The appearance of the 500 betrayed something of its heterodox origins. Although it was minuscule, and therefore wholly different to the outsize vehicles Italians were used to seeing in Hollywood films, it incorporated something of the streamlining of the American cars of the 1930s and employed chrome decoration as a sort of citation of this influence. Yet, like the best Italian design objects of the postwar years, it was elegant and functional. For the simplicity of its line, it drew on the German avant-garde.[27]

To understand the 500 fully, it is important to underline its connections with the one true innovation in private transport of the postwar years: the scooter. Although the car would eventually displace all other vehicles as the most desired object by Italians, the most genuine symbol both of Italy's recovery and of the changes in social relations of the 1950s was the Vespa. Invented in 1946 by Corrado D'Ascanio for Piaggio, it was one of a handful of objects which 'came to symbolise the new Italian democracy and to represent the essence of *ricostruzione*'.[28] The Vespa, like its rival, the Lambretta, promoted as a 'motorscooter for all' by Innocenti, was practical, youthful, stylish and cheap. In contrast to the darkly aggressive Fascist symbolism of the motorcycle, the scooter was clean, cheerful and, in marketing image, feminine.[29] It was cheaper and more accessible in the postwar years than any car. It was also uniquely Italian and as such it appeared in numerous films – from the 1951 romantic comedy *Roman Holiday*, starring Audrey Hepburn and Gregory Peck, to Nanni Moretti's 1995 film *Caro diario*.

Advertising: art or science?

Because of trade and international exhibitions, advertising was one of the fields in which ideas and techniques travelled most freely and frequently across frontiers. As Italy was a late developer industrially and its internal market was small, Italian poster artists often worked abroad and drew on foreign innovations. In the 1920s, advertising was not particularly developed, but several studios existed. Among these was the agency of poster impressario Giuseppe Magagnoli (Maga) whose philosophy was summed up in the title of his house organ *Il Pugno nell'occhio* (The Punch in the Eye). Advertisements used art to attract attention or evoke atmospheres that would have been recognizable as desirable to the relatively small numbers of fashionable consumers who frequented the boulevards and arcades of the centres of large cities.[30]

According to De Grazia, this Italian and European custom of artistic advertising went into crisis after World War One and was finished off by competition from American merchandising techniques and advertising strategies.[31] She suggests that this occurred as a result of the politicization of the poster in World War One and after. Doubts about the effectiveness of artistic motifs and styles, competition from other means of communication and a quickening-up of the pace of life, and the arrival on the market of new appliances which required more specific illustration and explanation also assisted in the decline. American-style advertisements prospered and triumphed, she argues, because they were meticulously designed and contained carefully argued explanatory texts. They were simple and uncluttered and usually relied on photographs to illustrate the product. They did not seek to evoke a 'tone' but rather to enter into a dialogue with the consumer and show the utility of an object. Thus they were better suited to an age in which consumerism was beginning to spread to wider social strata.

Is this account accurate? Certainly, there is evidence to support it. The American model made its appearance in the 1920s and this coincided with a widely recognized crisis of a certain type of poster art that had been intimately linked to Liberty style and the Belle Epoque. Magagnoli fought a rearguard battle in defence of artistic verve and against American scientific and academic notions of advertising up until the bankruptcy of his agency in 1932 and his death the following year.

But it would be mistaken to interpret the downfall of a certain set of practices and the appearance of American alternatives as a sign that Americanism was definitively displacing European and Italian models. In fact Italian practices relying on wit, artistry and idiosyncrasy proved to be very resilient and continued to prosper well after 1945, becoming a feature of the *Carosello* television advertisements from 1957.

As in the field of motor production, American innovations aroused interest and some emulation, but these tended to be of rather limited import and were not dominant. Ceserani argues that there was an ongoing conflict in Italian advertising between a rational, or practical, spirit on the one hand and an artistic, or creative, spirit on the other. The latter, not the former was dominant.[32] Its chief representatives were Dudovich, Boccasile and Sepo, poster artists of great creativity and flair who looked not to New York but to Paris. These artists *adapted* their work following the end of the Belle Epoque to suit the new climate of the 1920s and 1930s, and they did so again in the 1940s and 1950s. Their activity over a remarkably long period provided an important measure of aesthetic continuity in Italian advertising which meant that new products could at each juncture be presented in ways and with imagery that consumers found familiar and reassuring.

The 1930s were not a particularly propitious time for commercial advertising. The sector was drawn fully into the system of corporations, but in such a way that the various sub-professions (artists, producers of materials, copy-writers etc.) found themselves in separate associations. Moreover, in the phase of autarky, advertising's foreign connections were subject to rigorous control. In addition, there were restrictions on the type of images that could be used, with the regime preferring masculine associations to feminine ones.[33] Nevertheless, the development of radio, the press and cinema created new national communications networks and large scale collective campaigns were launched in favour of national products such as the wool substitute Lanital, beer and sugar.

A lot of commercial advertising was rather primitive and designed simply to astound or shock (although proposals to use illuminated signs in Venice and on the Asinelli Tower in Bologna were vetoed). Some, however, was of a higher standard. The magazine *L'Ufficio Moderno* kept alive some sort of debate about salesmanship and advertising, and an important role was played by Dino Villani, a prominent organizer of the advertising profession up until his death at age 90 in 1991. Villani was very much in the camp of imagination and creativity. In his books, he articulated a vision of advertising as gentle, cultural and explicitly different from the American way.[34] He took the view that conditions in Italy were simply too different for American techniques to work.

One of his most celebrated campaigns was for the Motta company's *panettone* Christmas cake, which began in the 1930s and continued after the war. In order to try and broaden the market for this mainly Milanese product, which in the 1920s was sold only by the Motta shop in Piazza Duomo, he sought to associate it with things that were already popular and had a national resonance. These included religious festivals, sport, and writers. *Panettoni* were given out as prizes at Christmas time to ordinary people who had performed good deeds, giant *panettoni* were presented to the winner of each lap of the Giro d'Italia cycle race, and endorsements were secured from D'Annunzio, Pirandello and others.

A second example of Villani's creativity was the campaign he organized for GVM toothpaste in conjunction with the illustrated weekly *Tempo*. In 1938 a competition was launched offering 'Lit.5,000 for a smile'. Open to everyone without distinction of age or sex, the competition invited members of the public to submit photographs of them in cheerful mode. A promotional popular song, a radio tie-in and open-air heats of the competition in holiday resorts amplified its resonance. The impact was considerable and after the war the competition evolved into the annual Miss Italy pageant. In time the toothpaste connection was dropped and a range of other products became associated with the promotion. This might be seen as an adaptation of an American technique of using euphoric attitudes and beauty contests to promote consumer goods. But in fact the contest grew out of Italian traditions; domestic criteria of beauty, privileging the closed-mouth smile and the face and personality over the figure, persisted well into the 1950s and arguably down to the present.[35]

In neither of these campaigns did Villani use science and instead employed improvisation and inventiveness. These methods were appropriate to a culture that was sceptical of commerce and in which consumer aspirations were developing rather than established. But their success and adaptability as well as the identification they provoked meant that they definitively shaped Italian advertising culture.

After 1945, in this sphere as in others, reconstruction occurred along established lines; there was no immediate 'Americanization' following the liberation. American models and ideas certainly exerted an influence, as they had done previously, but so did domestic, established ones and a wider range of foreign ones. Indeed, looking at the trade magazine *La Pubblicità*, it is apparent that Paris continued to be more frequently regarded as an example and a source of new techniques and ideas than

Madison Avenue. As far as advertising models are concerned, it was old models, with some renewal and openness to the new climate that prevailed. Statistics, psychology and market research remained virtually unknown.[36] Graphic art retained its central place and was used in advertisements for almost all products. Boccasile is an example of a well-known artist who provided a measure of aesthetic continuity in the transition from Fascism to the Republic. Creator in the 1930s of the saucy pin-up cover girl of the magazine *Le grandi firme*, he took an active propaganda role in the Republic of Salò. Like other artists who aligned themselves with Fascism even during the final years of the war, he avoided proscription and contributed to public advertising for the reconstruction. In his commercial work, he played a part in the return of the images of good-natured, easy-going, ruddy-faced old men that had been rigorously banned in the 1930s. He drew babies – another common theme of the postwar years – for Yomo yoghurt and Chlorodont toothpaste, and also images of shapely, slightly provocative young women that recalled his work of the 1930s. The most famous of these was his seductive 1947 illustration of an idealized semi-nude woman raising a basket of flowers over her head for Paglieri perfumes and face powder.

American advertising agencies began to arrive in Italy in the late 1940s in the wake of international companies like Phillips and Unilever, which preferred American techniques to what was on offer in Italy. Lintas, and Young and Rubicam opened Italian branches in 1948, J. Walter Thompson in 1951. Valeri writes that 'foreign inspired agencies preferred a more rational approach and a division of tasks, as well as serious treatment of themes on the basis of studies and research on consumer trends, and closer collaboration between strategists, copywriters and artists.'[37] Among Italian companies, Olivetti and Barilla were the first to use American style advertising. However, the conflict between the practical spirit and the creative spirit in advertising persisted. For some time, Valeri notes, Italian creativity and American capitalist realism existed side by side: 'two quite different methods, not yet a synthesis or a collaboration'. Only in the late 1950s, with the development of a wider consumer market among the middle classes, did local cultures and structures begin to give way to American ones. But, even then, the American triumph was mitigated and contested. For example, Armando Testa, a leading advertiser whose career began in the 1930s, in an article in *Notiziario Sipra*, protested publicly about the subordination of the advertiser as artist to the market.[38] His own agency (the most prominent Italian one) regularly produced 'arty' advertisements which employed

Dadaist references, most obviously reflected in animal imagery including the elephant allusion famously used in 1954 to promote Pirelli tyres.[39]

In the postwar years there was much more Catholic interest in advertising than there had been previously and representatives of the Church attended all the congresses of the advertising profession in Italy.[40] Catholics performed a double-edged mediating role that helped construct a bridge between tradition and modernity. On the one hand, the Catholic University of Milan, the first to establish courses in marketing, advertising and communications, acted as a channel of American influences. On the other, by its involvement, the Church aimed to control the impact of the market and protect moral values. Moreover, while the Communists produced their propaganda material in-house until the 1980s, the Christian Democrats used professional advertisers in all their campaigns from 1948.

Cinema and the development of consumerism

In the 1930s cinema was the most popular pastime in Italian cities, especially in the North and Centre. After 1945 many new cinemas were built in the South and in the provinces, turning film going into a routine practice for the lower classes.[41] Film undoubtedly contributed to the creation of a climate that was favourable to the promotion of and aspiration for material goods. It contributed to the privatization of leisure and to the spread of the idea that free time was properly spent consuming leisure goods and services. In this sense it may be said to have been an integral part of the development of a culture of consumerism. The vast majority of films exhibited in Italy between the 1920s and the late 1950s were American (with the exception of the years between 1938 and 1945) but does not mean that cinema was tied into networks of consumption in the same way that it was in the United States.

Italian cinemas in city centres were sometimes, although by no means always, purpose built. Their names – Lux, Eden, Excelsior, Smeraldo, Moderno and so on – suggested luxury and modernity. Moreover many films, including the Italian 'white telephone' films of the 1930s, offered images of up-scale lifestyles involving grand hotels, cruise-liners, beautiful people and carefree leisure. Both Gian Piero Brunetta and James Hay have argued that the opulence displayed on screen and fleetingly experienced in cinema auditoria directly contradicted the ambitions of the Fascists. Their campaigns for imperial expansion and custom reform were counter-balanced by the effects of films insofar as they pushed individual aspirations away from collective political goals and in the direction of full-fledged prosperity.[42]

This assertion is very difficult, if not impossible, to test; the evidence employed by Brunetta and Hay is drawn mainly from representations of lower middle class responses to wealth in comedy films such as *Giorno di nozze* (Wedding Day) and *Il Signor Max*. What must be underlined though is that the sort of connections which in America meant that movie-goers could buy into the images of luxury on the screen by purchasing products which were promoted in conjunction with films or by well-known stars was impossible in Italy. In the United States the histories of cinema and of consumerism were intertwined; the development of the exhibition sector and indeed of the film industry as a whole was part of the chain store revolution.[43] But in Italy, movie theatres were not modelled on department stores, which scarcely existed, and nor were films seen as having consequences for the retail industry. Rather, cinemas were modelled on theatres and the only product was the film itself.

For this reason American attempts to import promotional techniques tried and tested in the USA encountered little success. All the majors and some of the minor American companies had agencies in Italy that produced bulletins and press books suggesting strategies for publicizing first run films. For example, in 1936 the Twentieth Century Fox bulletin suggested that for the launch of *Music in the Air*, an operetta set in Bavaria, cinema foyers should be decorated in the style of a mountain village.[44] Although few of these bulletins have survived, it is striking in those which may be consulted how commercial tie-ups of any sort are virtually absent. In a rare example of a tie-up involving a department store, the Milan-based La Rinascente launched a line of little girls' clothes and dolls in 1936 to coincide with the release of a Shirley Temple film. Loudspeakers in the store broadcast the voice and songs of Shirley, posters and photographs were distributed, announcements were placed in newspapers and on the radio. In addition four publicity vans carried news of the event out into the provinces.[45]

Since the major studios were just developing systematic commercial tie-ins in the United States at this time, it was probably decided to try out such techniques in all major foreign markets.[46] But in Italy the experiment does not appear to have been repeated. At no time either before or after the war did film promotion become associated with general advertising or consumer practice. Not only were the necessary infrastructures and support systems insufficiently developed. But the climate was not favourable to such explicit commercialization of what were at least in part perceived as artistic products.

In order to promote their films successfully, American companies were obliged to rely on posters. Pasted on billboards, street corners and cinema fronts, posters played a vital role in communicating the themes and attractions of a film to its potential audience. In the Italian case at least, they were not imported ready printed from the US, as De Grazia states;[47] rather they were prepared on the spot by local artists who, the companies recognized, were better able to connect a film with the cultural codes of the audience. Often the artists used distinctive and personal styles that became easily identifiable.[48]

All of this does not mean that cinema was separate from consumerism. Films were of course commodities and cinema-going involved consumption in the form of purchase of a ticket. But it does mean that film going often did not lead directly into other consumerist practices, or that it did so in specific and original ways. Over the period from the 1930s to the 1950s, for example, films and film stars influenced models of appearance and beauty and contributed to greater attention to and care of self, practices which are commonly seen as precursors of a fully developed consumer culture.[49] This aspect was quite explicit as films often featured beauty parlours, perfume stores, hairdressers' salons. Beauty products were very occasionally advertised using the images of actresses like Alida Valli, or at any rate in a way that traded on the atmosphere of film. In the magazines for young women published by Rizzoli and other companies, Hollywood was the great beauty ideal. Stars were associated in the public mind with wealth, leisure, youth, beauty, travel, health and excitement.[50] To imitate stars was to position oneself in such a way as to be psychologically open to the dreams and possibilities of consumption. Cosmetics and cinema-related ideals of beauty began to spread to all urban classes at this time, albeit not without some resistance from the Church and from Fascists.

After the war, Hollywood cinema returned massively to Italian screens. In the new context, the beauty and luxury mythology of American films exercised a more far-reaching influence on Italian customs and mores than ever before. Beauty contests, dancing, mass interest in the seaside, and the idea of social mobility all prospered and fuelled the success of illustrated magazines like *Grand Hotel*, which adapted Hollywood ideology to Italian conditions for young women. The body ceased to be the bearer of a political project and instead became more completely a source of individual self-fashioning projected towards consumerism and well-being.

Italian cinema was no less important in changing mentalities and customs. Although the downbeat postwar cinema might be thought to be the very antithesis of consumerism, in fact the emphasis on war and social conflict of the first wave of neorealist films soon gave way to an emphasis on youth and beauty. In many popular films of the 1950s the young protagonists are poor; however, they are also beautiful and their beauty reflects their desire to escape from their poverty. In most films resignation is absent and poverty is perceived as a temporary rather than a permanent condition.[51] Yet this does not mean that the productivist, self-help ideology of the Marshall Plan was absorbed. Workers are often depicted, for example in *Vita da cani* (Dog's life), voicing desires for better clothes, a better life and so on. They are shown entertaining large-scale aspirations of the type US cinema catered for, but also smaller hopes for improvement. Cars, domestic appliances, fur coats, scooters all appear as desirable items.[52] But what is usually the means whereby achievement of the goal is conceptualized? Certainly not only productive labour and hard work, as Pullano suggests,[53] but perhaps more frequently through debt, black market trafficking, a big win in the lottery or the arrival of a windfall courtesy of some long lost American uncle. If, as has often been remarked, the proletariat is rarely present in Italian films of this period, the same cannot be said of the lumpenproletariat, its values and world-view. Prostitutes, thieves, tricksters, counterfeiters and black marketeers are rife. Dishonesty, that 'queer ladder of social mobility', appears as more readily attractive and sometimes reachable than more conventional routes.

The way film affected social trends and aspirations was also influenced by the two subcultures. In the interwar years, the Fascists influenced both the production and consumption of film. Although neither the Catholics nor the Communists financially supported more than a token number of films, they were able to some extent to influence the way they were watched and received. Both set up their own distribution circuits and covered cinema in all its facets in their many publications. By the mid-1950s, around one-third of the cinemas in the country were parish cinemas.[54] As Giuseppe Tornatore's Oscar-winning film *Cinema Paradiso* shows, parish cinemas, especially in the provinces, played a vital part in community life through the 1950s and beyond.

Conclusion

The development of consumerism was an important factor in the stabilization of Italian society. Although there were very significant moments of political conflict in the decade following World War Two, and again in the late 1960s and 1970s, the seeds were set in the 1920s of forms of privatized consumerism that would form the basis of the social and cultural integration of the 1950s. This provided Italy with a degree of shared culture and goals that it did not previously have. It has been shown here that the form modernization took in Italy was always influenced by American models, but that these were merely a factor in a process involving domestic actors and other foreign reference points. Americanism may have been exported with enthusiasm and verve, but Americanization did not involve the wholesale adoption of American techniques. America provided an imagery of modernity, important symbolic and material goods and a widc array of techniques. But Italians selected from these and rejected much. Essentially, the country found its own way to consumerized modernity. Only at the end of the 1950s did the internal equilibrium between tradition and modernity suddenly begin to unravel as modern, urban values and goals took over.

Particular attention has been paid here to the social and cultural role of political and religious forces. Far from being purely sources of tension, the conflict and rivalry between the Fascists, the Catholics and the Communists actually led to these forces seeking to stabilize their support in society. As part of this process, they set up institutions that shaped early patterns of consumption. Ultimately, mass consumption took over and the political factors that had inadvertently contributed to the process of extending consumption receded in influence and importance. But this does not mean that their role should be overlooked. Italians encountered consumerism in ways that reflected their own aesthetic preferences and values, the level of development of their own industries and the political history of their country. Moreover, both Catholics and Communists aimed to renew their associational networks to combat decline. In 1957 a new left-wing recreational association, ARCI, was founded which sought to supply the network of *Case del Popolo* with better quality and more demanding culture that would appeal to relatively sophisticated palates. It was still flourishing four decades later. The Catholic workers' association, ACLI, underwent a similar renewal and Catholic leisure became more decentralized. According to Diamanti and Pace, Catholic voluntary activities and sport continued to be the most significant provider of youth leisure in the Veneto even after the Church itself lost its central role in the everyday life of the community.[55] Organized leisure did not merely help make consumerism a mass rather than an élitist phenomenon. It remained an integral part of Italian modernity.

Notes

1. This aspect of American influence in postwar Europe is dicussed in D. W. Ellwood, *Rebuilding Europe: Western Europe, America and Postwar Reconstruction.* (London: Longman, 1992) Chapter 12.
2. See V. De Grazia, *The Culture of Consent: Mass Organization of Leisure in Fascist Italy.* (Cambridge: Cambridge University Press 1981); *How Fascism Ruled Women: Italy 1922–45.* (Berkeley: University of California Press, 1992); 'The Arts of Purchase: How American Publicity Subverted the European Poster, 1920–1940', in B. Kruger and P. Mariani (eds), *Remaking History.* (Seattle: Bay Press, 1989); 'Mass Culture and Sovereignty: The American Challenge to European Cinemas, 1920–60', *Journal of Modern History,* 61 (1989) 53–87; 'Nationalizing Women: The Competition Between Fascist and Commercial Models in Mussolini's Italy', in V. De Grazia and E. Furlough (eds), *The Sex of Things: Gender and Consumption in Historical Perspective.* (Berkeley: University of California Press, 1996). These works also treat broader issues relating to the export of Americanism to Europe.
3. G. Vené, *Mille lire al mese: vita quotidiana della familglia nell'Italia fascista.* (Milan: Mondadori, 1988).
4. C. S. Maier, *Recasting Bourgeois Europe: Stabilization and Change in France, Germany and Italy in the Decade After World War I.* (Princeton: Princeton University Press 1975), pp. 579–87.
5. De Grazia, 'Mass Culture and Sovereignty', pp. 54–6.
6. This assumption is also shared by Gary Cross. See *Time and Money: The Making of Consumer Culture.* (London: Routledge, 1993). For a contrary view, see Ellwood, *Rebuilding Europe,* p. 236.
7. For an attempt to develop an alternative model of Americanization to the 'informal empire' approach developed by De Grazia, see S. Gundle, 'L'americanizzazione del quotidiano: televisione e consumismo nell'Italia degli anni Cinquanta', *Quaderni storici,* XXI, 2 (1986) 561–94, reproduced in English as 'The Americanization of Daily Life: Television and Consumerism in Italy in the 1950s', *Italian History and Culture,* II (1996) 11–39.
8. See, for example, E. Mandel, *Late Capitalism.* (London: Verso, 1978) p. 393.
9. See De Grazia, *The Culture of Consent,* pp. 127–86.
10. Cross, *Time and Money,* pp. 99–127.
11. On the construction and development of the Communist subculture, see S. Gundle, *I comunisti italiani tra Hollywood e Mosca: la sfida della cultura di massa 1943–91.* (Florence: Giunti 1995). For reflections on continuities in political socialization and consensus formation between Fascism and the Republic, see S. Lanaro, *Storia dell'Italia repubblicana.* (Venice: Marsilio, 1992) pp. 47–8 and C. Levy, 'From Fascism to "Post-Fascists": Italian Roads to Modernity', in R. Bessel (ed.), *Fascist Italy and Nazi Germany. Comparisons and Contrasts.* (Cambridge: Cambridge University Press, 1996) pp. 179–82.
12. For a discussion of the persistence of political subcultures in Italy, and of their influence on voting behaviour even in the 1980s, see R. Mannheimer and G. Sani, 'Electoral Trends and Political Subcultures', in R. Leonardi and R. Y. Nanetti (eds), *Italian Politics,* Vol.1. (London: Pinter, 1986).

13. The close connection between Americanism and consumerism has been explored mainly by Stuart Ewen and Elizabeth Ewen in *Channels of Desire.* (Minneapolis: University of Minnesota Press, 1982).
14. F. Farina (ed.), *Il mare di Dudovich.* (Milan: Fabbri, 1991).
15. A. C. Quintavalle, 'L'auto-dipinta, eroi e popolo', in P. Barbaro and G. Bianchino (eds), *L'auto dipinta,* (Milan: Electa, 1992) pp. 33–4.
16. A. Bellucci, *L'automobile italiana 1918–1943.* (Bari: Laterza, 1984) p. 154.
17. *Ibid.*, pp. 126–32.
18. P. Sparke, *Design in Italy.* (New York: Abbeville Press, 1988) p. 47. On the limits of the impact of Fordist and Taylorist methods, see Levy, 'From Fascism to "Post-Fascists"', p. 174.
19. On Fascist modernism's emphasis on 'metallization' see, J. T. Schnapp, *Staging Fascism: 18BL and the Theater of Masses for Masses.* (Berkeley: University of California Press, 1996) p.xvii. The 'Fascistization' of motor cars is discussed in Quintavalle, 'L'auto dipinta', pp. 41–2.
20. Vené, *Mille lire al mese,* pp. 231–34.
21. A. Redaelli, *Le leggendarie Mille Miglia.* (Milan: Mondadori, 1989) pp. 11–66.
22. A. Santini, *Nuvolari.* (Milan: Rizzoli, 1987; first edn 1983) p. 228.
23. See M. H. Pierson, *The Perfect Vehicle.* (London: Granta, 1997) pp. 71–2.
24. G. Vené, *Vola colomba: vita quotidiana degli italiani negli anni del dopoguerra 1945–1960.* (Milan: Mondadori, 1990) p. 157. In *Fiat 500* (Turin: Lindau, 1992), p. 43, U. Castagnotto and A. M. Quarona state that in the early 1950s, the number of cars on Italian roads was a quarter of that in Britain.
25. Quintavalle, 'L'auto dipinta', p. 49.
26. Castagnotto and Quarona, *Fiat 500,* p. 55.
27. *Ibid.*, pp. 72–7.
28. Sparke, *Design in Italy,* p. 84.
29. See O. Calabrese (ed.), *Il mito di Vespa.* (Milan: Lupetti/Piaggio, 1996) pp. 84–101.
30. A. Valeri, *Pubblicità italiana: storia, protagonisti e tendenze di cento anni di comunicazione.* (Milan: Edizioni del Sole 24 Ore, 1986) pp. 29–31.
31. De Grazia, 'The Arts of Purchase', p. 231.
32. G. P. Ceserani, *Storia della pubblicità in Italia.* (Bari: Laterza, 1988) p. 131.
33. On Fascism's regulation of radio advertising, see R. Monteleone, *Storia della radio e della televisione in Italia.* (Venice: Marsilio, 1992) p. 67.
34. See especially D. Villani, *La pubblicità e i suoi segreti.* (Milan: Domus, 1946) pp. 225–7.
35. On the first eleven postwar pageants, see D. Villani, *Come sono nate undici Miss Italia.* (Milan: Domus, 1957).
36. Valeri, *Pubblicità italiana,* p. 96.
37. *Ibid.*, p. 135.
38. A. Testa, 'Punto franco', *Notiziario Sipra,* 12 October 1955, page unnumbered.
39. See G. Celant and G. Dorfles (eds), *Armando Testa: una retrospettiva.* (Milan: Electa, 1993). The Pirelli advertisement is reproduced on p. 62.
40. Valeri, *Pubblicità italiana,* p. 147.
41. For a detailed discussion of the expansion of cinema audiences after 1945, see S. Gundle, 'From Neorealism to *Luci rosse*: Cinema, Politics, Society 1945–85', in Z. Baranski and R. Lumley (eds), *Culture and Conflict in Postwar Italy.* (London: Macmillan, 1990) pp. 197–204.

42. Gian Piero Brunetta, 'Mille e più di mille (Lire al mese)', in M. Argentieri (ed.), *Risate di regime*. (Venice: Marsilio, 1991); James Hay, *Popular Film Culture in Fascist Italy: The Passing of the Rex*. (Bloomington: Indiana University Press, 1987) p. 62.
43. D. Gomery, *Shared Pleasures: A History of Movie Presentation in the United States*. (London: BFI, 1992) pp. 34–56.
44. *Bollettino 20th Century Fox Film*, January 1936.
45. *Bollettino 20th Century Fox Film*, September 1936.
46. J. Gaines, *Contested Culture: The Image, the Voice, the Law*. (London: BFI, 1992) pp. 158–9.
47. De Grazia, 'The Arts of Purchase', p. 234.
48. In several cases, the work of such artists has been repoduced in book form. See, for example, Egidio Mucci (ed.), *Il cinema nei manifesti di Silvano Campeggi, 1945–69*. (Florence: Giunti/Opus, 1988).
49. These issues are explored fully in David Forgacs, Stephen Gundle and Marcella Filippa, *Stolen Bicycles: Mass Culture and National Identity in Italy, 1938–54* (manuscript in preparation).
50. De Grazia, *How Fascism Ruled Women*, p. 130.
51. F. Pullano, 'Eccesso di gioventù: il cinema, i giovani e la società tra ricostruzione e boom economico' (Unpublished Tesi di laurea, University of Bologna, 1990–91), pp. 89 and 138.
52. G. P. Brunetta, *Cent'anni di cinema italiano*. (Bari: Laterza, 1991) p. 326.
53. Pullano, 'Eccesso di gioventù', p. 125.
54. G. Gori and S. Pivato (eds), *Gli anni del cinema di parrocchia*. (Rimini: Bianco e Nero, undated); Gundle, 'From Neorealism to *Luci rosse*', pp. 204–11.
55. Ilvo Diamanti and Enzo Pace, *Tra religione e organizzazione: il caso degli ACLI*. (Padua: Liviana, 1987) pp. 17–20.

8

Rationalizing Family Life – Stabilizing German Society: The 'Golden Twenties' and the 'Economic Miracle' in Comparison[1]

Carola Sachse

Europe's economic development after 1945 has been characterized as the 'short-lived dream of never-ending prosperity' (Burkart Lutz).[2] In West Germany, the 'economic miracle' was over by 1975 at the latest, although it took a while for the population to believe it. But if it was short-lived by one definition, the miracle had at least been incomparably more enduring than the 'golden' years of the Weimar Republic. Weimar had managed to maintain a 'semblance of normality' (Heinrich August Winkler) for at most five years, from 1924 to 1929.[3] The Federal Republic not only experienced over 25 years of sustained growth but, after the end of the economic miracle, remained far more stable than the Weimar Republic had been even in its few 'normal' years. In 1989/90, with unemployment over the two million mark, West Germany's image of freedom, prosperity and social security still proved extraordinarily attractive for the majority of East Germans. They hoped that their willingness to work in 'Germany, united fatherland' would enable them to partake of all the benefits of western modernity. Disappointment followed quickly and stayed. But this chapter will not speculate as to whether the second German democracy will successfully integrate the newcomers from the East. Nor does it aspire to predict the likely shape of the post-Cold War epoch. Instead, its aim is to compare the epochs after the two 'hot' wars. Using the example of one societal sector, the family, it seeks to answer the question why it proved possible only at the second attempt, and only in the western part of Germany, to create a democratic society with enduring social and political stability.

The fundamental differences in the starting position of the two postwar eras are obvious. In 1918 Germany was a country that had suffered military defeat beyond its borders, but at home remained an 'intact' class society, largely independent from foreign political control. In 1945, by contrast, German society was what Christoph Kleßmann has appropriately called a 'Society of collapse'. The pre-existing order had been totally defeated on its own soil. Germany had been placed under the political control of the victorious powers and stood accused of the greatest crimes in human history.[4] But at least collapse provided a new opportunity to create a stable domestic and international order. In comparing the two postwar eras, Charles S. Maier wrote some years ago about the process by which economic and financial élites in Western European and the United States learned to improve their national and international strategies of coordination and control.[5] In the case of West Germany, one could cite also as evidence of a learning process the constitutional changes introduced under the Allies' watchful eye or the progressive improvements to what was in any case a positive German inheritance in the field of social policy.

But is it possible that social change from one postwar period to the next was characterized also by learning processes which took place *below* the level of the political and economic élites? In other words, what kind of experiences contributed to the West German population's enduring acceptance of the market economy, the welfare state, democracy and federalism? If there was some kind of learning experience at this level then it was undoubtedly much more diffuse in terms of the actors, the spheres of activity and the political instruments involved than the kinds of change described by Maier. This chapter will concentrate on one such sphere, namely on what is conventionally termed the 'family'. Here 'family' is used as a collective concept for all the different kinds of social ensembles in which people conduct their intimate relationships and their daily life and which they refer to as family even when such groupings differ markedly from the ideal of the father-mother-child unit. Usually, when the 'family' is adduced as an explanation for the social stability of the first decades of the Federal Republic it is the ideal-type small family that is meant. But given that the reality of households in the postwar Federal Republic was extremely diverse, the ideal model is a poor guide to explaining why it was that a heterogeneous collection of family types was able to make such an important contribution to social stability. Why was the family apparently so much more successful than in Weimar? In Weimar, contemporaries repeatedly claimed to be witnessing the 'crisis of the family' as part of a wider societal crisis.[6] The present chapter, then, sketches in the outlines of a learning process that led to the 'family' changing from being a source of crisis to one of stability.

This process began with a set of linked discussions about social improvement conducted in Germany after World War One. The key term in the debate was 'rationalization', which contemporaries understood to include not just industrial rationalization, but rationalization of all spheres of social life. This utopian programme of social improvement however contained totalitarian elements which were to have disastrous consequences under the political conditions of National Socialism. After 1945, the rationalization movement was rejected in part, but only in part. On the one hand, the monstrous population- and racial policies of the Nazis were abandoned and more deference paid to the distinction between public and private spheres. This distinction was emphasized not just in contradistinction to the Nazi experience but also to the GDR, which, with its 'dissolution of the family' and obligatory work for women, was seen simply as the continuation of 'totalitarianism'. On the other hand, many of the ideas of the rationalization movement were not reversed and were instead transferred from the realm of public debate to that of reconstituted private life.

The utopia of rationalization

How was it possible that a whole epoch of German history, namely the period between the two World Wars, should have been so fascinated by the idea of rationalizing society that it failed to see the dangers inherent in such a project?[7] Contemporaries were bewitched not just by the basic idea of industrial rationalization – of using scientific methods to reduce the expenditure of time, material and manpower and thus optimize efficiency. Beyond the simple principle of 'less input, more output', the term 'Rationalisierung' seemed to hold out a richer promise. The term itself acquired far more complex and richer connotations than the similar concepts coined in other countries. In the Anglo-Saxon world, the principle of 'scientific management', after Frederick W. Taylor's book of the same name[8] was soon shortened simply to 'management'. In France, the discourse originally was of 'organisation scientifique du travail' but later simply of 'organisation'. Only in Germany, was the watchword 'Rationalisierung'.[9]

Originally rationalization was a term of the theological and philosophical enlightenment. It denoted liberation from old beliefs and their replacement by reasoned truths, the rational penetration of natural phenomena and social conditions, in short, the 'demystification of the world'. That was the phrase used in 1905 by the best known contemporary witness of the beginnings of the rationalization epoch, Max Weber. It was Weber too, who coined the idea of a 'rational way of life'. Weber used the example of Protestant sects of seventeenth- and eighteenth-century North America who in their rational and ascetic way accumulated wealth as proof of a god-fearing life.[10] Weber, however, coined the term within a context of profound cultural pessimism. For Weber, the Protestant ethic initiated a cultural development whose logical end was 'the powerful cosmos of the modern economic order, based on the technical and economic requirements of mechanical machine production. ... Every individual born into the machinery of this new order, and *not* just the directly economically productive individual, is driven by the overwhelming force of the economic machine. The force will abate perhaps only when the last pound of fuel has been burned up.'[11] Weber's speculation about the future society that would be created within the 'rigid steel cage' of the capitalist economic order was no less devastating. Echoing Friedrich Nietzsche he wrote: 'No one yet knows who in the future will live in that steel cage. No one yet knows whether at the end of this monstrous process new prophets will emerge or old ideas and ideals will be reborn. *Or* perhaps there will be neither and we will see instead mechanical stone men, taking themselves very seriously. These "last men" of the future will then indeed be "Specialists without spirit, hedonists without a heart: nothing-men who imagine they have reached a hitherto never attained stage of human evolution".'[12]

Both Weber and Nietzsche saw modernity as a self-destructive process in which human beings were degraded to narrow specialists, ignorant of everything that lay beyond their field. But their pessimistic vision did not dominate the debates about social rationalization after World War One, at least until the beginning of the world depression.[13] Instead, the term 'rationalization' basked in the allure of enlightenment, reason and truth. And to assuage the anxieties of those still influenced by cultural pessimism or who foresaw the danger of mass unemployment, the Latin-based 'Rationalisierung' was replaced by the soothing Germanic 'Gemeinschaftsarbeit' – cooperative work. The term 'Gemeinschaftsarbeit' implied that the different interest groups would cooperate with each other, transcend traditional gender and social boundaries and agree on norms and rules to reform production and reproduction for the good of all.[14]

From the early 1920s onwards, rationalization's appeal was reinforced by the promise of a better world emanating from the other side of the Atlantic and particularly from the automobile factories on the Rouge River. Employers' and trade union representatives flocked to the Ford works[15] and Henry Ford's memoirs appeared in German in 1923, rapidly going through several editions.[16] Ford's idea, like that of some other American contemporaries, was to create a profitable linkage between the rationalization of men's and women's lives. On the one hand, Ford introduced systematic conveyor belt production in his Detroit factories. On the other hand, the Ford worker's famous wage of five dollars a day – which exceeded the pay offered by any other factory – consisted of a basic wage and a bonus for clean living. To earn this bonus, Ford's workers had to meet certain conditions. Married workers had to live with their families and take care of them. The house had to be kept clean. All members of immigrant families had to prove themselves good American citizens, were not allowed to take on subtenants, had to maintain a close family life, eat American food and not exceed their spaghetti quota! Fifty inspectors of the department for social welfare controlled the employees' households according to the maxim of their boss: 'He who lives properly, works properly.'[17] In Germany, this message fell on fertile soil. It found resonance in Germany's own tradition of company social policy as practised since the Kaiserreich, for example, in the Krupp factories and factory estates. And it became part of a modern programme of 'social rationalization', extending beyond the factory to embrace the whole of society.[18]

A powerful combination of European enlightenment, American progress and the German idea of community thus helped to transform rationalization in Germany from a narrow factory programme to the watchword of social reform. Yet although the term's appeal derived from these many associations, in fact the meaning of 'rationalization' had been narrowed to simply 'achieving more with less'. This is clear from the first German lexicon in which the concept appears. Significantly, the lexicon appeared in 1916, at a time when the war had changed in character, quick victories had evaporated and supply and munitions were everything.[19] Once 'rationalization' had been thus narrowed to a simple means–ends relationship, its scope of application was progressively extended from the factory via work, the lifestyle of the workers to ever wider social spheres.[20] War and defeat had profoundly shaken up the society of the old Kaiserreich and contemporaries believed that Germany was now engulfed in a complex social crisis. In social policy journals and political pamphlets, we find continual reference to crisis – to the crisis of the family, the crisis of marriage, the health crisis of the Volk, the crisis of the work ethic and the crisis of social policy. However accurate their diagnoses, these articles reflected a comprehensive crisis of confidence in the existing social order. Moreover, they all prescribed the same medicine, namely, rationalization.[21]

Strange new ideas emerged: the rationalization of housework, the rationalization of sexuality and reproduction, the rationalization of the body of the 'Volk' or of its health. And thus, quite unexpectedly, the discourse of the 1920s brought together categories that the language of the nineteenth century had carefully kept separate: public and private; men and women; reason and feeling. As a result, rationalization came to be seen not just as means of producing more efficient strategies of management and control but also a means of emancipation from control – be it from 'capital', 'men' or inherited values. And social rationalization could be adopted at the same time by groups to the left and the right wing of the political spectrum, by academics from almost every discipline, and by state bureaucrats.[22]

The programme of rationalization in the Weimar Republic

When employers, economic politicians and economists spoke of rationalization, they were of course thinking primarily of the industrial context. Objectives such as standardizing product lines and setting common standards for suppliers, reorganizing the work process and combating waste in time, energy, raw materials and not least labour was the staple diet of a raft of new associations, research institutes and committees. The most important institutions were the Deutsche Normenausschuß, founded in 1917, and the Reichskuratorium für Wirtschaftlichkeit (RKW), created in 1921, both of which continue to play an important role today. However, when employers coined the term of 'cooperative work' ('Gemeinschaftsarbeit') for enhancing performance, they saw this idea as having application not only inside but also outside the factory gates.[23] In 1918 the journal of the German Employers' Association published an article with the title 'Rationalization of private life.' The article argued that, just as in the factory, the domestic sphere too 'requires savings. Domestic labour should be done in the most efficient manner, and should be reorganized in such a way as to produce the greatest and healthiest enjoyment of life with far less expenditure of effort than is currently the case.' 'Educating the masses', in such matters was 'decisive for Germany's economic development'.[24] Alongside the economic benefits, the employers also believed that social progress would follow. At the same time, however, they sought to dampen expectations of higher wages and cheaper consumer goods. The 'materialistic' part of the American dream, which indeed was not very realistic in the German economic context, was seen as incompatible with 'German quality work'. What remained was the 'idealistic' part of the dream, the education to a more rational way of life.[25]

Over the following years the masses were indeed deluged with a flood of texts seeking to provide enlightenment and advice. One best-seller was Gustav Großman's book 'Rationalizing yourself. Achieving your personal best with the least effort'. Another best-seller was 'The new household' from Erna Meyer, offering a 'rational' approach to domestic duties and child-rearing. By 1932 the book was in its forty-first edition. The famous book of marital advice from Van de Velde also appeared around this time, as did a growing specialist literature in the field of eugenics and social medicine. The size of the print-runs alone shows what hopes and dreams were aroused by such texts.[26] The gap between dream and reality remained nevertheless unbridgeable, as is evident when we turn to attempts to rationalize the household.[27]

In some senses, war and inflation had accelerated the process towards greater uniformity in women's situation as housewives. With the rapid reduction in the number of domestic staff, an increasing number of women now performed their own house-work, unpaid and without assistance. Nevertheless, there remained great differences between the social classes.[28] For the housewife of a middle-ranking white-collar employee, with two children and an easy to care for, centrally heated 'new apartment', equipped with a vacuum cleaner, an electric iron and washing machine, the domestic chores were a very different matter than for, say, the working class widow of fallen soldier. As well as earning her bread outside the house, there would be the daily battle of keeping a two-room proletarian apartment in a half-way decent condition without the help of electricity or a direct water supply. Yet the rationalization movement claimed to be able to surmount such obstacles. It placed its emphasis not on new equipment for the household but on rationalizing the activity of the housewife.

To be sure, the rationalization movement was also in part a promotional campaign by electrical engineering and power companies to increase the use of consumer durables and energy consumption. Many of the household machines now in daily use had, at least in their basic principles, been developed by the turn of the century. After 1910, the development of smaller motors allowed electrical power to be deployed in many hitherto purely mechanical pieces of equipment. However, with the exception of the electrical iron and to some extent of the vacuum cleaner, most of these new products found widespread use in German households only after 1950. The necessary infrastructure was lacking and above all the consumers simply did not have the money to buy them. There were far too few of the 'new', rationally designed and publicly funded apartments like those conceived by the Bauhaus architect, Bruno Taut.[29] Few workers or white-collar families could afford the so-called 'social rents' charged for them. During the years of the Weimar Republic the mass production of household goods – as indeed of many other products already well established in the USA – was hindered by widespread poverty and the consequent lack of demand on the home market.

The uneven standard of equipment in the households of different social groups led to a disastrous situation for poorer women. Lacking the technical backup, they were nevertheless expected by schools, welfare institutions and employers to meet all the new hygienic, nutritional and educational standards, never mind how inadequate the apartment or how over-worked the woman. The 'rationalization' of their housework was supposed to overcome inadequate conditions and income. Under the given conditions the outcome for most German women (assuming that they registered the demands of the rationalization movement at all) could be little more than an increase in their workload.

'Rationalization', according to the International Labour Office in 1932, 'is the replacement of traditional methods and habits with new, empirically based rules. It is the replacement of unplanned activity, driven by the demands of the moment, with systematic action. The most efficient method is worked out by scientific study, ensuring that the best possible results are obtained.'[30] Housework was seen as a haven of traditional habits and spur-of-the-minute activity and thus as ripe for countless rationalization proposals, in particular from the domestic economy section of the RKW. The RKW analysed almost all the work processes in the household such as washing clothes and dishes and cleaning floors and windows. It produced instructional material establishing scientifically the 'one best way' to carry out these tasks, based on an optimal calculation of energy, effort, time and material expenditure. Housewives were invited to reorganize all their household activity on scientific lines. They were supposed to produce exact schedules, planning the various domestic chores on a daily, weekly, monthly and annual basis. The Housewives' Associations drew up appropriate forms for such planning and also for keeping household accounts.[31] Housewives were invited also to give the furniture and appurtenances in their apartments a critical review and, as Erna Meyer never ceased to remind the readers of her book about the 'New household', to throw out all the dust traps. Furniture and equipment should be simple, without fine tracery or other such embellishments.[32] In 1929 the architect Franz Denner extrapolated from the individual household and calculated the potential time-saving for society as a whole. 'In 1927 there were 16 million furnished apartments in Germany. If, through introduction of more appropriate furniture and other equipment the removal of dust and dirt were to take just ¼ an hour less per week, this would produce a saving for Germany of 4 million working hours a week or 666,000 working hours every work-day.'[33]

But in what way could the housewife's 15 extra minutes or the 4 million extra hours for German households as a whole be used to benefit the economy? This is no rhetorical question. Social policy-makers, representatives of the women's associations, industrial managers, engineers and social scientists all had grand and worthy answers to offer. By reducing the burden on the housewife of all the 'household minutiae', the 'ethical quality of family life' could be 'brought all the more clearly to the fore'.[34] Thus, through rationalization of housework, the 'crisis of the family' could be overcome, young people's 'moral decline' reversed, and the health of the 'Volk' be raised.

By saving a minute here and a minute there and with the help of a rational time-budget, the housewife was expected over the course of the day to accumulate a substantial reservoir of additional time. Ergonomically appropriate methods would reduce physical exertion, while careful time-planning would prevent stress. Above all, the deliberate planning and organization of household jobs using modern work methods would raise the housewife's self-esteem, her energy and her 'joy' in her work. Of course, this extra energy was not left to the women to use for themselves – it was already planned for. There were two valuable tasks in particular to which the housewife could now devote more energy. On the one hand, she should contribute to generating the future labour-force through tender care for the infant and careful upbringing of the child. On the other, it fell to her to regenerate the adult labour force by gentle devotion to the needs of the husband. Women should thus no longer be the undemanding overtaxed proletarian workhorse or the proud bourgeois representatives of a separate and distinct female sphere. Instead, what was now called for was a healthy, qualified, active and up-to-date housewife and mother.[35]

For the most part, however, the real existing women of the Weimar Republic were neither willing nor able to meet these new demands.

A Social Democratic newspaper concluded resignedly in 1929, 'We women may surely take pride in the speed with which improvements have been made in the field of household rationalization. But if we pose the question to what extent the blessings of household rationalization have benefited the broad masses, the answer to which is essential for judging the significance of all innovations in this arena, we do not have so much to be proud of. The social circles which the new ideas have touched thus far remain extremely narrow, and far too few women have any inclination to apply these principles in their own homes.'[36] Despite the rationalization programme's ambitions, its impact was rather to destabilize society than to foster harmony and stability. True enough, it did not espouse some great utopian fantasy and instead invited people to enter a world of concrete possibilities – a world brought tantalizingly close by the new household goods on offer in shop windows and showrooms. But too many people soon discovered that this attractive new world was simply out of their reach and that rationalization of their lifestyle was no answer to the problems of poverty, downward social mobility and unemployment.

National Socialism and the realization of the utopian

For all the 'realism' and practicality, the rationalization movement nevertheless was about realizing a utopia. In the USA the dream was of integrating and Americanizing a comparatively open and multiethnic society by means of mass consumption. In Germany, it was about stabilizing and integrating a relatively closed society characterized by shortages and scarcity. The rationalization strategies of politicians, social reformers and population scientists were aimed at a social construct which they called the 'German Volkskörper', the body of the German people. They thus drew on a German tradition of treating the national society as a biological entity, the 'Volksgemeinschaft' or people's community.[37] Since the target was the 'body' of the Volk, it was no coincidence that it was women in whom the social experts took particular interest. They saw their task as adapting women to the conditions of a modern industrial society and reorganizing private life along the lines of the instrumental logic of the economic sphere.

Alongside the experts on domestic economy there were also those who sought to invade the intimate sphere of the family still further. Sexual advisors wanted to reduce the misery of abortions and to educate their clients about sensible sexual behaviour. Nurses involved in baby care wanted to encourage young mothers, if they insisted on having too few children, at least to raise them according to the latest medical and pedagogical knowledge. A reduction in infant mortality would compensate for the smaller number of births. Some humanitarian or religious, Social Democratic or Communist experts in the welfare offices and advice centres wanted to help their clients. Some wanted to reduce waste and increase the effectiveness of state expenditure. Many hoped that the concept of rationalization would allow both humanitarian goals and efficiency to be rationally combined.[38]

Once it was outside democratic control, however, this simple and universal programme of rationalization proved to be extremely dangerous. The racist-totalitarian regime applied rationalization with far more devastating impact than could Weimar's educational courses or books of advice. Above all, the Nazis revealed two key dangers to the rationalization idea. In the first place, the motif of 'rationalization' obscured the absence of a discussion about what were the desirable goals of social change. Rationalization had, as we have seen, come to mean nothing more than optimizing the relationship between means and ends. But where are those ends laid down and how are they morally or democratically legitimated? Who has the power of definition – and how is that power controlled? On these questions, the rationalization movement in the Weimar Republic had nothing to say. Rationalization became rather a comprehensive, self-justifying principle. The proposed social reforms did not need to be defended or explained, rather the simple label of 'rationalization' provided its own justification. The Nazi regime gladly adopted this winning formula to endorse its goals of eliminating 'useless mouths to feed' or restricting social spending to the 'racially valuable'. During the world economic crisis employers demanded with increasing vehemence the 'organic linkage of economic and social policy'. This demand, which the Nazis made their own after 1933, made selection seem rational, planned and efficient.

The danger inherent in rationalization was thus not only that it obscured a discussion of what should be the final ends of social policy. It was also the connection it established between rationalization, hierarchy and selection. When it comes to rationalizing the workforce (or the 'body of labour', as factory engineers, in analogy to the body of the 'Volk', liked to say) it remains a basic principle that labour should be deployed according to its (actual or assumed) qualities, knowledge and skills. Unsuitable individuals should be weeded out as early as possible.[39] What happens, however, when this principle of selection is applied to other areas of society? If the goal of social policy is changed from helping needy recipients to rationalizing the body of the 'Volk', then it is but a short step to selecting the recipients of social policy according to their ostensible 'value'.[40] This was inherent in the rationalization discourse of the 1920s but it took the National Socialist terror regime to put it mercilessly into practice. One of the regime's first actions, as Atina Grossmann has rightly emphasized, was to carry out a thorough purge of the personnel in the social policy institutions. Those male and female doctors, social workers and marital advice counsellors who as left-wingers and/or Jews were suspected of being unwilling to endorse a radical execution of the new social policy line, found themselves on the street, in prison, the torture chambers of the SA or in exile.[41]

What did it mean for the family as a social institution when economic and social policy came to be 'organically linked?' Let us take the example of 'Siedlungspolitik', a movement which began in the World Economic Crisis as a means of enabling workers to settle on unbuilt land, constructing their own cheap owner-occupied housing and planting market gardens.[42] The hope was that these would make them largely self-sufficient and thus relatively protected from the effects of economic crisis. In fact, the origins of the movement go further back to the independent efforts of hundreds of families in cities across Germany. Often unemployed and homeless, they would occupy land belonging to the German railway or the state over which the municipal authorities had no direct control. There, groups of families worked together to build simple but weatherproof homes, costing only around 400RM. In most cases, the women earned the necessary funds through washing, cleaning, sowing and other such tasks, while the men worked on building the houses themselves. These so-called 'unregulated' estates, with their extraordinarily low building costs, came to provide the model for a new housing policy. The authorities hoped to solve what had hitherto been the main obstacle to providing an adequate volume of workers' housing, namely, the workers' inability to afford the rents resulting from Weimar's relatively high building costs. In 1931 48 million Reichsmarks was made available for the first programme of 100,000 such self-help homes (Kleinsiedlungen). The programme was then progressively renewed in succeeding years and substantially expanded after the Nazi accession to power.

In 1930 the RKW looked at the 'unregulated' estates. That is not quite as surprising as at first appears, because alongside employers' representatives, the RKW also contained trade unionists and other groups and in addition enjoyed public funding. With the mass unemployment of the slump, often seen as a crisis of rationalization, the RKW had to prove its social worth. To ensure continued public funding it had to pay more attention to the 'human factor'. The RKW thus sought to rationalize unemployment itself. In Siedlungspolitik it believed it had found the philosopher's stone. In view of the very low costs involved, the RKW saw little scope for rationalizing the actual house building. So instead, it concentrated on the selection of the applicants. It developed a detailed questionnaire to assist in the process and laid down equally detailed selection criteria. There were sociological characteristics, such as the degree to which the applicant 'bonded with the land' and the 'female type' that was necessary to ensure the land would be successfully worked. There were physiological criteria such as the physical build and the energy of the settlers. And there were psychological criteria such as the settlers' 'drive', their 'capacity for quiet reflection' and their 'optimistic or pessimistic attitude to life'. The RKW also advised selectors to look for specific weaknesses such as proneness to drinking and fighting but also such things as a tendency to show off or to contradict others, over-sensitivity, dogmatism in any direction and so on. The 'techniques' to select the suitable settlers were 'psychological conversations' and 'researches' or, if a large number of applicants had to be dealt with in a short time, mass screening. The decisive factor in such investigations was often the domestic abilities of the wife.[43]

This approach to selecting the appropriate 'settlement material' was adopted by the relevant offices from 1931 onwards. Under the influence of rationalization, then, what had originally been a project of autonomous self-help was transformed into a measure of selective population policy. Soon this policy came to exclude the very unemployed and homeless who had given the settlement programme its original impetus. Here, the employers played an important role. Over several years of intense lobbying, they managed to get their company interests incorporated into the relevant laws and regulations. They did not want the unemployed. On the contrary, they wanted to give the estates to 'quality workers', thus providing them with supplementary income and rendering them secure from crises. Industry attacked the old-fashioned idea of self-sufficiency in the original 'full income' estates. Instead, they praised the moral and social-hygienic virtues of the so-called 'supplementary income' estates, with only a vegetable garden and a rabbit hutch. Such estates would provide the worker with a small amount of land and property, root him in the soil, fill his free time and provide a welcome additional income. A healthier lifestyle could thus be provided without additional wage costs and in crisis periods the worker could be put on short time without threatening the existence of his family.

Bit by bit the employers were able to influence state policy. They not only gained public funding for company housing schemes but were also able to ensure that only those whom they regarded as the 'most valuable human material' were the beneficiaries of all housing schemes. That meant above all those workers still in employment. Even the first Siedlungs programme in 1932, at the height of the slump, was not restricted to the unemployed; the employers received financial assistance for company housing if they could show that the recipients were working on short time. From 1933, the state funded *non*-company estates only where there was a clear expectation that the settlers would soon obtain employment. In 1935 the fully employed were made eligible for the programme and finally in 1936 only those people were entitled to become settlers who had a works certificate to prove that they were belonged to the 'core workforce' (Stammarbeiterschaft). The employers had thus succeeded in transferring the selection criteria of factory personnel policy to state social policy. In return, the employers agreed to take account of National Socialist race criteria, and to select only core workers of 'German and related blood' for company housing policy.

In the Nazis' approach to housing, company personnel policies and state racial policy became intermingled. At the beginning of World War Two, the responsibility for publicly funded housing was transferred to the German Labour Front (DAF) and its chief, Robert Ley. The DAF planned a giant housing programme to be implemented after the 'final victory'. The programme involved careful gradations. The best estates were to be limited to a specially selected élite of 'German-Aryan' and at the same time economically vital workers' families. Next came relatively spacious, hygenic 'people's apartments' which were designed for 'Aryan' families with four childen, where the father was a qualified and flexible worker. Families of 'German' and 'Aryan' workers who were not particularly valuable either on economic or on racial grounds should at most be offered the chance to move out of cellars and other such substandard dwellings and into very small apartments. 'Ethnically foreign' and 'racially inferior' workers could expect no more than camps of varying quality. The programme thus determined both who should decide on the allocation of life-chances to different families and what criteria they should adopt. Membership of a particular social class or stratum was no longer the decisive criterion – and certainly the wishes of the individual played no role in it at all. Instead, the decisive criterion was the father's economic status as core worker, flexible skilled worker or mobile unskilled worker, combined with the family's racial calibre.

The Nazi regime went a step further. Not only did it carry out selections to maximize the benefit to the 'people's community' of state social spending, but it also used the allocation of social benefits to promote the racial-hygienic selection of the population. As in the case of the settlers, the allocation of marriage loans and other social benefits came to be dependent on a painstaking 'racial', 'hereditary health' and social-medical investigation of the applicants. For the future bride or the wife in the settler couple, the investigation also involved assessing her housewifely abilities. The Nazis sought to create a 'hereditary register' of the German population that could in particular cases lead to the sterilization of the applicant.[44]

Such selective social policy sought to control families in their most intimate sphere. It threatened families with the withdrawal of social benefits, and individuals in the worst cases with sterilization and murder. Organizations for particular gender or generational groups such as the Hitler Youth, the League of German Girls, the NS Women's Organization, the SA and the National Socialist Factory Organization separated family members from one another. The NS regime restricted the content, space and time available to family life. At the same time it bestowed lavish praise on the 'family' as the 'germ' of the 'people's community'. Tim Mason has already shown the result of this contradictory set of pressures. Partly in reaction against the demands of the state, partly in response to the praise of the 'German family' a process was accelerated which had been underway since World War One, namely, the emergence of a 'modern form of domesticity'.[45] We will return to this in a moment.

The revival of private life in the Federal Republic

In two different guises, then, the family had been the target of social experts and policy-makers. In both cases the 'experts' were operating with a social construct or ideal type as much as responding to the realities of family life. In Weimar, experts wanted to transform the family into a functioning module of industrial society. In analogy to the search for greater efficiency in the economic sphere, they hoped that advice and instruction could, without the need for expensive technology or investment, create the effective and smoothly functioning family. Their promises of private prosperity and individual happiness were unrealizable under the conditions of the Weimar Republic but nevertheless aroused expectations that could not be suppressed. In the Nazi era, the family became the target of state racial policy. The Nazis sought to control and manipulate the family as the 'germ cell' of the 'body of the people'. Here too, as in Weimar, policy produced experiences that would not go away, above all the negative experience of being threatened, sometimes with death, by a state apparatus beyond individual control. Even the 'racially valuable' elements of the population experienced what it was like to have the state monitoring and controlling the family and their own reproductive behaviour.

These experiences could not be simply forgotten in 1945. After the carrot of unrealizable dreams in Weimar and the stick of state control in the Nazi era, people themselves – above all women – now took on the 'project' of the modern rationalized family. This project contained elements of the earlier policies and ambitions but also a new emphasis on the family as a space for the rediscovery of privacy.

In parallel to the rationalization, biologizing and politicizing of the family, but in a complex relationship to it, the first half of the twentieth century had seen the historical rise of the modern nuclear family as the most prominent institution of daily life. Influenced by Helmut Schelsky's 1953 study on 'Wandlungen der deutschen Familie in der Gegenwart', social historians have tended to see in the family an important source of postwar stability.[46] The family is seen as having played such a stabilizing role despite, or rather because it had itself initially been so destabilized by the peculiar conditions of the immediate postwar years. If we compare this thesis with that of Tim Mason for the Nazi period, it seems that the family as a social institution yet again developed in opposition to the demands placed on it from outside.[47]

By the end of the war Allied bombing had destroyed 25 per cent of housing stock and the population was swollen by the growing numbers of refugees. The result was that an increasingly heterogeneous population was forced to crowd into a dwindling number of apartments, many of them war-damaged. Life in emergency refugee camps or the imposition of subtenants, compulsorily assigned by the authorities, undermined the intimacy of family life and strengthened the yearning for the recreation of private space. Of the German population, 20 per cent had lost property, employment and/or social standing. Only the solidarity of the family provided a realistic springboard from which to work for a return to one's former position. Schelsky and many after him have argued that the absence of men at the front or in POW camps had damaged the hierarchy and material structure of family life. But it was precisely such 'damaged' families that ensured the survival and convalescence of the returning soldiers. All the evidence suggests that many of these families proved in fact to be the successful social 'modules' for promoting social recovery and recovery that they were supposed to have become in Weimar.

In order to understand the stabilizing function of these families (we should probable use the term 'households' in order not to lose sight of just how diverse were such family groupings in the postwar period), we ought to look a little more closely at the relationships prevailing between the sexes. Feminists and sociologists of the family still wonder why it was that women, who in the immediate postwar period seemed to have gained a great deal of independence, allowed it to be taken away again in the late 1940s and 1950s. They ask why women allowed themselves to be pushed out of the labour market and accept the dominant, usually termed 'conservative', family ideology. But it is questionable whether the assumption behind such questions, namely that female emancipation lies exclusively in paid work, really fits with the self-image of women and the values of the time. At least two corrections are necessary, both of which show that the 'Family' was not simply an ideology propagated from above. It was a social concept or model that ordinary men and particularly women made their own.

First, even in those 'traditional' families where both parents lived with their children, the division of labour did not necessarily conform to the classical pattern. Paid employment and house work may have been allocated along traditional lines, but the relationship between husband and wife was usually constructed as a partnership, with the husband only slightly dominant. This, at any rate, was the conclusion of contemporary family sociologists.[48] The role-allocation between husband and wife was thus more often based on consensus than on conflict. It was primarily understood as a functional division of labour in the best interests of the family as social unit and above all in the interest of the welfare and development of their children, on whom (particularly the boys) all hopes of regaining lost social standing or of social improvement were placed. In this combination of a consensual division of labour with marital partnership we see the result of the learning processes of the previous epochs. The idea of the marriage of 'comrades' stemmed from the youth movement of the late Kaiserreich. It was now combined with the idea of rational and skilled household-management as expressed in the commonly heard – and by no means derogatory – phrase, 'occupation: housewife'. In addition, the specific socialization of the Hitler Youth generation also played a part. For girls, the Nazi experience had not consisted simply of the propagandistic reinforcement of traditional sexual role models. Instead, in the League of German Girls many girls had for the first time been treated as part of 'youth' rather than as young ladies, and thus for the first time been allowed to enter a sphere previously the preserve of the boys. The state-organized leisure programmes of the 1930s, in which the Nazis typically downplayed the difference between boys and girls and emphasized instead their shared racial superiority, opened up new kinds of activity beyond the restricted world of family domesticity.[49]

Second, the standard model of the family with its father-mother-child constellation did not correspond to the reality as experienced by millions of women. Many lived in quite different family conditions.[50] Even when they were living on their own and in paid employment, they still insisted on being given public recognition as housewives. This was manifest in the 1950s in the hundreds of cases brought before the labour courts by West German female employees seeking to enforce one paid 'housework day' a month.[51] In several Federal states, women had enjoyed since 1948/9 a legal right to the housework day, even when they had no husband to look after. But employers often did not want to recognize this right. Those widowed employees denied the housework day protested against being seen as 'less valued' than married women or as being placed in the same category as single women.[52] Single women, like some employees in the Düsseldorfer Stadtwerke in 1961, felt obliged to defend their work as a 'vital necessity to support their existence'. In being denied the housework day, they argued that they were doubly disadvantaged in relation to those married women who were simply 'coearners'. They had not only to do the heavy duty work at home, such as bringing in the coal, without male help. Moreover, having 'through the effects of war been condemned to remain single', they were now being 'demoted behind the married women'.[53] To be a 'housewife', to have a 'family', was thus obviously an important matter of social standing, independent of the marital status of the individual. It provided social prestige and raised the individual's self-esteem. In the words of Lutz Niethammer, 'family' was for many women in the postwar period 'an obligation, a phantom and a project'.[54]

'Family' as individual task, as a space for new or revived privacy, as a motor for social mobility succeeded as a stabilizing factor in the second German postwar era above all because it was no longer a lifestyle available only to the better-off. The long-propagated ideal of the single-earner, housewife and child unit was for the first time a realizable goal for broad social strata. It was no longer the programme of social experts but something which many individuals chose for themselves, a social form to which even unmarried women laid claim.[55] Organized in a growing number of small households, these families were the appropriate counterpart to the 'social market economy', together contributing to the rapid emergence of the consumer society.

At the end of the 1950s, the ideal model of the nuclear family and the actual pattern of family lives were probably more closely aligned than ever before or since in German history. It was the successful conclusion of a social-political programme which had extended through a series of very different stages from the end of World War One to the end of the Adenauer Era. But was it also the beginning of the end of the era of the family? For Axel Schildt, the end of the 1950s was a turning point in German social history, a structural break on the way to a 'modernized modernity'.[56] In the new phase of social modernization that followed, the family, according to Schildt and others, lost cohesion and significance. But rumours of the death of the family have often been greatly exaggerated. As Yves Lequin once observed, the family has always proved extremely adaptable and able to take on new shapes in response to changing needs and social conditions. When the number of working mothers began to grow from the end of the 1950s it caused great doom and despair about the future of the family. But it turned out not to herald the end of the family after all. Nor did the vehement attacks by the '68 movement, including the women's movement, on the ostensibly 'reactionary nuclear family'. To be sure, new ways of living together emerged but they did not render the older forms obsolete. On the contrary, some gay and lesbian couples today want nothing more than to legalize their relationship and to enjoy equal status with conventional marriages.

It is hard to fit the history of the family into the conventional periods of political history. It may be possible to periodize family *policy* in terms of the major political turning points of twentieth-century political history – though even here there are important continuities and traditions that cross the conventional boundaries. But the history of the family itself has its own life, sometimes more sometimes less subject to pressures from 'above'. The family has been no more obedient to the dictates of prevailing family policy, than has the reality of family life conformed to the prevailing norms of what constitutes the ideal family. That, at least, is one fact that is as true of the prewar era as of the years after 1945.

Notes

1. Translated by Mark Roseman.
2. Burkart Lutz, *Der kurze Traum immerwährender Prosperität. Eine Neuinterpretation der industriell-kapitalistischen Entwicklung im Europa des 20. Jahrhunderts.* (Frankfurt a. M./New York: Campus Verlag, 1984).

3. Heinrich August Winkler, *Der Schein der Normalität. Arbeiter und Arbeiterbewegung in der Weimarer Republik 1924 bis 1930.* (Berlin/Bonn: J. H. W. Dietz, 1988).
4. Christoph Kleßmann, *Die doppelte Staatsgründung. Deutsche Geschichte 1945–1955.* (5. Revised and expanded edition, Bonn: Bundeszentrale für politische Bildung, 1991), S. 37ff.
5. Charles S. Maier, 'The Two Postwar Eras and the Conditions for Stability in Twentieth-Century Western Europe', *American Historical Review*, 86 2 (1981) 327–52.
6. On the discourse of crisis in the Weimar Republic, see Carola Sachse, *Betriebliche Sozialpolitik als Familienpolitik in der Weimarer Republik und im Nationalsozialismus. Mit einer Fallstudie über die Firma Siemens*, (Berlin, Hamburg, Hamburger Institute für Sozialforschung, 1987), esp. chapter III.
7. This article is based on long established international and inter-disciplinary debate about the phenomenon of rationalization in western modernity. This debate was instituted by the Haburger Institut für Sozialforschung and continued as a collaborative project by Atina Grossmann, Mary Nolan, Dagmar Reese, Carola Sachse and Tilla Siegel (financed by DAAD and ACLS) as well as Elisabeth Faue, Karen Hageman, Karin Hausen and Alice Kessler-Harris (financed by the Werner-Reimers-Stiftung). The debate has found expression in a number of journals and edited collections: Tilla Siegel (ed.), 'Fordism and Fascism', *International Journal of Political Economy*, 18, 1 (Spring 1988) Carola Sachse, Ilse Lenz und Tilla Siegel, 'Personnel Management as Gender Policy', (Diskussionspapier 10–90, Hamburger Institut für Sozialforschung 1990); Dagmar Reese, Eve Rosenhaft, Carola Sachse und Tilla Siegel (eds), *Rationale Beziehungen? Geschlechterverhältnisse im Rationalisierungsprozeß.* (Frankfurt a. M.: Suhrkamp, 1993); Tilla Siegel (ed.), 'Social Rationalization', *International Journal of Political Economy*, 24 4 (Winter 1994/95); Brigitte Aulenbacher und Tilla Siegel (eds), *Diese Welt wird völlig anders sein. Denkmuster der Rationalisierung.* (Pfaffenweiler: Centaurus-Verl.-Gesellschaft, 1995); *Social Politics. International Studies in Gender, State & Society*, special issue: 'Gender And Rationalisation In Comparative Historical Perspective – Germany and the United States', 4 1 (1997).
8. Frederick W. Taylor, *Die Grundsätze wissenschaftlicher Betriebsführung.* (Berlin: Oldenbourg Verlag, 1913).
9. See Kurt Pentzlin, Article: 'Rationalisierung', *Handwörterbuch der Sozialwissenschaften*, (1964), pp. 676–83, here p. 676. See also Tilla Siegel, 'It's Only Rational. An Essay on the Logic of Social Rationalization', in Siegel (ed.) *Diese Welt wird völlig anders*, pp. 35–70.
10. Max Weber, *Die protestantische Ethik und der Geist des Kapitalismus*, in Weber, *Gesammelte Aufsätze zur Religionssoziologie* I, (Tübingen: Mohr Verlag, 1920, reprinted 1988), pp. 1–206, here pp. 158 und 163.
11. Weber *Gesammelte Aufsätze*, p. 203 (emphasis in original).
12. *Ibid.*, p. 204 (emphasis in original).
13. On the cultural critical interpretation of rationalization above all from the vantage point of life philosophy, see: Gunther Mai, 'Die Ökonomie der Zeit. Unternehmerische Rationalisierungsstrategien und industrielle Arbeitsbeziehungen', *Geschichte und Gesellschaft*, 23 (1997), 311–27, here pp. 312–15.

14. On the notion of community in German industry, see Sachse *Betriebliche Sozialpolitik*, pp. 66–76 und Gertraude Krell, *Vergemeinschaftende Personalpolitik*, (Munich and Mering: Hampp, 1994), pp. 75ff.
15. On the fascination with America in the German rationalization movement, see Mary Nolan, *Visions of modernity: American business and the modernization of Germany* (New York: Oxford University Press, 1994).
16. Henry Ford, *Mein Leben und Werk*, (6. ed., Leipzig: Paul List, 1923).
17. Ford 1923, chapter. VIII (Quotation from p. 149).
18. See Sachse, *Betriebliche Sozialpolitik*, chapters II und III; see also Carola Sachse, *Industrial Housewives. Women's Social Work in the Factories of Nazi Germany*. (New York: Institute for Research in History and the Haworth Press, 1987) (also in: *Women & History*, (1987), No. 11/12).
19. Emil Lederer, 'Die deutsche Industrie im Weltkrieg', in: *Meyers Großes Konversations-Lexikon*. (6. edn, Kriegsnachtrag, Erster Teil, Leipzig/Vienna: Bibliographisches Institut, 1916) (Reprint 1920), pp. 416–19, here p. 418. A comprehensive lexicon article from J. Gerhard on rationalization in all sectors of the economy appeared 1929: *Handwörterbuch der Sozialwissenschaft*. (4. edn, Ergänzungsband, Jena 1929), pp. 708–817.
20. See for example the article by Fritz Giese, 'Rationalisierung', in F. Giese (ed.), *Handwörterbuch der Arbeitswissenschaft*. (Halle a. S., 1930), Vol. II, Columns. 3619–31 and his debate with Friedrich von Gottl-Ottlilienfeld, *Wirtschaft und Technik* (=Grundriß der Sozialökonomik, II. Abt.: Die natürlichen und technischen Beziehungen in der Wirtschaft, II. Teil), (2nd edn Tübingen, 1923) and *Ibid.*, *Vom Sinn der Rationalisierung*. (Jena, 1929).
21. See Carola Sachse, *Siemens, der Nationalsozialismus und die moderne Familie. Eine Untersuchung zur sozialen Rationalisierung in Deutschland im 20. Jahrhundert*. (Hamburg: Rasch und Röhring, 1990), pp. 27ff. On the 'Crisis of the work ethic' see: Joan Campbell, *Joy in Work, German Work. The National Debate, 1800–1945*. (Princeton, NJ: Princeton University Press, 1989).
22. On the ambivalent hopes of rationalization above all among the German left, see Atina Grossmann, *Reforming Sex. The German Movement for Birth Control and Abortion Reform. 1920–1950*. (Oxford: Oxford University Press, 1995), esp. chapters 4 and 5. There is a similar oscillation between fascination and criticism of the strategies of domination and control in Antonio Gramsci, 'Amerikanismus und Fordismus', in A. Gramsci, *Philosophie der Praxis. Eine Auswahl*. (Frankfurt a. M.: Fischer Verlag, 1967), pp. 376–404. See also Siegel 'It's only Rational', pp. 45–8.
23. On those rationalization institutions closely linked to industry, see Sachse *Betriebliche Sozialpolitik*, pp. 67–72 and Nolan 1994.
24. Erich Lilienthal, 'Rationalisierung des Privatlebens', in *Der Arbeitgeber* (1928) 9211f.
25. See Sachse, *Siemens*, pp. 27–35.
26. Gustav Großmann, *Sich selbst rationalisieren. Mit Mindestaufwand persönliche Bestleistung erzeugen*. (Stuttgart, 1927); Erna Meyer, *Der neue Haushalt. Ein Wegweiser zu wirtschaftlicher Haushaltsführung*. (Stuttgart, 1926, 29th edn 1928, 41st edn 1932); Theodoor Hendrik Van de Velde, *Die vollkommene Ehe*. (65th edn Rüschlikon-Zürich: Zurich, 1926).
27. The following remarks are based on: Carola Sachse, 'Anfänge der Rationalisierung der Hausarbeit. "The One Best Way of Doing Anything..."', in:

Haushaltsträume. Ein Jahrhundert Technisierung und Rationalisierung im Haushalt, ed. Barbara Orland (Arbeitsgemeinschaft Hauswirtschaft e.V. and Stiftung Verbraucherinstitut; Königstein im Taunus, 1990), pp. 49–61.

28. For more detail here and for comprehensive references to literature on the rationalization of houswework, see Karen Hagemann, 'Of "Old" and "New" Housewives: Everyday Housework and the Limits of Household Rationalization in the Urban Working-Class Milieu of the Weimar Republic', *International Review of Social History*, 41 (1996), 305–30.
29. Bruno Taut, *Die neue Wohnung. Die Frau als Schöpferin*, (3rd edn, Leipzig, 1925) (1st edn 1924).
30. Internationales Arbeitsamt (ed.), *Die sozialen Auswirkungen der Rationalisierung. Einführende Studien, Studien und Berichte, Reihe B (Wirtschaft und Arbeit)*, No. 18. (Geneva: ILO, 1932), p. 1.
31. Barbara Orland, 'Effizienz im Heim. Die Rationalisierungsdebatte zur Reform der Hausarbeit in der Weimarer Republik', *Kultur und Technik. Zeitschrift des deutschen Museums in München*, (1983) 4 221–7, here p. 226.
32. Meyer, 1928, pp. 71ff.
33. Quoted from Orland, 1983, p. 224.
34. This terminology stems from 1919 Claire Richter, *Das Ökonomiat*. (Berlin, 1919), p. 28; see Hiltraud Schmidt-Waldherr, 'Rationalisierung der Hausarbeit in den zwanziger Jahren', in: Gerda Tornieporth (ed.), *Arbeitsplatz Haushalt. Zur Theorie und Ökologie der Hausarbeit*. (Berlin: Reimer Verlag, 1988), pp. 32–54, here p. 42.
35. See Grossmann, *Reforming Sex*, pp. 3–13.
36. The article 'Rationalisierung des Arbeiterhaushalts' appeared in *Hamburger Echo*, No. 76, 17. 3. 1929, here cited from Hagemann 'Of "Old" and "New" Housewives', p. 305.
37. The complex German efforts at rationalization in the first half of the century find their closest analogy in the USA to the various efforts at Americanization by diverse social policy makers. See Atina Grossmann, 'Gender and Rationalization: Questions about the German–American Comparison', *Social Politics*, 4 1 (1997) 6–18.
38. See the comprehensive description of the policy of the sexual advisory centres in Grossmann, *Reforming Sex*, chapters. 2 and 3.
39. On analogies with the body in the social policy discussions of the time, see for example the lecture of the head of one of the biggest German companies of 1917, Carl Friedrich von Siemens, 'Die Bedeutung der Wohnungsfrage für die Industrie', in: *Großstadt und Kleinhaus. Vorträge und Verhandlungen der 3. Huaptversammlung des Groß-Berliner Vereins für Kleinwohnungswesen am 6.2.1917 im Rathause der Stadt Berlin*. (Berlin 1917), pp. 3–11; see Sachse 1990, pp. 149–51.
40. For a detailed analysis of racism as Nazi social policy see Sachse, *Siemens*, pp. 42–7.
41. Grossmann, *Reforming Sex*, chapters 5 and 6.
42. The following is based on a study of company housing, Carola Sachse, 'Werkswohnungsbau und betriebsinterne Arbeitsmarktpolitik in Deutschland von 1880 bis 1945'. *Studien zur Geschichte betriebsinterner Arbeitsmärkte in Deutschland, Teil 2, Arbeitspapiere aus dem Arbeitskreis Sozialwissenschaftliche Arbeitsmarktforschung (SAMF) 1994–3*. (Gelsenkirchen 1994), pp. 48–76.
43. *RKW-Nachrichten*, (1931) Nr. 11, Sonderbeilage. The questionnaire is reproduced in: Sachse 1994, S. 53f.

44. For a detailed account, see Gabriele Czarnowski, *Das kontrollierte Paar. Ehe- und Sexualpolitik im Nationalsozialismus.* (Weinheim: Deutsche Studien-Verlag, 1991). On compulsory sterilization, see Gisela Bock, *Zwangssterilisation im Nationalsozialismus. Studien zur Rassenpolitik und zur Frauenpolitik.* (Opladen: Westdeutscher Verlag, 1986).
45. Timothy W. Mason, 'Zur Lage der Frauen in Deutschland 1930 bis 1940: Wohlfahrt, Arbeit und Familie', *Gesellschaft. Beiträge zur Marxschen Theorie 6,* (Frankfurt/M., 1976), pp. 118–93, here p. 120, 179 (An English version can be found in, 'Women in Nazi Germany, 1925–1940: Family, Welfare and Work', *History Workshop*, 1 & 2, (1976).
46. Helmut Schelsky, *Wandlungen der Familie in der Gegenwart. Darstellung und Deutung einer empirisch-soziologischen Tatbestandsaufnahme.* (2nd edn, Stuttgart: Enke Verlag, 1954).
47. The following remarks are drawn from Kleßmann, *Doppelte Staatsgründung,* particularly chapter. II 'Die Zusammenbruchsgesellschaft'.
48. Gerhard Wurzbacher, *Leitbilder gegenwärtigen deutschen Familienlebens, Methoden, Ergebnisse und sozialpädagogische Folgerungen einer soziologischen Analyse von 164 Familienmonographien.* (Dortmund: Ardey Verlag, 1951). See also Sibylle Meyer and Eva Schulze, *Auswirkungen des II. Weltkriegs auf Familien. Zum Wandel der Familie in Deutschland.* (Berlin: Technische Universität-Berlin, 1989), pp. 79–94.
49. These are the conclusions of Dagmar Reese, *'Straff, aber nicht stramm – Herb, aber nicht derb'. Zur Vergesellschaftung von Mädchen durch den Bund Deutscher Mädel im sozialkulturellen Vergleich zweier Milieus.* (Weinheim: Beltz-Verlag, 1989).
50. Meyer and Schulze, *Auswirkungen des II. Weltkriegs*, p. 394.
51. Hans Grewe, 'Die arbeitsgerichtliche Rechtsprechung zum Gesetz des Landes Nordrhein-Westfalen über den Hausarbeitstag für erwerbstätige Frauen mit eigenem Hausstand. Eine kritische Untersuchung über die Anwendung der Prinzipien für die Rechtsfindung und Rechtsfortbildung durch die Gerichte', (jur. Diss., Freiburg i.B. 1968). On the political and trade union debate see Carola Sachse, 'Ein "heißes Eisen". Ost- und westdeutsche Debatten um den Hausarbeitstag', in: Gunilla-Friederike Budde (ed.), *Frauenarbeiten. Weibliche Erwerbstätigkeit in Ost- und Westdeutschland nach 1945.* (Göttingen: Vandenhoeck und Ruprecht, 1997), pp. 252–85.
52. Bundesarchiv Koblenz, B 106/7352, Bl. 300 (Letter from Frau K. to the Federal Interior Ministry, 7.5.1958) ; See. Sachse, 'Ein "heißes Eisen"', p. 272.
53. Hauptstaatsarchiv Düsseldorf, NW 285–32, Bl. 188 (Letter from Frau P. to the Interior Ministry of North-Rhine Westphalia, 28. 11. 1961).
54. Lutz Niethammer, 'Privat-Wirtschaft. Erinnerungsfragmente einer anderen Umerziehung', in. Niethammer (ed.), *'Hinterher merkt man, daß es richtig war, daß es schief gegangen ist.' Nachkriegserfahrungen im Ruhrgebiet. Lebensgeschichte und Sozialkultur im Ruhrgebiet 1930 bis 1960*, vol. 2. (Berlin, Bonn: J. W. W. Dietz Verlag, 1983), pp. 17–105, here p. 54.
55. In similar vein, Maier 'Conditions', p. 349: 'Harder to measure, but just as important, was the yearning for private goals in countries where Fascists had sought to politicize all aspirations and relationships.'
56. Axel Schildt, *Moderne Zeiten. Freizeit, Massenmedien und 'Zeitgeist' in der Bundesrepublik der 50er Jahre,* (Hamburg: Christians Verlag, 1995), p. 450.

C. Between Post-Materialism and the End of the Cold War

9

1968/1989: Social Movements in Italy Reconsidered

Robert Lumley

This chapter will consider social movements in Italy in relation to two key dates in postwar European history – 1968 and 1989. Through an analysis of the main features of those movements it will focus on the continuities and breaks in the forms of oppositional politics for the period concerned. In broad terms, the argument will be that 1968 ushered in a period of left-inspired movements that were active until the beginning of the 1980s. The decade that followed witnessed a general decline in mobilization and oppositional politics in Italy as in other European countries. But by 1989 a strong current of regionalist and autonomist politics had developed. This, in the case of the Leagues of Northern Italy, had distinct social movement components but these combined with party organization and charismatic leadership to produce an identifiably right-wing populism. '1989' provided an international frame of reference for an oppositional politics with forms in part analogous to those of the previous decade but one that put particularism in the place of universalism and difference in the place of equality.

I

If 1989 marked the end of the Cold War, 1968 represented an important moment of transition with respect to the *status quo* of the postwar settlement. On the one hand, there was a revival of older political forms – a reversion to Cold War scenarios of confrontation; on the other, signs of new forms that did not fit into the existing repertoire. Italy was a key European country in the waging of the Cold War because of the borders with Yugoslavia, the sheer size of the Italian Communist Party, and the role of Rome as the centre of the Roman Catholic faith.[1]

It was not surprising, therefore, that the events of 1968 and the Hot Autumn of workers' action of 1969 had such repercussions. The strategy of tension initiated by the Piazza Fontana bomb of December 1969, the plans for *coup d'état*, and the manipulation of the terrorist emergency in the late 1970s all contributed to conserving the dominance of the Christian Democrats in a political deep-freeze. At the same time, this period was also characterized by counter-tendencies that cut across the red/white sub-cultural divide. The emergence of the women's movement and the referendum votes in favour of divorce (1974) and abortion (1981) signalled the decline of Church influence. Secularization was accompanied by a growing sense that religious belief was a personal matter. Meanwhile the affirmation of the 'consumer society' undermined the Communist project of cultural hegemony.[2] Signs of fragmentation within both the Catholic and Communist 'worlds' were further indicators of a weakening of those loyalties that were to go into crisis after 1989. It is to 1968, moreover, that accounts have dated the origins of the spirit of independence among magistrates, the professional group that did most to attack the citadels of 'partitocrazia' in 1992.

1968 also has a longer-term historical significance. As Charles Maier has observed, it signalled the end of Taylorism and Socialism as models and the beginning of the 'postmodern' era. The May events in France spelt this change more clearly than conflicts in Italy, with Guy Debord's *Society of the Spectacle* of 1967[3] prophesying the new era. Although in Italy much of the oppositional political discourse at the time sprang out of a preoccupation with the factory as the organizing force of society, it was from this moment in time that the factory was to lose its central place. What we have therefore is a date that has become a metaphor, condensing change at a number of levels – social, political, and symbolic – into a composite image.

For the purposes of this chapter, the focus will be on the 'new social movements' associated with 1968. The new social movements, as they are called in the sociological literature, first emerged in the United States with the movement for civil rights, the women's and gay movements, and the ecology movement.[4] Each movement is obviously a complex and variegated phenomenon in its own right. An adequate historical analysis would have to enter into their specific characteristics; as Judith Adler Hellman has shown for feminism in Italy, the situation of women in Caserta, just south of Naples, was very different from that of their sisters in Milan.[5]

However, this analysis will follow Ron Eyerman and Andrew Jamison in using a comparative approach centred on the concept of 'cognitive space' and 'public space'. For Eyerman and Jamison, the 1960s movements 'opened a space for the later movements to fill with specific meanings'. The migration of ideas and activists between forms of activity made it a differentiated but shared political space, a space created *partly* through reaction to earlier 'old movements', which had become institutionalized, *partly* through innovation and experimentation leading to redefinitions of what was called 'politics'.[6]

This process can be understood in relation to critiques in three areas – the routinization of politics, institutionalization of knowledge, and the idea of progress. The questioning of the routinization and professionalization of politics concerned the language of politics that had become a discourse internal to the political class and impervious to popular opinion. In Italy the circumlocution and complex rhetoric of politicians required the kind of decoding practised by Kremlinologists.[7] Decision-making likewise appeared as remote and representatives as unaccountable. Indeed, as the history of the centre left demonstrated, coalition governments successively avoided taking divisive decisions whenever possible.[8] The absence in political discourse of precise programmes harmonized with this procrastination. Politics was identified with political parties; even in the PCI, which remained in opposition, the organization in the 1960s was increasingly dominated by full-timers for whom it was a career. The contemporary debate about the apathy and de-politicization of youth marked unease at the perceived gap between representatives and represented.[9] Membership and participation in parties and unions was worryingly in decline. Subsequent studies have spoken of 1968–9 in terms of a 'crisis of representation'.[10]

The mobilizations of 1968 and the industrial action of the Hot Autumn were in large measure anti-party, anti-state movements. For the students, the PCI represented centralism, the PSI (Socialists) another party of government, and parliamentary democracy a denial of grass-roots democracy. The refusal to delegate ('we are all delegates') and the sovereignty of the general meeting were hailed as bringing back the *agora* into public life. Norberto Bobbio, reflecting on this experience, wrote:

> Democracy is subversive in the most radical sense of the word, because, wherever it spreads, it subverts the traditional conception of power, one so traditional it has come to be considered natural, based on the assumption that power – i.e. political or economic, paternal or sacerdotal – flows downwards. By conceiving of power flowing upwards, democracy is in some ways more subversive than socialism,

> if we use 'socialism' in the limited sense of transfer of ownership of the means of production.[11]

In the case of the workers, there was a turn towards the unions and away from the parties. The unions, moreover, were reformed with greater powers going to newly constituted factory councils. A process accompanied by theorizations that counterposed direct democracy and self-management to bureaucracy and hierarchy. A utopian and council communist tradition, associated in Italy with the young Gramsci, underwent a rapid revival.

This moment of democratization in which the professional politicians and officials were spectators was short-lived, a phase in social movements that the sociologist Francesco Alberoni baptized '*statu nascenti*'.[12] But while it lasted, the protagonists were vociferous. Freedom of speech in places, such as factories and offices where it was denied to trade unionists, was established by taking direct action. It is not by chance that political satire in Italy was reborn in the midst of this babble, opening up a new symbolic battlefield in which official discourses were put under systematic attack.[13] Nor was it an accident that the libertarian politics of the following decade developed a new awareness of the relationship between power, identity and language. The individual as well as the collective subject entered the scene under the aegis of the slogan 'the personal is political'.[14]

The critique of the institutionalization and specialization of knowledge relates closely to the theme of democratization. The political class's monopolization of politics was seen to be part of a wider tendency within 'neo-capitalism' towards the effective disenfranchisement of the masses. It was thought to be visible in the factory, where the worker was reduced to a set of simple physical movements, in the school, where the disadvantaged pupils were labelled ignorant, and in asylums, where mental patients were treated as purely physiological beings. These 'institutions' became the target of social movements that championed subjectivity and the liberation of individuality in the face of the objectivity of science and the rule of the experts. In Italy figures such as Franco Basaglia became emblems of a revolt that was not only against the paternalist and repressive state as such but against the social and ideological constructs that legitimated its powers.[15] New forms of self-knowledge (as developed, for instance, by feminist 'consciousness-raising') and the valorization of forms of knowledge deemed exotic, irrational or archaic led to the creation of alternative practices, especially in relationship to the treatment of the human body.

The ideals of progress and modernity revived during the postwar long boom underwent severe criticisms after 1968. Already the diffusion of Frankfurt School Marxism and the persistence of Catholic social thought fed scepticism about the benefits of material progress and the neutrality of science and technology. But these ideas were perhaps more widespread in the student movement, and subsequently in the women's and ecology movements, which had a predominance of activists of middle-class origin, than among workers many of whom could only afford a car thanks to successful strikes following the Hot Autumn. It is the activists of the student movement who are crucial in constituting that differentiated but shared public space that the new social movements occupy. Indeed, ecological politics in Italy developed a critique of industrialism and Marxism that signalled the end of the hegemony of the traditional left parties and trade unions.[16] Their hegemony had been affirmed in 1968–9, even if in retrospect the recycling of the repertoire, from the red flag to the political vocabulary, looks distinctly 'postmodern'.[17] By the end of the following decade, with the movement of 1977 marking the break, the older political framework was held in place by exceptional circumstances of the anti-terrorism emergency. The older forms of identification according to class and religious belief were ceasing to be the bases for political mobilization.

By the early 1980s the cycle of protest that had begun in the late 1960s was at an end. The experience of terrorism culminating in the assassination of Aldo Moro, the defeat of the Fiat workers' occupation in 1980, the crisis of Marxism and disillusionment on the left, and the electoral decline of the PCI marked the demise of a politics of social solidarity.[18] The abolition of wage indexation following a referendum in 1985 highlighted the loss of influence of the trade unions whose memberships went into steep decline with the acceleration of restructuring, automation and relocation. Meanwhile the 'Third Italy' of small and medium sized companies looked distinctly healthier than the large corporations that had traditionally headed the Confindustria.[19] Political defeat and economic reorganization paved the way for the Leagues. But while these declared their contempt for 1968 and all it represented, there were links and continuities that need to be noted.

II

The biographies of two leaders of the Lega Lombarda are a case in point. Roberto Maroni, who was a student activist in 1968, abandoned the left in 1979 because of a feeling that it was 'destined not to lose but not to win'. Yet he claims that, 'blasphemous though it might seem, I believe my decision was consistent. I kept faith with the idea of wanting to make a revolution because in Italy replacing the Christian Democrats in government, bringing down the regime that had lasted since 1946, is a revolution'.[20] Umberto Bossi, who was to convert Maroni to his ideas on regional autonomy, read Marcuse and absorbed the political debates of the New Left in the 1970s as an onlooker. But he too acquired a belief in grass-roots movements as the only viable vehicle for bringing about change. Bossi's earliest political acts – writing graffiti, producing and distributing leaflets, drawing up manifestos – were learnt from this ambience. Likewise his shock tactics derive from the example of movements not parties.[21]

There are undoubtedly elements in the anti-system, anti-state, anti-Christian Democrat rhetoric of the 1970s movements that carried over, but more important than the contents of the political discourse is the process of constructing new identities they manifested. Whereas the main parties depended on core constituencies and the loyalty of the so called '*voto di appartenza*', the new social movements invented hitherto unimagined identities based on gender, sexual preference and ecological awareness. This freedom of symbolic elaboration was not created by them and has to be related to wider social processes encouraging the need for self-realization.[22] Yet these movements played a key role in producing new cultural codes. In this perspective, the invention of a Lombard identity with its medieval warrior symbol is consonant with the possibilities already exploited by ecological activists in creating myths. The televisualization of politics in the 1980s contributed considerably to the staging of events like the gathering at Pontida to celebrate the defeat of Emperor Barbarossa by the united communes of the Carroccio. It was paradoxical, as Adrian Lyttelton has pointed out, that just as Italians were becoming more unified in their habits, tastes and language due to the penetration of the mass media, the spread of consumer culture and massive interregional migration, such importance should be attached to cultural differences.[23] The Lega Lombarda, along with the other five leagues operating in Northern Italy, developed its own rudimentary means of communication independently and in opposition to the national media. Yet their radical attacks on the media *both* helped to reinforce a sense of Them and Us on the part of the Leagues *and* helped maximize coverage thereby giving them a much higher public profile. The apparent crudeness of the 'barbarians' disguised effective news manipulation in reverse.

However, much more striking is the reaction against the post-1968 movements. Bossi's own use of sexist, homophobe and racist expressions were a violent assault on the sensibilities of those who identified themselves with feminism, gay politics or egalitarian values more generally. His was the blunt and colourful language of the bar room, not the politesse of the political class. Resort to dialect was also a way of speaking in the words of his people rather than in those of the '*Palazzo*' or Establishment.[24] The new social movements were generically anti-capitalist. Capitalism was thought to create material and social inequalities, regional imbalance (not to say Northern exploitation of the South), destruction of the natural environment, and cultural homogenization and uniformity. The principles of the redistribution of wealth and the abolition of forms of discrimination tied them, albeit involuntarily, to the unitary state. Above all, economics had to be subordinated to political decision-making for the common good. In its way, the New Left too subscribed to the project of 'making Italians'.

The Leagues, on the other hand, espoused a post-ideological neo-materialism based on free market ideas and the work ethic of the small businessman.[25] A hard-headed realism was counterposed to utopian alternatives. This was tellingly revealed by a document on educational reform that aimed to 'bring back a school that prepares young people for work and for the professions without indulging in experiments that create demotivation and the failure to adapt to the rules of our civilization'.[26] As for redistribution, League proposals demanded direct regional control to ensure that taxes went to the producers of wealth and not to 'parasites' in the form of politicians, state bureaucrats and the non-productive South. Inequality, in this view, was a natural condition, and material affluence a sign of virtue. There were certainly no alternatives to capitalism.

This neo-Calvinism was not invented by the Lega Lombarda: rather it represented sets of assumptions that were distinctive to the communities produced by an industrialization accompanied by limited urbanization and continuity with the old rural economy that ensured minimal social conflict and disruption. It was a different route to modernization to that of the cities of the industrial triangle. The new social movements had their strongholds in the major cities in whose universities their activists were educated in lay ideas and where cultural diversity and cosmopolitanism were celebrated. Here, by contrast, in Lombardy and the Veneto of small-scale industry, communities were traditionally tight-knit, inward looking, suspicious of outsiders, and bound by a strong sense of place.[27] When the ecology movement introduced questions of environment into politics it did so within a universalist discourse with little capacity to mobilize. It was simply too inclusive and abstract. By contrast, the Leagues in their formative years 1983–7 began by evoking an imaginary community based on differences and particularities of language, custom and tradition that overtly excluded those that did not belong. 'The identity, which was otherwise impossible to pin down, was defined in relation to enemies from whom it had to be protected. One is Lombard, Piedmontese or from the Veneto in being against Rome, against the national parties, against the State, against Southerners, against immigrants, against drug addicts, against homosexuals and so on'.[28]

The importance of exclusionary mechanisms to the construction of identity brings into focus the role of the Lega Lombarda and Lega Nord as political actor or 'political entrepreneur' to use Diamanti's term.[29] Rather than seeing the new identity as a something that already existed but needing to be articulated politically, this approach stresses the agency of the movement itself in bringing that identity into being. This helps explain the Lega's capacity for metamorphosis, notably its continuous redefinition of what it represented. In its initial phase the definition was essentialist – 'you are where you were born'. Ethnicity was understood culturally rather than genetically but there was a racist subtext that characterized Southerners as being imbued with *mafiosità*. Subsequently, as electoral support extended beyond the heartlands, belonging was defined principally in terms of a community of economic interests. Membership was opened to people with five years residence, whatever their origins. Bossi's model was that of an anti-institutional party in which symbolic elements were played down and instrumental ones privileged, in contrast to the Liga Veneta's ethno-regionalism.[30]

The effectiveness of the Leagues as a political force contrasts with the relative electoral weakness of the new social movements. Symptomatically, the latter stemmed from a left that called itself 'extraparliamentary' and only stood candidates as a propaganda exercise. Their activity centred on workplaces, educational institutions and neighbourhoods and they saw the 'old left' as the parliamentarism's prisoner. Going one step further, feminists and ecological activists theorized a micropolitics in which changes in attitudes and situations would be brought about within civil society. Theirs was a cultural politics that treated political parties as antithetical to change by their very nature. They adopted loose structures based on federations of independent often *ad hoc* bodies as opposed to the democratic centralism.[31] Umberto Bossi, on the other hand, pursued a strategy that was akin to a reversion to Leninism. As the charismatic leader who exercised iron control over the movement, he established a party with collateral organizations for workers, farmers and youth in the manner of the old PCI. Annual congresses were plebiscitary.

Membership was rigorously supervised to prevent infiltration and the formation of factions. Inspired political opportunism not ideological coherence characterized a leadership that claimed to speak for the people and against the *Palazzo*.[32] Whereas the Christian Democrats arose in postwar Italy in the context of an established Catholic subculture, the Leagues, which emerged in the very same areas, were a political organization first and foremost. It is true that there was the establishment of cultural associations, such as the Venetian Philological Society, in the 1970s, but the movement developed in the following decade through participation in elections and the mobilization of existing networks of family, friends, professional associations and sports clubs. The electoral successes then led to the setting up of an organization with its own headquarters and personnel.

The record of mounting successes created a momentum and the sensation that history was on their side. Standing in the local elections in 1985 the Lega Lombarda won seats in Varese and Gallarate. In the June 1987 it won a seat in each house and 3 per cent of the vote in the seven constituencies it contested for the Chamber of Deputies. In the 1989 European elections it received 6.5 per cent of the vote in Lombardy and in the 1990 regional elections the share had risen to 16.4 per cent. Geographically it was strongest in the small and medium sized towns, reaching 20.8 per cent in Varese and 20 per cent in Brescia as against 12.9 per cent in Milan. At the general elections in 1992, now part of the Lega Nord, it got 8.7 per cent of the national vote for the Chamber of Deputies while in Lombardy it totaled 20.5 per cent, making it the largest party in Northern Italy. In June 1993 it became the largest party in the Milan City Council with its candidate Marco Formentini elected mayor.[33]

The dramatic support for the League between 1987 and 1990 was due to a haemorrhaging of votes from the Christian Democrat Party. Already there were strong indications that traditional loyalties were under strain. However, the collapse of Communism in Eastern Europe and the PCI leader's call to abandon the party name in order to make clear its democratic credentials swiftly removed the threat of the enemy without and within against whom the Christian Democrats had offered protection since 1947.[34] There was no longer sufficient reason to 'hold your nose and vote DC' or to follow the counsel of the parish priest regarding political allegiances. For the League the events presented a historic opportunity which it was well positioned to exploit. The activists of the new social movements had become largely marginalized. In Germany, the paralysis of the German Greens when faced with German unification was symptomatic of the inability of the wider ecology movement to grapple with non-environmental political issues. The PCI was riven with internal disputes, and the parties of government tried to carry on as if nothing had changed.[35]

In the shorter term, the impact of the Lega was visible in the crisis of the First Republic. Crucially, the Lega was the most articulate actor in denouncing corruption and financial mismanagement just when monetary affairs were put to the top of the political agenda by external pressures. The Maastricht Treaty on monetary union of December 1991, which set down strict guidelines on inflation and government debt, highlighted the parlous state of public finances. Then in February 1992 the Milanese magistrates arrested the Socialist Mario Chiesa, setting in motion the *tangentopoli* scandals which within a couple of years saw three out of four politicians of the governing parties charged with criminal activities. As has been seen, the Lega championed the values of thrift and hard work that were perfectly antithetical to the immorality of the corrupt politicians. Although the magistrates acted independently, it is arguable that they could only do so without political impediment because of the climate of opinion in 1992 that meant that 20 per cent of the voters in Lombardy supported the Lega.[36] Whether the destruction of the Christian Democrat and Socialist Parties constituted a 'revolution' is obviously questionable. After 1968 there was a 'kind of social revolution', particularly with respect to women's position in society; after 1989 there was a 'kind of political revolution' in that a political class was virtually destroyed. But the word 'revolution' is used here in a weak sense and has lost its classic meaning of overthrow of a state and a social class. Instead, it borrows the language of the protagonists themselves to refer to a process of accelerated change within the framework of parliamentary democracy, itself a significant development within a country that in the twentieth century had experienced incipient civil war.

III

What was new after 1989 was that issues the League had previously raised on the periphery now entered the mainstream. It was able to link its own destiny to greater historical developments. The end of the Cold War and the ensuing thaw brought to the surface realities long hidden or suppressed as if natural forces had been released from under the ice. Small nations, like those of the Baltic States, re-emerged. Maps were being re-drawn, streets renamed, statues pulled down, memories voiced, and histories re-written. Assumptions about what was durable and what was ephemeral, what artificial and what authentic were suddenly called into question. Above all it was a moment for movements struggling against one-party states. Class politics and egalitarianism were associated with the *ancien régime*, not with utopias as in 1968.[37]

The events of 1989 could be read in very different ways. At the time the benign aspects of nationalism were uppermost and the destructive ones revealed in Yugoslavia in 1992 not yet apparent. What is important here is to show the way that the League was able to make connections between the international and domestic situation in order to set political and cultural agendas. Arguably the Eastern European analogy was forced; Italy had after all been a parliamentary democracy since 1945. But that did not stop talk of a regime in the form of a *partitocrazia* with its own *nomenklatura*. Nor did it stop the League from identifying itself with the revolt of civil society against an overweening state. Crucially the League was able to open up a debate about Italian history that questioned the orthodoxies. Already in 1986 Senator Spadolini's visit to celebrate the centenary of the inclusion of the Veneto in the united Italy had met with protests from the Venetian League and claims that the plebiscite had been rigged. In April 1990 Franco Rocchetta, leader of the Liga Veneta, returned to the theme, equating the annexation of the Veneto to that of Lithuania in 1940 and calling Garibaldi the Risorgimento equivalent of Renato Curcio of the Red Brigades. National unification was criticized not because it was a 'failed revolution' or defective but as the imposition of an artificial political order from outside.[38]

Apart from the polemics, there was an intellectual struggle in the making. The League had an ideologue and political theorist in Gianfranco Miglio, professor at the Catholic University of Milan. Miglio played an important part in reviving interest in federalist thought, re-reading Carlo Cattaneo and translating American writings by Hamilton and others.[39] A tradition that had previously been associated with the 'losers' – fascinating, but marginalized by the march of History – was now seen as having anticipated the decline and fall of nation-states. The regional movements, far from being the remnants of older formations, prefigured a future political organization of society. In the case of Italy, Miglio proposed a tripartite division into macroregions of Padania, Etruria and Sud.

These formulations were much criticized and derided for their artificiality and Miglio himself resigned from the Lega Nord when he found his utopian ideas not being adopted by the leadership. However, it is worth bearing in mind how mental maps create and consolidate divisions: the cartography that helped develop a sense of Italy as a unitary nation was being undermined by alternative maps that circulated in the manner of 'urban myths'.[40]

The very fact that the newspapers discussed the question of Italian national identity on an almost daily basis reflected the Lega's success in agenda-setting and the uncertainties of a national political culture whose founding myth was the Resistance. Claudio Magris, the Trestine novelist, wrote on the front page of *Il Corriere della Sera* in November 1993:

> For some time now, one has had the almost tangible sensation that for the first time the country may disintegrate and that very soon Italy – as a political and thus cultural entity – may cease to exist. This is extremely bewildering because Italy, for all the cancerous growths now thankfully being exposed, is our reality and imagining something different is difficult and unacceptable. Every day the papers are filled with a crescendo of news of decomposition, disintegration and erosion affecting the central nervous system of the country, leading to an inflation and devaluation of information itself.[41]

It was, he said, like the situation of a person so preoccupied about overcoming his insomnia that he struggles to get any sleep. The problem was to counteract a tendency that was assuming day by day an air of inevitability.

Whether the actions of the Lega spelled the beginning of the end of the Italian nation state is a matter for speculation. Commentators observed that several factors have concurred to make the Lega into a 'normal' political actor. First, electoral successes drew it into increasingly into a national political framework and into practices such as forming alliances and coalitions typical of party politics in Italy.[42] Second, it threatened to use tactics such as non-payment of taxes but preferred symbolic gestures to concerted lawbreaking. Third, its attempts to create a macroregional identity faced internal divisions within the movements not to mention resistance from an entrenched legacy of 'micro' identities of a municipal and local nature. Finally, the Roman Catholic Church, an enemy of the united Italy from its inception in 1860, has continued to assume positions favourable to the unitary state and critical of the Lega even after the demise of the Christian Democrat Party.

On the other hand, the Lega has consistently confounded expectations in the 1990s that it would be integrated into the existing political framework. It maintained consistent electoral support in the 1994 and 1997 general elections. In the first, it obtained about 8 per cent of valid votes, which translated into 106 seats in the Chamber of Deputies thanks to the deal done with its electoral allies. In 1997 the League got fewer seats (59 in the Chamber of Deputies, 27 in the Senate) but its vote rose in the North, replacing Forza Italia as the biggest party in Lombardy. Commentators had predicted that its moment had passed, but the adoption of a more radical tone in favour of secession paid political dividends. Although it formed a government with Forza Italia and Alleanza Nazionale in April 1994 it brought that government down the following December. For the rest of the 1990s, according to Walter Veltroni of the Democratic Party of the Left, it pursued a strategy that would provoke the secession of the North from the nation. Far from trying to promote reform of the institutions, through participation in them, it has cynically disrupted proceedings from within.[43] Moreover, symbolic acts, such as the proclamation of the founding of the Republic of the North, the occupation of the *campanile* of St Mark's in Venice on 5 May1997, and the call for the election of a constituent assembly in Padania in August 1997, had serious objectives. In the words of Ilvo Diamanti, 'With the election of a parliament in Padania the Lega is in the process of constructing a plan of legitimation with respect to that State. The electoral ritual forms the threshold, the creation of a "counter-power" that challenges the official one by mimicking its forms and mechanisms. And that makes the Lega community even more estranged from the national state.'[44]

IV

The politics of the Lega has thrown into relief and challenged the consensus about the nature of the Italian state established between 1945 and 1948. The Constituent Assembly elected in June 1946 drew up a Constitution that laid down the political ground-rules accepted by the parties. After two decades of dictatorship followed by a war in which Italy was divided into warring states, there was fundamental agreement over the need to forge national unity and prevent the emergence of civil war. It was symptomatic that the common credo – anti-Fascism – to which all the parties subscribed (with the exception of the neo-Fascist Movimento Sociale Italiano) was defined in the negative. There were severe limits to cooperation. Yet the replacement of Fascism by Communism as the enemy drew attention away from the consensual aspects of the relationship that developed between government and left opposition. While the anti-communism of the Cold War ensured that the PCI would not enter government, their electoral strength made it necessary to include them in the decision-making process. A form of consensus politics was elaborated in order to prevent the deep ideological cleavages in society from giving rise to dangerous social and political conflicts. The term '*consociativismo*' was later used by political scientists to describe this arrangement.[45]

In 1968–9 there was a rebellion against this conduct of politics. The political parties, including the PCI, were by-passed by the social movements. However, the language of that protest shared much of the vocabulary and many of the frames of reference created by the left in the wake of 1945. The PCI was criticized for its failure to live up to the ideals of the Resistance, and the Republic under Christian Democratic leadership was accused of maintaining laws and institutions inherited from the Fascist period. A touchstone in this respect was the South. If there were disagreements over how the Southern Question was to be solved, there was consensus across the whole political spectrum that state intervention was desirable.[46]

It is in the context of this consensual politics that the radicalism of the Lega can best be understood. '*Antimeridonalismo*', for instance, provided a perfect wedge with which to prize open the fragile unity of the dominant political discourse. Similarly, the attack on '*partitocrazia*' offered an opportunity for criticizing the very way the First Republic had been founded. The adoption of aggressive and uncivil language represented a further assault on the cosy world of a political class that included left and right.

Indeed the left/right dichotomy that had historically structured political discourse began to be called in question in unprecedented ways. It is true that the new social movements had anticipated this development but they had done so within a 'cognitive space' connoted as 'on the left'. The decision of the PCI to abandon its name, the foundation of Alleanza Nazionale and the invitation of the 'post-Fascists' into the political mainstream in the mayoral elections of autumn 1993, and the emergence of the leagues as a new force created a dramatic realignment in politics. Now the consensus had been enlarged to include the historic enemies of parliamentary democracy to both right and left. But the 'resolution' of the conflicts that had produced and maintained a Cold War which included a ferocious if marginal struggle between the political extremes resulted in a paradox – the removal or drastic diminution of the conflict also meant undermining the conditions that had secured consensual politics in Italy. The enlargement of consensus about the desirability of parliamentary democracy and the capitalist economic system took away the ideological cement that had held 'left' and 'right' in place and defined the political space. By an irony of history old political enemies now found themselves on the same side in the struggle to maintain the unity of the nation-state against the threat of secession – a possibility indicative of the degree to which the consensus necessary for a revision of the constitution has been eroded.

Notes

1. C. Duggan and C. Wagstaff (eds), *Italy in the Cold War: Politics, Culture and Society*. (Oxford: Berg, 1995); F. Romeo, 'Gli Stati Uniti in Italia: il piano Marshall e il Patto atlantico', in *Storia dell'Italia Repubblicana*, 1. (Turin: Einaudi, 1994) pp. 234–82.
2. S. Gundle, *I comunisti italiani tra Hollywood e Mosca: la sfida della cultura di massa*. (Florence: Giunti, 1995).
3. G. Debord, *The Society of the Spectacle*. (Detroit: Black and Red, 1977). (Original French text Paris: Buchet Castel, 1967).
4. M. Mayer and R. Roth, 'New Social Movements and the Transformation of Post-Fordist Society', in M. Darnovsky, B. Epstein and R. Flacks (eds), *Cultural Politics and Social Movements*. (Philadelphia: Temple University Press, 1995) pp. 299–320.
5. J. Cohen, 'Rethinking Social Movements', *Berkeley Journal of Sociology*, XXVIII (1995) 99–113; J. Adler Hellman, 'The Riddle of New Social Movements: Who are They, What They Do', in S. Halebsky and R. L. Harris (eds), *Capital, Power and Inequality in Latin America*. (Boulder CO: Westview Press, 1995) pp. 165–83.
6. R. Eyerman and A. Jamison, *Social Movements: A Cognitive Approach*. (Cambridge: Polity, 1991).
7. U. Eco, 'Political Language: The Use and Abuse of Rhetoric', in R. Lumley (ed.), *Apocalypse Postponed*. (Bloomington and London: Indiana University Press, 1994) pp. 75–86.
8. G. Tamburrano, *Storia e cronaca del centro sinistra*. (Milan: Biblioteca universale Rizzoli, 1990).
9. E. Capussotti, 'La rappresentazione della gioventù come metafora culturale: discorsi, discipline e giovani negli anni cinquanta in Italia', Unpublished paper, European University Institute, 1997.
10. For a theorization of this crisis, see A. Pizzorno, 'On Gramsci's Method', *First Italo-Hungarian Conference of Sociology*, 1967; for studies on the period, S. Tarrow, *Democracy and Disorder: Protest and Politics in Italy, 1965–75*. (Oxford: Clarendon, 1989); R. Lumley, *States of Emergency: Cultures of Revolt in Italy from 1968 to 1978*. (London: Verso, 1990).
11. N. Bobbio, 'Alternatives to Representative Democracy', in *Which Socialism?* (Cambridge: Polity, 1988) p. 74.
12. F. Alberoni, *Statu nascenti*. (Bologna: Il Mulino, 1966).
13. A. Chiesa, *La satira politica in Italia*. (Bari: Laterza, 1990).
14. L. Passerini, 'Gender Relations', in D. Forgacs and R. Lumley (eds), *Italian Cultural Studies*. (Oxford: Oxford University Press, 1996) pp. 144–59.
15. F. Basaglia, *L'istituzione negata*. (Turin: Einaudi, 1968); and *Morire di classe*. (Turin: Einaudi, 1969).
16. M. Diani, *Green Networks*. (Edinburgh: University of Edinburgh Press, 1995).
17. M. Perniola, *La società dei simulacri*. (Bologna: Cappelli, 1983).
18. G. De Luna, 'Dalla spontaneità all'organizzazione. La resistible ascesa della Lega di Bossi', in G. Della Luna (ed.), *Figli di un benessere minore. La Lega 1979–1993*. (Scandicci: La Nuova Italia, 1994) pp. 21–5.
19. A. Bagnasco, *Tre Italie. La problematica territoriale dello sviluppo italiano*. (Bologna: Il Mulino, 1977).

20. R. Maroni, 'Come la vedo io', in G. Pajetta, *Il grande camaleonte. Episodi, passioni, avventure del leghismo.* (Milan: Feltrinelli, 1994) p. 142.
21. U. Bossi (with D. Vimercati), *Vento del nord.* (Milan: Sperlong and Kupfer, 1992) p. 33.
22. In relation to the Lega, see C. Donegà, 'Strategie del presente. I volti della Lega' in G. Della Luna (ed.), *Figli di un benessere minore,* pp. 83–4; on the growth in importance of a politics of identity, see A. Melucci, *Altri codici.* (Bologna: Il Mulino, 1984).
23. A. Lyttelton, 'Shifting Identities: Nation, Region and City', in C. Levy (ed.), *Italian Regionalism. History, Identity and Politics.* (Oxford: Berg, 1996) p. 49.
24. P. Allum and I. Diamanti, 'The Autonomous Leagues in the Veneto', in C. Levy (ed.), *Italian Regionalism,* pp. 155–6.
25. A. Cento Bull, 'The Politics of Industrial Districts in Lombardy: Replacing Christian Democracy with the Northern League', *The Italianist,* 13 (1993) 209–29.
26. P. P. Poggio, 'Il naturalismo sociale e l'ideologia della Lega', in G. De Luna, *Figli di un benessere minore,* p. 160.
27. A. Cento Bull, 'Ethnicity, Racism and the Northern League', in C. Levy (ed.), *Italian Regionalism,* pp. 171–88.
28. G. De Luna, 'Dalla spontaneità all'organizzazione' in G. Della Luna (ed.), *Figli di un benessere minore,* pp. 58–9.
29. I. Diamanti, *La Lega: Geografia, storia e sociologia di un nuovo soggetto politico.* (Rome: Donzelli, 1993) p. xv.
30. P. Allum and I. Diamanti, 'The Autonomous Leagues in the Veneto', in C. Levy (ed.), *Italian Regionalism,* pp. 151–70.
31. D. Della Porta, *Movimenti collettivi e sistema politico in Italia, 1960–1995.* (Bari: Laterza, 1996) pp. 91–128.
32. I. Diamanti, *La Lega,* pp. 80–5.
33. J. Farrell and C. Levy, 'The Northern League: Conservative Revolution?', in C. Levy (ed.), *Italian Regionalism,* pp. 131–50.
34. M. Calise, *Dopo la partitocrazia.* (Turin: Einaudi, 1994) p. 139.
35. M. J. Bull, 'The PDS, the Progressive Alliance and the Crisis', *Modern Italy,* Autumn, 1 (1995) 30–9.
36. M. Donovan, 'The Referendum and the Transformation of the Party System', *Modern Italy,* Autumn, 1 (1995) 60–4; D. Della Porta, 'La capitale immorale: le tangenti di Milano', in S. Hellman and G. F. Pasquino (eds), *La politica in Italia.* (Bologna: Il Mulino, 1993).
37. S. Allievi, *Le parole della Lega.* (Milan: Garzanti, 1992), p. 38.
38. '[Franco Rocchetta] ritiene di avere un bel numero di frecce al proprio arco, grazie anche – dice – al crollo, del comunismo. Ed emerge così una catena di equazioni avventurose: il Veneto come la Lituania, l'annessione all'Italia come i patti Molotov–Ribbentrop e così via. Fino a Garibaldi come Renato Curcio e Mazzini come Toni Negri'; M. Bellu, 'La Liga contro i patrioti', *La Repubblica,* 20 April 1990.
39. For his political ideas, see G. F. Miglio, *Come cambiare. Le mie riforme.* (Milan: Mondadori, 1992); 'Io e la sinistra', *Micromega,* 2, 1992.
40. J. Dickie, 'Fantasy Maps', in D. Forgacs and R. Lumley (eds), *Italian Cultural Studies,* pp. 102–4; for an examination of the process whereby 'Padania' became 'normalized', see A. Destro, 'A New Era and New Themes in Italian Politics: the Case of Padania', *Journal of Modern Italian Studies,* 3 (1997) 358–77.

41. C. Magris, 'Ne' disgregazione ne' assuefazione', *Il Corriere della Sera*, 2 November 1993.
42. J. Agnew, 'The Rhetoric of Regionalism: the Northern League in Italian Politics, 1983–94', *Transactions of the Institute of British Geographers*, NS 20 (1995) 156–72.
43. W. Veltroni, 'Non si rompe l'Italia per un assessorato', *Il Corriere della Sera*, 19 August 1997.
44. Quoted in W. Veltroni, *ibid.*
45. A. Pizzorno, 'Le difficoltà del consociativismo', in *Le radici della politica assoluta.* (Milan: Feltrinelli, 1994) pp. 285–313; S. Fabbrini, 'The End of Consensual Politics in Italy', Paper delivered at the Conference 'Contesting the Boundaries of Italian Politics', Carleton University, Ottawa, Canada, 22–23 March 1996.
46. G. Gribaudi, 'The Mezzogiorno Seen Through the Eyes of Insiders and Outsiders', in R. Lumley and J. Morris (eds), *The New History of the Italian South: The Mezzogiorno Revisited.* (Exeter: University of Exeter Press, 1997) pp. 83–113.

10

The Youth Question: Generations, Stability and Social Change in France since 1945

Chris Warne

Historians seeking to understand the evolution – and the stability – of the Fifth Republic remain divided as to what constitute the major moments of change. Whereas 1945 used to be seen as the watershed in the emergence of the 'new France', in the eyes of many analysts now the end of the war appears of little significance. After all, following the brief period of tripartism, the Cold War revived precisely the unstable coalition politics of the Third Republic that had seemingly been rejected in 1945. A more suitable 'postwar' date for France might be seen as 1962, when de Gaulle, in effectively ending the colonial era, also confirmed the presidentialization (and stabilization) of politics with a referendum on constitutional reform that instituted direct election of the president. For other authors, however, it was only the revolt of May 1968, with all its attendant political and cultural fallout, that constituted the end of French 'exceptionalism'.[1] This claim in turn has now begun to be subjected to critical analysis. With the benefit of hindsight, the upheavals in May 1968 may seem to have had fewer lasting consequences than the depoliticization inaugurated in the early 1960s.[2] The events of 1989 have added a new element to the riddle of continuity and change in modern France: if there was some kind of postwar stabilization in France – has it now begun to unravel?

This chapter addresses these questions obliquely by looking at French youth and its relationship to adult society. This generational approach recommends itself partly out of general considerations and partly in response to specific features of modern France. On a general level, the emergence of generational identities often serves as a useful index of change. In stable periods, the transition between generations is a gradual process within professions, institutions and structures – a process experienced more at the individual than the group level. But during periods of discontinuity and change we see the emergence of more clearly defined and self-conscious generations – not necessarily the clear-cut entities posited by Mannheim[3] but ones at least characterized by the broadly shared set of values and assumptions that Jean-Pierre Terrail has summarized under the term 'disposition'.[4] The emergence, at any given time, of such generational identities may be a sign that some discontinuity in *past* experience is now becoming politically significant – for example the coming of age in postwar France of a generation united by the fact that they were too young to have fought in the war. Or it may indicate that society is currently finding it difficult to negotiate rapid change, change which highlights differences between old and young. Finally, it may be – as is frequently the case in modern societies – that more general anxieties about the current state of society are being projected by the adult establishment on to what it imagines to be the 'youth of today'.

A more specific reason for studying modern France from this particular vantage-point is that since the end of the war seemingly every important moment of crisis or transition has been associated by contemporary commentators with the emergence of a new 'youth' or with significant generational conflict. We might mention the strong feeling in 1944–5 that Pétain's fall and the collapse of Vichy's aspirations represented the discrediting of an older generation and its replacement by a new one. Or the fact that social change in the 1950s saw repeated reference to the dangers of a new youth culture. The events of 1968, in which an activist youthful minority brought the Fifth Republic to its knees, would alone suffice to justify an analysis of youth's place in postwar France. For their part, the 1980s saw a renewed bout of speculation and concern at the changing face of French youth.

The present chapter investigates the development of generational disposition and distinctiveness at three points in French history since 1945. Such distinctiveness will be measured by reference to the social representation of youth, that is to say, the prevailing way in which the young are characterized and understood as a discrete group, whether in spectacular media set-pieces, or in the more mundane patterns of social and political discourse employed by institutions, social groups and communities. At each of these three points, an assessment will be made of the relationship between heightened generational identity, on the one hand, and patterns of social change and stability, on the other. Finally, some conclusions will be drawn about change and stability in France since 1945.

1945: a postwar era that never happened?

1945 undoubtedly marks a break in the process of generation transition in many areas of French life. The experience of the war in France had contributed to the possibility of generation consciousness, particularly among young males: a significant slice of the male population (the age group that fell into the conscriptable category in 1939) was effectively exiled after the defeat of 1940, and spent most of the war as prisoners. Young men too young to fight in 1939 were to be directly affected by the compulsory work service introduced in 1943, targeted on those in a specific age range. It is a commonplace that after 1943 the character of the French resistance was profoundly affected by the influx of young men seeking a way to avoid the labour draft.

Two points can therefore be made about the relationships between this younger group and their elders. In the first place, the war had undoubtedly disrupted the processes of male socialization; the absence of male authority figures (not compensated for in the fatherly presence of Pétain) provoked an anxiety about the destiny of those young men left at home. This anxiety is reflected in the range of Vichy policies aimed at the social control of the young, and in the panic surrounding the 'zazou' youth sub-culture, where the evils of jazz, hedonism and ostentatious fashion were denounced in collaborationist circles as part of an American–Bolshevik plot to corrupt the nation's youth.[5] Second, in the immediate postwar period, the generational break acted as a catalyst for change in a range of areas. It has been argued, for example, that the impact of young men could be observed in a number of economic sectors, and particularly in agriculture, where a new generation of farmers was (albeit briefly) given the chance to try out different methods and techniques.[6]

However, when the term the 'generation of 1945' became a cliché in French historical writing, it tended to be invested with a much more specific set of characteristics. Usually male, members of this group were depicted as having lost the connection with their parents as a result of the displacements inherent in wartime. With a record of participation in the resistance, their experience of war left them with a profound commitment to social justice and internationalism, expressed in the first instance by a commitment to the communist party, and by a more general commitment to social revolt and to challenging the existing social order. Discussion of this group occurs most often in relation to intellectual and cultural developments in the postwar period. The images most commonly associated with it derive from the postwar subculture that developed in the bars and cafes of the St-Germain-des-Près district of Paris. This subculture was populated by followers of Sartre and his existential philosophy, tailor-made for the new era of moral uncertainty and nuclear insecurity. The participants expressed their ennui in endless philosophical discussion, against a soundtrack of imported American jazz and a reinvigorated style of socially aware and intellectually respectable French chanson.[7]

What is striking about this picture of an ostensible generational identity is that it applies at most to a narrow, active élite, and one whose influence derived more from its control of key areas of literary and cultural life than because it reflected a wider set of social changes. Indeed, in more recent work in the developing field of cultural history, the same group of historians who had initially identified 1945 as a turning point now offer a more nuanced picture. Though they still posit the existence of a new postwar generation, they also identify a great deal of continuity with the culture and society of the prewar era. The contemporary celebration of the St-Germain subculture by the press and the cinema is now seen as deriving from that culture's inaccessibility, its very otherness in relation to the majority.[8] Jean-François Sirinelli employs the phrase 'the post-war era [that] never happened', arguing that, despite the hopes raised at the liberation, the radical social and cultural changes that had been wished for during the occupation were not realized.[9] The same story of widespread continuity from the prewar and wartime periods had already been identified by writers such as Robert Paxton and René Remond, when they showed that the economic policies of the Liberation were simply putting into effect a technocratic style of economic management pioneered by groups within the Vichy nexus.[10] Thus what is celebrated at the Liberation is not youth's distinctiveness, despite the emergence of a 'generation of 1945': this group is an exotic exception to a more general rule of surprising continuity, a return to the normal, to the known (in)stabilities of the Third Republic, whatever its problems. For radical discontinuities in the patterns of youth representation, we must turn to the early years of the Fifth Republic.

The 1960s: generations in conflict and revolt

The first signs of a potential crisis in the succession of the generations in France coincided with the advent of the Fifth Republic. Indeed, a general shift in the social representation of youth can be observed at this point. Whereas in the earlier postwar years youth tended to be depicted as having the energy and dynamism necessary for national reconstruction, by the end of the 1950s a series of more negative portrayals had emerged.[11]

This negative social representation of youth coincides with the teenage years of the first cohorts of the postwar baby-boom. In particular, it focused on the spectacular return of the juvenile gang (first noted as part of the criminal underworld of the Belle Epoque) and a real rise in rates of juvenile crime and delinquency. That there appeared to be a direct link between growing prosperity, stability and this juvenile crime wave, made its appearance all the more baffling. 1959 was baptised 'the summer of the gang' by social work and educational specialists, as France's southern coastal holiday resorts became the scenes of massed gatherings of apparently aimless young, taking advantage of the availability of longer summer holidays and forming the bulk of a new casual labour force associated with the nascent mass vacation industry.[12] The written press in particular concentrated on reports of gang violence and criminality, whether directed at property, police or innocent bystander.[13] One figure dominates these reports: the 'jeune voyou' (young lout) or 'blouson noir', so-named after the black leather jacket popularized in the cinematic representation of youthful rebellion by Marlon Brando and James Dean in films such as 'The Wild One' and 'Rebel without a Cause'. That the models for such youthful revolt were American and therefore imported, undoubtedly reinforced the anxiety prevalent among social commentators concerning the negative effects of modernization on the young. The link between the new prosperity, the development of a consumer society, and the prospects of France thus becoming increasingly Americanized had already been drawn by many politicians and intellectuals of both left and right. Now France's future generation seemed to have succumbed to such alien influences: consequently, the continuity of France's national traditions appeared to be in question.

This anxiety was further reinforced by the emergence of an apparently more benign figure of youth in the early to mid-1960s, namely the 'copain' or pal. Often presented as a contrast to the alienated blouson noir, the copain came to be seen as representing the adolescence of the later cohorts of the postwar baby-boom, and in particular their appearance as active consumers.[14] The copain phenomenon centred very specifically around the emergence of a teenage market for music and the development of rock'n'roll in France. In 1959, the same year that saw the crisis of youth gangs, Daniel Filipacchi, a DJ on Europe 1, altered the format of his weekly broadcast of jazz and blues ('Pour ceux qui aiment le jazz') to take account of the new music. The success of the modified programme, christened 'Salut les Copains', was immediate, and Europe 1's peripheral commercial rivals soon followed suit. While to some Anglo-Saxon observers, the French artists promoted by Filipacchi purveyed no more than pale imitations of their American inspirations, they performed an important dual function. First, they sang in French, thus domesticating what was an apparently alien culture. Second, the new heroes of French rock'n'roll were overwhelmingly of the same age and generation as their target audience. The best-known example is Johnny Hallyday. Born and raised in the itinerant culture of the music hall, Hallyday was fascinated by the images of America presented in the cinema of James Dean and the music of Elvis Presley. His attempts to copy his idols found an immediate echo among a circle of young Parisians who gathered at the Golf Drouot, a bar-cum-youth club whose main attraction was a jukebox which played the latest American hits. This venue soon became the launch pad for a series of teenage singers and groups who were to be the central figures in the wave of teen idols that hit France in the early 1960s.[15] Hallyday's 1960 tour of France following his record deal soon became a media event, with the press focusing on the excitable crowds and frequent violence accompanying his appearances. Worried mayors cancelled concerts, and there were calls for Hallyday's music to be banned. Others were nonetheless impressed by the possibilities represented by the evidence of a new young public with obvious purchasing power. In summer 1962 Filipacchi himself launched a magazine, the first in France specifically aimed at a young audience and concerned exclusively with the new idols of pop and rock music. Using the same title as his radio show, within a year the circulation of *Salut les Copains* had topped the million mark.[16] Contemporary surveys revealed that it drew its readership in equal proportions from lycéens and college students, from apprentices and young workers, indicating that it touched young people from all social backgrounds and classes. The extent of its success can be measured in the impact of the now infamous 'Nuit de la Nation', a concert organized by Filipacchi on the Place de la Nation in Paris in June 1963. Advertised simply by word of mouth and over the airwaves of Europe 1, contemporary observers were astounded when over 150,000 young people turned out to witness their heroes perform. Such was the crush, that Hallyday, Richard Anthony, Sylvie Vartan and other performers required a police escort to reach the stage. The notoriety of the event was guaranteed when the evening ended in violence: in a foreshadowing of the events of May 1968, cars were overturned, trees uprooted, shop windows smashed and crowds were dispersed by riot police.

The 'Nuit de la Nation' brought to a head a growing wave of comment, analysis and reportage devoted to the question of youth and its place within French society.[17] While the analyses differed widely, both in their starting point and in their conclusions, all were united in portraying youth as a problem to be solved, as a group to be contained, managed and organized. Calls for the state to play a greater role in education and training, and in providing suitable cultural and social facilities were given greater urgency both by the feeling that the problem was only going to get worse (demographic projections showed that the peak of the baby boom would only reach adolescence later in the decade, threatening to overwhelm the institutions dedicated to the socialization of the young), and by the decline in membership of the civil organizations and youth movements such as the scouts or young communists. The success of *Salut les Copains* confirmed to many that the marketing men were all too successful in seducing the young with false promises of consumer happiness and prosperity.[18]

What is interesting about these reactions is that they are united by a common theme: the problems faced by the young in France were a direct consequence of the processes of modernization. Rapid urbanization was blamed for throwing together large numbers of young people together on housing estates that had little sense of community or social provision. Family structures and traditional communities were deemed to be under pressure from the too rapid evolution in work and domestic life, leaving the young to seek compensation in materialism and devotion to their new idols. In other words, the processes of technocratic and industrial management that had created the conditions for France's postwar stability were now being held responsible for causing social instability. Just at the time when de Gaulle appeared to be providing long-sought for political stability, the relative social stability of France was being challenged by the very modernizing processes that had produced it.

Few called in to question, however, the basis of the state's role in technocratically managing the modernization of French society. Gang activity was observed to proliferate in the more traditional working class quarters of France's industrial cities,[19] and the consensus here was that it was precisely a *lack* of modernization that was to blame. Thus, the state was frequently criticized for not doing enough, for merely being concerned with the economic at the expense of the social. Rather than calling modernization into question, the majority of social analysts of the youth question in the 1960s called for more rational involvement of the technocratic state to ensure the smooth integration of the new generation into existing social structures. It is perhaps not surprising that state action in response to the 'problem' of youth, seen in both the massive educational expansion of the 1960s at secondary and tertiary level, and in the first efforts at sociocultural provision in the shape of a national network of youth cultural centres (*Maisons des Jeunes et de la*

Culture), was marked by a certain paternalism. The young were to be protected not only from negative influences outside, but also from themselves. This paternalistic aspect of the institutions that dealt with the young was to be one of the key targets for the protestors of May 1968.

If the appearance of the 'blouson noir' and the 'copain' are symptomatic of new generational distinctions, what can be concluded about the disposition of these new groups? Many contemporary observers, while emphasizing the novelty of the youth phenomenon, were quick to point out the political apathy that characterized even the most alienated of the young.[20] If this was youth in revolt, then it had easily been recuperated by the capitalist order, a recuperation best pictured in the transformation of a star like Johnny Hallyday from his early launch as a James Dean-style rebel, to the more socially integrated teen idol of the mid-1960s, patriotically accomplishing his military service, and forming the ideal aspirational young couple with fellow singer and teen idol Sylvie Vartan.

This picture of the docile, apathetic young might seem odd when juxtaposed to the student revolts of May 1968. But in generation terms, May 1968 involved a complex three-way interaction. In the first place there was a small, highly politicized cohort of leaders drawn mostly from the age group equivalent to the blouson noir (but from the opposite end of the social spectrum), a group which had been formed in the protests against the Algerian war of the late 1950s. Second, there was a second, younger group, largely made up of high school students, for whom the May events themselves were the catalyst for the formation of a sense of their own generation identity (the 'real' 1968 generation). In between the two was a middle group, drawn from the supposedly docile 'copain' audience for the teen idols of the earlier part of the decade.[21] As Jean-François Sirinelli has pointed out, the image of this middle group being lulled to political sleep by the rhythms of over-commercialized pop-music, only to wake overnight to the sound of revolution in the streets, is close to a cliché, and over-emphasizes the ideological veneer that the articulate few gave to the May events.[22]

What linked May 1968 with the generation distinctions evident earlier in the decade is that it confirmed (to use economist Alfred Sauvy's expression) 'the rise of youth' within French society,[23] a rise seen at the time as posing a threat to hard-won social stability and continuity. Yolande Cohen has argued that May 1968 marked the moment when a specifically student movement, with a history dating back to the beginning of the twentieth century of seeking and failing to win autonomy and acceptance as a viable force within existing political structures and organizations, finally accepted its own destructuration within a wider youth revolt, by exploiting the themes of generation conflict to register its dissidence.[24] This meeting between a radical student movement and the new kind of youth signified by the generation conflicts of earlier in the decade, would not have been possible without the prior development of a youth-oriented culture. As sociologist Edgar Morin observed in a contemporary study of the copains, the youth subculture was characterized above all by a new set of aspirations, above all the pursuit of personal fulfilment through the activation of an individualized, autonomous social sphere.[25] This drive for increased freedom of expression and autonomy undoubtedly provided common ground for the otherwise heterogeneous revolts of May 1968.

Against this background, it is not surprising that the overwhelming consensus regarding the pattern of postwar French history has been to see the 1960s as a key decade in the shift from one kind of social order to another.[26] But as the cursory examination of generation representation and self-awareness above suggests, in explaining this shift we need to move our attention away from May 1968 (and also away from the rather fruitless ideological debates about the revolutionary nature of 1968). Rather than being the key moment of change, May 1968 now seems rather more the symptom and culmination of a series of ruptures initiated in the post-1945 modernization and accelerated in the early years of the Fifth Republic. Viewed in this light, it becomes less surprising that the '1968 generation' should have come to terms so quickly with the existing social order. Many of the changes demanded by the protesters of 1968 had already been set in motion at a deeper level by the discontinuities inherent in economic and social modernization. It was the rigidity of France's institutional life, symbolized by the petty restrictions experienced by students in the newly expanded university sector, that had failed to keep pace with these underlying developments. The political and economic stability offered by the Gaullist settlement had come at the price of a certain social instability, a misalignment that was to a large extent corrected as the 1968 generation made its peace with the system over the two decades that followed their protests. However, it was precisely at the time when many observers were celebrating the establishment of this social stability in the late 1980s,[27] that concerns over its long-term viability re-emerged in the shape of a new youth panic.

1989: social exclusion and the 'prison-ship generation'

In the mid-1980s, French sociologists working within a number of very different paradigms and perspectives began to reach a common conclusion: fundamental and long-term changes were taking place in the way in which youth was defined as a social category.[28] At the heart of these changes was an extension of the phase of youth and adolescence beyond the teenage years with which it had been traditionally associated. A number of factors had combined to produce this 'new social age group' – above all, the far greater numbers of young people staying longer in some form of educational institution. The second phase of massive postwar educational expansion in France dates from this period, and was clearly itself a response to profound changes in the nature of work and the economy inherent in the adjustment to the postindustrial order.[29] Thus, prolonging education can be seen as a strategic response to changes in the availability and nature of employment. However, we should not lose sight of other factors contributing to educational expansion, not least the general rise in expectation on the part of girls and young women as to what they could achieve in education and beyond.[30] This rise in expectation was only reinforced by those parents seeking a better status for their children, or anxious that they should take opportunities that had not been open to them.

Another feature of the now extended youth phase was a rise in the average age of those getting married for the first time. Clearly, young people were choosing to defer the day when they finally established a new family unit, a trend only reinforced by the tendency to experiment with alternative living arrangements such as cohabitation, or by remaining longer in the family home. Even when the prolonged process of education was complete, increasing numbers of young people were entering the job market in a markedly different fashion, deferring the moment when a professional identity was fixed, and preferring or being obliged instead to take a series of short-term jobs as stages towards the fixing of a professional status. The combined effect of these changes in the domestic, educational and employment realms was to prolong that period of social experimentation associated with youth, such that the boundaries of that age group were increasingly being extended beyond the teenage years, into the 20 to 30 year-old age group, and even beyond.

For the 1960s we argued that youth's changing social and economic circumstances helped to give rise to a new youthful identity, or disposition. Can we similarly conclude that the new circumstances of the 1980s not only changed the pattern of youth in a quantifiable sense (the sociologist Olivier Galland's 'nouvel âge social'), but also gave rise to a new generational self-awareness? The problem with reaching such a conclusion is that the changes in the 1980s do not seem to have enhanced youth's homogeneity. Instead, the changes taking place were experienced in very different ways according to the cultural and economic capital available. For those with the support structures of relative prosperity and stability at home, and at ease in their negotiation of the sometimes bewildering range of educational options on offer, this new age of uncertainty could be embraced as a set of opportunities to experiment with and exploit. For those less well endowed with such capital, the experience was more likely to be undergone and endured rather than embraced. Indeed, in what became acknowledged as a pioneering study of those young people who were most likely to suffer the negative aspects of such changes – children and adolescents living on the working-class housing estates of large outer-city suburbs – the sociologist François Dubet coined a term borrowed from the language of incarceration (*la galère* or prisonship) to capture their experience of marginalization and frustration.[31] He identified their response in an unfocused, destructive rage, expressed in delinquency, vandalism, violent and aggressive relationships with the social system (and particularly the police) and in the growth of drug taking and suicide rates. Thus all young people experienced these new set of circumstances, and the generational distinction comes from their being the first to do so. However, not all young people experienced these new circumstances in the same way or with the same results, thus it is still appropriate to stress the plurality of youth, and remain cautious about the possibility that this rather diffuse generational consciousness would produce decisive collective interventions in the social field, or even a clearly easily identifiable disposition.

Indeed, what is noticeable is that despite the real change in the social conditions experienced by the young, the prevailing representation of youth in France throughout the 1980s generally failed to acknowledge this. The mid-1980s in particular marked a key moment in the definition and characterization of youth that owed nothing either to the general work of Galland and others like him, or to the more focused work of Dubet on 'la galère'. The proposed reform of the French university by Chirac's right-wing government of cohabitation in 1986 was originally conceived as part of a more general policy aim to reduce the role of the state in areas of the economy and of industry. It was also an attempt to streamline a higher education system widely accepted to be facing a series of problems, not the least of which was the high drop-out rate, a consequence of forms of selection being used at the end of the first cycle of study, rather than at the baccalauréat level and point of entry to the university. This attempt to engineer the movement of university population was based on giving more autonomy to the universities themselves in terms of setting entry criteria, tuition fees and determining the nature of qualifications awarded. Some reversal of post-1968 reforms was also envisaged in the reduction of student representation on management committees. The strength of opposition to these proposed reforms was a surprise. A student population that had been relatively calm for over a decade organized itself into a series of strikes and demonstrations that lasted throughout the autumn, a response supported by members of the teaching unions, and by high-school students fearful that their access to higher education might be curtailed. Fearful as they were of the erosion of nationally determined diplomas, opposition was perhaps strongest from students at provincial universities and at those institutions created in the wake of the 1968 events. While the largest demonstration in Paris in December ended in violence, and resulted in the death of a student at the hands of CRS riot police, and while the government quickly dropped the planned reforms in face of this opposition, what is striking about this episode are the widespread conclusions that were drawn about the condition of French youth.[32] Two features mark these conclusions. The first is to do with the political outlook of the young. Drawing an obvious comparison with 1968, most commentators and analysts were struck by the limited aims of the movement, by its pragmatic rejection of excessive political idealism. The strikes and demonstrations were organized around the specific goal of forcing the withdrawal of a particular reform, and refrained from any wider call for social change or revolt. Attempts to channel discontent in any other direction failed. Similarly, the search for 'star' leaders who would use the movement as a launch pad for careers in the politics of social reform was also fruitless. The overwhelming conclusion therefore was that youth as socially deviant category had simply ceased to exist: young people were (depending on the interpretation) either too docile to be a threat, or were so successfully integrated into the patterns of republican politics and citizenship, that they were now behaving as any other section of the population. This analysis of the student population was further reinforced by the second conclusion that was drawn from the movement, namely that it signalled the successful integration of the young ethnically mixed populations of the suburbs (the banlieue) into the wider political solidarities of the republic.

Widespread attention had been given to those born in France, but of immigrant parentage, since the summer 1983 'March for Equality and against Racism' ('Marche pour l'Égalité et contre le Racisme').[33] Starting as an improvised protest by local associations in the Lyons suburbs of Les Minguettes, against on the one hand, police methods and attitudes employed in the banlieue, and on the other, against the growing influence of the far right at local level, an influence increasingly connected to a series of racist attacks, the march grew in momentum and ended, amidst considerable national media coverage, with an official reception at the Presidential palace. It was the spur for a flurry of debate on the situation of France's ethnic minorities, and more specifically the younger sections of these groups. However, by 1986 the movement which grew out of the 1983 march had begun to divide into several factions, unable to agree on either philosophy, aims or tactics. The successful groups at a national level (SOS-Racisme and France Plus) had prospered by establishing clear links with existing parties and groups on the left with a longer-term involvement in the anti-racist movement.[34] The slogan of SOS-Racisme ('Touche pas à mon pôte' – 'Leave my mate alone') summed up neatly the aim of building a form of social solidarity in opposition to the rise of the new right, not only in government (represented by the hardline interior minister Charles Pasqua), but in the more sinister form of the extreme nationalist Front National, whose big electoral breakthrough had come earlier in the decade. This tactic was criticized by some as selling out to the short-term electoral concerns of the socialist party, especially as the latter's own record on both immigration and social exclusion had proved so disappointing. Whatever the grassroots differences and debates that took place over the direction of the movement, among those same commentators who had celebrated the moderation of the student demonstrations, there was an equal willingness to celebrate the presence among the student demonstrators of young 'Beurs' as a signal that those born of immigrant parentage in France, and particularly those of North African descent, were being successfully integrated into the styles and patterns of republican citizenship. Some argued that the term 'Beur' had ceased to be meaningful: the particular struggle against the social exclusion of the suburbs and against racism that had propelled the 'Beur' into the public eye, had now been successfully absorbed into a wider struggle for democracy, solidarity and human rights, at the head of which was a reinvigorated socialist party fresh from its post-Keynesian reinvention. The 'hot summer' of riots and joyriding on some of the larger outer-city housing estates that had followed Mitterrand's election in 1981 now seemed a distant memory.

What is distinctive therefore about the representation of youth that emerged from the reaction to the student movement of 1986 is the complete absence of any notion of the radical alterity of youth and of youth experience. Despite the developing analyses on the part of certain sociologists and academics that pointed to a new social age group with distinct characteristics and facing new circumstances, the overwhelming sense is of youth as a category, whether from the ethnic minorities or the majority, as being essentially 'integrated', successfully positioned to assure the stability of the post-Keynesian political settlement between left and right, symbolized by the relatively easy period of cohabitation, from which the left had undoubtedly benefited more than the right. It is not until the disruption that 1989 causes to this settlement that the radical alterity of youth experience, as identified by Galland and others, can actually emerge in the concrete shape of an acknowledged youth subculture. It is perhaps not coincidental therefore that the first year of this postwar era (1990) sees the emergence of another panic over youth, with many echoes of the one that accompanied the foundation of the Fifth Republic.

At the heart of this panic was a series of violent incidents involving the young ethnically mixed populations of the banlieue: riots at Vaulx-en-Velin near Lyons in November followed the death of a young motorcyclist in collision with a police car; student demonstrations in the same month against a proposed reform of the lycée ended in violence as hooded 'casseurs' embarked on a spree of looting through central Paris, and throughout the summer, reports in the press of confrontations between exotically named gangs disputing territory and control of the drugs trade, a violence that seemed all the more threatening as it appeared to be spilling over from the banlieue into the centre of Paris (in particular the areas around the La Défense and Les Halles). The accumulated effect of this was to refocus political and public attention on the banlieue. Increasingly, these areas were characterized as lawless zones, populated by gangs of alienated youth, victims of unemployment, social deprivation, prone to delinquency and drug abuse, and most significantly, whose alienation from the system was such that ethnicity and locality now were the key factors in determining their social position. More than once in media reporting of these events, the American ghetto is evoked as both marker and the shape of what is to come.[35] The anxiety is evident: from the picture of youth as being 'part of us' in the mid-1980s, the situation has changed fundamentally to focus on the presence of the young who now seem out of reach and alien. By adopting overtly ethnic loyalties, they reject assimilationist and integrationist models of French citizenship. Their ready resort to violence seems to indicate a profound rejection of the paths of negotiation and dialogue so clearly adopted by the social movements of the 1980s.[36] This impression of radical alterity was only confirmed in the concurrent attention given to the re-emergence of French hip-hop, whose practitioners often originated from the very same banlieues that were now the focus of such public concern: the unfocused anger of 'la galère' first identified by Dubet now seemed to be finding an outlet, but in a culture that was to many disconcerting in its confrontational use of the word, its espousal of tagging and graffiti that many equated with simple vandalism, and in its exotic and strange dance styles. It was almost as if the uncertainties of the international situation, the reawakening of ethnic and tribal particularisms consequent on the break up of the Eastern bloc, had their counterpart within the nation itself. The postwar era was not simply 'out there'. It was 'in our midst' and posing a very direct challenge to the grounds on which consensual stability had been finally achieved in France.

As in the early 1960s, there were calls for the state to respond to the perceived challenge of youth. As in the early 1960s too, much of this response has been in the form of reforms in the areas of education or employment training, reforms which have met with mixed results. However, what is perhaps more significant is the willingness of state institutions to adopt an apparently more flexible approach than their counterparts in the early 1960s. Running through these policies has been a concerted attempt to give young people their voice, and a readiness to acknowledge and give status to their concerns. Thus a range of initiatives have been launched at both local and national level aimed at encouraging grass-roots cultural movements and associations.[37] While these policies are not without their ambiguities and problems,[38] and while there is much ground to be covered before the problems associated with and experienced by the young excluded in France can be properly addressed, this less rigid response is perhaps indicative of the more fundamentally stable nature of the social and political system in France. Despite the problems revealed in this latest postwar era, there are reasons to believe that the equilibrium not achieved in the postwar era of 1945, but put in place by the conflicts and revolts of the 1960s, has not been thrown too far out of balance by the adjustment to 1989.

Conclusion

This survey of generational identities and relationships in postwar France has revealed a pattern of continuity and change in postwar France, in which the 1960s play the crucial role. True, in 1945 and even more in 1989 we find accepted assumptions and attitudes being widely challenged – a process in which youth played a central role both as active subject and as object of concern. But in the making of a stable political and social system it is the 1960s which are the real watershed. The 1960s marked the culmination of a first phase of modernization, largely economic and structural, to some extent initiated in 1945, and typified most of all by the Gaullist political settlement of the Fifth Republic. And the decade also saw the start of a new phase of modernization, in the course of which the aspirations and ideals expressed during the 1960s by the younger generation began to inflect the social styles and mores of France's institutional and political life. So that when in the 1980s changes in economic and social circumstances produced another phase of strong generation distinction (even isolation), a process highlighted by the end of the Cold War, the response of the adult world, represented by the institutions of state, was despite its shortcomings and inefficiencies, characterized by a desire to take young people seriously as subjects, rather than as a problem to be directed and managed.

Notes

1. This was the view expressed by Peter Morris at the original conference on which this volume is based. Sadly Peter died before he was able to put his views on paper.
2. For a survey of the debates on depoliticization in early 1960s France, see J. Capdevielle and R. Mouriaux, *Mai 68. L'Entre-deux de la modernité* (Paris: Presses de la Fondation Nationale des Sciences Politiques, 1988) pp. 53–5.
3. Mannheim's now classic theory of generation formation is found in 'The Problem of Generations', in *Essays on the Sociology of Knowledge*. (London: Routledge & Kegan Paul, 1954) pp. 276–322.
4. J.-P. Terrail, *La Dynamique des générations: activité individuelle et changement social 1968–1993*. (Paris: L'Harmattan, 1995).
5. J.-C. Loiseau, 'Les zazous (la culture populaire française pendant l'occupation allemande)', *Historia*, no. 521 (1990) 97–104. For a survey of Vichy's paternalistic policies on youth, W. D. Halls, *The Youth of Vichy France*. (Oxford: Clarendon Press, 1981), pp. 132–57.
6. For a description of the impact of a new generation of farmers, symbolized by the activist and reformer Michel Debatisse, see D. Borne, *Histoire de la société française depuis 1945*. (Paris: Armand Colin, 1992, 3rd edn) pp. 28–30.
7. S. Berstein and P. Milza, *Histoire de la France au XXe siècle 3. 1945–1958* (Bruxelles: Éditions Complexes, 1991) pp. 203–8.
8. J.-P. Rioux and J.-F. Sirinelli (eds), *Histoire culturelle de la France 4. Le Temps des masses*. (Paris: Seuil, 1998) p. 224.
9. *Ibid.* pp. 216–30. Sirinelli's phrase – 'l'après guerre n'a pas eu lieu' – is a deliberate echo of the title of Jean Giradoux's prewar pacifist play *La guerre de Troie n'aura pas lieu*.
10. R. O. Paxton, *La France de Vichy, 1940–1944* (Paris: Seuil, translated 1973) pp. 325–7; R. Rémond, *Histoire de France 6. Notre siècle, de 1918 à 1995* (Paris: Fayard, 1996) pp. 298–9.
11. F. Tétard, 'Face à la montée des jeunes (fin des années 1950-début des années 1960). Les réponses de la société adulte' in B. Francq, F. Goffinet, J.-C. Lagrée and M. Vuille (eds), *Générations de jeunes* (Bruxelles/Genève: Éditions SECJ/AISLF, 1988) pp. 17–35.

12. A typical contemporary analysis is B. Abel, 'La saison des bandes', *Les Cahiers de l'enfance*, 8th année, no. 62 (January 1960) 36–9. For retrospective accounts, see M. Fize, *Les Bandes, l'"entre-soi" adolescent* (Paris: Desclée de Brouwer, 1993) pp. 26–68; F. Tétard, 'Le phénomène "blousons noirs" en France, fin des années 1950-début des années 1960', in *Révolte et société. Actes du IV*[e] *Colloque d'Histoire au Présent, Paris, mai 1988*, vol. 2, pp. 205–14.
13. For an analysis of press reporting of the blouson noir phenomenon, see P. Macaigne, 'Quelques réflexions sur la présentation par la presse écrite des "blousons noirs"', *Annales de Vaucresson*, no. 2 (1964) 233–55.
14. It is perhaps indicative of the rapidity of change in this period that the figure deemed representative of youth as a whole has also changed so quickly.
15. J.-P. Rioux, 'La France yé-yé des années 60', *L'Histoire*, no. 182 (November 1994) 16–25.
16. M. Winock, 'Années 60: la poussée des jeunes', in *L'Histoire, Études sur la France de 1939 à nos jours* (Paris: Seuil, 1985) pp. 304–22.
17. J. Jenny, 'Les discours sociaux sur "la jeunesse" dans les années 60: production, circulation, évolution et articulation aux pratiques sociales et représentations collectives', in J.-C. Lagrée and P. Lew-Faï (eds), *La Jeunesse en questions.* (Paris: La Documentation Française, 1983) pp. 19–44 provides an exhaustive analysis of this output.
18. This theme is central to the otherwise sympathetic accounts of youth culture to be found in Y.-M. Cloître, *Johnny Hallyday. Les Idoles et les jeunes.* (Paris: Casterman, 1964) and J. Marny, *Les Adolescents aujourd'hui. Culture, loisirs, idoles, amour, religion*... (Paris: Centurion, 1965).
19. A typical contemporary sociological account of such working-class areas is P. Robert, *Les Bandes d'adolescents*. (Paris: Editions Ouvreres, 1966).
20. Jean-Paul Sartre, in the first issue of *Le Nouvel Observateur* in November 1964, deplored the lack of political consciousness among the young, and stated that they had been betrayed by their idols for the sake of 'daddy's profits'. Cited by J.-F. Sirinelli, 'Les jeunes', in J.-P. Rioux and J.-F. Sirinelli (eds), *La France: d'un siècle à l'autre. Dictionnaire critique.* (Paris: Hachette-Littératures, 1999), p. 439.
21. For a detailed examination of this three-way interaction, see D. Bertaux, D. Linhart and B. Le Wita, 'Mai 68 et la formation des générations politiques en France', *Le Mouvement social*, 143 (April–June 1988) 75–89.
22. J.-F. Sirinelli, '1968: les fleurs de mai', in Rioux and Sirinelli *La France: d'un siècle à l'autre.* pp. 91–2.
23. Translation of the title of Sauvy's 1959 pioneering book *La Montée des jeunes.* (Paris: Calmann-Lévy, 1959).
24. Y. Cohen, 'Mai 68: le mouvement étudiant comme mouvement de génération?', *L'Homme et la Société*, issue 111–12, (January–June 1994), 119–36.
25. Morin's initial analysis of the copain sub-culture was originally published as a series of articles in *Le Monde* during the weeks following 'La Nuit de la Nation'. They were republished as part of his *Introduction à une politique de l'homme.* (Paris: Seuil, 1965) pp. 213–20. He later explored the links between this youth culture and the May 1968 events in 'Culture adolescente et révolte étudiante', *Annales ESC*, 24 3 (May–June 1969) 765–76.
26. The sociologist Henri Mendras sees this decade as initiating a 'second French Revolution', particularly in the realm of values and attitudes: *La*

Seconde révolution française 1965–1984 (Paris: Gallimard, 1988). In a similar vein, Jean-François Sirinelli sees 1965 as commencing a period of 'Twenty Decisive Years' ('Les Vingt Décisives'), which intersect with economist Jean Fourastié's 'Thirty Glorious Years' ('Les Trente Glorieuses') of postwar economic expansion (1945–1975): 'Les Vingt Décisives. Cultures politiques et temporalités dans la France fin du siècle', *Vingtième Siècle. Revue d'histoire*, 44, (October–December 1994), 112–19. Finally, political scientists Jacques Capdevielle and René Mouriaux see the decade as marking a watershed between two kinds of modernity in France: *Mai 68. L'Entre-deux de la modernité*, pp. 9–21.

27. One such case would be the analysis of the 'The Republic of the centre' by François Furet, Jacques Julliard and Pierre Rosenvallon. See their essays published in *La République du centre: la fin de l'exception française.* (Paris: Calmann-Lévy, 1988).
28. The two most prominent examples are: J.-C. Chamboredon, 'Adolescence et post-adolescence: la "juvénisation". Remarques sur les transformations récentes des limites de la définition sociale de la jeunesse', in A.-M. Alléon, O. Morvan and S. Lebovici (eds), *Adolescence terminée, adolescence interminable.* (Paris: Presses Universitaires de France, 1985) pp. 13–28 and O. Galland, 'La prolongation de la jeunesse: vers un nouvel âge de la vie?', *"Jeunes et société", Contradictions*, 40–41, (Summer–Autumn 1984) 7–16, a perspective Galland has subsequently developed in numerous articles and books, most notably in his *Sociologie de la jeunesse: l'entrée dans la vie* (Paris: Armand Colin, 1991). Given that the new conditions identified by such sociologists seemed likely to produce a sense of generation distinction, it was perhaps no coincidence that at the same time the generation as a mode of historical and social analysis was also making a comeback in the work of social scientists in France, having previously enjoyed only a brief period of favour in the wake of the 1968 events, for example: D. Kessler and A. Masson, *Cycles de vie et générations.* (Paris: Economica, 1985), J.-F Sirinelli (ed.), 'Générations intellectuelles', special issue of *Cahiers de l'IHTP*, no. 6, (November 1987), C. Attias-Donfut, *Sociologie des générations, l'empreinte du temps.* (Paris: Presses Universitaires de France, 1988).
29. A. Prost 'L'Éducation nationale depuis la Libération', in P. Tronquoy (ed.), 'Le Système éducatif', *Cahiers français*, 285, (March–April 1998), 3–11.
30. On the changing place of girls and young women as contributing to the formation of a new generation, see J.-P. Terrail, *La Dynamique des générations*, pp. 75–113.
31. F. Dubet, *La Galère: les jeunes en survie* (Paris: Seuil, 1987).
32. A typical analysis was one offered by the then editor of the left-wing *Libération* newspaper, Laurent Joffrin in his *Un Coup de jeune: portrait d'une génération morale.* (Paris: Éditions Arléa, 1987). See also R. Duclaud-Williams, 'Student protest: 1968 and 1986 compared' in D. L. Hanley and A. P. Kerr (eds), *May '68: Coming of Age* (Basingstoke: Macmillan, 1989) pp. 43–61.
33. 'Beur' is backslang for 'Arabe', and was coined to describe young descendants of North African immigrants, experiencing the particular problems of growing up in areas of social exclusion. The phrase enjoyed considerable currency in the media, and was subsequently disowned by the groups who had originally used it to describe themselves.

34. A critical account of this phase of the movement's development has been provided by one of its participants: S. Bouamama, *Dix ans de marche des Beurs. Chronique d'un mouvement avorté.* (Paris: Desclée de Brouwer, 1994) pp. 77–191.
35. For a survey of press coverage of the gang phenomenon, see A. Negroni, 'De bande à gang: la presse fait le pas', in CFREPJJ, *L'Actualité des bandes*. (Vaucresson: CFRES, 1991) pp. 1–8. The notion that the American ghetto is comparable to the French banlieue is challenged by L. Wacquant, 'Banlieues françaises et ghetto noir américain: de l'amalgame à la comparaison', *French Politics and Society*, 10 4 (Fall 1992) 81–103.
36. M. Kokoreff, 'Tags et zoulous: une nouvelle violence urbaine', *Esprit*, new series 169 (February 1991) 23–36 outlines the challenge posed to republican institutions by these new cultural forms. A perspective on ethnic identity in the French context can be found in O. Roy, 'Ethnicité, bandes et communautarisme', *Esprit*, new series 169 (February 1991) 37–47.
37. Many of these initiatives emanate from the Ministry of Culture: the new attitude is perhaps best represented by state support for the Festival of Urban Dance held at the Parc de la Villette exhibition site in Paris, and for endorsement of the Techno Parade, a festival of club culture also held in Paris.
38. These problems and inconsistencies are clearly highlighted by F. Menard, 'La rue: une forme d'intégration sociale', *Informations sociales*, 60 (1997) 36–43.

Part III

Political Frameworks Across the Three Postwar Eras

11
France's German Question, 1918–1945–1989

Douglas Johnson

I

Pierre Renouvin left a lasting mark on the study of French diplomatic history during the twentieth century. His influence was felt, not only through his books and articles, but also through his lectures at the Sorbonne during the Fourth and Fifth Republics. Many generations of students sat in crowded amphitheatres and heard him explain how France was fortunate in its natural frontiers, as it was protected by mountains and seas. Only to the east were the plains open. France was also fortunate in its immediate neighbours, who were either small states (such as Switzerland, Belgium and Luxemborg), medium-sized powers which never considered attacking France (Italy and Spain), or Great Britain which was barred from the continent by the sea and which had never possessed a powerful army. Only Germany remained. The only potential enemy. The enemy which had invaded France three times in 70 years.

More sophisticated historical and geo-political arguments have been put forward to describe this situation. France and Germany have been condemned to be enemies or they have been condemned to partnership. Successive French governments have had to search for security or to search for a means of cooperation. 'France has a German policy. She has no other.'[1]

Germany has haunted the French. After the defeat in 1870 when Gambetta described France as having been 'degraded, disarmed and betrayed', the Ligue des Patriotes organized collective mourning as a patriotic religion, making pilgrimages to the battlefields and to the symbolic sites of war. In this way the lost provinces of Alsace and Lorraine would be remembered, Germany would constantly appear as the enemy of France, and as in the Christian religion, the patriotic belief was that suffering would be followed by redemption.[2] In the twentieth century the battle of Verdun had become the symbol of the most terrible of wars and if it has figured intensely in the national memory, it has stood for German aggression as well as for French heroism and sacrifice.[3]

Clemenceau, in March 1919, pleaded that the French position should be understood. 'America is far away and protected by the ocean; England could not be reached by Napoleon himself. You are sheltered, both of you; we are not.'[4] He believed in the inevitability of another German attack on France, as did Poincaré who, famously, would show visitors in his house in Lorraine where Germany was and who would say, 'They'll come again, they'll come again.' Another man who believed in the certainty of another Franco–German war was the ex-prisoner of war in Germany, Charles De Gaulle, who wrote about the vulnerability of France's north-western frontier and who rejected any idea of a reconciliation between France and Germany. 'Between the Gauls and Germans the victories of the one over the other decided and resolved nothing!'[5] After the war, in 1945, his opinion of the German nation seemed to be unchanged. 'The Germans are a great people who perpetually turn to war, who never cease to dream of dominating, and who will applaud anyone who promises them conquest even if this leads them into crime.'[6] When faced with the imminence of a re-united Germany, President Francois Mitterrand said that it was necessary to re-establish close relations between England and France, as in 1913 and 1938.[7] Earlier, when irritated by German policies within Europe and attracted by the reforms in the Soviet Union carried out by Gorbachev, he spoke nostalgically of turning to the English and the Russians. 'We will return', he said, 'to 1913.'[8]

Certain statistics loomed large in French apprehensions of Germany and have remained a constant factor. Prior to 1914 the Germans had more than three times the number of men from whom they could choose front-line troops. They could return more than half of the men who were called up to their homes and jobs. For the French there was no possibility of doing this and they were forced to take men with real disabilities into the active service units, even though a steady drop-out rate was inevitable.[9] After the war, Briand's chief assistant Philippe Berthelot envisaged a future when Germany would have some 70 million 'organized and industrious men' in contrast to the stagnating French population of 38 million.[10] The statistics seemed more optimistic in 1985 when the French population at 55.2 millions was compared to that of the German Federal Republic with 61 millions, and history seemed to be on the side of France when future population growths were calculated. Eurostat, the Statistical Office of the European community claimed that in the year 2000 the French population at 57.9 millions would almost equal that of the Federal

Republic with 59.2 millions, but most important of all, in the year 2020 the French population would outnumber the declining German population. This would have dropped to 51.2 millions, while that of France, at 58.7 millions would have been the highest of any of the 12 countries which then composed the European Community (narrowly outnumbering the British population which would have grown to 58.5 millions). But the consideration of these projections became otiose with the re-unification of Germany, with the United Nations estimate of its population in 1994 being 81,410,000, in contrast to the metropolitan French population of 57,747,000.

With this constant and visible comparison of populations, which always reflected in the public and political view a comparison of relative strengths, it was necessary for the French to realize, and to make it clear to other peoples, that France was not only a European power in danger of being overshadowed by a mighty neighbour. France was also a world power. During and after World War One this was obviously true. Nearly a million men from French colonies and protectorates were mobilized; some 450,000 served in the army, and 70,000 were killed. The presence of such units was vital in the manpower shortage which was recognized as being acute in January 1918; the colonial troops took part in many of the most important battles of the war, such as the recapture of the fort at Douamont, in Verdon, by the Régiment colonial du Maroc.[11]

This was one of the reasons why, after the war, colonial ventures became more popular. The French empire had grown as the German empire had been confiscated. While many French businesses profited from increased trade and new opportunities for growth, it has often been remarked that it was not French economic interests that explain the preoccupation with colonial possessions. The administrator played a more prominent role than did the trader; the military were often more involved than the merchants. French rule was an expression of power; the greater the area ruled then the greater the power of the state that lay at the centre of this organization. Thus France possessed a certain rank. This was important in world affairs and it was hugely important in domestic politics when a statesman could claim to represent the authority that ruled over vast areas of the world.

But France also expressed universal values. French rule was a mission, 'la mission civilisatrice'. The French language was the key to enlightenment and progress. The French educational system would bring the masses of backward peoples out of ignorance and superstition. The aim of this colonization was to make the colonized French by assimilation or to help and influence them by association. For all of them Paris became the centre of the world.

A more practical demonstration of the importance of the empire occurred in 1940. On 7 August 1940 the British Prime Minister and General de Gaulle signed a letter of agreement. Before the month was out Chad, the Cameroons and French Equatorial Africa had declared their allegiance to De Gaulle's Free French movement. The British Foreign Office complained that they had signed an agreement recognizing General de Gaulle as the leader of a committee. But suddenly he had become someone who ruled over territories. This was undoubtedly an important element in the rise of De Gaulle's power and influence, a stage in the process which culminated in his famous appearance as the Liberator of Paris, on the Champs-Elysées, 26 August 1944. When François Mitterrand remarked that without Africa there would be no history of France in the twenty-first century, we can be sure that he was not thinking specifically about General De Gaulle, but it is certain that without Africa the history of France in the twentieth century would be very different.[12]

After 1945, in spite of the movement of decolonization which swept the world, the French were so determined to maintain their empire, and therefore their rank as a world power, that they fought the unsuccessful wars of Indo-China and Algeria, and asserted French power in many other overseas possessions, such as Madagascar, where the insurrection of March 1947 was repressed with extreme severity. It was only after military disaster in May 1954, that Pierre Mendès France was accepted as Prime Minister, with the obligation of arranging an armistice to bring the Indo-Chinese war to an end. And yet it was the same statesman, who had claimed that the war was endangering France's economic progress and competetiveness, who reacted traditionally to the first manifestations of the insurrection, that was to become the war, in Algeria. On 12 November 1954 Mendès France declared 'Algeria is French and has been French for a long time. There is no question of secession!' François Mitterrand then Minister of the Interior declared 'Algeria is France'.

It is not necessary to recount the story of how De Gaulle led the French nation to accept the independence of Algeria. It was the only way he could find of getting out of 'the tragic labyrinth'.[13] But he claimed that the greatness of France was enhanced rather than diminished by this. For the direct power of France in overseas territories he substituted influence, and Jacques Foccart, who was the Elysée official responsible for organizing this influence, was among his most frequent interlocators.

When it came to direct negotiations with Germany, de Gaulle and his advisers emphasized France's continuing importance as a world power. A member of the Security Council, a nuclear power (having exploded its first atomic bomb in the Sahara in January 1960), a state that was totally independent of the American and Soviet blocs. When De Gaulle met Chancellor Adenauer it was the meeting between a world statesman and a local politician. The General, and his successor as President, Pompidou, both believed and said that there was a difference between France and Germany that was fundamental. Germany had been a European power, but only a European power, and the German language had never been an international language.[14]

We have been told by Hubert Védrine, the former spokesman and Secretary-General of the Elysée (who became Minister for Foreign Affairs in June 1997) that President Mitterrand adhered largely to what he called 'the national myth' concerning French influence in Africa.[15] However for some time the idea was correct that Africa was a continent where France could make its influence felt, where the presence of 500 men could change the course of history.[16] And in Mitterrandian policy to Africa, while we can see the continuation of the Foccart policies of exerting influence through networks and personal relationships, there has been an even greater emphasis than before on maintaining and extending the French language, 'la Francophonie'. One commentator has stated clearly, 'Francophonie is what remains of the French colonial empire.'[17] According to the *Atlas de la langue française* French is the sole official language of 12 countries out of the 18 members of Francophone 'Afrique noire'. The French language is in itself the sign of civilization and the demonstration of French importance.

II

During 1914–18 France's primary war aim was the restitution of Alsace and Lorraine, annexed by Germany after the Franco-Prussian War of 1870–1. The commitment to this national claim was made public by the Prime Minister, on 22 November 1914 (although it had been stated officially, by Gaston Doumergue, the Minister for Foreign Affairs, on 5 August).

France's other war aims tended to be vague and shifted during the course of the war. But some of those that did not create general agreement concerned the future economy. Only too conscious of the French failure to compete with the Germans in the years before 1914, both the government and private business interests hoped to benefit from the blockade imposed by the Allies during the war and the peace terms which a victorious France could impose after the war, to oust Germany from markets and to acquire new sources of raw material. In the course of 1916 especially, a variety of plans were put forward which did not meet with universal approval. Some of them were far-reaching, such as the setting up after the war of an independent Westphalia with frontier control of its customs. Others more commonly involved the annexation by France of the Saar, with its coal mines. By 1918, in economic terms, it was clear that France wished for Allied cooperation to continue. Otherwise there was the possibility of an economic union with Luxembourg and the Rhineland, a customs union with Belgium and a far-reaching agreement with Italy. In this way, it was argued, France would become the dominating economic power of Europe. Such a programme was attractive to the small producers and to what has been called 'le milieu des chambres de commerce', since a series of special agreements would not affect the general principal of protection. But the banks and the heavy metallurgical industries were more interested in central and eastern Europe, and the Assembly was worried about the customs union with Belgium.[18]

As is well known, Clemenceau described his thoughts when he heard of the impending armistice as revolving round two considerations. One, that his country had suffered terribly and that the Germans should be made to compensate the French people in some way for the destruction that they had wrought. The other that a means should be found to give France security.

It was not easy for these French objectives, for all their vagueness, to be met in the peace settlement, either in the Treaty of Versailles or the years of negotiations that followed. The immediate settlement was clear enough. Germany restored Alsace and Lorraine to France, Eupen and Malmédy to Belgium. Germany also lost Posen and West Prussia to Poland and Danzig was made a free state under the League of Nations administration. The Saar was placed for 15 years under international administration giving France the use of its coalfields. Germany was forced to abandon its colonies and was disarmed, except for a small defence force. The land west of the Rhine was placed under allied administration for 15 years, the lands east of the Rhine were demilitarized to a depth of 50 miles. Alsace and Lorraine had the right to export duty free to Germany for 5 years. The Allies were given most favoured nation treatment for 10 years. Germany and her allies were held responsible for the war and for the destruction it had caused and therefore had to pay reparations. The treaty details were placed within a framework consisting of an Anglo-American guarantee of assistance to France in the event of an unprovoked aggression and the creation of the League of Nations.

It was clear that this treaty satisfied few in France. Would 60 million Germans accept to pay tribute to 30 million French over an endless period of years? Would 60 million Germans accept the division of Prussia in two by an independent Polish state? Since the tragedy of four years of war had brought no reward to France, many French people became extreme nationalists seeking to remedy an injustice, and many became pacifists, swearing that never again would they allow such a war to be repeated. There was thus an increasing difference in outlook.

Successive governments maintained their efforts to achieve security and economic benefits. Sometimes they did this by forceful means. Sometimes by the adoption of a new policy.[19]

III

The period of French history that follows the Armistice and the Peace has usually been shown as a period of decline. It is the story of a nation proceeding from victory to defeat. On 11 November 1918 Germany signs the Armistice, after 4 years of terrible war and slaughter; on 22 June 1940 France signs an armistice, after a German offensive that has lasted 43 days. In 1919 the Peace Conference took place in Paris, under the Presidency of the French Prime Minister, Clemenceau; between 1943 and 1945 the United States, Great Britain and the Soviet Union, in the absence of France, took decisions about the postwar settlement. On 26 March 1914, General Foch was named commander-in-chief of the allied forces in Europe, and it was the French who equipped the American army as it arrived in Europe; in 1944 the Liberation of France depended largely on the decisions of an American general and on American military and civilian material.[20]

It was as if France could not recover from the war. The date, 11 November, had retained its significance. A sombre significance for it became the day when the dead were remembered, and a national significance; it became the day when the unity and heroism of the French people had achieved victory. The tomb of the Unknown Soldier, the symbol of those who had died, was placed under the Arc de Triomphe in 1921. This changed the geography of Paris. It became the symbolic centre of the city. It was there that General De Gaulle went on 26 August 1944. Then he went down the Champs Elysées, thus demonstrating that Paris was liberated.

The effects of the war were obvious. There was the destruction in the north and east of the country, and as the houses were re-built, the bridges repaired and the fields restored to agriculture, so the war memorials were built in every town and village. There were 700,000 women who had been made widows by the war, many of whom would wear mourning. More than a million men had been wounded and had suffered permanent disabilities. There were old men who had lost the sons who had supported them, there were children who had lost their father. Books, films, arts, all spoke about the war. Associations of former soldiers, veterans, were created, the Anciens Combattants and they made their presence felt in may aspects of social and political life.[21]

The Treaty of Versailles was a good treaty for France (in spite of the criticisms which were made at the time and which have largely dominated the thought of historians since then). Germany was no longer an important military power; the French hoped that they would replace Germany as the leading industrial power. The Habsburg Empire had been broken up. Russia, preoccupied with civil war was no longer a power on the world stage. Everywhere European countries were in crisis. The great parade of 14 July 1919 demonstrated that France possessed the most powerful army in Europe and was allied to the two greatest world powers, Britain and the United States. For the first time since Napoleon it seemed that France could establish predominance on the continent.

But the pessimism that was felt at the time by many French leaders, such as Clemenceau and Poincaré, turned out to have been largely justified. To consider only external events, the recovery of Germany was rapid, and by 1925 Germany was once again a state that commanded support in Europe and possessed a certain national force. Several German governments believed that they would be able to bring about a successful revision of the Versailles Treaty. Great Britain insisted on its world role and found itself in opposition to France in this sphere. The United States retired into isolation and rejected the world role which President Wilson had envisaged. The emergence of Italy as a fascist state posed certain problems. And the Soviet Union was to play a particular role in French domestic politics.

Two fundamental facts remained. Germany had lost population through the casualties of war and through the terms of the Treaty. But its population stood at over 60 millions, whereas the French population, even after the return of the lost provinces, was around 40 millions. Furthermore the demographic future was worse for France than for Germany, the German losses in the war being in a young population with potential for growth, were less catastrophic. Second, the ambition of making France, in spite of its lack of coal and coke, the leading industrial power of the continent came up against the hostility of British and American financiers who worked for the economic recovery of Germany. There was also a certain timidity on the part of French industrialists who, with the exception of Eugene Schneider, were not tempted by the imperialist project of creating installations in Poland and Czechoslovakia.[22] The whole economic project which would have made France the principal steel producer on the continent collapsed at the Spa conference of July 1920 when Germany was allowed a 43 per cent reduction in the coal that was to be delivered to France. By 1922, through importing Swedish and Spanish ore and by constructing new steel works, Germany had regained its superiority in terms of steel.

The issue of reparations was another source of French disappointment. For some French politicians and for much of the public, the issue was simple. Germany had to pay. But the argument (associated with the famous publication by John Maynard Keynes) that it would be foolish to burden Germany with debts that were over heavy, especially at a time when Germany was in difficulty, had made progress, sometimes among French officials. More particularly the implications of enforcing a rigorous policy was being recognized even by those who were most vociferous in their demands that Germany must pay. It would mean breaking with Britain, having to face demands for debt repayments from Britain and the United States, and being forced to see the franc depreciate.[23]

It must be emphasized that at this time France was in a position that was to recur throughout the century. Whereas the French public and French politicians were normally ready to leave matters of foreign policy to experts, events in 1921 and 1922 were such as to make the economic welfare of France dependent upon the outcome of negotiations with other European powers. The number of meetings that were taking place on the continent, the number of international committees that were in process of negotiation and the only-too vivid remembrance of French suffering during the war, meant that all French politicians insisted that they should have their word to say about policies and objectives. France was also adversely affected by the evolution of policies in other countries. Thus in December 1922 the British Foreign Secretary Lord Curzon was scathing in his condemnation of the way in which French governments went in for 'relentless promotion of French prestige' and the British Cabinet laid down that Germany was the most important country for Britain in Europe.[24] The surprise announcement that Germany and the Soviet Union had signed an agreement at Rapallo on 16 April 1922 increased the confusion. The French denounced British policies in the past and in the present and there were those among the French who urged a rapprochement with Germany or, at least, the establishment of an economic cooperation that would transform the insoluble problems of reparations. As Professor Maier has put it, 'indecision itself became too costly to maintain in terms of domestic support'.[25]

When Poincaré returned to power in 1922, a personal element was added to the confusion, since intense German propaganda was suggesting that it was he who was responsible for the outbreak of war and therefore that the 'war-guilt' clause in the Peace Treaty was in no way justified; hence Germany need to pay no reparations. But as Poincaré's British biographer has pointed out, although he was deeply affected by these allegations, they do not explain his actions. He firmly believed that for France to be in a position to resist Germany, it was necessary for the 'union nationale' to persist, but this was increasingly difficult because of left-wing opposition, pacifism and the creation of the French Communist party. It was necessary for France to maintain her alliances with Britain and with the United States but experience was showing almost daily the impossibility of doing this; the British government had virtually stopped collaborating with France, while the British Foreign Secretary was indulging in extraordinary outbursts, accusing France of attempting to dominate Europe.[26]

On 11 January 1923 French and Belgian troops began the occupation of the Ruhr. Officially this took place because Germany was not supplying France with the goods that were stipulated in the Treaty of Versailles. Poincaré claimed, when speaking in the Assembly, that they were only there in order to fetch coal. But whatever Poincaré's sentiments, there were plans afoot which involved greater changes. There was the idea of creating a territory in the Rhineland that would be autonomous, producing its own currency. The thought behind these schemes was well expressed by a French General in 1922, who asked whether it might not be possible, in the near future, to speak of 'les Allemagnes', as in the days of Napoleon, rather than 'l'Allemagne'.[27]

The French government could be said to have gained the first stage of the occupation, when the Germans abandoned the policy of passive resistance with which they had greeted the French troops. But Poincaré's position was undermined by the decline of the French franc and by his inability to devise an acceptable form of financial retrenchment in domestic policy. Speculation against the franc, combined with the knowledge that a general election would be held in the spring of 1924, compelled the government to accept an American loan and to accept the consequent obligation that an international committee of experts, presided over by the American banker Dawes, would decide on the future of reparations. It has been said that the very acceptance of the loan and of the obligation to attend the meetings of the Dawes Committee implied the abandonment by the French of all their postwar policy towards Germany. Others have stressed the weakness of the new government of the Cartel des Gauches which came to power after the election of 11 May 1924 without a coherent majority in the National Assembly. It embarked on a new policy, that of an attempted reconciliation with Germany.[28]

The radical leader, Edouard Herriot, accepted the Dawes Plan, which stabilized the German economy and which abolished France's legal authority to force Germany to pay through unilateral action. He attempted to strengthen the League of Nations by a Franco-British initiative, but this failed. He recognized the Soviet Union as an attempt to strengthen the French position in eastern Europe, but French secret diplomacy, which sought to organize a union of certain states around Hungary and thereby to create a bulwark against Germany and improve conditions for French trade, also failed.[29]

From 1925 to 1929 French policy was largely dominated by Aristide Briand, who sought for reconciliation between France and Germany and who believed that this would lead to European cooperation. France would, in this situation, achieve a vital role as the animator and leader of international conciliation. The League of Nations, where the French delegation was carefully chosen, would function in support of France. In this way France would attain security and governments would be able to reduce taxation on rearmament.

In October 1925 the international meeting at Locarno gave France guarantees by Britain and Italy that the existing frontiers of Germany, France and Belgium were permanent, as was the demilitarization of the Rhineland. Germany was admitted to the League of Nations. There followed in 1926 an agreement between the steel producers of France, Germany, Belgium, Luxemborg and the Saar. In 1927 France and Germany signed a trade agreement. The spirit of Locarno received much publicity. It seemed to have given France security, and this impression was all the greater since the years that followed Locarno were years of relative prosperity.

However, optimism faded when it was realized that Britain had not become more active or devoted as an ally, always giving priority to Dominion affairs and to the future government of India; nor had the Locarno agreement concerned itself with eastern Europe. The issue of the Versailles Treaty returned when it was known that the German statesman, Stresemann had accepted Locarno only as a stage in the process whereby he was about to ask for a revision of the Treaty. The Treaty came alive again when, faced by the worsening economic crisis of the depression years, on 20 June 1931, President Hoover proposed a temporary moratorium on all intergovernmental debts, including war debts and reparations. French opinion was indignant that the sacred right to reparation for their suffering in the war should be treated like an interallied loan. This, in French eyes, weighed heavier than the American and British assessment of the fact that France was suffering less from the depression than other countries. In January 1932 a press leak suggested that the

German government had declared that it could not pay any reparations either then or in the foreseeable future. The French government immediately ordered a concentration of forces on the German frontier.

It has been said that on three occasions France had the legal right to use military sanctions against Germany: 1923, when the Ruhr was occupied (but when according to some historians, the opportunity was not taken to extend this operation much further);[30] 1932, and 1936, when Hitler ordered the military reoccupation of the Rhineland. On all three occasions Paris sought an international solution based upon the cooperation of Britain and the United States. In 1932 all that happened was that the reparations conference was postponed from January until June, when the Hoover monatorium was due to expire. Twelve days after the invasion of the Rhineland France, Britain, Belgium and Italy, renewed their Locarno obligations. The military support that they promised was minimal and France's dependence on Britain was maximized. Most historians believe that the movement towards the war of 1939 dates from this period.

Thus it appears that in the 20 years that followed the Armistice, France was dominated by the peace arrangement of Versailles. The new developments that had occurred in Europe, this is to say the founding of Soviet Russia, the development of a Fascist state in Italy, and the Spanish Civil War, prevented any new diplomacy. Although attempts were made to create a meaningful Franco-Russian agreement, notably in 1935, the presence of a Communist Party in France which followed the policies of the Comintern contributed to the unpopularity of any such move. The prospects of an Italian alliance, that had seemed promising at the beginning of 1935, were destroyed by the Italian attack on Abyssinia in October 1935. The French government attempted to compensate for the Italian alliance by hoping that England would extend its Locarno limits but this was refused. The Abyssinian affair, with the revelation of the Laval agreement with the British Sir Samuel Hoare on 3 October 1935, ceding two-thirds of Abysinia to Italy, weakened France's position in the League of Nations.

Further new elements in the French position were the extent of pacifist sentiments at home, the weakness of French finance which meant that diplomatic pressure could be applied through the money markets, and the emphasis of French military policy on defence. Finally there came the hope, prominent from 1936 to 1938, that France and Germany could come to an understanding. There could be an economic agreement; some revision of the Versailles peace could lead to Germany recovering her lost colonies. The past was recalled. Daladier remembered that at

Verdun he had thought that between the French and German peoples, there were strong ties of mutual respect which could lead to loyal collaboration between the two peoples. But in the late 1920's Edouard Herriot found himself wondering if Germany would attack France as she had in 1914. In the early 1930s it was said that Germany was hypnotizing France as it had in the 1890s. The French diplomat René Massigli asked if Europe was to become German.[31]

IV

It must be remembered that the military defeat of France in 1940 was followed by the years of German occupation. During this period there were some who considered that the real enemies of France were the Communists. There were those who believed that Europe would be unified under German rule and that France would have an important role to play in the new Europe. It is known that the vast majority of the population accepted the German presence and tried to adapt to it. These attitudes changed as a result of German defeats, and more particularly in reaction against German atrocities and the Vichy government's cooperation with the policy of rounding up Jewish men, women and children and transporting them to an unknown fate. But while a hatred of the Germans undoubtedly existed in 1944 and 1945, it is possible to remember a time when occupation did not mean complete hatred.

However in 1945 it seemed as if the period after 1918 was to be repeated. Before the Liberation the Provisional Government in Algiers, and later General de Gaulle in 1945, were to make the same demands for French security against Germany. He told *The Times* of London that the Potsdam agreements had amputated Germany in the east but not in the west. Hence German aggressiveness would again face westward (10 September 1945). Therefore the Saar should be attached to France, a French protectorate established in the Rhineland, the Ruhr should be internationalized and centralized government within Germany should be replaced by a loose confederation. It looked as if the same policies and demands would be followed by a weary repetition of the occupation of the Ruhr, the diplomacy of encirclement and all the rest.

But it was not to be. The Soviets, the British and the Americans rejected the French proposals. The French themselves, whether it was General De Gaulle in 1945 or Georges Bidault in 1946, became aware of the dangers of Soviet policy and realized that it was necessary to build up Germany so as to resist the Soviets.

But above all there was the new attitude which was present among certain French officials, and which had been discussed both in Paris and in Algiers. It has been described as consisting of three items. The first was 'grandeur'. This meant something different from military power. It meant that France would be great, assuming a preponderant place in a European ensemble. The second item was 'security'. This was to be attained by removing the causes which had made the German Nazi movement possible, and these were seen as the weaknesses of the German political system. Therefore Germany must become a democracy. The third item was 'coal'. This was the first need. The economic modernization and development of France must take place, but since it was to exist in a European ensemble it must not mean the plundering of Germany. The order went out that when it came to requisitioning in Germany, 'one must not kill the goose that lays the golden eggs'. It has been claimed that these preoccupations made the French occupation zone in Germany quite unlike the other allied occupation zones. The French possessed a particular educational and cultural programme that could be said to lay the groundwork for better relations between the French and German peoples.[32]

One can interpret France's European policy in two ways. The one is that ideology and reason came together. The three wars between France and Germany since 1870 were not only tragic, they were ridiculous. The French and the Germans were Europeans, as were their neighbours. As Europeans they should write and abolish war altogether. The other interpretation is more political. It was obvious that the days of military control were limited, and the presence of American and West European troops in Germany were protecting the west against the Soviet Union. Therefore the Federal Republic of West Germany had come into independent existence. The only way that the French government could retain control over the new state would be to place it in a European grouping.

Thus whether it was through the 'constructions intellectuelles' of Jean Monnet, or through the calculations of politicians, it was Robert Schuman, having himself acquired French nationality only in 1919, who proposed the establishment of a European Coal and Steel Community. This was 9 May 1950. The Germans preferred to be under the High Authority of the Coal and Steel Community to that of an Allied Control Commission. Within France, although both Gaullists and Communists opposed the move, and although French business was hesitant and apprehensive, what else was France to do? Its leaders did not want to repeat the trauma of the 1920s.

Hostility to Germany resurfaced in France when a treaty was proposed that would involve German rearmament. But it was noticed that within Western Germany itself there was also opposition to rearmament. In October a limited German army was integrated into the Brussels Treaty Organization under the auspices of the North Atlantic Treaty Organization. When there was complete disagreement between France and Germany there was invariably an international intervention to break the deadlock. In spite of disadvantages, France could still claim superiority over Germany. France was a world power, even after being forced to withdraw from Indo-China and being in a crisis over Algeria. Western Germany still had to expiate her guilt over the war and the Holocaust.

De Gaulle took a new view of Europe. The union was not simply a means of controlling Germany. It was a means, first, of assuring that the two superpowers should not extend their control over any of the European members, and second that France should be the first of the six countries and thereby, for the first time since Waterloo, should become the first in the world.[33] De Gaulle also endeavoured to change the nature of Franco–German relations with the Franco-German Friendship Treaty, signed in January 1963. It laid down the objectives of coordinating foreign policies and of arranging for economic, military and educational cooperation. But although it alarmed some by establishing a Paris–Bonn axis that threatened to become overpowerful, it proved to be a failure. The German government was not prepared to abandon its links with the USA and the NATO agreement. Nor did the Friendship Treaty have any meaning when De Gaulle, paying no heed to German wishes, rejected British membership of the European Community, took France out of NATO and established closer links with Moscow. General De Gaulle had seriously overestimated his influence.

For nearly 15 years after De Gaulle's resignation the Franco–German relationship was the subject of endless meetings, conferences, speeches and communiqués, but it did not evolve significantly. President Pompidou was worried about the Federal Republic coming to agreements with the Soviet Union and states in eastern Europe. President Giscard d'Estaing abolished the national holiday on 8 May, which was the commemoration of the German capitulation in 1945. Under Raymond Barre French farmers protested that German farmers were getting unfairly high cash benefits from the Common Agriculture Policy.

West Germany became economically more powerful, and the new generations of West Germany were said to have outgrown any sense of culpability about past history. They were said to have assimilated democratic principles, to have gained an independence with regard to America, and to maintain a hatred of the Soviet system as it existed. A perfect symbiosis was possible between France and Germany, but on two conditions: that the Germans did not regard the European Community as a purgatory for their past, and that the French did not treat the Community as a means of holding Germany in check.[34]

For France, the Cold War was a moment of satisfaction. France was the power most needed on the continent of Europe. Western Germany looked to France for protection. France could help to organize further means of protection as was shown when President Mitterrand spoke in the Bundestag on 20 January 1983 recommending the West Germans to maintain American missiles on their land. It was France which was the intermediary between Europe and the Soviet Union. It was to France that President Gorbachev came when he made his first official visit outside the Soviet Union. This was, according to Mitterrand, natural because it brought together the two people whose peoples had organized great revolutions. Mitterrand was able to multiply visits of French ministers and officials to Western Germany and to encourage German visitors in return. He created the idea that it was the Paris–Bonn axis that was the motor of the European Union. The symbol of Franco–German friendship was Mitterrand and Kohl, standing together, clasping hands over the tombs at Verdun, in September 1984. The nature of Franco–German cooperation is measured by the statistic of Mitterrand and Kohl meeting together on 13 separate occasions between January 1985 and June 1986.

France was able to demonstrate its international importance by its military interventions in Africa. It was a nuclear power and western Germany was not. Above all, it did not seem to the French government or to French observers that there was any possibility of a reunification of Germany. It was not feasible, the idea of the German nation was only a vague idea in Germany. The new Germans were said to be both irritated and impressed by France, 'nation par excellence'.[35] This was just as well since François Mitterrand had gone on record in 1978 as declaring that given the European balance of power, the security of France and the maintenance of peace, German reunification was neither possible nor desirable.[36] A remark which was a throw-back to earlier years.

V

On the morning of 10 November 1989 France awoke to the realization that the Berlin Wall had been destroyed and that the frontier between the two Germanies had been abolished. On 3 November President Mitterrand had declared that he was not hostile to reunification, but on 15 November Foreign Minister Roland Dumas declared to the National Assembly that reunification was not 'un problème d'actualité'. The President echoed this statement in December, and on 9 December the European summit held in Strasbourg decided that the future of East Europe had to be seen in terms of assimilation to Europe.

Undoubtedly the French government was surprised by the Federal Republic's failure to give advance notice of Chancellor Kohl's Ten Points of 28 November. The French had accepted West German economic superiority since the late 1980s. But they had never accepted German independent diplomatic initiatives, hence the emphasis on frequent meetings and the framing of joint communiqués. President Mitterrand made great efforts to bring other powers into the settlement of the question. He consulted President Bush and Mrs Thatcher; he travelled to eastern Germany in the hope of propping up the moribund government there; above all he went to Kiev on 6 December, where he appears to have laid down the principle that in the existing situation which was the result of the war, no country in Europe could take action without consulting other countries. He seems to have repeated the idea, which he expressed in 1986, that with a Soviet Union that had become democratized it would be possible to construct a new Europe which would be more independent of the United States. However he had always been thinking of a Europe evolving over a period of some ten to fifteen years.[37]

The United States supported German reunification. From February 1990 Gorbachev admitted that the process could not be stopped. In March it was accepted by the French government and immediately Mitterrand returned to his idea of 1986, that a profound reconstruction of Europe should take place. In March 1990 it was announced that a European Community policy on foreign policy and security would be proposed and on 6 December 1990 Mitterrand and Kohl sent a joint letter to their European partners. The eventual result was the Treaty of Maastricht, and subsequent decisions concerning the introduction of European Monetary Union. It could be said that this European Union meant that France was in a totally new era of international politics, with profound results upon its domestic history.

One aspect of French policy in the early 1990s was short-circuited. There was the idea that a rapprochement could take place between France and the Soviet Union. This would be ideological, and would repair the rupture that had taken place between the social democracies of France and Russia, on account of the Bolshevik Revolutions, and it would be a question of power, France and the Soviet Union controlling Germany and dispensing with dependence on the United States. But the Soviet Union disappeared. The desire to diminish the importance of the North Atlantic Treaty Organization on the European continent was not shared, either by the states of the European Union or by certain of the leaders of the states of central Europe, such as President Havel.[38]

One could conclude by quoting *Le Monde* of 2 February 1991, stating that Franco–German relations had become a vast building site out of which anything might emerge. There are those who believe that French and German leaders understand the dangers and the historic status, and that divorce between the French and the Germans is impossible, although they inevitably ask whether the widespread intuition of today will remain deeply rooted in the next generation.[39] Yet there are those who protest that France has become the vassal of Germany, and who list the occasions when Germany has cheerfully disregarded French wishes. In the unilateral recognition of Croatia and Slovenia, the interest rates policy of the Bundesbank, the strict interpretation of the rules laid down by the Maastricht Treaty, the location of the Central European Bank in Frankfurt, the decision to call the European currency the 'euro' rather than the 'ecu', the refusal to accept the French candidate for the governorship of the European Bank, these are some of the examples given.[40]

Germany has alternative policies. Given a recovery of Russian power. Germany could become the ally of Russia and seek to dominate eastern and central Europe. But there are French observers who see rather that while German industry is moving to Moravia in Czechoslovakia and Silesia in Poland, it is also moving towards North Carolina. Germany seeks nuclear protection from the United States. A special relationship between Germany and the United States (with or without Great Britain) would have a considerable effect on the defence industries, on agriculture, on investments and on cultural matters.[41] Thus Germany has alternative policies both within and outside the European Union.

But France has nowhere else to go. In this sense, France at the end of the 20th century resembles France in 1920.

Notes

1. This remark has been made by many French politicians and by commentators, both French and non-French. In the form quoted it is usually attributed to André Fontaine of *Le Monde*, writing in 1952.
2. Robert Gildea, *The Past in French History*. (New Haven, CT and London: Yale University Press, 1994) pp. 119–21.

3. Antoine Prost, 'Verdun', in Pierre Nora, *Les Lieux de Mémoire.* (Paris: Gallimard, 1997), vol. 2, *La Nation*, pp. 1755–80.
4. Clemenceau, 27 March 1919. Paul Mantoux, *Paris Peace Conference 1919: Proceedings of the Council of Four.* (Geneva: Librairie Droz, 1964) pp. 24–9.
5. Charles De Gaulle, *La Discorde chez l'ennemi.* (Paris: Berger-Levrault, 1934); *Vers l'armée du métier.* (Paris: Presses Pocket, 1934) pp. 18–22.
6. Charles De Gaulle, *Discours et messages.* vol. 1. (Paris: Plon, 1970) p. 497. Quoted in Maurice Vaïsse, *La Grandeur.* (Paris: Fayard, 1998) pp. 30–1.
7. Jacques Attali, *Verbatim III.* (Paris: Fayard, 1995) p. 369.
8. Mitterrand made this remark to François Léotard, footed in François-Olivier Giesbert, *Le President.* (Paris: Seuil, 1990) p. 378.
9. J. C. Hunter, 'The problem of the French birth-rate on the eve of World War I', *French Historical Studies*, (1962) 490–503.
10. Georges Suarez, *Briand: Sa Vie, Son Oeuvre*, Vol. 5. (Paris: Plon, 1941) p. 429.
11. See Claude Carlier and Guy Pedroncini, *Les Troupes coloniales dans la Grande Guerre.* (Paris: Economica, 1997).
12. Quoted by Tony Chafer, 'France and Black Africa: a very special relationship', *Modern and Contemporary France*, No.4 (1996) 427.
13. Alain Peyrefitte, *C'était De Gaulle*, vol. 1. (Paris: Fayard, 1994) p. 139.
14. This argument was used by both General De Gaulle and by President Pompidou in their respective interviews with the American journalist Cyrus Sulzberger, 14 February 1969 and 29 July 1969. See his *An Age of Mediocrity.* (New York: Macmillan now Palgrave, 1974) pp.165, 563.
15. Hubert Védrine in Samy Cohen (ed.), *Mitterrand et la sortie de la guerre froide.* (Paris: Presse Universitaire de France, 1998) p. 286.
16. Louis de Guiringaud, *L'Express*, 23 December 1979, quoted in Samy Cohen, p. 275.
17. Gabrielle Parker, 'French Language Policy in Sub-Saharan Africa', *Modern and Contemporary France*, 4 (1996) 477.
18. For the economic war aims see Georges-Henri Soutou, *L'Or et le sang.* (Paris: Fayard, 1989) and M. Trachtenburg, 'A New Economic Order: Etienne Clémentel and French Economic Diplomacy during the First World War', *French Historical Studies*, X (1977) 315–41. More generally see D. Stevenson, *French War Aims against Germany 1914–1919.* (Oxford: Clarendon, 1982).
19. Anthony Adamthwaite, *Grandeur and Misery: France's Bid for Power in Europe 1914–1919.* (London: Edward Arnold, 1995); Charles S. Maier, 'The Truth about the Treaties?', *Journal of Modern History*, 51, 1 (1979) 56–67; Jon Jacobson, 'Strategies of French Foreign Policy after World War I', *Journal of Modern History*, 55, 1 (1983) 78–95.
20. See the introduction to Claude Paillat, *Dossiers secrets de la France contemporaire*, Vol. 1 *1919: Les Illusions de la Gloire.* (Paris: R. Laffont, 1979).
21. These have been studied by Antoine Prost, *Les Anciens Combattants et la Société française*, 3 vols. (Paris: presses de la Fondation Nationale des Sciences Politiques, 1977).
22. G. Soutou, L'Impérialisme du pauvre: le politique économique du government français en Europe centrale et orientale de 1918 à 1929, *Relations internationale*, 7 (1976).
23. J. F. V. Keiger, *Raymond Poincaré.* (Cambridge: Cambridge University Press, 1997) p. 270.
24. *Documents on British Foreign Policy, 1919–1939.* Series I. vol. 16, p. 867.

25. Charles S. Maier, *Recasting Bourgeois Europe*. (Princeton: Princeton University Press, 1975) p. 285. See also the relevant chapter (5) in Walter A. McDougal, *France's Rhineland Diplomacy 1914–1924. The last Bid for Power in Europe*. (Princeton, Princeton University Press, 1978).
26. J. F. V. Keiger, pp. 274 ff.
27. See the research carried out by Stanislas Jeanneson, *La France, Poincaré, et la Ruhr 1922–1924*. (Paris: Presses Universitaire di Strassbourg, 1997).
28. Stephen A. Shuker, *The End of French Predominance in Europe*. (Chapel Hill, University of North Carolina Press, 1976).
29. François Fetjo, 'La Petite Entente, la France et Benes', *Vingtième Siècle*, January–March (1991) 11–15.
30. Maier, *Recasting Bourgeois Europe*, pp. 392–3
31. See the chapters by Douglas Johnson, Neville Waites and Maurice Baumont in Neville Waites (ed.), *Troubled Neighbours Franco–British Relations in the Twentieth Century*. (London: Weidenfeld and Nicolson, 1971), and Anthony Adamthwaite in W. J. Mommsen and L. Kettenacker (eds), *The Fascist Challenge and the Policy of Appeasement*. (London: Allen and Unwin, 1983).
32. Rainer Hudemann, 'L'Occupation française dans les relations franco-allemandes depuis 1945', *Vingtième Siècle*, July–September (1997) 58–68.
33. De Gaulle to Alain Peyrefitte, 22 August 1962. Alain Peyrefitte, *C'était De Gaulle*, pp. 158–9.
34. Gerhard Kiersch, *Les Héritiers de Goethe et d'Auschwitz*. Translated from the German. (Paris, 1986).
35. Michel Meyer, 'Quoi de neuf? L'Allemagne', *L'Express*, 18 April 1986.
36. Louis Wiznitzer, *Le grand gáchis or la faillite d'une politique ètangère*. (Paris: First, 1991) p. 125.
37. In a posthumous work François Mitterrand seeks to minimize his hesitations and hostility to changes in Germany. See his *De l'Allemagne et de la France*. (Paris: O. Jacob, 1996). It is well known that he has questioned the conversations reported in Jacques Attali, *Verbatim III*. See Georges-Henri Soutou, 'La France et les Bouleversements en Europe', *Histoire, Économic et Société*, 1 (1994) 190–214 and *L'Alliance Incertaine*. (Paris: Fayard, 1996); Sami Cohen, *Mitterrand et la sortie de la guerre froide*, Douglas Johnson, *How European are the French?* (Reading, University of Reading Press, 1996).
38. See the article by Pierre Mauroy, 'Construire l'eurogauche', *Le Monde*, 31 March 1989. On President Havel and the role of the USA in the defence of Europe, Claire Tréan, *Le Monde*, 24–25 September 1989.
39. David Calleo in Patrick McCarthy (ed.) *France–Germany 1983–1993*. (Basingstoke: Macmillan now Palgrave, 1993) p. 197.
40. Edouard Husson, *L'Europe centre l'amité Franco-Allemand des malentendus à la discorde*, (Paris: F.-X/Guibert, 1998).
41. See Alexandre Adler, 'L'Allemagne irremplaceable', *L'Express*, 26 June 1997.

12
Defeat and Stability: 1918, 1945 and 1989 in Germany[1]

Mark Roseman

For Germany more than any other country under review in this volume, the three ends of wars brought dramatic change. Each involved fundamental alterations to Germany's internal political and social structure. Each confronted Germany with a new international environment, in particular with a new political constellation on its Eastern borders. Yet the significance of these turning points for Germany's ability to maintain a stable democracy was vastly different. The new democracy that emerged in 1918 was contested from the start, subject to violent attack from within and gave way after 15 years to one of the most murderous regimes in human history. After 1945, in the western part of Germany at least, a much more successful democracy emerged. The Federal Republic became as indelibly associated with stability as Weimar was with crisis. The third turning point 1989, despite increasing the size of the population by a third and fundamentally altering the Federal Republic's geopolitical situation, has until now had a much more limited impact on Germany's political system.

The contrast between 1945 and 1918 is particularly striking because so many of the postwar problems adduced to explain Weimar's downfall were equally present after World War Two. Take the Versailles Treaty, which imposed on the Weimar Republic territorial losses, demands for substantial reparations and, in the eyes of most Germans, a loss of status and honour. As well as fostering bitter resentment against their former enemies, the Allies also helped alienate many Germans from their own Republic. Weimar appeared dishonourable not just because its statesmen had, by signing, made themselves a party to the Versailles peace treaty; but also because in the eyes of many the domestic political system itself bore the taint of Allied imposition. After all, the pressure to depose the Kaiser became unstoppable only following Wilson's hint of better treatment if the Kaiser went. Yet the demands made by the Versailles peace treaty on Germany were as nothing compared to the territorial loss and division of the post-1945 period. There was, to be sure, not the huge reparations bill to be faced – except in the Soviet Zone. Yet even in the western Zones reparations were substantial – in the form of dismantling, under-priced coal exports, stolen patents and the like.[2] In the hunger years after 1945, the potential for an explosive interaction between Germans and occupiers seemed even greater than in 1923, when the French occupation of the Ruhr met such determined opposition from a coalition of government, employers and miners.[3] In addition, the large number of refugees and expellees on German soil seemed to offer a festering sore that – as in the interwar period but far worse – would permanently undermine any chance of political normalization. And if after World War One democracy was tainted by the sense that it had been imposed by the Allies, how much stronger in 1949 must the awareness be of a link between Allied pressure and the adopted form of government!

Another obvious parallel between the two postwar situations was provided by the very serious economic and financial consequences of the war. The costs of war in 1945 were even greater than they had been in 1918. Apart from the destruction and erosion of plant and capacity (soon to be compounded by dismantling) and the loss of overseas assets, the massive shortages and the millions of refugees to be supported, there was the burden of occupation costs to be carried (though it has to be acknowledged at the outset that the British and Americans bore a considerable part of that charge themselves).[4] The mortgage on future growth prospects thus seemed all the greater in 1945. Moreover, the same problem of wartime inflation applied. In the immediate postwar years there was no hyperinflation, to be sure, but the vast prices of the black market accurately reflected the imbalance between available cash and supplies of real goods. The 1948 currency reform, though differing from the 1923–4 stabilization in some key respects, left millions of savings accounts holders with only a fraction of their former assets and generated mass unemployment that lasted well into the 1950s.

Yet the political outcome of these challenges was very different. Why?

I

In the 1950s and 1960s, when observers began to try to account for Bonn's success, two answers were ready at hand. One was that for all the economic pain of its opening years, the FRG rapidly moved into an almost miraculous period of sustained growth. Prewar output levels were surpassed by the early 1950s and grew initially at around 10 per cent per annum. Thus, whereas in 1929, ten years after the Weimar Republic's creation, Germany's first unhappy democracy found itself engulfed in the consequences of the Wall Street Crash, in 1959, a decade after the Federal Republic's foundation, Germany was entering an era of full employment and unparalleled prosperity. Apart from German hard work, the cause of this prosperity was believed to be the Federal Republic's Economics Minister, Ludwig Erhard, and his policy of the 'social market economy'.[5] There is no question that Erhard helped to introduce some positive modifications to the economic and financial system. The creation of a central bank independent of political control helped ensure public confidence in the stability of the currency. Following the introduction of the DM in June 1948, Erhard not only rapidly dismantled much of the control apparatus which had hitherto administered the postwar economy but also went further in the direction of a market economy than the framework of the interwar period: cartels were outlawed and the protectionist trend of the interwar years was replaced by a more consistently free trade approach.

The social element of the social market economy, however, was initially no more than an ideological fig-leaf. It is also open to question how consistent the authorities were in their commitment to the free-market. Fear of inflation led the government to hold down prices in so many key areas of the economy that this in turn distorted investment flows, requiring some rather unmarket-like expedients. Nor is it clear how far Erhard's policies were actually responsible for later prosperity.[6] Most industrial countries grew far faster in the 1945–73 era than they had before the war and many of them pursued different policies to Erhard. All benefited from a more propitious external framework, thanks to structural change, institutional innovation and coordination by the USA. The USA, for reasons to which we must return, had also worked hard to help revive acceptance for German goods in other European markets. This was the principal benefit of the Marshall Plan for Germany. Wartime innovation and the dispersal of production sites away from bomb-hit areas meant that German economic capacity in 1945 was much higher than the ruined cities led observers initially to believe. The huge influx of expellees, refugees and economic migrants from the Soviet Zone more than made good wartime labour losses in western Germany. Though a difficult social problem initially, in the medium term the influx of willing and qualified labour was a boon.

But more significant than the debate about the causes of the FRG's economic growth, however, is the fact that the political process by which the economy was reformed in the late 1940s suggests that – well before prosperity had kicked in – government and society were already operating in very different ways to their Weimar forebears. A glance at Niall Ferguson's chapter shows what is distinctive about the 1948 reforms: relatively early on, and without being forced into it by hyper-inflation, the German administration (in partnership with the Military Government) proved willing and able to risk unpopularity and unemployment for the sake of longer-term economic benefits. From 1948 until the early 1950s, although growth was already rapid, the widespread unemployment and economic hardship led to great uncertainty among the population at large about the development of the economy. In 1950, Germany's workers were little better off than they had been in 1913 and a year later, Erhard was the most unpopular minister in the cabinet. It was only in 1953 that the majority of the population showed any confidence in the market economy and only at the end of the 1950s that real prosperity began to change the lives of Germany's working class.[7] The story of the introduction of the 'social' market economy thus begs more questions about Bonn's early stability than it answers. What is particularly interesting is why the German administration felt able and willing to introduce a fairly naked capitalist order, despite being backed by only a minority among Germany's political leaders, let alone its population, and how it could be sustained for the first few years without causing the sort of political fall out that might have weakened democracy, forced the political parties further apart, and reduced investor confidence. We must return to this in a moment.

The other standard explanation for Bonn's success was that the constitution and policy-makers had learned from their mistakes and created a Republic able to respond to the challenges of reconstruction and international integration.[8] Certainly, Bonn's federal system was not burdened by the presence of an overweening Prussia, as Weimar's had been. Bonn's system of proportional representation was complemented by a first-past-the-post first vote and a 5 per cent electoral hurdle, both designed to trip up small extremist parties before they could gain the light and sustenance which Weimar had so naively allowed them. Not only the radicals, but the people themselves were prevented from disturbing the reasoned deliberations of the parliamentarians: Weimar's panoply of plebiscites, referenda and Presidential elections had no place in Bonn's Basic Law. The President was to be largely ceremonial. And parliament itself had responsibility enjoined upon it – votes of no confidence were not allowed unless a viable coalition was ready to take over government. But while the constitution-makers in Bonn had indeed lasting cause to be proud of their handiwork, it is not clear that their changes – with the exception of the destruction of Prussia, a step for which the Allies and not they were responsible – made such a difference. Until 1957, for example, the electoral hurdle was enforced only in a watered down version – yet the emergence of a strong, stable centre-right electoral block was already clearly apparent in the early 1950s. In any case, the constitution makers had restored as much or more than they had changed. Both Republics were capitalist democracies with a federal structure based (largely) upon proportional representation. Large parts of Weimar's constitution and legal code were readopted or remained in force in Bonn. It seems unlikely that the modifications, valuable though they were, could really account for Bonn's triumph and Weimar's tragic demise. No politician would ever again dare to draw up a constitution, if so much were to hinge on a paragraph or two! And in institution after institution, where the Allies had attempted to impose reforms – be it in the civil service, in schools, universities or in local government – most of their changes never found their way to the German statute book, or were reversed once the Federal Republic regained sovereignty.[9]

Instead what is striking is that despite great institutional and personnel continuity from previous eras (and at a time when such political reforms as had taken place had had little time to bite), government already seemed firmer, the electorate less bitterly divided, extremism was off the stage and violence absent from politics. Military government, of course, had a lot to do with the maintenance of public order. And yet the Allies' very presence, which in Weimar had aroused so much opposition and done so much to discredit the institutions to which they helped give shape, did not seem now to be weakening the Federal government's position. The nature of Bonn's institutions cannot explain this any more than can the later diffusion of prosperity.

II

Institutional comparisons rest not only on a misapprehension of the process by which the Federal Republic gained strength and stability after the war, but also on a misguided reading of Weimar's problems. Recent research suggests that Weimar's principal problem was not its constitution *per se* but the enormous crisis of adjustment (political, economic, social and psychological) thrust upon it by losing a major war.

As Richard Bessel among others have shown, it was the scale and simultaneity of the postwar challenges that was the primary problem.[10] The argument here, then, is that neither institutions nor indeed even social structures and attitudes in Bonn were initially very different from those of Weimar. What was different was the process of managing the transition from war to peace, from the old regime to the new and from defeat to reintegration into the international community.

In 1945 the Allies were in a far better position to impose their blueprints onto postwar Germany than they had been in 1918. This was partly because the objective imbalance in power was now so much greater. In 1918, the Allied superiority of forces had begun to tell only in the closing months of the war, and the German army remained largely intact even at the close of hostilities. In 1945 the Wehrmacht was in tatters, while the Allies controlled armies of millions of men with equipment replenished by the massive resources of the US. Germany itself was overrun, with Allied tanks on every street corner. In 1918 it had not been occupied.

Moreover, there was in 1945 no organization or movement that could speak for Germany and articulate a counter-position. In November 1918, it is true, there was a brief period when the old Germany had faltered, and for a few weeks the established apparatus of power was sidelined by the élan of a revolutionary movement. But there was only a relatively short period in which the confused power situation meant that there was no one to speak for Germany in relation to the Allies. In 1945, however, Allied insistence on unconditional surrender had denied any chance that vestiges of the old regime might preserve themselves in office. Even with such Allied prohibitions, an alternative national voice might have emerged had there been any sort of successful national resistance movement against Hitler analogous to the popular fronts of France or Italy. But in Germany such movements had not gained any momentum before the final collapse of the regime. The Nazis had murdered many of their potential leaders; and the failure to achieve anything undermined the moral claim that the resistance might have had. The left did, it is true, move quickly after the defeat to create workers committees in many towns and just possibly these might have formed a new kind of public representation – but the Allies moved in to squash them before they could do so.[11]

The élites that did emerge in the occupation years were ones whose composition was heavily influenced by the Allies. With the partial exception of the church, it was some two years before German institutions emerged that could operate at a high enough level to supply a leadership role – and they operated in circumstances very much dictated by the Allies. Thus, while the Allies could not control it completely, the whole process of opinion formation was far more subject to their decree than it had been in 1918.

Germany lay prone to the invaders also in a psychological sense. Whereas in 1918 the nationalist spirit was in many cases unbroken or only temporarily dented and resentment against the peace terms very rapidly reached fever pitch, in 1945 it remained only in the persistence of the widespread belief that somewhere Germany had been wronged and that the whole mess somehow went back to Versailles. There were also plenty who could still find much that was good in National Socialism, or believed that the Jews were somehow Germany's misfortune. For the rest of it, the massive destruction and the overwhelming evidence of the Allies' superiority ended any plausibility which nationalist politics might have had. In 1918 it had been possible to believe the undefeated army had been stabbed in the back. In 1945, as the wretched ragged remains of German units plodded desperately homewards, it was clear that the country had been monumentally defeated. The scale of defeat was written everywhere, both in small details and the large picture, and the German people were drained of energy, and for the most part without hope. It is only this spiritual exhaustion that can explain, for example, how in its zone the Soviet Union could so easily carry out the Communization of an advanced industrial society. In such a context, even if the underlying values about the Jews or Versailles persisted, nationalist politics made little sense. The realities of power were against it.[12]

But even with Germany so weak, a stable settlement would require some common ground between victors and vanquished. In 1945 there was some basis to hope that such common ground could be found. The Allies, for their part, had adopted at Teheran the positive goal of democratizing German society. True, the decision to define positive war aims was taken for largely tactical reasons. In 1945, security ranked higher for all the Allies, with reparations also a top priority for France and the Soviet Union. The fact remains that the Allies presented themselves to the Germans as coming with positive as well as punitive intentions, an important prerequisite for German initiatives. Moreover, however vague or tactical the intentions at Teheran, they revealed that Allied planning staffs had learned a lot from the debacle of the interwar period. It was unlikely that a stable Europe could be built upon a disgruntled Germany. One of the distinctive features of wartime thinking in Britain and the USA, and to a certain extent among the De Gaulle's advisors who were later to make up the staff in the Quai d'Orsay, was also the degree to which they understood that a stable postwar settlement could be built only on sound *economic* foundations. It was hard to imagine a stable Europe that was not reasonably prosperous, and hard to imagine a prosperous Europe without a functioning German economy in its midst. The British foreign office, in particular, was well aware of the danger of starving the Germans. Despite briefly signing up to the ludicrous Morgenthau plan, Churchill too declared he would like to see the Germans 'fat but impotent'. Many French experts too were conscious of the need to establish a more productive relationship between the Ruhr and the Lorraine, though these insights were initially unable to assert themselves in general French policy.[13]

On the German side, too, a number of important groups saw in the Allies a favourable opportunity for change or at least a force with which they could cooperate. In part, this was simple opportunism, as leading German figures trimmed their sails to the new wind. In the closing years of the war even a leading SS figure such as Otto Ohlendorf encouraged economic experts to plan out what Germany's policies would have to look like in an American dominated world.[14] But there were also other groups who had more principled reasons for working with the Allies. The willingness of bourgeois democrats like Konrad Adenauer to cooperate with the Allies reflected, apart from simple realism, three major insights. The first was that the experience of Fascism had vastly upgraded the priority of establishing the rule of law and a sober political system as against, say, articulating national interests against the former enemy. Thus the common ground they shared with the western Allies seemed far greater than it had in the interwar period. Second, as early as 1945 observers like Adenauer saw the threat of Communism, and believed that only close cooperation with the West could halt it. But third, and more unexpectedly, the turn to the Allies also reflected some politicians' fear of what Germany itself was capable of – in Adenauer's case expressed as a fear of Prussia. The Allies' involvement and close ties to the west, could help rescue Germany from itself.[15]

From the German left's point of view, the greater potential for cooperation in 1945 than in 1918 rested in part on the new fact that the former enemy was – in the British and Soviet cases – now governed by representatives of organized labour. Moreover, like their bourgeois counterparts, many labour leaders now laid far greater emphasis than hitherto on re-establishing and protecting civil liberties and the rule of law – giving them a basis to cooperate with the capitalist Americans as well as with the British. Many had spent years of exile in Britain and the USA and had developed considerable sympathy with the host societies to whom they owed their personal survival. When they returned from exile to rebuild the labour movement in 1945, they felt often profoundly out of synch with a workforce which had so docilely and sometimes enthusiastically sustained the Hitler regime to the bitter end. In particular the returning leaders did not know what to make of the younger generation of workers, with whom they had had no contact, and to whom they had provided no schooling. With such an uncertain mass basis, Military government support looked set to play a vital role in carrying out major structural change.[16]

The other crucial contrast between the two immediate postwar periods related to the inner divisions within German society. After World War One, Germany had experienced a revolution and in its aftermath been plunged into civil war. The fears and antipathies aroused on the right by the revolutionary overthrow of the state in the November days, and on the left by the sight of the SPD using ruthless and ill disciplined Freikorps to crush the revolution and by the disappointment of many of the hopes of 1918, created a chasm in the heart of Germany society that no subsequent Weimar government was able to heal.

One reason that this did not happen in 1945 was, of course, that Allied troops prevented a power vacuum from emerging. A revolution was simply not possible. Yet there is reason to imagine that, even in the absence of Allied troops, German society would not have plunged into the conflicts of 1918. The only clearly positive outcome of World War Two in comparison with 1918 (apart from the public acknowledgement of defeat), was that it had blurred rather than reinforced class divisions. The relative 'success' of the rationing system (that is, the privileging on racial lines of the 'Aryan' German population at the expense of other 'racial' groups), the fact that every class grouping had been almost equally hit by bombing and expulsions, and that all classes felt somehow implicated in the crimes which they at least half knew had been carried out in their name, had created the sense of *Schicksalsgemeinschaft*, or community of fate, that the Nazis had invoked so fervently. That fact, together with the exhaustion of the population, was to help secure the postwar settlement when it emerged.[17]

Moreover, just as in France and Italy in 1944–5, the right was in disarray. And as in those countries the left was committed to a broad popular front strategy, concentrating on reconstruction with the hope of future structural reform, rather than revolution now. Germany's Social Democratic leadership had in reality long advocated a cautious pragmatic approach, but unlike Weimar they were not now being outflanked by the Communists. In line with the Soviet popular front strategy adopted in the 1920s, the Communists were keen to work within the framework of a broad anti-Fascist alliance, embracing bourgeois elements without precipitately pushing forward to revolution. As in other countries, the notion that some sort of front might be created, or at least that different groups might cooperate in pursuit of certain shared aims, was reinforced by the fact that among many bourgeois political leaders, too, there existed a strong sense in 1945 of the need to create a more socially minded and caring society. The collapse of the economy and the level of destruction inclined many Christian Democrat politicians, for example, to call for the nationalization of basic industries and the introduction of other forms of public control into the economy. The CDU's 1947 Ahlen programme is the most famous expression of this line.

Of course, there were many factors in the immediate postwar period less propitious for the creation of stability. The biggest problem of the opening years was the fact that the struggle between the Allies to find a common line undermined attempts to restore democracy and prosperity in Germany. Soviet reparations demands, French security fears, the punitive and restrictive climate of early US policy-making and British worries about over-burdening the exchequer could not, despite almost two years of trying, be fit together to create a common policy. As a result, the years 1945–8 were immensely testing for German society. Food fell for many to near starvation levels; the black market thrived as normal channels of distribution failed, there was a massive increase in criminality, particularly youth criminality and prostitution. In the face of this chaos, opinion polls revealed that a growing proportion of the population were prepared to look back on National Socialism favourably, as 'a good idea that had been badly executed'.[18] The left too was growing disillusioned at the failure of the British to engage in constructive rebuilding or the hoped for structural change. For the left, there were disturbing signs that the employers were regrouping and regaining influence.

By some obvious yardsticks the immediate postwar years were thus years of disintegration rather than stabilization, leaving many people frustrated or yearning for the ordered certainties of the Nazism of the 1930s. Many British observers certainly felt that in early 1947 that they were walking back into a repeat of the struggles between victors and vanquished which had so poisoned the post-1918 settlement.[19]

III

By then, however, Britain and the USA realized that they could no longer allow policy to drift for the sake of trying to reach some kind of accommodation with the Soviet Union. For the USA, it was the failure of the Moscow Conference in April 1947 to reach any positive conclusions that ushered in a very rapid shift of policy. America now committed herself to rapid German economic revival within the context of an integrated European economic recovery programme (the Marshall Plan was announced in June) and to the creation of a Western German state. The logic to these moves was initially more economic than anti-Soviet, but the introduction of the Marshall Plan produced such a rapid worsening of East–West relations that the Cold War soon became the principal factor shaping both Allied policy towards western Germany and German responses to the Allies. In Allied eyes, the Cold War lent a strategic value to Germany and to West German public opinion.[20]

Over the period 1947–9 increasing pressure came from the USA for the rapid creation of a West German capitalist democracy. At the London conference in May 1948, the Americans finally persuaded the French to agree to the creation of a West German state, though with a more protracted timetable than Britain and the USA had originally envisaged. Western German politicians were induced to accept a separate West German state now, in the hope of attaining German unity later. For German conservative and pro-nationalist opinion, fear of the Soviet Union was undoubtedly the crucial motive in acceding to this request. They accepted the need to give rapid reconstruction of capitalist democracy in western Germany priority over the struggle to ensure the unity of Germany. This relationship between Cold War and cooperation was apparent at all levels. It was given a radical new twist by the Berlin blockade in 1948, which brought home the potential threat posed by the Soviet Union. The level of anti-Soviet sentiment among the general public reached new heights.[21]

Even so, in view of the demands being made of Germany, it is at first sight surprising that there was not more tension between Germans and Allies over the terms under which the new German state was to be formed. When Germany's leaders were presented in July 1948 with the Frankfurt documents which were to be the basis of deliberations of the future state, they learned that an enormous list of prerogatives were to be retained by the Allies, that foreign control of Ruhr production was to continue indefinitely, that industrial dismantling would continue – a series of demands against which those of Versailles pale into insignificance. To understand the process by which they came to be accepted and how it was that a system that in many ways was so clearly imposed from outside nevertheless came to seem democratically legitimated, we need to look more closely at the relationship between the Allies and the German political élites.

For, in one key respect, the inception of the Federal Republic presented an ironic mirror image of Weimar's demise. In Weimar, democracy had collapsed because a democratic vote willed it so: in the summer of 1932 the two extremist parties polled over 50 per cent of the vote. The people had been allowed to decide, and the people had voted away their own power of decision. In postwar west Germany, on the other hand, the outlines of a democratic capitalist system were laid down with virtually no popular involvement at all. In Weimar the people had voted themselves out of power; now in Bonn they were not to be involved in granting themselves back in power again. The curiously undemocratic process of creating Germany's second democracy began in 1948 with the far reaching decisions about the introduction of a market economy decided upon by a bizonal administration, in coordination with the Allied authorities. The bizonal administration was not directly elected, it was rather nominated by the Bizonal Economic Committee which itself had been elected from the regional Land parliaments. Those parliaments were to remain the only directly elected bodies above municipal level until the election of the first Federal Government in September 1949. (Incidentally, where the directly elected Länder parliaments tried to carry out fundamental reforms to the economic structure – for example in nationalizing key industries – they were prevented from doing so by Military Government with the argument that only a future National Parliament could take such decisions. And this while indirectly- or non-elected bodies were taking the most far-reaching decisions about the future!) After the London conference 1948, when the Allies set the wheels in motion to create a West German state, two German bodies were decisive in creating the new constitution. The body formally entrusted with the task was the so-called Parliamentary Council, again only indirectly elected by the regional parliaments. The Parliamentary Council was however heavily influenced by the draft presented by a committee appointed by the Minister Presidents of the Länder. Many of the members of the committee were administrative and technical experts rather than party political figures. To underline the remoteness of the process from popular involvement, the decision was taken deliberately not to put the proposed constitution to popular vote. Instead, it was to be ratified by the regional parliaments.

Why did the western Allies find indigenous élites willing to cooperate with them, despite the very narrow room for manoeuvre which the Allies left? The principal reasons were undoubtedly fear of the Soviet Union and a general feeling of there being little alternative. But German political élites were also constrained in how much which they wished or were able to appeal directly to the German people. For one thing, the fact that the bizonal representatives had no direct mandate made it harder for them to speak in the name of the people. On the other hand, many bizonal politicians (particularly on the left) did not want the more directly elected Länder politicians to gain too much profile either – keen as they were to prevent the Länder from gaining too much independence – particularly in view of the known Federalist views of both French and Americans. Certainly, the SPD pushed hard and with some success for the strongly Federalist ideas advanced by some quarters to be replaced by greater emphasis on the authority of the Bund.[22]

A crucial motive for seeking to limit public involvement in the constitution-making process was the desire to avoid making the new West German state seem anything other than a temporary and provisional expedient. That is why it was decided not to call the Parliamentary Council a constituent assembly (which is what it was), nor to choose its members by national election nor even to put its final deliberations to a referendum! An equally important motive for limiting public involvement was the fact that many West German leaders remained rather fearful of the instincts of the German people. Adenauer favoured the creation of strong ties between Germany and the West not least because of his fear of the revival of Prussianism and his desire that *his* Germany, Rhinish Germany, the Germany that looked West, would triumph over the other Germany with its autocracy and eastern ambitions. For other politicians, too, the attitudes of ordinary Germans were something of an unknown territory. There was therefore considerable reluctance to exploit even the limited opportunities offered by the occupation regime to rouse nationalist sentiment and create a popular platform to offset against the allies. Not surprisingly, then, the Basic Law which emerged from the Parliamentary Council's deliberations abolished many of the popular prerogatives enshrined in Weimar's constitution: the president was to be only indirectly elected, and the extensive powers to hold plebiscites and referenda were largely removed.[23]

Once Germany's political élite were set on a course of cooperation with the Allies, the interplay between the two sides brought a number of bonuses for the emerging Federal Republic. Above all, it had the effect of blurring many of those fronts of confrontation which had arisen between government and people, or left and right, in the post-1918 period. Consider the relationship between labour and capital. On the one hand, until the early 1950s the Allied presence gave labour leaders considerable leverage in economic policy-making that was not dependent on the unions' ability to get labour on to the streets. The employers' need to get union support in opposing Allied plans for deconcentration, the government's desire to enlist their involvement in plans for the European Coal and Steel Community or, at a more local level, the employer's wish to get labour leaders to endorse them before a denazification panel, all gave labour a voice. This encouraged union leaders not to indulge in strike activity which might compromise their claim to be part of responsible policy-making (and perhaps also misled them as to the amount of power they could expect to enjoy in the new system). On the other hand, the frustrations with the 'uncontrolled' economy of the immediate postwar years, when collisions with the Allies were at least as likely as conflict with the employees, and when many workers had become small scale capitalists on the black market, led many workers to give plans for the creation of a socialist or mixed economy less priority than getting the factories working in something like an efficient economic order. But perhaps the most important example of Allied involvement defusing confrontation was the currency reform of 1948 we have already mentioned. The potentially explosive decision to expropriate millions of small Reichsmark holders was seen largely as an Allied fiat. The deflation was thus in political terms relatively harmless for the *German* system – a development reinforced by the way the hardships of the war and immediate postwar period had vastly suppressed popular expectations. A modest stability was all that was demanded.[24]

Another virtue of the relationship between Allies and political class was that, because of the Allies' role in suppressing and containing the disorder of the postwar period, the new government, unlike those of Weimar, did not emerge the prisoner of army and administration. Admittedly the enormous centralization of power under the Nazis had already gone a long way to weakening the informal power which civil service, army and also other groups like the industrialists had wrested from central government under Wilhelm II and Weimar. But the framework of the occupation period reinforced the trend. There was no cartel of big industry and big labour calling the shots on wage and pricing policy; nor were the civil service and army offering Groener-style deals as the precondition for cooperating with government. The army was of course completely out of action – as in Japan a major contrast with the situation in the interwar period. And, of course, the Christian Democratic achievement in creating a large broad-based party of the centre ground reinforced the government's preeminence.

Thus, by dint of the shock effect of war and defeat, the role and function of the Allies, and the pro-western élites who had managed to positions themselves as makers of public opinion, neither public behaviour and attitudes nor the results of the first Federal elections in September 1949 pointed to the public alienation, disaffection or radicalization which had been such a feature of the Weimar period. The radical right had been so discredited (and, it has to be said, discriminated against by Allied electoral practices) and the Communists so marginalized that the politicians of the centre ground had emerged at least as strong as they had ever been. True, there were no simple majorities – the proliferation of parties (12 were represented in the first Federal parliament) showed that the new constitutional provisions had not succeeded in ending the problem of political fragmentation. But Germany in 1949 seemed a far less openly embittered or divided society that it had been at the end of its post-World War One stabilization in 1924.

IV

This explains the oddity of the postwar period: that the Federal Republic felt from an early stage very different to its Weimar forebear, despite the fact that in a great many respects public attitudes towards democracy had not significantly changed. Many left-wing observes bemoaned the degree of 'restoration'. And certainly, opinion polls from the first half of the 1950s suggested that the population was not much more influenced by democratic ideas than a generation earlier.[25] Erich Kuby wrote bitterly in 1957 that 'With the flag of freedom in his hand, the Nazi who disappeared from the stage of history now returns to the stage unchanged'.[26] As already argued, the emergence of a stable settlement in Germany had as much to do with the German political élites' fears that the people had learned nothing, as it did with changes in popular consciousness.

Of course, for all the continuities, there were important changes in the wider ideological climate. The most important difference was the marginalization of aggressive nationalism and the emergence of new attitudes towards Germany's place in the wider world. The sense of the new realities of world power penetrated to every aspect of German life.[27] When it came to attitudes on more domestic matters, it is true, there were many continuities – in middle class anti-Communism, for example, and a strong desire for order. Yet whereas in Weimar, the bourgeoisie had shown itself willing to embrace a culture of violence in order to crush the left, restore order and reestablish Germany's place in the world, after 1949 there was a very conscious effort to return to old niceties. Guides to etiquette and good behaviour, to 'guten ton', sold in hundreds of thousands.[28] While for left-wing critics this emphasis on decency and order was both stifling and hypocritical, and was often not particularly democratic (aiming to produce the decent, loyal state citizen rather than the active democrat), it gave the old civic virtues of the bourgeoisie a place they had not enjoyed in Weimar.[29] Moreover, in Weimar, many on the right had sought to unify society by crushing the organized left. In post-1949 Germany, a strong, anti-pluralistic yearning remained. But instead of aspiring to create unity by force there was an almost wilful desire to believe that German society was *already* unified. The popular sociologists of the time – Geiger, Schelsky and others – reflected and reinforced the desire to believe that here was a society where class divisions were a thing of the past. As a result, even when the rhetoric of political leaders still had a strident Weimar tone, contemporaries often experienced this rhetoric as being out of keeping with the times, a 'ghost-like' reminder of social divisions that ostensibly no longer existed.[30]

There is no doubt that there was considerable obfuscation of the past, denial of involvement, indeed a conspiracy not to mention it. Most German people were unwilling to confront their role in Germany's crimes. But the hegemonic myths of the post-1945 era were far more constructive than those that had held sway in the interwar period. After all, the twists and turns that allowed a whole generation of civil servants and businessmen to emerge with careers intact from the denazification panels, nevertheless at the same time did involve acceptance of the postwar settlement: individuals may have concealed their pasts but they also distanced themselves from them. This was very different from the glorification of tradition or the stab in the back legend which had so undermined Weimar. The kinds of narratives that Germans privately and publicly constructed after 1945 to make sense of what had happened revolved round the lessons that had been learned from the defeat – lessons such as the ability to put your shoulders to the wheel and build a better society, or the ability of European nations to work together. They did not involve denying the defeat or plotting ways to overturn the terms of the postwar settlement.

V

Since the 1950s, of course, the Federal Republic's political culture has deepened and broadened. Attitudes to democracy transformed over the decades as did the nation's willingness to confront its past. By the 1970s and 1980s, West Germany had one of the most pluralist and open political cultures in Europe. As a result, the system was able to surmount a series of challenges and changes without difficulty – be it Germany's repositioning of its foreign policy towards the East 1969–72, dealing with world recession and mass unemployment from 1974/5 onwards, or responding to the challenge of unification at the end of the 1980s. As far as unification is concerned, major problems remain to be faced. But the extraordinary ease with which the West German system accommodated the economic, political and social challenges thrown up since 1989 is surely testament to the Federal Republic's enduring strength and stability. This stability, as we have seen, did not derive from a particular policy blueprint or institutional mix. Instead, the impact of Nazism and war, conjoined with the new geopolitical realities facing Germany after defeat, allowed a partnership between Allies and German political élites to emerge that steered a sceptical and exhausted people towards the unheroic but palpable blessings of a smoothly functioning capitalist democracy.

Notes

1. This is a revised and abridged version of 'Restoration and Stability: The Creation of a Stable Democracy in the Federal Republic of Germany', in John Garrard and Ralph White (eds), *European Democratisation since 1800.* (London: Macmillan – now Palgrave, 2000), pp. 141–63.
2. Werner Abelshauser, 'American Aid and West German Economic Recovery: A Macroeconomic Perspective', in Charles S. Maier (ed.), *The Marshall Plan and Germany.* (Oxford: Berg, 1991), pp. 367–409.
3. Barbara Marshall, 'German Attitudes to British Military Government 1945–1947', *Journal of Contemporary History,* 15, 4 (1980) 655–84; Barbara Marshall, *The Origins of Post-war German Politics* (London: Berg, 1988).
4. Abelshauser, 'American Aid'.
5. The best statement of this view is A. J. Nicholls, *Freedom with Responsibility. The Social Market Economy in Germany.* (Oxford: Oxford University Press, 1994).
6. Not least because success stories were achieved in postwar Western Europe with such a rich and varied array of policies. Doubtless currency stabilization and some relaxation of price controls *were* crucial but in themselves they hardly constituted an institutional revolution. For a critical view of Erhard, see Alan Kramer, *The West German Economy 1945–1955.* (Oxford: Berg, 1991).
7. Thomas W. Neumann, 'Kompensieren und Kaufen – die Währungsreform zwischen Alltagsereignis und identitätsstiftender Legende', in Thomas W. Neumann (ed.), *'Da ist der Aufschwung hochgekommen...' 50 Jahre Deutsche Mark.* (Lüdenscheid, 1998), pp. 41–54; Axel Schildt, *Moderne Zeiten Freizeith Massenmedien und 'Zeitgeist in der Bundesrepulik der 50er Jahre.* (Hamburg: Christians, 1995), esp. pp. 310–11; Michael Wildt, *Am Beginn der 'Konsumgesellschaft'*

Mangelerfahrungen, Lebenshaltung, Wohlstandshoffnung in Westdeutschland in den fünfziger Jahren. (Hamburg: Ergenbnisse Verlag, 1994).

8. On all this, see Kurt Sontheimer, *The Government and Politics of West Germany* (London: Hutchinson, 1972).
9. Christoph Kleßmann, *Die doppelte Staatsgründung.* (Göttingen: Vandenhoeck & Ruprecht, 1991), p. 98.
10. Richard Bessel, 'Why Did the Weimar Republic Collapse', in Ian Kershaw (ed.), *Weimar: Why did German democracy fail?* (London, 1990); Richard Bessel, *Germany after the First World War.* (Oxford: Oxford University Press, 1993).
11. On the absence of any kind of national voice in Germany, see Lutz Niethammer, 'War die bürgerliche Gesellschaft in Deutschland 1945 am Ende oder am Anfang', in Lutz Niethammer *et al.*, *Bürgerliche Gesellschaft in Deutschland.* (Frankfurt/Main: Fischer Taschenbuch-Verlag, 1990), pp. 515–32.
12. On the immediate postwar period, see Kleßmann, *Die Doppelte Staatsgründung 1945–1955.* (Göttingen 1991), pp. 53ff.
13. For an English-language discussion of recent literature on Allied aims, see Mark Roseman, 'Division and Stability. Recent Writing on Post-war German History', in *German History*, 11, 3 (Sept. 1993) 363–90 and Mark Roseman, *Neither Punitive Nor Powerless. Western Europe and the Division of Germany.* (Birmingham: Aston Modern Language Department, Research Papers, 1993).
14. Ludolf Herbst, *Der totale krieg und die Ordnung der Wirtschaft.* (Stuttgart: Deutsche Verlags-Anstalt, 1982).
15. On Adenauer, see Hans-Peter Schwarz, *Konrad Adenauer*, Vol. 1. (Providence and Oxford: Berghahn, 1995).
16. See Lutz Niethammer, 'Rekonstruktion und Desintegration. Zum Verständnis der deutschen Arbeiterbewegung zwischen Krieg und kaltem Krieg', in Heinrich August Winkler, *Politische Weichenstellungen im Nachkriegsdeutschland 1945–1953.* (Göttingen: Vandenhoeck & Ruprecht, 1973), pp. 26–43.
17. Wolfgang Werner, *'Bleib Übrig'. Deutsche Arbeiter in der nationalsozialistischen Kriegswirtschaft.* (Düsseldorf: Schwann, 1983); Ulrich Herbert, *Fremdarbeiter. Politik und Praxis des 'Ausländer-Einsatzes' in der Kriegswirtschaf des Dritten Reiches.* (Berlin/Bonn: J. H. W. Dietz Verlag, 1985); on the widespread knowledge of the Holocaust, see David Bankier, *The Germans and the Final Solution. Popular Opinion under Nazism.* (Oxford: Oxford University Press, 1992).
18. Kleßmann, *Doppelte Staatsgründung*, p. 56.
19. Marshall, 'German Attitudes'.
20. Michael Hogan, *The Marshall Plan.* (Cambridge: Cambridge University Press, 1987).
21. Wilfried Loth, *The Division of the World, 1941–1955.* (New York: St Martin's Press, 1988).
22. H. J. Grabbe, 'Die Alliierten und das Grundgesetz', *Vierteljahreshefte für Zeitgeschichte*, 26 (1978) 393–418.
23. This suspicion of the people remained a remarkably consistent feature in German politics. See Ian Buruma, *Wages of Guilt. Memories of War in Germany and Japan.* (London: Vintage, 1995), p. 28.
24. Lutz Niethammer, 'Privat-Wirtschaft. Erinnerungsfragmente einer anderen Umerziehung', in Lutz Niethammer (ed.), *'Hinterher merkt man, daß es richtig war, daß es schiefgegangen ist'. Nachkriegserfahrungen im Ruhrgebiet.* (Berlin/

Bonn: J. H. W. Dietz Verlag, 1983), pp. 17–107; Mark Roseman, *Recasting the Ruhr 1945–1958*. (Oxford: Berg, 1992), p. 315.

25. See the detailed discussion in Schildt, *Modern Zeiten*, pp. 314ff.
26. Cited in Schildt, *Modern Zeiten*, p. 316.
27. Even German cook-books from the 1950s showed a new receptivity to international influences (albeit with a Germanified touch), see Wildt, *Am Beginn der 'Konsumgesellschaft'*.
28. Schildt, *Modern Zeiten*.
29. On the bourgeosie's embrace of violence in Weimar, see Bernd Weisbrod's excellent essay 'The crisis of bourgeois society in interwar Germany' in Richard Bessel (ed.), *Fascist Italy and Nazi Germany*. (Cambridge: Cambridge University Press, 1996), pp. 23–39.
30. On the discussion in the 1950s, see Birgit Mahnkopf, *Verbürgerlichung. Die Legende vom Ende des Proletariats*. (Frankfurt: Campus Verlag, 1985), pp. 124ff.

13
The Roots of the Italian Political Crisis: A View from History, 1918, 1945, 1989...and After

Paolo Pombeni

It is questionable whether Italy's postwar eras can be understood using the ideal type of stabilization. Certainly the concept is not applicable to the upheavals of the post-1918 period, upheavals that gave rise to a Fascism that itself helped little in solving Italy's historical problems. Probably it is not true either for 1989, when the collapse of bipolar confrontation between the Great Powers and the new settlement of Central Europe coincided in Italy with the end of a form of party-based democracy and a move toward a still not clearly discernable type of new politics, and which is still not ready to be interpreted in terms of stabilization. The question is more open in relation to the post 1945 era, when we find the beginnings of a more substantial form of political stability, even if it developed in the presence of the bitterest ideological struggle in Italian history.

There are many different ways of looking at crisis and stabilization:[1] my own will be, following my own previous work, that of constitutional history and of constitutional reform. This does not imply that I will not take into account social crisis, but simply that I will read it as part of political change. I will not go into details, since I presume some knowledge of constitutional history in the European tradition from Bryce to Weber and from Maine to Hintze survives.[2] It can be argued that the constitutional legacy of 1948 has affected the whole of the subsequent postwar period. Until 1948 the problem was that of writing the new constitution of the republic. Afterwards, the problem became, amidst heated debate, how to interpret it.[3] Finally the post-1989 period brought to the fore the so-called 'question of institutional reforms', practically speaking a re-writing of at least a part of the constitution.

I

Bracketing events of the post-1918 era with this constitutional historical periodization might itself seem questionable. The events of 1918 were in fact dependent on the crisis of a nineteenth-century constitution based on a troublesome combination of English political and French/ German legal models. In other words, Italy had a parliamentary system that lacked the tools to help foster either ideological flexibility or a socially rooted ruling class, with the added complication of a legal system informed by the principles of the German *Rechtsstaat* and of the French system of public administration.[4]

It is a curious fact that political reforms in Italian history have very rarely been achieved in ordinary times and have proved ineffective in transforming political life. During the nineteenth century, and to some extent also during the twentieth century, Italian political thinkers have been fascinated by the English political system as a model of evolutionary change. England was assumed to be a country able to adapt its institutions to changing times without recourse to violent revolutions and with a certain spirit of cooperation among the main political actors.[5]

Very little of this can be detected in Italian constitutional history. Modern Italy has formally had only two constitutions. The first was the so-called Albertine Statute of 1848, originally given to the Kingdom of Piedmont and extended problematically to the Kingdom of Italy.[6] It lasted until 1946 when a constituent assembly was elected to write the new constitution promulgated on 1 January 1948 and is still basically in place today.[7]

Of course in the hundred years of the Albertine Statute many things changed in the political field and in the organization of power. To mention only the major case, Fascism had no difficulty in transforming a parliamentary system into a dictatorship.[8] What needs to be stressed is that formally speaking all this happened in an ambiguous way so that nobody could claim to have changed the rules of the game while everybody knew that the rules were absolutely different.[9]

To understand this paradox one needs to bear in mind the constitutional crisis of 1918. Italy came out of the war as a winner, but as a winner of nothing. France had had a clear goal in its war (to destroy its historical enemy), Britain was in a similar position (to overturn German continental hegemony and introduce an international balance of power). In a word, they were looking at their defeated foe and were able to be satisfied. Italy had a much more ambiguous goal in its war: to show that it was a great power, playing in the same big league as the others.[10]

This was not especially rooted in popular culture; instead, it was the ruling élite that embraced the great-power project with more enthusiasm than chance of success.

An additional problem was that Italy's contribution to the war had been underrated. Italy's enemy, the Austro-Hungarian Empire, had collapsed at the end of the war, leaving the impression that no effort had been required to hasten the end of an empire whose downfall was attributed to the internal cancer of nationalism. This analysis was profoundly mistaken. The Habsburg Empire was a powerful enemy, and the Italians had fought a brave and costly war against it. However in the eyes of contemporaries it was Germany that was the great power and it was the defeat of Germany that gave one the right to speak in the name of a new era.[11] And Italy had had practically no war with Germany; even the formal declaration of war against Germany had been postponed by the Italian Government until August 1916.[12]

The old Italian ruling élite thus found itself deprived of victory and of any form of legitimacy deriving from it: they were no longer political leaders and lost the support and attention of the war veterans. At the same time political leaders on the parliamentary fringe of the political system, moderate socialists and Catholics who in the last phase of the war had accepted a more or less hidden form of *union sacrée*,[13] were calling for political reform in the name of democracy. Calls for a constituent assembly were relatively widespread among the general public. But mainstream Italian liberalism was able to respond to them employing very traditional 'English' theory according to which a constituent power is always present in any form of parliament, making it unnecessary expressly to elect an assembly for carrying out constitutional reform.[14]

In fact, Italian liberals did not think that real constitutional reform was possible. They tried – as usual – to solve the problem by introducing a new electoral law,[15] in the hope that this would act as a way of checking political change, forcing all those fearful of revolution toward the political centre. This strategy is not unusual in political disputes. But it is worthwhile drawing attention to the heart of liberal strategy. This saw the passage of an electoral law, which introduced proportional representation and the *panachage*, that is, the possibility for electors to add to their choice of a list of candidates (a party-oriented vote) another 'free vote' for somebody else outside the chosen party.[16] The liberals hoped that this 'additional vote' would suffice to maintain the position of the prewar notables. But the strategy failed completely and the liberal area (divided into many small 'parties') was no longer dominant, even if it remained the largest group in parliament.[17]

What is interesting is that the Italian liberal élite was unable to govern without an absolute majority: they had no strategies for alliance building, no perspective for dealing with new situations. The electoral law failed to reestablish liberal power, and no other constitutional strategy was available for the liberal élite. From this point on the only strategic issue among the old ruling élite was how to regain hegemony (it was no coincidence this word would be chosen by Gramsci as crucial in Italian politics). And thus the reason why they surrendered to the Fascist movement was because this seemed the only plausible way to attain that goal.

To be sure, the Italian crisis could also be analysed from a social point of view. Deep discontent was widespread across the country and nearly every social group had its own reasons for considering itself robbed of some of its historical conquests. Industrial workers could no longer count on a war-driven economy. Public sector workers felt threatened both by the inflation, which bit into their purchasing power and by the change in cultural attitudes which now painted the state's bureaucratic machine as of little importance and parasitic. There is a huge amount of literature on this phenomenon[18] and the debate about the 'real dangers' of the social unrest in the years 1919–21 is unending. In my opinion what matters in this case is not to measure the extent of the discontent, but to stress that it was seen as 'dangerous' for the post-1918 era because of the combination of two factors. First, the myth of the Soviet revolution frightened the ruling classes into fearing for the future of their social system. Second, the more immediate reality of the established power at certain levels (local administrations, trade unions, some intellectual circles) of new political forces such as the Socialists and the Catholics challenged the established power of the liberal ruling élite.[19]

Of course the seizure of power by Fascism did not restore liberal hegemony, but introduced a new one, even if to classify it is far from easy. The experience of Fascism was a highly ambiguous episode in the history of modern Italy, because it passed through many different phases. In the first phase (1922–4), it could be seen as a new right-oriented coalition but within the context of an authoritarian, albeit still parliamentary constitution. In a second phase, that of 1925–32, it seemed a sort of temporary but unavoidable dictatorship necessary for the restoration of the state. In a third phase, 1933–7, Fascism could be seen as a regime, but only for the lifetime of Mussolini. From 1938 few doubts survived as to the true nature of the new regime, even if some individuals were still confident that the death of Mussolini would bring the adventure to an end.[20]

The Italian constitution was radically changed during these years, even though the previous Albertine Statute had neither been abolished nor changed by direct legal procedure (in spite of many requests to this end by radical Fascist jurists).[21] This gave rise to a peculiar form of 'dual state' (to borrow Ernst Fraenkel's famous definition).[22] According to this view, a 'Fascist revolution' had allowed the monarchy and the old élite to join the new order and had therefore made it possible for elements of the old regime to survive. According to another view the monarchy had coopted Mussolini and his regime as a temporary stopgap measure in order to head off the threat of a revolution and restore, in due time, the *ancien régime*.

II

When Fascism fell on 25 July 1943 nobody had a precise idea of what would happen at a constitutional level.[23] The monarchy, which had been heavily involved in and compromised by Fascism, thought it could cancel 20 years of history and restore, more or less intact, the pre-Fascist political system. This dream was not so far-fetched if we remember that in Italy, and even more so in Germany, the 'dual state' was in place even if the terms of this duality were different in each case. The Fascist system could be seen as a totally new order, which for historical reasons maintained the older figure of the monarch and his statute. Or else it was the recreation of the true conditions for a purely monarchical system, without cabinet government, which for the time being owed this restoration to the extraordinary figure of Mussolini and to the fighting capacity of his political movement.

Many civil servants, therefore, were able to believe, more or less opportunistically, they were serving the king and his legal system in much the same way as others were convinced that they were servants of the Fascist revolution. Both sides to this constitutional comedy thought they could decide at their pleasure to eliminate their competitors and remain alone in power. Both sides were wrong, since the upshot was that the legitimacy of the system as a whole was undermined and than disappeared. Italy became a country without a constitution and without political legitimacy for the last few years of the war.

In this particular case a much more deep-rooted social crisis was at work, than that in the post-1918 era. Fascism, it seems to me, had broken with its social base as of 1938, by which time Mussolini thought he was entitled to enter world history as a great figure.[24] This idea or, rather, feeling, led Mussolini to break with the 'bourgeoisie', regarded as a class interested only in conserving its privileges and resisting any strategy premised on blood and tears in the name of future glory that would follow world revolution. A vast majority of the Italian people reacted with a degree of scepticism to this vision of grandeur proposed by the *Duce*. At this point the regime's legitimacy began to decline in their eyes. It was no longer seen as a 'restoration' of old values (and the old social order), but as a regime with in mind dangerous adventures based on a dubious ideology that was every day farther from the roots of the culture of the middle classes (the original backbone of Fascism). Thus the social unease and discomfort of the traditional Italian civic culture with this new wave of Fascist radical ideology explains the downfall not only of the regime but of the 'establishment' which had patronized its seizure of power in the name of a restoration of the traditional social order.

The only forces that were able to claim a degree of political legitimacy were the political parties who fought against the seizure of power by Fascism and organized a form of resistance inside the country or in exile: the Communists, the Socialists, left-wing liberals and radicals, the Catholics. While very different forces each with its own particular history, each represented a centre of recognized resistance.[25] This is obvious in the case of the communists and socialists, much more intriguing for left-wing liberals and Catholics. Despite the compromise that many leading groups of Catholics (and *in primis* the Holy See), the Catholic Church at large regarded the independence of the Catholic movement as an eternal force, defeating in some cases the attempt of Fascism to control or marginalize it. More generally, it was also true that some elements among the intellectuals and the economic élite refused to be merged totally with Fascism, maintaining a snobbish attitude towards those they thought were mere parvenus.[26]

After 1945 political parties became the watchdogs of the new constitution. Thus if Fascism had rejected party-based politics, it would be party-based politics that would forge a new democratic Italy. Let us not forget that political parties had fought the war against German occupation and its Fascist allies. And let us also not forget that they were the only forces able to sustain a minimum of legitimacy and public life when all the official authorities, beginning with the army, collapsed overnight.[27]

Of course the landscape was more crowded than I have sketched. The main political parties themselves tried to enlarge their consensual base by enlisting to their side other political currents that enjoyed less legitimacy: the right-wing liberals for instance, or newly invented groups of 'democratic labourism' intended to draw in an older generation of Socialists or radicals of Marxist leanings.

This development extended the legitimacy of the political parties over forces and groups of the old élite that were not equipped to cope with the new democratic order. It would however have been difficult to stop this process, given that more or less the same phenomenon was at work in the Catholic party. Being a confessional group, it had to transcend a 20 year history of ambiguous and shadowy relationships that had been built up between the Church and the Fascist regime.

The situation at the end of the war can then be described broadly as follows. No constitution had survived the conflict: there was no trust in constituted power as such, in contrast to France, where de Gaulle depicted himself as the man who would restore republican legality.[28] The only legitimacy on hand was that provided by political parties to the extent that they were indispensable vehicles for securing the trust of the general public in the name of the government. A purely negative attitude toward the reorganization of the state prevailed, in the sense that everybody was eager for a totally new and just system, but they had no clear idea about how to achieve it.

Of course one cannot deny the presence of a deep social crisis in the country. The material reconstruction of society and economy after a disastrous defeat and a war fought across large tracts of the country presented major problems. The integration of the various disbanded groups into society (war prisoners, partisans, soldiers of the Fascist army of Salò) and the continuation of violence and the memory of violence sustained the atmosphere of civil war for several years.[29] Instability was also generated by the great expectations of the winners to 'purify' society and with fear of the defeated of losing their position (a phenomenon that especially affected the large majority of those employed in the civil service).[30] In addition there was a nationwide economic crisis, with industry undergoing radical change and experiencing heightened tension in its industrial relations. This also helps explain why political parties became so deeply rooted in social life because they represented and defended the corporate interests of different social groups in this economic crisis.[31]

The upshot of all these pressing issues meant it was seriously difficult to deal with the constitutional question. The Constituent Assembly was very large but selected on a narrow 'political' basis, with very few of its members having any real experience or training to help them perform their task. The easiest issue to deal with was the introduction into the new constitution of a special section devoted to fundamental rights and guiding principles that were to inform the new state. All the rest was vaguely planned expectations, especially high the hope of creating some sort of economic or industrial democracy.

But in the end a large section of public opinion was confused.[32] No one, or very few individuals, recognized in the text of the constitution their own ideology. Many political leaders argued that the reason for the lack of any specific reference to their party's professed ideology was due to the fact that this had been the price they had had to pay to reach an accommodation with the ideology of their opponents. This is why many politicians and journalists spoke of a compromise constitution, the fruit of uninspired political negotiations that lacked any guiding spirit. Out of these less than inspired results a myth of origins arose. In the decades that followed 'lay', liberal sections of the old and new ruling class tried to explain their less than influential role by pointing to a document written, as it was put, half in Latin and half in Russian. In other words, a constitutional compromise championed by the Catholics was fashioned in which they obtained many privileges for the Church in return for a certain number of social measures favourable to the working class. With more realism, however, the radical jurist Piero Calamandrei believed the Communist party had given up the possibility of changing the ruling classes in the aftermath of the Resistance in exchange for a vague promise of a future social revolution.[33]

But things were actually quite different. In the first place, the proceedings in the Constituent Assembly reveal that no real bargaining took place between the different parties.[34] The role of the Communist party as an institution was virtually non-existent and its secretary, Palmiro Togliatti, was a lone participant in the working committee that agreed to support in large part the ideas and proposals of the Christian democratic left. It was this group, led by Giuseppe Dossetti, that planned the architecture of the new charter. It imparted that peculiar mood to the Italian constitution that promoted as its chief constitutional subject 'the person' rather than the 'individual' of liberalism, a more social interpretation than classical liberalism, but not as economic as he/she was defined in Soviet-style constitutions.[35]

The constitutional debate on these matters was very high-minded, sometimes dramatic, full of political passion. It forced all other problems into the shade. The attempt to engineer real economic democracy produced miserable results: there were no clear suggestions, and the articles dealing with this problem are more rhetorical than effective. The problems of state organization were underestimated, remaining topics for specialists and drawing precious little attention.

The subsequent difficulties for the post-1948 constitutional order are all rooted in this story. The optimistic attitude of the main protagonists of the Constituent Assembly caused the new political class to think that problems could only be solved in a directly political way, that is, open fighting between parties. But an older liberal culture that was predominant among jurists hindered the explicit inclusion in the constitution of the idea of a strong and institutional presence of political parties. Albeit the whole functioning of the political system with its 'secret efficiency' (to use Bagehot's famous formulation) was based on the parties.

Unlike the previous constitution the new document of 1948 was received as a fresh start. It was assumed that Fascism has been able to seize power because no explicit mechanism existed for changing the constitution. Therefore, it was argued, the Fascists had manipulated the old Albertine constitution to achieve their dictatorship. In the 1948 an attempt was made to keep this devil at bay by introducing a very complicated mechanism for amending any part of the constitution (except the treaties with the Church, whose revision did not need the same procedure as that laid down for constitutional amendments).

The possibility of amendment did not exist in the Albertine Statute. The 1848 constitution was a charter *octroyèe*, which explains why there were no procedures for amendments.[36] Only the monarch could have changed what he had granted. The fact that afterwards this had been forgotten did not nullify existence of this great power. Indeed, if one looks carefully at Italian constitutional history, one sees that all the changes took place within the framework of the Albertine Statute and changes that ran counter were rejected. In fact the only real exception to this rule came relatively late on during the last period of the Fascist regime, in 1939, when the Chamber of Deputies was abolished in favour of a new Chamber of Corporations.

Setting up a system based on cabinet government had not caused any problems in post-1860 Italy since this could be explained by the king voluntarily giving up his right to appoint a government without taking into account the wishes of parliament. In fact, during the Liberal period a debate erupted about the possibility of 'going back to the Statute', that is, reestablishing the royal right to appoint the 'Government of His Majesty', and thus ending the practice of appointing the government in line with the wishes of the parliament majority.[37] The success of this drive was very limited and the cabinet system remained dominant in Liberal Italy. But when, as in Mussolini's case, the king decided to act in the old way, choosing his Prime Minister without taking into account the opinion of parliament, no one was allowed to object.

The reform of the Senate under the Liberal and Fascist regimes also displays the tenacity of the Albertine Statute but in this case the issue of will of the representative parliament did not enter. The Senate was a body whose political weight declined rapidly.[38] It consisted of men appointed by the king from among prominent categories of citizens, but had no real representative legitimacy, its political capacity being increasingly undermined. It turned into an honorary body for retired politicians or for prominent members of society.

Before the Fascist dictatorship it was the Senate's majority, composed of liberals, that proposed reform of the Senate, and some eminent senators and political notables such as Fedele Lampertico or Giorgio Arcoleo produced papers on the issue. But nothing changed. Fascism also tried to modify this old-fashioned body, and once again nothing ensued. In both cases nobody put up resistance to the idea of change, nobody objected. The proposals fell short simply because to change the Senate meant admitting that the Statute could be modified and that this constituent power was in the hands of somebody other than the king – parliament, the Fascist regime, or whatever.

Seen in this light, therefore, there was much less room than has been generally assumed for changing the political rules of pre-Fascist Italy: the scope for experiments was limited to electoral legislation that formally did not form part of the constitution. But even the seizure of power by Fascism and its transformation into political regime was achieved by exploiting the silences and ambiguities in the old constitutional charter. The Fascist regime never took account of the requests of its integralist jurists to create a new 'Fascist constitution' appropriate for the new order.

In this respect the fears expressed by the founders in 1948 regarding the possibility of constitutional manipulation were excessive. The old constitution was sufficiently flexible to live happily in Liberal Italy and the Fascist regime without having to be amended or suspended. Rather the rigidity of the amendment process in the new constitution was a product of the mutual suspicion between Christian Democrats and the left (especially the Communist party). Thus the post-1945 settlement and particularly the emergence of Cold War Europe, rather than the putative lessons of Italian constitutional history left their mark on the constitutional settlement of 1948.

Thus the main political parties involved in the creation of the new constitution did not agree on first principles. Meanwhile the opinions expressed by the established mostly moderate-liberal broadsheets were unsympathetic to the conclusions of the Constituent Assembly.[39] In 1948 it was therefore far from clear that the new constitution would be an effective or popular document. In fact a popular and effective constitutional patriotism arose in Italy only several decades later.

In spite of the partisan political disputes of the 1950s and early 1960s, the growing affluence of Italian society and increasing experience of parliamentary democracy led the political establishment to see the constitution as common ground for what could be defined as a 'western liberal-democratic' system. But the inherent tensions present in the constitution of 1948 became evident in the late 1950s and 1960s. Thus the need to spell out the rights of citizens found in the constitution was placed against the defence in the same document of the rights of property and the Catholic religion. In the late 1950s and 1960s, once the first intense period of Cold War confrontation (in which the left had been marginalized) had come to an end, the left pressed for constitutional values and for the defence of the constitution to regain lost political space. Furthermore, this attempt at reformism that invoked the constitution occurred just as the economic miracle rapidly transformed Italian society. Mass migration from the south to the north of Italy broke down regional barriers and consumerism began to undermine the appeal of the older rigid working-class culture that viewed the governments of Cold War Italy with great suspicion. Therefore, economic change and the endorsement of reform through the constitution by the mainstream left transformed the political scene in the 1960s.[40] And in the 1970s and 1980s when terrorism was at its height, constitutional values became a common ground for resistance to subversion and for the legitimacy of the state, to a greater degree than many of the keener supporters for constitutional patriotism had predicted.

Nevertheless this apparent legitimacy was not enough to give stability to a system that did not work properly. As we have seen, the political parties were the guardians of the constitution and the legitimacy of the system was reflected in the public trust shown them both individually and as a party system. But this public trust started to wane at the end of the 1960s.[41] The terrorists of the 1970s believed that lack of trust in the parties would mean the growing delegitimation of the present system and the opportunity to press for revolutionary change. But the terrorists were mistaken. Indeed as has been suggested, under the threat of terrorism the party system enjoyed a resurgence of legitimacy, especially as it afforded the opportunity for the political order to involve the left-wing opposition in parliamentary support for an emergency government. In this way the system reaped the benefit of the added legitimacy it received from bringing on board the 'virgin' opposition without feeling obliged to include the opposition in government.[42]

But when terrorism was defeated and tension eased, the crisis of public trust in the political parties once again appeared. This time, however, the decline in trust also affected the power base of the Communist party, which had lost its supposed political innocence and was seen as part of a broader system. Since the 1970s the left had secured powerful governing positions in local government in many regions and cities. In many respects, the left used (and uses) the same dubious methods of governance as had the Christian Democrat-led national governments since 1948. In both cases the lack of moral rigour or neutrality in favour of a spoils system that allocated public moneys and resources to 'friends', and therefore implicitly relied on a complicated mechanism of allocation and regular corruption to obtain results. It was this that fuelled the distrust of public opinion in a political system based on political parties organized to include and control the different sectors of society.

Out of this discontent the demand for institutional reforms started to grow. The debate was initiated at the end of the 1970s on the occasion of the celebration of the thirtieth anniversary of the end of the 'War of Liberation' and of the Constituent Assembly.[43] This centred on the reform of the power of the political parties in order that the constitutional order laid down in 1948 could be improved. The attempts at institutional reform in the early 1980s centred on the need to diminish the role of the party machinery in the selection of candidates for elections. The need to contain the power of political parties in the formation of national and local governments was also raised. Anticipating the scandals of the 1990s, the early 1980s also witnessed a series of scandals that limited the power of the Christian Democrats. Furthermore, the perennial demand for simplification of the administrative and political machinery was addressed in the present context because its notorious byzantine complexities and abuse of legal technicalities by professional politicians had allowed them to strengthen their hold on power.

III

All this was under way well before the events of 1989,[44] which in a certain sense did not affect Italy. Only with a great effort of the imagination could the Italian Communist Party at that time be regarded as a 'communist' party. There might have existed relics of the romantic left, or the more important presence of a rather crude trade unionist influence. But in a certain sense they were the folklore of the Italian Communist Party. At its centre the party was composed of machiavellian politicians interested only in political games and in controlling the administrative machinery of the party, recalling more the stereotypes of American political bosses rather than the Soviet *nomenklatura*. Nobody in the PCI wanted the Soviet model, neither did the extreme left.[45] And it was generally regarded as completely unsuited to Italian conditions (and more generally for Western developed countries).[46]

Meanwhile ideological weakness and corruption characterized the opponents of Communism (including the new-style Socialist Party of Bettino Craxi). The Christian Democrats were already, in any case, a declining force in terms of political inventiveness or in the capability to plan a future.[47]

Why then can 1989 also be regarded in Italy as the beginning of a new era? I do not share the opinion that the demise of the Soviet system deprived the Italian ruling class of American protection so that it now proved possible to attack the privileges of the governing groups. In this perspective it would have been easier for those attacking these groups that held power to fight for hegemony from within the existing parties as had been done on other occasions in the past. Destroying the system was felt to be dangerous. Thus at first this led to a kind of benevolent attitude toward Christian Democrat rule in the early 1990s and even toward its most compromised leaders, such as Giulio Andreotti, on the part of 'lay' public opinion, traditionally unsympathetic towards the ruling Catholic establishment as a whole.

But instead of the expected moderate transition from the old political ruling class to a replacement gradually rising from it, after 1989 we witnessed the sudden collapse of all the traditional parties of government. The Christian Democrats, the smaller players such as the Republicans, the Social Democrats and the Liberals vanished from the scene. The Italian political landscape has in consequence totally changed. Even the former Communist party was not able to survive this storm, and not because it had to change its name (an irrelevant fact), but because it was completely unable to maintain its leadership of the reformist forces, as it had done in the 1970s and 1980s. During the 1990s the post-communists emerged as leader of the 'conservative' forces fighting to preserve as best it could the *ancien régime*, even at the price of entering a confused alliance with all the surviving groups of political professionals from the previous political establishment.

The year 1989 marked the beginning of all this transformation simply because it provided the Italian people with vivid examples that times could change. One of the most famous statements of Andreotti was, 'Power wears down people who do not have it'. This had been his reply to the prophecy that Christian Democracy was destined to fall because of its long period in government. In fact for many years it appeared impossible to overthrow the 'stabilization' of post-1945. Even the challenge made by Craxi, his attempt to cope with changing times before 1989 through constructing an alternative to the cooption of the Communists. In the 1980s Craxi was unable to cope with the slowness of historical evolution in the absence of any accelerating factors. He thought he could lubricate change through corruption and thus gradually 'buy' off the ruling powers. It turned out to be a naive approach and destroyed not only the personal fortunes of Craxi, but also the chances of creating a rational project aimed at reforming the state and thus providing a basis for a new stabilization.

If I am allowed an oversimplification, Italian political history in the 1980s seemed blocked because world history appeared in stasis. 1989 showed that history goes on, and that Italian history too had to march forward. In this sense 1989 has its true historical parallel in 1848, the mechanisms behind the two events being, *mutatis mutandis*, remarkably similar.

Once more the break from the old regime was sought through electoral reform.[48] The Italian political system was unable to cope with the demand for a new constituent assembly. This was due to series of factors in play in the 1990s. Italy lacked a viable centre of political thought (which in the past, such as during the 1970s, had been the political parties). The ruling classes were worried at the potential lose of their autonomy with the creation of potentially effective future constitutional regulation. In general it was thought that Italian democracy did not have to be rethought, rather the major issue was who dominated and coordinated the Italian 'empire' (to borrow the definition proposed by Charles Maier Chapter 2). Because Italy in the 1990s, as in 1918, was much more an 'empire' than a 'nation'; the presence of the Northern League, with its vague demand for federalism that then turned into a frantic clamour for secession, is proof of this reality.

IV

For much of its modern history Italy has tried to find a solution to the problem of governing its 'empire' of widely differing social, political, cultural and regional constituents. Before 1918 this meant searching for the political leadership that could unify the country through a kind of benign dictatorship tempered by acceptance of a framework of constitutional parliamentarianism. After the 1918 crisis, it was decided that a soft dictatorship was no longer possible and that the preservation of the Italian 'empire' called for outright dictatorship. Then, after 1945, Italy tried to become a 'nation'. The shock of Fascism accelerated the quest to create a common national identity and a common political culture underwritten by a new constitutional settlement. But it was only half-successful. On the one hand, Italian culture was pervaded by a sort of *Verfassungspatriotismus* that safeguarded the peculiar balance of power between the older components of the 'empire' – even if shared historical legitimacy for this constitutional patriotism was sometimes limited to the Resistance and sometimes extended to other periods of Italian history. But on the other, the Cold War prevented the rotation of power at the helm of the petrifying Italian 'empire' and without the exchange of government and opposition the integration of two different political cultures and Italian 'nations' was far more difficult.

The events of 1989 might have provided an opportunity for finishing the work that had been begun in 1945. But the ruling classes and social élite seemed very hesitant to accept the risks such an operation implied and to pave the way for a real transition towards a different political system outside the older framework. What was lacking was quite simply the requisite 'culture'. De Tocqueville splendidly illustrated this cultural landscape in his *The Ancien Régime and the Revolution*; John Maynard Keynes wrote famous lines on a similar type of cultural blockage Italy has experience since 1945 at the time of an equally famous crisis. I do not think it is necessary to add any more words to explain what the nature of the cultural blockage was (or perhaps still is) in post-1989 Italy.

Notes

1. Charles Maier has drawn the attention of historians to this pair of concepts. See, C. Maier, *In Search of Stability: Explorations in Historical Political Economy*. (New York: Cambridge University Press, 1987). In classical historiography, attention was mainly focused on crisis; what followed a crisis was thought as *transition*, more than as *stabilization*. I think that the question is much more complicated than a naive usage of these different terms would suggest. In classical terms a crisis is a sort of final judgment which leads to the dissolution of an ancient order and to the establishment of a new one. In the new usage derived from Maier's approach, a crisis seems to be the loss by a socio-political system of its 'foundation'. This then leads to the rearrangement of the system in a new shape that protects it for a certain time against credible challenges (and this new arrangement seems to be in fact what he means by stabilization).
2. For the study of constitutional history the obvious reference is to the works of Otto Hintze and Otto Brunner. For the first author see, G. Gilbert, *Otto Hintze,*

1861–1940, introduction to, *The Historical Essays of Otto Hintze*. (Oxford: OUP, 1975). For the general framework of constitutional history, including its dependence on Max Weber's works, P. Pombeni, *Partiti e sistemi politici nella storia contemporanea*. (Bologna: Il Mulino, 1994, 4th edn.) (French translation of the third edition, *Introduction a l'histoire des partis politiques*. (Paris: PUF, 1992).)

3. The quarrel about the 'application' of the constitution lasted until the 1970s, but was essential in the development of Italian political life until the beginnings of the centre-left experiment. See F. Bonini, *Storia Costituzionale della Repubblica*. (Rome: NIS, 1993).
4. The best illustration of this peculiarity of the Italian constitution is in, M. Fioravanti, 'Le dottrine dello stato e della costituzione', in R. Romanelli (ed.), *Storia dello stato italiano dall'unità ad oggi*. (Rome: Donzelli, 1995), pp. 407–57.
5. For the fascination of the English model in Liberal Italy, see, Fulvio Cammarano, 'Il modello politico britannico nella cultura del moderatismo italiano di fine secolo', in R. Camurri (ed.), *La Scienza moderata*. (Milan: Angeli, 1992), pp. 309–38. The phenomenon did not end with World War One: it was still alive in Fascist Italy, until the Abyssinian crisis. It returns at the beginning of Republican Italy with a fascination for the Labour government of 1945.
6. The Mazzinians thought that only a constituent assembly could legitimate the rise of a New Italy, which was circumvented by Cavour and the House of Savoy both for diplomatic reasons and political fears of revolution. Formally the new 'Kingdom of Italy' was presented as an enlargement of the older Kingdom of Piedmont, from which it inherited laws, institutions and in the initial period the ruling élite.
7. For a sketch of Italian constitutional history, see P. Pombeni, *La costituente. Un problema storico-politico*, (Bologna: Il Mulino, 1995).
8. There is a good deal of literature about the transformation of the Italian political system under Fascism: I will simply recall my own contribution to it (*Demagogia e tirannide. Uno studio sulla forma partito del fascismo*. (Bologna: Il Mulino, 1984)) and the collected essays in A Del Boca, M. Legnani and M. G. Rossi (eds), *Il regime Fascista*. (Roma-Bari: Laterza, 1995).
9. This opened a heated debate among jurists in order to interpret this strange case of constitutional transformation. For a highly technical analysis of it, see, M. Fioravanti, 'Dottrina dello stato persona e dottrina della costituzione. Costantino Mortati e la tradizione giuspubblicistica italiana', in M. Galizia and P. Grossi (eds), *Il pensiero giuridico di Costantino Mortati*. (Milan: Giuffré, 1990), pp. 45–185. I am reluctant to quote only Italian works, but the international literature, so rich in titles on Fascism, has more or less completely missed these approaches.
10. The most recent examinations of Italian politics in the Great War are the first chapter of N. Tranfaglia, *La prima guerra mondiale e il fascismo*. (Turin: Utet, 1995), and G. Procacci, 'L'Italia nella Grande guerra', in G. Sabbatucci and V. Vidotto (eds), *Storia d'Italia*, vol. IV. (Roma-Bari: Laterza, 1997), pp. 3–99.
11. The fact is plainly evident in the debate among the so-called 'Big Four', where Wilson, Lloyd George and Clemenceau regarded the Italian representatives

(Orlando and Sonnino) as not representative of the new era: cf. *The Deliberations of the Council of Four (March 24-June 28, 1919). Notes of the official interpreter P. Mantoux*, trans. and ed. by A. S. Link. (Princeton: Princeton University Press, 1992).

12. See, L. Riccardi, *Alleati non amici. Le relazioni politiche fra l'Italia e l'intesa durante la prima guerra mondiale.* (Brescia: Morcelliana, 1992).
13. In fact Catholics displayed nationalist attitudes from the beginning of the war, even if the Catholic peasantry and their clergy displayed a more diffident spirit. As is well known, the Socialists employed the very ambiguous formula: 'neither adhesion nor sabotage' (né aderire, né sabotare). But after the heavy Italian defeat at Caporetto (October 1917), when the nation seemed in mortal danger, nearly all the Socialists rediscovered the older 'Garibaldinian' spirit of the left and assumed a patriotic attitude. On this see the old, but still valid collection of essays, *Il trauma dell'intervento.* (Firenze: Vallecchi, 1968). On the problem of the relationship between Nationalsm and Catholic culture in Italy, see G. Formigoni, *L' Italia dei cattolici: fede e nazione dal Risorgimento alla Repubblica.* (Bologna: Il Mulino, 1998).
14. For this see, P. Pombeni, 'Potere costituente e riforme costituzionali. Note storiche sul caso italiano 1848–1948', in P. Pombeni (ed.), *Potere costituente e riforme costituzionali.* (Bologna: Il Mulino, 1992), pp. 81–105, and the documents in the appendix of that volume at pp. 201–24.
15. This way of using electoral reform to avoid conflict over major constitutional questions is illustrated by M. S. Piretti, *Le elezioni in Italia dal 1848 ad oggi.* (Roma-Bari: Laterza, 1996). See also, P. Pombeni, 'La rappresentanza politica', in R. Romanelli (ed.), *Storia dello Stato Italiano.* (Rome: Donzelli, 1996), pp. 73–124.
16. The details in this passage can be found in M. S. Piretti, *La giustizia dei numeri. Il proporzionalismo in Italia dal 1870 al 1923.* (Bologna: Il Mulino, 1990).
17. On this point within the framework of the crisis of Liberal Italy, in addition to the above quoted essays, see, F. Grassi Orsini and G. Quagliariello (eds), *Il partito politico dalla grande guerra al fascismo. Crisi della rappresentanza e riforma dello stato nell'età dei sistemi politici di massa (1918–1925)*, (Bologna: Il Mulino, 1996); G. Sabbatucci, 'La crisi dello stato liberale', in G. Sabbatucci and V, Vidotto (eds), *Storia d'Italia*, vol. IV, pp. 101–67.
18. To start with see, C. Maier, *Recasting Bourgeois Europe: Stabilization in France, Germany and Italy in the Decade after World War I.* (Princeton: Princeton University Press, 1988). A more recent analysis of the unrest in the state bureaucracy can be found in G. Melis, *Due modelli di amministrazione tra liberalismo e fascismo. Burocrazie tradizionali e nuovi apparati.* (Rome: Pubblicazioni degli Archivi di Stato, 1988).
19. During the prewar years many different strategies were experimented to come to terms with these two forces, both by trying to integrate them in various ways into the existing establishment and by excluding them definitively from political competition. The apparent failure of both these strategies only increased fears for a breakdown in the political order. On the problem of social power in Italian history, see, P. Pombeni, *Autorità sociale e potere politico nell'Italia contemporanea.* (Venezia: Marsilio, 1993).
20. This chronology is my own: I am aware that different dates could be proposed with equal plausibility.

21. The more coherent on this matter was Carlo Costamagna with his journal *Lo Stato*. See on this point M. Foravanti, *Dottrina dello stato-persona* and, F. Lanchester, *Momenti e figure del diritto costituzionale in Italia e in Germania*. (Milan: Giuffré, 1994).
22. E. Frankael, *The Dual State. A contribution to the theory of dictatorship*, (1941). (New York: Octagon Books, 1969). In fact Frankael's theory is not completely applicable to Fascism because in this latter case there never had been a legal break with the *Rechtsstaat* (the rule of law). It had established that the 'will' of the *Duce* was considered law even in absence of a legal registration of this through the normal ways of parliamentary acts or governmental decrees. In contrast, under the Nazi regime, it was openly stated that 'the *Fuhrer*'s word is law': the so-called *Führerprinzip* that allowed Frankael to speak about a 'prerogative state').
23. The collapse of the Italian system is now the object of a heated debate among Italian historians. The debate was opened by Renzo De Felice's book on Mussolini's fall (*Mussolini l'alleato.1940–45. I L'Italia in guerra 1940–43*. (Turin: Einaudi, 1990) and continued in a series of different essays: that of Elena Aga Rossi on the crisis of the 8 September 1943 (*Una nazione allo sbando.L'armistizio italiano del settembre 1943*. (Bologna: Il Mulino, 1993) and that of Ernesto Galli Della Loggia on the so called 'Death of the fatherland' (*La morte della patria*. Roma-Bari, Laterza, 1996). On this perspective I have expressed my opinions in, 'Discussione: La morte della patria', *Il Mulino*, 45 (1996) 810–15.
24. I have developed this point in my essay, 'Il Partito Nazionale Fascista nel declinare del regime 1938–1943', in A. Ventura (ed.), *Sulla crisi del regime fascista 1938–1943*. (Venezia: Marsilio, 1996), pp. 3–19 where a more developed argument can be found.
25. In fact the events known as the 'Aventino' (the retreat from the Parliament of the non-Fascist members in the summer/autumn of 1924 after the assassination of the socialist parliamentary deputy Giacomo Matteotti) left the impression of a general rift between Fascists and the traditional parties. The members of the ruling élite that supported Fascism on that occasion simply changed their shirts for black ones; their Aventine opponents were forced to stay outside of political life, and sought solace by privately criticizing in bitter and snobbish terms the regime.
26. The most obvious cases were the vitality of the mass movements of Catholic Action during the regime, in the Catholic organizations of university students and the academic professions. See, R. Moro, *La formazione della classe dirigente cattolica (1929–1937)*. (Bologna : Il Mulino, 1979); A. Giovagnoli, *La cultura democristiana*. (Bari-Rome: Laterza, 1991).
27. An impressive account of the incapacity of the public authorities to deal with the emergency of the summer of 1943 is in Alfredo Pizzoni's memoirs. Pizzoni, a banker and a bourgeois liberal not particularly imbued with anti-Fascist feelings, became through this experience not only a member of the Resistance movement, but the President of the Comitato di Liberazione nazionale Alta Italia (CLNAI). He was brutally sidelined by the political parties on the eve of the Liberation. See, A. Pizzoni, *Alla guida del Clnai*. (Bologna: Mulino, 1995).
28. cf. J. Lacouture, *De Gaulle. Le politique*. (Paris: Seuil, 1985); O. Wieviorka, *Une certaine idée de la Résistance. Defense da l France 1940–1949*. (Paris: Seuil, 1995), pp. 211–74.

29. Recent research has tried to deal with this until now neglected problem. See G. Ranzato, *Il linciaggio di Carretta. Roma 1944. Violenza politica e ordinaria violenza.* (Milan: Il Saggiatore, 1997). P. Pezzino, *Anatomia di un massacro. Controversia sopra una strage tedesca.* (Bologna: Il Mulino 1997).
30. This fear led to the establishment of a specific political movement called *L'Uomo Qualunque* (the ordinary man). It fought against the 'power of the parties' and presented itself as a defender of the ordinary apolitical man in the street who had served his country but was now treated as a servant of Fascism. The movement fed on the resentment of those who feared the loss of government jobs through political purges. This movement performed astonishingly well at the 1946 election, but disappeared in 1948, when it became clear that no real purge was planned inside the civil service at any level. On this see, S. Setta, *L'Uomo Qualunque 1944–1948.* (Rome-Bari: Laterza, 1975). On the question of the political purges, see C. Maier, 'Fare giustizia, fare storia: epurazioni politiche e narrative nazionali dopo il 1945 e il 1989', *Passato e Presente,* 34 (1995).
31. On this see, L. Musellla, 'Formazione ed espansione dei partiti', in F. Barbagallo (ed.), *Storia dell'Italia repubblicana,* vol. II/2. (Turin: Einaudi, 1995), pp. 153–212.
32. There is an old, but still valid, study which deals with the relationship between public opinion and the 'constitutional strategies' (in fact they were purely political strategies) of the parties: R. Ruffilli (ed.), *Costituente e lotta politica. La stampa e le scelte costituzionali.* (Florence: Vallecchi, 1978).
33. On all this see, P. Pombeni, *La costituente,* and also, P. Pombeni, *Il gruppo dossettiano e la fondazione della democrazia italiana (1938–1948).* (Bologna: Il Mulino, 1979).
34. This is another of the never-ending quarrels in Italian historiography. Of course, in the Constituent Assembly, as in every political assembly, the debate aimed at a final decision which could claim to be a synthesis of many different positions. The general trend was in this case reinforced by the so-called 'ideology of the 30s': during the climatic phase of the anti-Fascist alliance the idea was popular that the great ideologies of the last centuries, socialism, communism, Christian Democracy, had a lot in common in their fight to defend social rights and in their hope to reach a settlement for a better world. But the term 'compromise' is totally inappropriate to describe what actually happened; there was no bargaining process or compromise in the 1940s between Christian Democrats seeking rules that looked after the position and interests of the Catholic Church and left-wing parties (especially the PCI) wanting rules that helped the lot of the trade unions and the working class. I have showed this in all my works on this period already quoted.
35. This is a highly interesting, but also highly technical point that can not be dealt with in this chapter. I have analysed this in detail in my essay, 'Individuo/Persona nella costituzione italiana. Il contributo del dossettismo', *Parole Chiave.* (1996), 10/11 197–218.
36. The long accepted validity of the division of constitution-types into 'rigid' and 'flexible' (those constitutions that did not have rules for their amendment, presupposing that this absence had been the intention of those who had drawn them up) is now being questioned. Jurists are stating to reconsider

the issue in a more historical framework, recognizing that for many eighteenth-century constitutions that absence was simply due to the fact that the constitution did not take into account the idea of a change of its rules. See, A. Pace, *La causa della rigidità costituzionale.* (Padua: Cedam, 1996).

37. The champion of this political campaign was Sidney Sonnino in 1897. In his article *Torniamo allo Statuto* he pleaded for a return to the so-called 'pure constitutional method' against the existing cabinet system. See, R. Nieri, 'Sidney Sonnino e il "Torniamo allo Statuto"', *Rassegna storica del Risorgimento*, 83, (1996) 463–512.
38. See, E. Lanciotti, *La riforma impossibile. Idee, discussioni e progetti sulla modifica del Senato Regio e vitalizio (1848–1922).* (Bologna: Il Mulino, 1993); N. Antonetti, *Gli invalidi della Costituzione.Il Senato del Regno 1848–1924.* (Bari-Rome: Laterza, 1992).
39. One of the most prominent and influential journalists at that time, Mario Missiroli, who edited *Il Messaggero* in Rome, was a distinguished champion of this hypersceptical, snobbish attitude toward the Constituent Assembly. He regarded it as a conclave of lazy time-consuming politicians. See, M. Bonomo, *Giornalismo indipendente e scelta moderata: 'Il Messaggero' di Missiroli*, in R. Ruffilli, *Costituente e lotta politica*, pp. 203–33. *Il Corriere della Sera* was more measured in its opinion, but started with the same biases: see, M. S. Piretti, 'Il rapporto costituente-paese nelle relazioni dei prefetti, nelle lettere alla costituente e nella stampa di opinione', in *La fondazione della Repubblica.* (Bologna: Il Mulino, 1979) pp. 443–504.
40. Research into the 1950s and 1960s is quite limited and marked by the political partisanship. I have tried to sketch in a more detached perspective these years in my essay, 'I partiti e la politica dal 1948 al 1963', in G. Sabbatucci and V. Vidotto (eds), *Storia d'Italia*, vol. V. (Bari-Rome: Laterza, 1997), where you can find a bibliography on this period.
41. An excellent illustration of the climate of that years in, P. Craveri, *La repubblica dal 1958 al 1992.* (Turin: Utet, 1995).
42. A positive view of this phase is, P. Scoppola, *La repubblica dei partiti. Profilo storico della democrazia in Italia (1945–1990).* (Bologna: Mulino, 1991), pp. 355–93; a more critical evaluation in, P. Craveri, *La Repubblica.*
43. The main cultural endeavour that celebrated that event was a large research project sponsored by the (left-oriented) regional government of Tuscany. This employed the best 'intellectuals in politics' of the 'constitutional arc'. (All the parties in Parliament bar the neo-Fascists.) For a sketch of that climate I take the liberty to cite an essay in memory of one of this men, the historian and later Senator of the DC, Roberto Ruffilli, who ended his life killed by terrorists of the 'Red Brigades' in 1988. (Ruffilli was my teacher at the University of Bologna). See, P. Pombeni, 'Roberto Ruffilli e la storiografia sullo stato contemporaneo', in M. Ridolfi (ed.), *Roberto Ruffilli. Un percorso di ricerca.* (Milan: Angeli, 1990), pp. 109–31.
44. The struggle against 'partitocracy' (*partitocrazia*) started with the already cited episode of the *Uomo Qualunque*, but in this case the movement was regarded as a nostalgic semi-Fascist development (also Fascism had pleaded against 'camarillas and parties' in its struggle against the Liberal state). A new spin was put on the term by two different personalities. The senator for life, Luigi Sturzo (the old founder of the Catholic Popular Party in 1919), and

a professor of politics at the University of Florence, Giuseppe Maranini. The first, who spent his exile in the US, could never accept a party-based democracy, which he found foreign both to his nineteenth-century political culture and from the new interpretation of democracy he gathered from the American context. In the 1950s he criticized the growing power of political parties over civil society, their 'occupation' of the economic sphere, and the predominance of party apparatuses over parliamentary life. To this criticism Giuseppe Maranini added an academic approach, writing in 1967 a book – *Storia del potere in Italia 1848–1967.* (Firenze: Vallecchi, 1967) – where he built up an interpretation of Italian political history showing the pernicious effects of party factionalism and party predominance.

45. The models were typically the Chinese Cultural Revolution, Castroite Cuban communism or the Marxist revolutionary groups of Latin America.
46. An analysis of the evolution of the PCI can be found in P. Ignazi, *Dal Pci al Pds.* (Bologna: Il Mulino, 1992).
47. The DC's decline began during the Second Vatican Council: this great event in Catholic life diverted Italian Catholic intellectuals from politics, involving them in a much more interesting debate about the reform of the Catholic Church. The traditional linkage of the DC with the Catholic youth organization ended. It had supplied the DC with new blood and new ideas, in an atmosphere that was cushioned from the political factionalism of the party itself.
48. The dynamics of this event are reconstructed in, A. Pappalardo, 'La nuova legge elettorale in parlamento. Chi, come e perché', in S. Bartolini and R. D'Alimonte (eds), *Maggioritario manon troppo.* (Bologna: Il Mulino, 1995). My reflections on this last phase of the old Italian party system are in, P. Pombeni, 'La rappresentanza politica', in Romanelli (ed.), *Storia dello stato Italiano*, pp. 120–4.

Index